Lecture Notes in Computer Scien. 1500

Edited by G. Goos, J. Hartmanis and J. van Leeuwen

Springer

Berlin
Heidelberg
New York
Barcelona
Hong Kong
London
Milan
Paris
Singapore
Tokyo

Hideki Imai Yuliang Zheng (Eds.)

Public Key Cryptography

Second International Workshop on Practice
and Theory in Public Key Cryptography, PKC'99
Kamakura, Japan, March 1-3, 1999
Proceedings

 Springer

Series Editors

Gerhard Goos, Karlsruhe University, Germany
Juris Hartmanis, Cornell University, NY, USA
Jan van Leeuwen, Utrecht University, The Netherlands

Volume Editors

Hideki Imai
The Third Department, Institute of Industrial Science
University of Tokyo
7-22-1, Roppongi, Minato-ku, Tokyo, 106-8558, Japan
E-mail: imai@iis.u-tokyo.ac.jp

Yuliang Zheng
School of Computing and Information Technology
Monash University
McMahons Road, Frankston, Melbourne, VIC 3199, Australia
E-mail: yzheng@fcit.monash.edu.au

Cataloging-in-Publication data applied for

Die Deutsche Bibliothek - CIP-Einheitsaufnahme

Public key cryptography : proceedings / Second International
Workshop on Practice and Theory in Public Key Cryptography, PKC
'99, Kamakura, Japan, March 1 - 3, 1999. Hideki Imai ; Yuliang
Zheng (ed.). - Berlin ; Heidelberg ; New York ; Barcelona ; Hong
Kong ; London ; Milan ; Paris ; Singapore ; Tokyo : Springer, 1999
    (Lecture notes in computer science ; Vol. 1560)
    ISBN 3-540-65644-8

CR Subject Classification (1998): E.3, G.2.1, D.4.6, K.6.5, F.2.1-2, C.2, J.1

ISSN 0302-9743
ISBN 3-540-65644-8 Springer-Verlag Berlin Heidelberg New York

© Springer-Verlag Berlin Heidelberg 1999
Printed in Germany

Typesetting: Camera-ready by author
SPIN: 10702882   06/3142 – 5 4 3 2 1 0   Printed on acid-free paper

Preface

The PKC'99 conference, held in the ancient capital of Kamakura, Japan, March 1-3, 1999, represents the second conference in the international workshop series dedicated to the practice and theory in public key cryptography.

The program committee of the conference received 61 submissions from 12 countries and regions (Australia, Canada, Finland, France, Japan, Saudi Arabia, Singapore, Spain, Taiwan, UK, USA, and Yugoslavia), of which 25 were selected for presentation. All submissions were reviewed by experts in the relevant areas.

The program committee consisted of Chin-Chen Chang of the National Chung Cheng University, Taiwan, Yvo Desmedt of the University of Wisconsin-Milwaukee, USA, Hideki Imai (Co-Chair) of the University of Tokyo, Japan, Markus Jakobsson of Bell Labs, USA, Kwangjo Kim of Information and Communications University, Korea, Arjen Lenstra of Citibank, USA, Tsutomu Matsumoto of Yokohama National University, Japan, Eiji Okamoto of JAIST, Japan, Tatsuaki Okamoto of NTT, Japan, Nigel Smart of HP Labs Bristol, UK, and Yuliang Zheng (Co-Chair) of Monash University, Australia. Members of the committee spent numerous hours in reviewing the submissions and providing advice and comments on the selection of papers. We would like to take this opportunity to thank all the members for their invaluable help in producing such a high quality technical program.

The program committee also asked expert advice of many of their colleagues, including: Masayuki Abe, Kazumaro Aoki, Daniel Bleichenbacher, Atsushi Fujioka, Eiichiro Fujisaki, Chandana Gamage, Brian King, Kunio Kobayashi, Tetsutaro Kobayashi, Phil MacKenzie, Hidemi Moribatake, Kazuo Ohta, Amin Shokrollahi, Shigenori Uchiyama, and Yongge Wang. We thank them all for their help.

The conference would not have been successful without the skillful assistance of the members of the organizing committee. Our special thanks go to Takashi Mano of IPA, Japan, Kanta Matsuura and Hidenori Shida, both of University of Tokyo, Japan.

Last, but not least, we would like to thank all the people who submitted their papers to the conference (including those whose submissions were not successful), as well as the workshop participants from around the world, for their support which made this conference possible.

March 1999
University of Tokyo, Japan
Monash University, Melbourne, Australia

Hideki Imai
Yuliang Zheng

PKC'99

1999 International Workshop on Practice and Theory in Public Key Cryptography

Kamakura Prince Hotel, Kamakura, Japan
March 1-3, 1999

In cooperation with
The Technical Group on Information Security, the Institute of
Electronics, Information and Communication Engineers (IEICE)

Organizing Committee

Hideki Imai, Chair   (University of Tokyo, Japan)
Takashi Mano   (IPA, Japan)
Kanta Matsuura   (University of Tokyo, Japan)
Hidenori Shida   (University of Tokyo, Japan)
Yuliang Zheng   (Monash University, Australia)

Program Committee

Hideki Imai, Co-Chair   (University of Tokyo, Japan)
Yuliang Zheng, Co-Chair   (Monash University, Australia)
Chin-Chen Chang   (National Chung Cheng University, Taiwan)
Yvo Desmedt   (University of Wisconsin-Milwaukee, USA)
Kwangjo Kim   (Information and Communications University, Korea)
Markus Jakobsson   (Bell Labs, USA)
Arjen Lenstra   (Citibank, USA)
Tsutomu Matsumoto   (Yokohama National University, Japan)
Eiji Okamoto   (JAIST, Japan)
Tatsuaki Okamoto   (NTT, Japan)
Nigel Smart   (HP Labs Bristol, UK)

Contents

A New Type of "Magic Ink" Signatures — Towards Transcript-Irrelevant Anonymity Revocation

Feng Bao and Robert H. Deng

Information Security Group
Kent Ridge Digital Labs
Singapore 119613
Email: {baofeng, deng}@krdl.org.sg

Abstract. The *magic ink signature* recently proposed in [11] is a *blind signature* which allows "unblinding" of a signature by authorities to establish what is known as *audit trail* and *anonymity revocation* in case of criminal activities. In [11] as well as in all the previous fair blind signature schemes (e. g., [2] and [10]), trustees need to search a database maintained by signers to obtain a transcript of the corresponding signing protocol instance in order to trace the signature receiver. In other words, to establish anonymity revocation, the trustees need to know some information which was produced in the signing stage and kept by the signers. This is clearly not convenient for the anonymity revocation in certain applications. In this paper, we propose a new type of magic ink signature scheme. The novel feature of the new scheme is that anonymity revocation is made transcript irrelevant. That is, the trustee can revoke a receiver's anonymity based solely on the information embedded in a signature, not on any additional information; therefore, it is possible that the trustee revoke the anonymity without the help from the signer, therefore, without the signer knowing who is being traced.

Key Words: blinding signatures, anonymity revocation, traceability, e-commerce.

1 Introduction

The concept of blind signature was first proposed by Chaum [3]. It is a protocol for a receiver to obtain a signature from a signer such that the signer's view of the protocol cannot be linked to the resulting message-signature pair. The physical analog of blind signatures of Chaum is the following: *the receiver writes a message on a paper, puts the paper and a carbon paper into an envelope. The signer writes his signature on the envelope. Due to the carbon paper, the signature is copied onto the paper. Only the receiver can present the signed message and the signer cannot get hold of the signed message and the signature.* Blind signature schemes have been used in various cryptographic protocols to provide anonymity of some of the participants, including the generation of anonymous access tokens and credentials, voting protocols, and electronic payment systems [1, 3, 5].

All the existing blind signature schemes (e.g., [3, 5]) were designed to provide *perfect anonymity*. That is, it is impossible for anyone except the receiver to link a message-signature pair to the corresponding instance of the signing protocol. However, it has been noted that perfect anonymity could result in *perfect crimes* [16]. In the case of anonymous access tokens, a malicious user could access a system and create a lot of damages without being traced back. In the case of anonymous electronic payment, blind signatures prevent anyone (except the payer) from linking the withdrawal of cash and the payment made by the same payer. This could result in perfect black-mailing or money laundering. Therefore, it is necessary to design blind signature schemes which provide receivers' anonymity in normal circumstances, and should need arises (e. g., for law enforcement and audit trail), it allows a trusted party (trustee) to revoke receivers' anonymity.

Blind signature schemes allowing anonymity revocation by a trustee or trustees have been studied in some literatures. In [14], *fair blind signature* is proposed; one of the their scheme requires the trustee(s) to be on-line during the signing stage. The other two schemes use off-line trustee(s) by exploiting cut-and-choose technique. In [2] and [10], anonymity revocation can be achieved without the trustee(s) being involved in the signing stage. For a good survey on this subject, the reader is refereed to [6].

Most recently, a *magic ink signature* scheme is proposed in [11]. It is a group blind signature scheme which requires n signers to take part in the signing stage and allows $k < n$ signers (instead of trustees) to perform anonymity revocation. The physical analog of this magic ink signature is the following([11]): *the signer puts a paper and a carbon paper into an envelope. The receiver writes the document on the envelope using magic ink – the ink that is only visible after being "developed". The signer then writes his signature on the envelope. Due to the carbon copy, both the receiver's document and the signer's signature appear on the internal paper. Finally, the receiver gets the paper and the signer keeps the envelope with the magic ink on it. Should the signer need to unblind the document, he can then get the document copy on the envelope by developing the magic ink.*

In this paper, we propose a new type of "magic ink" signatures from a completely different approach. Our "magic ink" signatures have the following physical parallel: *the receiver places a document with a carbon paper on top in an envelope and hands it over to the signer. The signer signs on the envelope. Due to the carbon paper, this results in the signature being written on the document paper. Then the signer writes the receiver's identity on the back of the envelope using our new "magic ink" – an invisible ink that penetrates the envelope and be written on the back of the document paper where it becomes visible only after being "developed" by a trustee. Finally, the receiver gets the document paper with the signer's signature on one side and the invisible ink on the other side. The receiver may pass the paper to anyone, who in turn may pass it further. To revoke a receiver's anonymity, the trustee and only the trustee can develop the magic ink on the signed document. As a result, there is no need for anyone to keep the used envelopes. They can be thrown away after the signing stage.*

In the original magic ink signatures [11] as well as in all the previous fair blind signature schemes ([2] and [10]), trustees need to search a database to obtain a transcript of the corresponding signing protocol instance in order to trace the signature receiver. In other words, to establish anonymity revocation, the trustees need to know some information which was produced in the signing stage and kept by the signers. This means that the trustees must get assistance from the signers in order to do anonymity revocation. The novel feature of the new magic ink scheme proposed in this paper is that anonymity revocation is made transcript irrelevant. That is, the trustee can revoke a receiver's anonymity based solely on the information embedded in a signature, not on any additional information; therefore, it can be completely accomplished by the trustee along. Hence, no one else, except the trustee, knows who is being traced. This might be a required feature for law enforcement in certain cases.

The rest of the paper is organized as follows. In Section 2 we first present the concept of *disjoint orbits* and then describe the basic idea of the proposed new scheme. In Section 3 we introduce a few cryptographic protocols for concealing *starting points* of disjoint orbits and for proving equality of logarithms respectively. The proposed new scheme is formally described in Section 4 which is then followed by illustration on its security in Section 5. A discussion on our protocol implementation is given in Section 6. Finally, Section 7 contains our concluding remarks.

2   Disjoint Orbits and Outline of the New Scheme

The concept of *disjoint orbits* is to partition a signature "space" into "disjoint orbits" and confine each user or receiver to a different one. One method to realize disjoint orbits as proposed in [7] by Desmedt is as follows.

Let $p, q_1, q_2, \cdots, q_n$ be all (odd distinct) primes such that

$$p = 2 \prod_{i=1}^{n} q_i + 1.$$

Let g_p be a generator of $\mathbf{Z}_p^*$ (i.e., $\mathbf{Z}_p^* = \langle g_p \rangle$) and let $g = g_p^2 \bmod p$. Then g is a generator of $G_Q \subset \mathbf{Z}_p^*$, where $Q = \prod_{i=1}^{n} q_i$ and G_Q is the subgroup of $\mathbf{Z}_p^*$ of order Q. Later, all our discussions are restricted within $G_Q = \langle g \rangle$. Let α be a binary string of length n, say $\alpha = (b_1 b_2 \cdots b_n)_2$ with b_i being 0 or 1. Define

$$g_\alpha = g^{\prod_{i=1}^{n} q_i^{b_i}} \bmod p.$$

Apparently, g_α has order $Q/\prod_{i=1}^{n} q_i^{b_i}$ for $\alpha = (b_1 b_2 \cdots b_n)_2$. For any α, if s is relatively prime to Q (i.e., $\gcd(s, Q) = 1$), then g_α and g_α^s have the same order.

We are now ready to state the outline of our scheme. A trustee constructs many disjoint orbits which can only be distinguished by himself. Then he shows the starting points g_α of these orbits to the signer, where α is a binary string of length n (hence the maximum number of disjoint orbits is $2^n - 2$, excluding the cases of $\alpha = (0 \cdots 0)_2$ and $(1 \cdots 1)_2$). The signer places each receiver on a different starting point g_α by assigning α as the receiver's identity (ID). A blind signature on a message issued to a receiver is based on g_α. To provide receiver anonymity, in addition to the message, g_α is also blinded to

$$G = g_\alpha^s \bmod p$$

with s randomly chosen by the receiver. With negligible probability, the receiver can choose an s such that g_α^s has different order from that of g_α (i.e., to randomly choose an s such that s has non-trivial common factors with Q). To revoke the receiver's anonymity on the signature, the trustee, who knows $q_1, q_2, \cdots, q_n$, can trace the receiver from G by calculating its order as follows. First assume its order is $\prod_{i=1}^{n} q_i^{b_i}$, with $b_1, ..., b_n$ unknown. Then, for $i = 1, 2, ..., n$, check to see if $G^{Q/q_i} \equiv 1 \pmod p$ or not. If the equality holds, let $b_i = 1$; otherwise $b_i = 0$.

3 Cryptographic Protocol Building Blocks

Before presenting the details of our scheme, we describe some protocols for generating blind signatures and for proving equality of logarithms respectively. These previously known protocols will be used as building blocks in constructing the new scheme in the next section.

3.1 Blind Signature Concealing the Starting Point

Let p and q be primes such that $q \mid p - 1$, g be an element of $\mathbf{Z}_p^*$ of order q, $x \in \mathbf{Z}_q$ be the private key of the signer and $h = g^x \bmod p$ be the corresponding public key. Further, let $\mathcal{H}$ denote a cryptographic one-way hash function from arbitrary length input to fixed length output and m denote the message to be signed. To make our notations compact, we will assume that all the exponential computations are done in $\mathbf{Z}_p^*$, and all the computations between components are done in $\mathbf{Z}_Q$.

Protocol 1

1. The signer randomly chooses $w \in \mathbf{Z}_q$, sets $a' = g^w$ and sends a' to the receiver.
2. The receiver randomly chooses $u, v \in \mathbf{Z}_q$, calculates $a = a'g^v h^u$, $c = \mathcal{H}(m, a)$ and $c' = c + u$, and sends c' to the signer.
3. The signer sets $r' = w + c'x$ and sends r' to the receiver.
4. The receiver checks whether $a' = g^{r'} h^{-c'}$. If yes, he accepts r' and sets $r = r' + v$.
5. The receiver outputs (r, c) as the signature of m. The verification of the signature is to check $c = \mathcal{H}(m, g^r h^{-c})$.

Protocol 1 is developed based on the Schnorr signature and has been discussed in many references, such as in [1, 2, 5, 9, 12, 13]. The central idea of the

Schnorr signature is to use a hash function as a random oracle in place of the random challenge generated by the verifier in the Schnorr identification protocol.

We will use Protocol 2 below, a variant of Protocol 1, in our new magic ink signature scheme. In Protocol 2, besides g and $h = g^x$, we also have g_α and $h_\alpha = g_\alpha^x$. The pair g_α and h_α are specified as the base for the receiver with identity α. Protocol 2 is a blind signature protocol which conceals g_α and h_α.

Protocol 2

1. The signer randomly chooses $w \in \mathbf{Z}_q$, sets $a' = g_\alpha^w$ and sends a' to the receiver.
2. The receiver randomly chooses $s, u, v \in \mathbf{Z}_q$, calculates $a = (a'g_\alpha^v h_\alpha^u)^s$, $G = g_\alpha^s$, $H = h_\alpha^s$, $c = \mathcal{H}(m, a, G, H)$ and $c' = c + u$, and sends c' to the signer.
3. The signer sets $r' = w + c'x$ and sends r' back to the receiver.
4. The receiver checks whether $a' = g_\alpha^{r'} h_\alpha^{-c'}$. If yes, he accepts r' and sets $r = r' + v$.
5. The receiver outputs (r, c, G, H) as the blind signature on m. The verification of the signature is to check $c = \mathcal{H}(m, G^r H^{-c}, G, H)$ and $\underline{H = G^x}$.

Note that in Protocol 2, it is essential to check the condition $H = G^x$ in verifying the signature; otherwise, anyone without knowing x, can find (r, c, G, H) such that $c = \mathcal{H}(m, G^r H^{-c}, G, H)$ by arbitrarily choosing G and y and then setting $H = G^y$. Checking the validity of $H = G^x$ is equivalent to proving that $\log_G H = \log_g h$. Such a proof cryptographically binds G, H to the signer (since g and h are publicly known to be from the signer). Fortunately, this can be done without revealing x as described in the next Paragraph.

3.2 Proving Equality of Logarithms

The method of proof of equality of logarithms [1, 4, 2, 15] enables a prover to prove to a verifier that $\log_G H = \log_g h$ without revealing x, where $H = G^x$ and $h = g^x$.

Protocol 3

1. The prover randomly chooses $w \in \mathbf{Z}_q$, computes $a = g^w$, $A = G^w$ and sends a and A to the verifier.
2. The verifier randomly chooses $c \in \mathbf{Z}_q$ and sends c to the prover.
3. The prover sets $r = w + cx$ and sends r back to the verifier.
4. The verifier checks whether $a = g^r h^{-c}$ and $A = G^r H^{-c}$. If yes, the proof is accepted.

For discussions on the security of the above protocol, the reader is referred to [15]. Replacing the random challenge c by the output of a hash function, Protocol 3 can be modified to Protocol 4 in which a prover issues a certificate to prove that $\log_G H = \log_g h$.

Protocol 4

1. The prover randomly chooses $w \in \mathbf{Z}_q$, calculates $a = g^w$, $A = G^w$ and sends a and A to the verifier.
2. The verifier calculates $c = \mathcal{H}(g, h, G, H, a, A)$ and sends c to the prover.
3. The prover sets $r = w + cx$ and outputs (r, c) as the certificate of $\log_g h = \log_G H$.
4. The verification of the certificate is to check whether

$$c = \mathcal{H}(g, h, G, H, g^r h^{-c}, G^r H^{-c})$$

holds.

Note that Protocol 4 can be non-interactive by having the prover computes $c = \mathcal{H}(g, h, G, H, a, A)$ in Step 2.

In the next Section, we combine disjoint orbits, Protocol 2 and Protocol 4 to arrive at the new magic ink signature scheme.

4 Description of the New Scheme

Environment Description There are less than $2^n - 2$ users or receivers. Each receiver has an identity α which is a binary string of length n ($\alpha \neq (0 \cdots 0)_2$ and $(1 \cdots 1)_2$). There are a number of signers and one trustee.

Set-up of the trustee The trustee secretly generates n primes $q_1, \cdots, q_n$ such that $p = 2 \prod_{i=1}^n q_i + 1$ is a prime. For each $\alpha = (b_1 b_2 \cdots b_n)_2$, he computes $g_\alpha = g^{\prod_{i=1}^n q_i^{b_i}}$, where g is an element of $\mathbf{Z}_p^*$ of order $Q = \prod_{i=1}^n q_i$. The trustee then publishes g and all g_α while keeps all the q_i secret. We assume that factorizing Q is difficult. Under this assumption, a randomly chosen number from $\mathbf{Z}_Q$ will have common factors with Q with negligible probability.

Signers' Keys Each signer randomly chooses a $x \in \mathbf{Z}_Q$ as its private (signing) key and publishes $h = g^x$ and $h_\alpha = g_\alpha^x$ for all the α as the public keys. By Protocol 4, the signer can prove to anyone that $\log_g h = \log_{g_\alpha} h_\alpha$ for all α, i.e., the signer has published correct h and h_α.

The Signing Protocol When a receiver (with identity α) goes to a signer (with signing key x), the receiver gets a blind signature on a message m by running the following protocol with the signer.

Protocol 5

Part I

1. The signer randomly chooses $w \in \mathbf{Z}_Q$, computes $a' = g_\alpha^w$ and sends a' to the receiver.
2. The receiver randomly chooses $s, u, v \in \mathbf{Z}_Q$, computes $a = (a' g_\alpha^v h_\alpha^u)^s$, $G = g_\alpha^s$, $H = h_\alpha^s$, $c = \mathcal{H}(m, a, G, H)$ and $c' = c + u$, and sends c' to the signer.

3. The signer sets $r' = w + c'x$ and sends r' back to the receiver.
4. The receiver checks whether $a' = g_\alpha^{r'} h_\alpha^{-c'}$. If yes, he accepts r' and sets $r = r' + v$.

Part II

5. The signer randomly chooses $W \in \mathbf{Z}_Q$ (W must be different from w), computes $A' = g_\alpha^W$ and $B' = g^W$, and sends A' and B' to the receiver.
6. The receiver randomly chooses $U, V \in \mathbf{Z}_Q$, calculates

$$A = (A')^s G^V H^U$$

for the same s, G, and H as in Part I, and $B = B' g^V h^U$. Then he calculates $C = \mathcal{H}(A, B, G, H, r, c)$ for the same r and c as in Part I, sets $C' = C + U$, and sends C' to the signer.
7. The signer calculates $R' = W + C'x$ and sends R' back to the receiver.
8. The receiver checks whether $A' = g_\alpha^{R'} h_\alpha^{-C'}$ and $B' = g^{R'} h^{-C'}$. If yes, he accepts R' and sets $R = R' + V$.

Finally, the receiver outputs (r, c, R, C, G, H) as the blind signature of m. The verification of the signature is to check for equality of both

$$c = \mathcal{H}(m, G^r H^{-c}, G, H) \text{ and } C = \mathcal{H}(G^R H^{-C}, g^R h^{-C}, G, H, r, c).$$

Anonymity The receiver can later show (r, c, R, C, G, H, m) to anyone, including the signer. The signer has $(w, W, r', c', R', C', a', A', B')$ as the transcript of the instance of the corresponding signing protocol. Knowing the signature even by the signer does not reveal any correlation between (r, c, R, C, G, H, m) and $(w, W, r', c', R', C', a', A', B')$ nor does it reveal the receiver's identity (i.e., α). We will explain this in detail in the next Section.

Anonymity Revocation When need arises, (r, c, R, C, G, H, m) is brought to the trustee who can find out the receiver's identity α by computing the order of G. As has been shown in Section 2, computing the order of G is very easy with the knowledge of $q_1, q_2, \cdots, q_n$. Hence, the trustee can easily trace the receiver directly from the signature. However, to ensure correct anonymity revocation, the signing protocol must guarantee that the resulting G is really obtained from g_α raised to sth power, where s has no common factor with Q. We will explain in the next Section that this is indeed achieved by the protocol except for a negligible probability.

5 Security Of the New Scheme

In this Section, we present some discussions on the security of Protocol 5, the main result of this paper.

Correctness The correctness of Protocol 5 is easy to see since we have

$$G^r H^{-c} = G^{r'+v} H^{-c'+u} = G^{r'} H^{-c'} G^v H^u = (a')^s G^v H^u = a,$$
$$G^R H^{-C} = G^{R'+V} H^{-C'+U} = G^{R'} H^{-C'} G^V H^U = (A')^s G^V H^U = A,$$
$$g^R h^{-C} = g^{R'+V} h^{-C'+U} = g^{R'} h^{-C'} g^V h^U = (B')^s G^V H^U = B.$$

Hence, we have

$$c = \mathcal{H}(m, G^r H^{-c}, G, H) \text{ and } C = \mathcal{H}(G^R H^{-C}, g^R h^{-C}, G, H, r, c),$$

assuming that both the signer and the receiver execute the protocol correctly.

Soundness First we show that, without knowing $\log_g h$, it is computational infeasible to find C and R such that $C = \mathcal{H}(G^R H^{-C}, g^R h^{-C}, G, H, r, c)$. To this purpose, we view $\mathcal{H}(G^R H^{-C}, *, G, H, r, c)$ as a new hash function $\mathcal{H}'(*)$. Then finding C and R such that $C = \mathcal{H}'(\}^R (^{-C})$ is computational infeasible without knowing $\log_g h$. The Schnorr signature scheme also requires this property.

Secondly, we show that

$$C = \mathcal{H}(G^R H^{-C}, g^R h^{-C}, G, H, r, c)$$

guarantees $\log_G H = \log_g h$ except for a negligible probability. Here we can ignore the items r, c, which are used for another purpose (to be explained later). Hence, we can write $C = \mathcal{H}(G^R H^{-C}, g^R h^{-C}, G, H, r, c)$ as $C = \mathcal{H}'(\mathcal{G}^R \mathcal{H}^{-C}, g^R h^{-C}, G, H,)$, which is like Protocol 4. Since Protocol 4 is derived from Protocol 3, we consider Protocol 3 here (the validity of evolving Protocol 3 to Protocol 4 has been discussed in previous literatures). The difference between the environment of Protocol 3 and that of Protocol 5 is that q is a prime in the former while Q is a composite in the latter. *However, this difference does not affect the validity of Protocol 5 since Q is the product of n large primes with n comparatively small.* Suppose $H = G^{x'}$, $h = g^x$ and $x' \neq x$. The prover can succeed in cheating if and only if he can find w and w' such that for the challenge c given (after choosing w and w') by the verifier, $G^r = G^{w'} H^c$ and $g^r = g^w h^c$ hold for some r. That is, $r = w' + x'c \bmod \text{ord}(G)$ and $r = w + xc \bmod \text{ord}(g) = Q$. Hence, we should have at least one q_i such that $w' + x'c = w + xc \bmod q_i$, i.e., $c = (w' - w)/(x - x') \bmod q_i$. This implies that for any given w and w', the probability that the verifier chooses the "right" c is at most $1/q_i$.

Anonymity We now show that the signer is unable to trace any signature, say, (r, c, R, C, G, H, m), to the transcript $(w, W, r', c', R', C', a', A', B')$ produced by the corresponding signing protocol instance. Observe that $c' = c+u$ and $r = r'+v$ for randomly chosen u and v, and u and v are kept secret by the receiver. Hence, r and c are perfectly blinded. Similarly, we have $C' = C + U$ and $R = R' + V$, where U and V are also secretly and randomly chosen by the receiver. Therefore, R and C cannot be determined from R' and C'. We also have $G = g_\alpha^s$ and $H = h_\alpha^s$ for secret s. As a result, g_α can not be linked to G.

Trying to "match" (r, c, R, C, G, H, m) with $(w, W, r', c', R', C', a', A', B')$ by checking $C = \mathcal{H}(G^R H^{-C}, B'g^{R-R'} h^{C'-C}, G, H, r, c)$ does not help at all. This is because we have $B' = g^{R'}h^{-C'}$ for every transcript. Hence, every transcript $(w, W, r', c', R', C', a', A', B')$ can "match" every signed message

$$(r, c, R, C, G, H, m),$$

i.e., they "match" even they are produced from different signing protocol instances.

Anonymity Revocation This is the central function of Protocol 5. We need to show that it is impossible, except with negligible probability, for the receiver to mislead the trustee by present G and H other than specified by the protocol.

Apparently, the receiver can find c and r satisfying $c = \mathcal{H}(m, G^r H^{-c}, G, H)$ by simply choosing G and H such that $H = G^y$ for some y. However, our protocol requires that G and H must satisfy $C = \mathcal{H}(G^R H^{-C}, g^R h^{-C}, G, H, r, c)$. This in turn implies that the G and H chosen by the receiver must satisfy $\log_g h = \log_G H$, i.e., $x = y$. This can only happen with a negligible probability; otherwise, the receiver can find the signer's private key.

Protocol 5 is divided into two parts, Part I and Part II. This is necessary since otherwise, the receiver can present G and H as powers of g and h. In this case, the signature will be verified as valid but the order of G will be different from that of g_α. To avoid this from happening, we have r and c appear in $C = \mathcal{H}(G^R H^{-C}, g^R h^{-C}, G, H, r, c)$. By doing so, we force Part I to be completed before Part II. In this way, the receiver has no other choice than setting $G = (g_\alpha)^s$ for some s, since only $a' = g_\alpha^w$ is given to the receiver in Part II.

The only way for the receiver to present a G having different order from that of g_α is that he chooses a s such that it has a common factor with Q. This happens with a negligible probability.

6 Implementation

In the security proof in Section 5, we imply an assumption that each receiver goes to each signer to get blind signature only once. Therefore, the application of this scheme is limited to the situation where each receiver gets each signer's signature only once, such as for registration scenario.

For multiple signing application, such as bank and users, the implementation should be like this: α is divided into two parts, $\alpha = \alpha_1 \alpha_2$, where $|\alpha_1| = n_1$, $|\alpha_2| = n_2$ and $|\alpha| = n = n_1 + n_2$. α_1 is used as the identity of a user while α_2 is the index to show that this is the α_2-th time the user α_1 coming for blind signature.

The signer, therefore, needs to keep a counter for each α_1. The content of the counter is α_2. When α_1 comes for blind signature, the signer does it with $g_{\alpha_1 \alpha_2}$ and then updates the counter to $\alpha_2 + 1$.

In this case, we can have 2^{n_1} receivers and each receiver can have 2^{n_2} blind signatures from each signer. (But receivers $(00 \cdots 0)_2$ and $(11 \cdots 1)_2$ can only have $2^{n_2} - 1$ blind signatures.)

The trustee need not go to any signer for just tracing the receiver, but needs to check with the signer for tracing each transaction(or tracing coin).

It should be pointed out that our scheme is less computationally efficient than the previous schemes. For example, we take the sizes of $p, q_1, q_2, ..., q_n, n$ in our scheme as follows: $n = 30$ and each q_i has 300 bits. Let $n_1 = 20, n_2 = 10$. The scheme can support about one million users. Each user can have 1000 blind signatures from each signer.

With these parameters, p has about 9000 bits which is about 8.8 times larger than the typical value of p (i.e., 1024 bits); To increase the speed of Protocol 5, we can restrict the size of $x, w, s, r, -c, u, v, W, R, -C, U, V$. It is not necessary to choose them from $\mathbf{Z}_Q$ for the security purpose. By suitable adjustment, we can make all the exponential computations in the protocol have relatively small power, independent to Q. Therefore, computing exponential mod p in our scheme is about $8.8^2 = 77$ times slower than a 1024-bit exponentiation. In fact, the exponential computation for large modulus p with small exponent has complexity smaller than $O(|p|^2)$. This is because FFT-based multiplication plus Montgomery's method can reduce the complexity to $O(|p| \log |p| \log \log |p|)$. FFT method is efficient only to large p, therefore, meets our setting very well.

Of course, above parameter sizes may be not sufficient for certain applications. Then we can enlarge the parameter sizes at low extra cost. For example, if we enlarge n to 60, the system can contain 2^{40} users with each user having one million possible signatures from each signer. On the other hand, the system is slowed down by a factor smaller than $2^2 = 4$.

Remarks on the Factorization of Q The security of our scheme is based on the hardness of the factoring Q. Here Q is a product of some 300-bit primes. Q itself has nearly ten thousand bits. It is apparently that any factoring algorithm whose complexity depends on the size of Q cannot be feasible for factorizing Q. Currently two factoring algorithms have complexity dependent on the size of the prime factors. One is Pollard's algorithm which requires the prime factors being smooth. Therefore, this algorithm can be resisted by choosing secure prime factors. The other is so-called Elliptic Curve Factoring. It is estimated that ECF so far is infeasible to factor the integer with 300 bit prime factors. In our scheme, the ECF is more infeasible due to the large size of Q(the ECF needs to do exponential computations over $\mathbf{Z}_Q$).

7 Conclusions

The new magic ink signature scheme we have presented in this paper is a blind signature scheme with anonymity revocation. The major difference between our scheme and the previous schemes is that our scheme is transcript irrelevant in performing anonymity revocation while the previous schemes are not. More specifically, the trustee can trace a receiver's identity directly from a signature; he does not need to search the transcript of the corresponding signing protocol instance. Therefore, in our scheme the trustee can do the anonymity revocation along. In addition, each signer need not maintain a huge database to store all the transcripts for later revocation.

Acknowledgment The authors would like to thank Stadler for pointing out an error in the early version of this paper and to thank the anonymous referee for his valuable suggestions, on improving the sizes of the parameters and referring us to some important references.

References

1. S. Brands, "An efficient off-line electronic cash system based on the representation problem", Technical Report of CWI, CS-R9323, pp. 1–77, 1993.
2. J. Camenisch, U. Maurer and M. Stadler, "Digital payment systems with passive anonymity-revoking trustees", *ESORICS '96*, LNCS 1146, Springer-Verlag, pp. 33–43, 1996.
3. D. Chaum, "Blind signature for untraceable payments", *Advances in Cryptology — Proc. of Crypto '82*, Plenum Press, pp. 199–203, 1983.
4. D. Chaum, J. Evertse and J. van de Graff, "An improved protocol for demonstrating possession of discrete logarithm and some generalizations", in the Proceedings of Eurocrypt'87, LNCS, Springer-Verlag pp. 200-212.
5. D. Chaum and T. P. Pedersen, "Wallet databases with observers", *Advances in Cryptology — Proc. of Crypto '92*, LNCS 740, Springer-Verlag, pp. 89–105, 1993.
6. G. Davida, Y. Frankel, Y. Tsiounis and M. Yung, "Anonymity control in e-cash systems", *Financial Cryptography*, in LNCS, Springer-Verlag.
7. Y. Desmedt, "Securing traceability of ciphertexts – Towards a secure software key escrow system", *Advances in Cryptology — Proc. of Eurocrypt '95*, LNCS 921, Springer-Verlag, pp. 147–157, 1995.
8. Y. Desmedt and Y. Frankel, "Threshold cryptosystems", *Advances in Cryptology — Proc. of Crypto '89*, LNCS 435, Springer-Verlag, pp. 307–315, 1990.
9. A. Fiat and A. Shamir, "How to prove yourself : Practical solutions to identification and signature problems", Proceedings of Crypt'86, LNCS, Springer-Verlag, pp. 186-194.
10. Y. Frankel, Y. Tsiounis and M. Yung, "Indirect discourse proofs: achieving efficient fair off-line e-cash", *Advances in Cryptology — Proc. of Asiacrypt '96*, LNCS 1163, Springer-Verlag, pp. 286–300, 1996.
11. M. Jakobsson and M. Yung, "Distributed "magic ink" signatures", *Advances in Cryptology — Proc. of Eurocrypt '97*, LNCS 1233, Springer-Verlag, pp. 450–464, 1997.
12. T. Okamoto, "Provable secure and practical identification schemes and corresponding signature schemes", *Advances in Cryptology - Proc. of Crypto '92*, LNCS 740, Springer-Verlag, pp. 31–53, 1993.
13. T. Okamoto and K. Ohta, "Divertible zero-knowledge interactive proofs and commutative random self-reducibility", *Advances in Cryptology — Proc. of Proc. of Eurocrypt '89*, LNCS 434, Springer-Verlag, pp. 134–149, 1990.
14. M. Stadler, J-M. Piveteau and J. Camenisch, "Fair blind signatures", *Advances in Cryptology — Proc. of Eurocrypt '95*, LNCS 921, Springer-Verlag, pp. 209–219, 1995.
15. E. R. Verheul and H. C. Tilborg, "Binding ElGamal: a fraud-detectable alternative to key-escrow proposals", *Advances in Cryptology — Proc. of Eurocrypt '97*, LNCS 1233, Springer-Verlag, pp. 119–133, 1997.
16. B. von Solms and D. Naccache, "On blind signatures and perfect crimes", *Computers and Security*, 11(6):581–583, 1992.

A New Aspect of Dual Basis for Efficient Field Arithmetic

Chang-Hyi Lee[1] and Jong-In Lim[2]

[1] Samsung Advanced Institute of Technology,
chang@saitgw.sait.samsung.co.kr
[2] Korea University,
jilim@tiger.korea.ac.kr

Abstract. In this paper we consider a special type of dual basis for finite fields, $GF(2^m)$, where the variants of m are presented in section 2. We introduce our field representing method for efficient field arithmetic(such as field multiplication and field inversion). It reveals a very effective role for both software and hardware(VLSI) implementations, but the aspect of hardware design of its structure is out of this manuscript and so, here, we deal only the case of its software implementation(the efficiency of hardware implementation is appeared in another article submitted to IEEE Transactions on Computers). A brief description of several advantageous characteristics of our method is that (1) the field multiplication in $GF(2^m)$ can be constructed only by $m+1$ vector rotations and the same amount of vector XOR operations, (2) there is required no additional work load such as basis changing(from standard to dual basis or from dual basis to standard basis as the conventional dual based arithmetic does), (3) the field squaring is only bit-by-bit permutation and it has a good regularity for its implementation, and (4) the field inversion process is available to both cases of its implementation using Fermat's Theorem and using *almost inverse* algorithm[14], especially the case of using the *almost inverse* algorithm has an additional advantage in finding(computing) its complete inverse element(i.e., there is required no pre-computed table of the values, x^{-k}, $k = 1, 2, \ldots$).

1 Introduction

Field arithmetic is fundamental in the implementation of Elliptic Curve Cryptosystem(ECC), one of the public key cryptosystems suggested by N. Koblitz [1] and V. Miller [2]. To achieve an effective ECC, there needs efficient implementations of field arithmetic operations. Among these operations, the field multiplication and the field inversion are very critical to the time/hardware complexity of their software and hardware implementations. In general, there are three methods to represent the field elements in $GF(q^m)$ depending upon what type of basis is used for the field, polynomial basis(standard basis), normal basis, or dual basis. It is known that the dual basis multipliers are the most hardware efficient multipliers available, both in bit-serial and in bit-parallel designs [3],

[4], [5]. But in its software implementation as well as such a hardware implementation with dual basis, one should pay some additional costs, such as basis conversion and a little of additional complexity in the implementation of field squaring. Here, in this manuscript, we insist that there exists a special type of dual basis over which the performance and implementing effectiveness of field arithmetic(field multiplication and field inversion) surpass those over optimal normal basis[7][8][9] or trinomial standard basis(optimized polynomial basis).

Whatever basis is used to represent the field elements of $GF(2^m)$, each of them has its simplified and effective form, so called *trinomial standard basis*, optimal dual basis(which is dual to a trinomial basis)[5], optimal normal basis[10](of which multiplication table has the least number$(2m - 1)$ of nonzero entries).

As said previously, in our special type of dual basis of $GF(2^m)$ over $GF(2)$, the field arithmetic operations can be accomplished with gaining both benefits of dual basis and normal basis(or optimal normal basis), where m is the field extending dimension over $GF(2)$ on which the first type of optimal normal basis exists, i.e.

$$m = 4, 10, 12, 18, 28, 36, 52, 58, 60, 66, 82, 100, 106, 130, 138, 148,$$
$$162, 172, 178, 180, 196, 210, 226, 268, 292, 316, 346, 348 \cdots$$

Note that our dual basis is not a self-dual normal basis[11]. In the following subsection, we describe some mathematical background for general dual basis and in section 2, there is presented our method to implement field arithmetic operations. In section 3, we describe our implementing algorithms(for the aspect of their VLSI design, we have described it in another article).

1.1 Dual Basis

Throughout this paper it is assumed that the reader is familiar with the basic theory of finite fields, and for more details one may refer to [12]. Let $Tr(\cdot)$ be the trace function of $GF(q^m)$ to $GF(q)$ defined by

$$Tr(a) = \sum_{i=0}^{m-1} a^{q^i},$$

which is a special type of linear functional(linear transformation) of $GF(q^m)$ to $GF(q)$. In general, there are q^m linear functionals of $GF(q^m)$ to $GF(q)$ and by them we can define the general duality between two bases $\{\varphi_i\}$ and $\{\psi_i\}$ for $GF(q^m)$ such as the following.

Definition 1. *Let f be a nontrivial linear functional of $GF(q^m)$ to $GF(q)$. Any two bases, $\{\varphi_i\}$ and $\{\psi_i\}$, are called dual with respect to f if they satisfy the following equation.*

$$f(\varphi_i \psi_j) = \begin{cases} 1 & ,if\ i = j \\ 0 & ,if\ i \neq j \end{cases}$$

Theorem 1. *Every basis for $GF(q^m)$ has its unique dual basis with respect to any given nontrivial linear functional f of $GF(q^m)$ to $GF(q)$.*

Theorem 2. *If $\{\varphi_i\}$ and $\{\psi_i\}$ are dual bases for $GF(q^m)$ to each other, then any element $a \in GF(q^m)$ represented via $\{\varphi_i\}$ can be rewritten in the form of*

$$a = \sum_{i=0}^{m-1} f(a\varphi_i)\psi_i$$

via the basis $\{\psi_i\}$.

Here we describe a bit serial multiplier due to Berlekamp[3] which uses a self-dual basis representation. Let

$$\varphi = \{1, \alpha, \alpha^2, \cdots, \alpha^{m-1}\}$$

be a polynomial(standard) basis of $GF(2^m)$ over $GF(2)$, $p(t)$ is the minimal polynomial of α, and let

$$\psi = \{\psi_0, \psi_1, \cdots, \psi_{m-1}\}$$

be its self-dual basis with respect to trace function $Tr(\cdot)$, i.e. $\psi_j = \alpha^j$, $j = 0, 1, \cdots, m-1$ and $Tr(\alpha^i \psi_j) = 1$ if $i = j$ and $= 0$ if $i \neq j$. And let $p(t) = \sum_{i=0}^{m-1} p_i t^i$ is the minimal polynomial of α over $GF(2)$,i.e. the field defining irreducible polynomial for $GF(2^m)$. Then for each $x \in GF(2^m)$, we have

$$x = \sum_{i=0}^{m-1} x_i \alpha^i = \sum_{i=0}^{m-1} Tr(x\alpha^i)\psi_i = \sum_{i=0}^{m-1} [x]_i \psi_i,$$

where $[x]_i$ are the coordinates of x with respect to the dual basis ψ. Then we have

$$[\alpha x]_j = Tr(\alpha x \cdot \alpha^j) = Tr(\alpha^{j+1} x) = [x]_{j+1},$$

for $0 \leq j \leq m-2$, and

$$[\alpha x]_{m-1} = Tr(\alpha^m x) = Tr(\sum_{i=0}^{m-1} p_i \alpha^i x)$$
$$= \sum_{i=0}^{m-1} p_i Tr(\alpha^i x) = \sum_{i=0}^{m-1} p_i [x]_i.$$

This mechanism is in charge of the very critical role in the field multiplication process based on a dual basis. For the concrete explanation, let $y = \sum_{i=0}^{m-1} y_i \alpha^i \in GF(2^m)$, then for each k, $0 \leq k \leq m-1$,

$$[xy]_k = \left[x \sum_{j=0}^{m-1} y_j \alpha^j \right]_k = \sum_{j=0}^{m-1} y_j [\alpha^j x]_k = \sum_{j=0}^{m-1} y_j [\alpha^k x]_j.$$

Thus the product of x and y with dual based coordinates can be obtained by the computation diagram in Fig.1, in that figure, $\oplus$ denotes the bit-by-bit XOR

Fig. 1. Block diagram for general dual basis multiplication

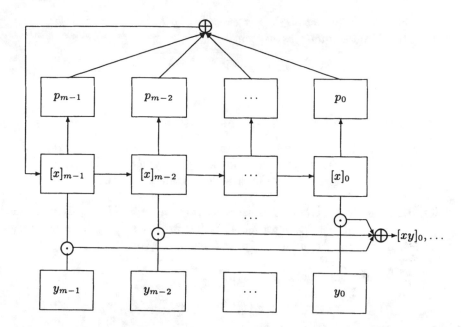

operation and $\odot$ denotes the bit-by-bit logic AND operation which are the two field operations in $GF(2)$.

As seen in Fig.1, in the general case(non self-dual), the product of two elements in $GF(2^m)$ using dual basis representation requires the extra work to convert one of the two elements into the representation over its dual basis(or from dual to standard basis) and it can be easily checked to note that for the simplicity of the upper XOR-summation part in Fig.1, one selects a very simple(small number of nonzero terms) irreducible polynomial, i.e., trinomial, etc., for *optimized dual basis*[10].

From the Fig.1, we can easily get the following theorem in generalized form.

Theorem 3. *Let α be a root of the irreducible polynomial defining the field, $GF(q^m)$. And let $\psi = \{\psi_i\}$ be the dual basis to the standard basis $\varphi = \{\alpha^i\}$ with respect to a linear functional f of $GF(q^m)$ to $GF(2)$.*

If, for $x, y, z \in GF(q^m)$, $xy = z$ then the following relation holds. (in the following, $[\cdot]_j$ means the jth coefficient over the dual basis ψ.)

$$\begin{bmatrix} f(y) & f(y\alpha) & \cdots & f(y\alpha^{m-1}) \\ f(y\alpha) & f(y\alpha^2) & \cdots & f(y\alpha^m) \\ \vdots & \vdots & \ddots & \vdots \\ f(y\alpha^{m-1}) & f(y\alpha^m) & \cdots & f(y\alpha^{2m-2}) \end{bmatrix} \begin{bmatrix} x_0 \\ x_1 \\ \vdots \\ x_{m-1} \end{bmatrix} = \begin{bmatrix} f(z) \\ f(z\alpha) \\ \vdots \\ f(z\alpha^{m-1}) \end{bmatrix} \quad (1)$$

$$= \left([z]_0, [z]_1, \cdots, [z]_{m-1}\right)^t$$

Let's denote the above matrix equation by $M(\mathbf{y}) \cdot \mathbf{x}^t = \mathbf{z}^t$, where the superscript, t, denotes the transposition.

2 Description of the theoretic evolution

2.1 Circular Dual Basis

Throughout the following, it is assumed the characteristic of $GF(q)$ is 2, i.e. q is a power of 2. In this section we propose a new type of dual basis named *circular dual basis* and extract some useful results from it for the field arithmetic.

Definition 2. *Let $p(t)$ be a nonzero polynomial over $GF(q)$, where q is a prime power, and $p(0) \neq 0$. Then the least positive integer e for which $p(t)$ divides $t^e - 1$ is called the order(or period) of p and denoted by $\mathrm{ord}(p(t))$.*

For the convenience, let's call the polynomial

$$p(t) = 1 + t + t^2 + \cdots + t^m \in GF(q)[t]$$

by *compact polynomial* of degree m over $GF(q)$.

Theorem 4. *For a positive integer $m \geq 2$, if $m+1$ is prime number and m is the multiplicative order of q modulo $m+1$, then there exists a unique irreducible compact polynomial $p(t)$ of which degree m and of which order is $m+1$. That is, $p(t) = 1 + t + t^2 + \cdots + t^m$ is irreducible over the field and it divides $t^{m+1} - 1$.*

Proof. By theorem 3.5 in [12], the number of monic irreducible polynomials in $GF(q)[t]$ of degree m and order e is equal to $\phi(e)/m$, where ϕ is a Euler's function. And in our case, $e = m+1$, and so $\phi(e) = m$. Hence the unique monic irreducible polynomial of degree m which divides $t^{m+1} - 1$ is the very *compact polynomial.* $\square$

We call by *circular polynomial* such compact and *irreducible* polynomial of which order is $m+1$ as in the above and call by *circular dual basis* the dual basis of circular polynomial. For the concrete example, considering those over the field $GF(2)$, we are led to the following result.

Theorem 5. *Over the field $GF(2)$, there are circular polynomials of which degrees are one of the following values m;*

$$m = 4, 10, 12, 18, 28, 36, 52, 58, 60, 66, 82, 100, 106, 130, 138, 148,$$
$$162, 172, 178, 180, 196, 210, 226, 268, 292, 316, 346, 348 \cdots$$
$$= \text{the set of all dimensions for which the first}$$
$$\text{type of optimal normal basis over } GF(2) \text{ exist.}$$

Proof. By the previous theorem, each degrees m of the circular polynomial must be a positive number such that $q = 2$ is a primitive element modulo the prime number $m + 1$. And these are the same with the set of numbers which are the degrees on which the first type of optimal normal basis exists[10][13]. □

Throughout the following, it is assumed that $p(t) = \sum_{i=0}^{m} t^i$ is a circular polynomial of degree m over $GF(q)$, i.e. the irreducible polynomial over $GF(q)$ of degree m which divides $(t^{m+1} - 1)$. The m-dimensional extended field $GF(q^m)$ over $GF(q)$ defined by the circular polynomial $p(t)$ has the standard basis

$$\varphi = \{1, \alpha, \alpha^2, \cdots, \alpha^{m-1}\},$$

where α is a root of $p(t)$.

Theorem 6. *If we fix the linear functional in theorem 2 by the trace map $Tr(\cdot)$ of $GF(q^m)$ to $GF(q)$, the dual basis $\psi = \{\psi_0, \psi_1, \cdots, \psi_{m-1}\}$ to the standard basis φ are represented in the following form:*

$$\psi_i = \alpha + \alpha^{-i}$$
$$= \alpha + \alpha^{m+1-i}.$$

Those can be also represented in the basis elements α^i's of φ such as;

$$\psi_0 = 1 + \alpha, \tag{2}$$

$$\psi_1 = s + \alpha, \ s = \sum_{i=0}^{m-1} \varphi_i, \tag{3}$$

$$\psi_j = \alpha^{m+1-j} + \alpha, \ j = 2, 3, \cdots, m - 1. \tag{4}$$

Proof. By the theorem 1.5 in [13], if

$$g(t) = (t - \alpha)(\beta_0 + \beta_1 t + \cdots + \beta_{m-1} t^{m-1}), \tag{5}$$

then the dual basis is $\psi = \{\psi_i\}$, where

$$\psi_i = \frac{\beta_i}{g'(\alpha)}, \ i = 0, 1, \cdots, m - 1. \tag{6}$$

Through the expansion of equation(5), we can easily get the representations of β_i's in the polynomial form of α^{-1};

$$\beta_i = \sum_{j=1}^{i+1} (\alpha^{-1})^j, \ i = 0, 1, \cdots, m - 1.$$

Furthermore $g'(\alpha) = 1 + \alpha^2 + \alpha^4 + \cdots + \alpha^{m-2}$, and note that

$$(1 + \alpha)g'(\alpha) = 1 + \alpha + \alpha^2 + \cdots + \alpha^{m-1} = \alpha^{-1}$$

$$\Rightarrow g'(\alpha) = \frac{1}{\alpha(1 + \alpha)}. \tag{7}$$

Hence, by equation(6) and equation(7), we get

$$\psi_i = \frac{\beta_i}{g'(\alpha)}$$

$$= (\alpha + \alpha^2) \sum_{j=1}^{i+1} (\alpha^{-1})^j$$

$$= (\alpha + \alpha^2)(1 + \alpha + \alpha^2 + \cdots + \alpha^{m-i-1})$$

$$= \alpha + \alpha^{m+1-i}.$$

□

From the above, we easily get the following basis changing matrix D_0 from the dual basis ψ to the standard basis φ;

$$(x_i)^t = D_0([x]_i)^t = \begin{bmatrix} 1 & 1 & 0 & 0 & \cdots & 0 & 0 & 0 \\ 1 & 0 & 1 & 1 & \cdots & 1 & 1 & 1 \\ 0 & 1 & 0 & 0 & \cdots & 0 & 0 & 1 \\ 0 & 1 & 0 & 0 & \cdots & 0 & 1 & 0 \\ \vdots & \vdots & \vdots & \vdots & \ddots & \vdots & \vdots & \vdots \\ 0 & 1 & 0 & 1 & \cdots & 0 & 0 & 0 \\ 0 & 1 & 1 & 0 & \cdots & 0 & 0 & 0 \end{bmatrix} \begin{bmatrix} [x]_0 \\ [x]_1 \\ [x]_2 \\ [x]_3 \\ \vdots \\ [x]_{m-2} \\ [x]_{m-1} \end{bmatrix} \tag{8}$$

Here we introduce one(bit) additional coefficient $s[x]$ for the utilized representation of $\mathbf{x} = ([x]_i) \in GF(2^m)$ over the circular dual basis such as the following:

$$s[x] = \sum_{i=0}^{m-1} [x]_i$$

$\mathbf{x} = ([x]_0, [x]_1, \ldots, [x]_{m-1})$ over the dual basis

$$\bar{\mathbf{x}} := ([x]_0, [x]_1, \ldots, [x]_{m-1}, s[x]) \tag{9}$$

We call the representation $\bar{\mathbf{x}}$ by circular dual based representation. By this notion, the equation(8) can be rewritten as:

$$\begin{bmatrix} x_0 \\ x_1 \\ x_2 \\ x_3 \\ \vdots \\ x_{m-1} \\ 0 \end{bmatrix} = \begin{bmatrix} 1 & 1 & 0 & 0 & \cdots & 0 & 0 & 0 \\ 0 & 1 & 0 & 0 & \cdots & 0 & 0 & 1 \\ 0 & 1 & 0 & 0 & \cdots & 0 & 1 & 0 \\ 0 & 1 & 0 & 0 & \cdots & 1 & 0 & 0 \\ \vdots & \vdots & \vdots & \vdots & \ddots & \vdots & \vdots & \vdots \\ 0 & 1 & 1 & 0 & \cdots & 0 & 0 & 0 \\ 0 & 0 & 0 & 0 & \cdots & 0 & 0 & 0 \end{bmatrix} \begin{bmatrix} [x]_0 \\ [x]_1 \\ [x]_2 \\ [x]_3 \\ \vdots \\ [x]_{m-1} \\ s[x] \end{bmatrix} \tag{10}$$

$$\Rightarrow \text{ let's abbreviate this eq. by } \mathbf{x}^t = D\bar{\mathbf{x}}^t \tag{11}$$

Using the above utilities, we got the following theorem.

Theorem 7. *Let* $\mathbf{x}, \mathbf{y}, \mathbf{z} \in GF(2^m)$, $\mathbf{z} = \mathbf{xy}$, *and let*

$$\bar{\mathbf{x}} = ([x]_0, [x]_1, \ldots, [x]_{m-1}, s[x])$$
$$\bar{\mathbf{y}} = ([y]_0, [y]_1, \ldots, [y]_{m-1}, s[y])$$
$$\bar{\mathbf{z}} = ([z]_0, [z]_1, \ldots, [z]_{m-1}, s[z])$$

be their circular dual based representations. Then, the equation(1) can be rewritten as the following form:

$$\bar{\mathbf{z}} = \bar{\mathbf{x}} \begin{bmatrix} [y]_0 & [y]_1 & [y]_2 & \cdots & [y]_{m-2} & [y]_{m-1} & s[y] \\ s[y] & [y]_0 & [y]_1 & \cdots & [y]_{m-3} & [y]_{m-2} & [y]_{m-1} \\ [y]_{m-1} & s[y] & [y]_0 & \cdots & [y]_{m-4} & [y]_{m-3} & [y]_{m-2} \\ \vdots & \vdots & \vdots & \ddots & \vdots & \vdots & \vdots \\ [y]_2 & [y]_3 & [y]_4 & \cdots & s[y] & [y]_0 & [y]_1 \\ [y]_1 & [y]_2 & [y]_3 & \cdots & [y]_{m-1} & s[y] & [y]_0 \end{bmatrix}$$

$$= \sum_{i=0}^{m} [x]_i Rot_r(\bar{\mathbf{y}}, i), \ [x]_m := s[x], \tag{12}$$

where $Rot_r(\bar{\mathbf{y}}, i)$ denotes the rotated vector of $\bar{\mathbf{y}}$ to the right by i positions.

Proof. Note that

$$Tr(\mathbf{y}\alpha^i) = [y]_i \ \ i = 0, 1, \ldots, m-1,$$
$$Tr(\mathbf{y}\alpha^m) = Tr(\mathbf{y}\sum_{i=0}^{m-1}\alpha^i) = \sum_{i=0}^{m-1}[y]_i = s[y],$$
$$\alpha^{m+1} = 1.$$

Using these notions, the equation(1) can be rewritten as in the following one bit expanded form.

$$\begin{bmatrix} [y]_0 & [y]_1 & \cdots & [y]_{m-1} & s[y] \\ [y]_1 & [y]_2 & \cdots & s[y] & [y]_0 \\ \vdots & \vdots & \ddots & \vdots & \vdots \\ [y]_{m-1} & s[y] & \cdots & [y]_{m-3} & [y]_{m-2} \\ s[y] & [y]_0 & \cdots & [y]_{m-2} & [y]_{m-1} \end{bmatrix} \begin{bmatrix} x_0 \\ x_1 \\ \vdots \\ x_{m-1} \\ 0 \end{bmatrix} = \begin{bmatrix} [z]_0 \\ [z]_1 \\ \vdots \\ [z]_{m-1} \\ \delta \end{bmatrix}, \tag{13}$$

$$\Rightarrow \text{let's abbreviate this eq. by } M(\bar{\mathbf{y}})\mathbf{x}^t = \bar{\mathbf{z}}^t \tag{14}$$

where δ is not determined yet. It will be turn out to be $\sum_{i=0}^{m-1}[z]_i$. Now, using the equation(10) and (11), we replace the standard based representation of $\mathbf{x}$ appeared in the above equation by our circular dual based representation, then we got:

$$MD\bar{\mathbf{x}}^t = \bar{\mathbf{z}}^t \tag{15}$$

Take the transposition of the both sides, then we are led to the new equation:

$$\bar{x}D^t M^t = \bar{z} \tag{16}$$

Hence we get to know that the left hand side of equation(16) is the right hand side of the theorem. Furthermore, the fact that the sum of all row vectors in $D^t M^t$ is zero-vector gives us the result $\delta = \sum_{i=0}^{m-1}[z]_i$. This completes the proof. □

In the following section, with these results we deal the field multiplication, squaring, and field inversion.

3 Description of the technique(algorithm)

In this section we describe the algorithms for efficient field arithmetic operations based on the previous results.

3.1 Field Multiplication

As one sees in the previous section, we got to know that

$$\begin{aligned}
\mathbf{x} &= ([x]_0, [x]_1, \ldots, [x]_{m-1}, [x]_m), \quad [x]_m = \sum_{i=1}^{m-1}[x]_i \\
\mathbf{y} &= ([y]_0, [y]_1, \ldots, [y]_{m-1}, [y]_m), \quad [y]_m = \sum_{i=1}^{m-1}[y]_i \\
\mathbf{z} &= \mathbf{xy} \\
&= \sum_{i=0}^{m}[x]_i Rot_r(\mathbf{y}, i).
\end{aligned}$$

From this we can easily construct the following very simple field multiplication algorithm in pseudo-code(Table 1); But note that $\sum_{i=0}^{m} Rot_r(\mathbf{y}, i) = zero\ vector$.

Table 1. Field multiplication algorithm(1)

INPUT : $\mathbf{x}$, $\mathbf{y}$: circular dual based elements in $GF(2^m)$.
OUTPUT : $\mathbf{z} = \mathbf{xy}$ in circular dual based representation.
$\mathbf{z} \leftarrow 0$ /* initialize $\mathbf{z}$ to be zero vector */
for $(i = 0; i \leq m; i++)$
{
    if $([x]_i \neq 0)$ $\mathbf{z} \leftarrow \mathbf{z} \oplus Rot_r(\mathbf{y}, i)$;
}

From this notion, we get more developed algorithm(see Table 2, but if we prepare the pre-computed table of rotated vectors of $\mathbf{y}$ then the above algorithm would be more effective);

Hence we can achieve $\mathbf{z} = \mathbf{xy}$ only by $k(\leq \frac{m}{2})$ vector rotations and the same amount of vector XOR operations.

Table 2. Field multiplication algorithm(2)

INPUT : x, y : circular dual based elements in $GF(2^m)$.
OUTPUT : z = xy in circular dual based representation.
z ← 0 /* initialize z to be zero vector */
if ((# of nonzero entries of x)$> \frac{m}{2}$) negate x;
for $(i = 0; i \leq m; i++)$
{
    if $([x]_i \neq 0)$ z ← z ⊕ $Rot_r(y, i)$;
}

3.2 Squaring

From now on, it is assumed that all coefficients of any element in $GF(2^m)$ over $GF(2)$ were represented over the circular dual basis defined in the above.

Theorem 8. *Let* x, y $\in GF(2^m)$, y $= x^2$, *and*

$$\mathbf{x} = ([x]_0, [x]_1, \cdots, [x]_{m-1}, [x]_m = s[x])$$
$$\mathbf{y} = ([y]_0, [y]_1, \cdots, [y]_{m-1}, [y]_m = s[y]).$$

Then the following equation holds;

$$\mathbf{y}^t = \begin{bmatrix} 1 & 0 & 0 & \cdots & 0 & 0 & 0 & \cdots & 0 & 0 \\ 0 & 0 & 0 & \cdots & 0 & 1 & 0 & \cdots & 0 & 0 \\ 0 & 1 & 0 & \cdots & 0 & 0 & 0 & \cdots & 0 & 0 \\ 0 & 0 & 0 & \cdots & 0 & 0 & 1 & \cdots & 0 & 0 \\ \vdots & \vdots & \vdots & \ddots & \vdots & \vdots & \vdots & \ddots & \vdots & \vdots \\ 0 & 0 & 0 & \cdots & 0 & 0 & 0 & \cdots & 1 & 0 \\ 0 & 0 & 0 & \cdots & 0 & 0 & 0 & \cdots & 0 & 0 \\ 0 & 0 & 0 & \cdots & 0 & 0 & 0 & \cdots & 0 & 1 \\ 0 & 0 & 0 & \cdots & 1 & 0 & 0 & \cdots & 0 & 0 \end{bmatrix} \mathbf{x}^t \qquad (17)$$

That is,

$$[y]_{2i} = [x]_i, \ i = 0, 1, \ldots, \frac{m}{2} \qquad (18)$$

$$[y]_{2j-1} = [x]_{j+\frac{m}{2}}, \ j = 1, 2, \ldots, \frac{m}{2}. \qquad (19)$$

Proof. Since the characteristic of $GF(2^m)$ is 2, the squaring map is a linear transform. So it is sufficient for us to check the behavior of basis elements(ψ_i's) via the squaring transformation. First, recall that $\psi_j = \alpha + \alpha^{-j} \bmod(m+1)$ for $j \neq 1$, then

$$\psi_j^2 = \alpha^2 + \alpha^{-2j}$$

$$= (\alpha^2 + \alpha) + (\alpha^{-2j} + \alpha)$$

$$= \psi_{m-1} + \psi_{2j}, \quad \text{for } j = 0, 1, \cdots, \frac{m}{2} - 1$$

$$\psi_{m/2}^2 = \alpha^2 + \alpha^{m+2}$$

$$= \alpha^2 + \alpha, \quad \text{since } \alpha^{m+1} = 1$$

$$= \psi_{m-1}$$

$$\psi_{m/2+j}^2 = \alpha^2 + \alpha^{m+1-(2j-1)}$$

$$= (\alpha^2 + \alpha) + (\alpha^{m+1-(2j-1)} + \alpha)$$

$$= \psi_{m-1} + \psi_{2j-1} \quad \text{for } j = 1, 2, \cdots, \frac{m}{2} - 1$$

Hence

$$[y]_{2j} = [x]_j, \quad j = 0, 1, \cdots, \frac{m}{2} - 1,$$

$$[y]_{2j-1} = [x]_{m/2+j}, \quad j = 1, 2, \cdots, \frac{m}{2} - 1$$

$$[y]_{m-1} = \sum_{i=0}^{m-1} [x]_i = s[x]$$

and moreover,

$$s[y] = \sum_{i=0}^{m-1} [y]_i$$

$$= \sum_{i=0}^{m/2-1} [x]_i + \sum_{i=1}^{m/2-1} [x]_{m/2+i} + s[x]$$

$$= [x]_{m/2}.$$

This proves the theorem. □

In the above theorem, the squaring is only a bit-by-bit permutation based on the circular dual basis, that is this squaring process needs no logic operations in its hardware implementation. Let $EXPAND_k(\cdot)$ be the function of $GF(2^k)$ to $GF(2^{2k-1})$ defined as, for given $\mathbf{x} \in GF(2^k)$:

$$EXPAND_k(\mathbf{x})_{2j+1} = 0, \quad j = 0, 1, 2, \ldots, k-2$$
$$EXPAND_k(\mathbf{x})_{2j} = \mathbf{x}_j, \quad j = 0, 1, 2, \ldots, k-1$$

Then the squaring can be described by the following simple algorithm(Table 3), in pseudo-code;

where the function $EXPAND_k(\cdot)$ can be easily implemented by small memory of table.

3.3 Conversion to Standard Basis

We showed that the basis conversion matrix of circular dual basis to its standard basis is the matrix D_0 appeared in the equation(8). From that equation, we get

Table 3. Squaring algorithm

INPUT : $\mathbf{x} = ([x]_0, [x]_1, \ldots, [x]_{m-1}, [x]_m = s[x])$;
OUTPUT : $\mathbf{x}^2$ in circular dual based form;
$\mathbf{x}^L \leftarrow ([x]_0, [x]_1, \ldots, [x]_{\frac{m}{2}})$;
$\mathbf{x}^H \leftarrow ([x]_{\frac{m}{2}+1}, [x]_{\frac{m}{2}+2}, \ldots, [x]_m, 0)$;
Return $\mathbf{x}^2 \leftarrow EXPAND_{\frac{m}{2}}(\mathbf{x}^L) \bigoplus (EXPAND_{\frac{m}{2}}(\mathbf{x}^H) >> 1)$;

---

the following conversion equation in one bit expanded form(here, x_i's denote the coordinates over the standard basis and $[x]_i$'s denote the coordinates over its circular dual basis of $\mathbf{x}$):

$$
\begin{bmatrix} x_0 \\ x_1 \\ x_2 \\ x_3 \\ \vdots \\ x_{m-1} \\ 0 \end{bmatrix} = \begin{bmatrix} 1\,0\,0\,0\,\cdots\,0\,0\,0 \\ 0\,0\,0\,0\,\cdots\,0\,0\,1 \\ 0\,0\,0\,0\,\cdots\,0\,1\,0 \\ 0\,0\,0\,0\,\cdots\,1\,0\,0 \\ \vdots\ \vdots\ \vdots\ \vdots\ \ddots\ \vdots\ \vdots\ \vdots \\ 0\,0\,1\,0\,\cdots\,0\,0\,0 \\ 0\,1\,0\,0\,\cdots\,0\,0\,0 \end{bmatrix} \begin{bmatrix} [x]_0 \\ [x]_1 \\ [x]_2 \\ [x]_3 \\ \vdots \\ [x]_{m-1} \\ [x]_m \end{bmatrix} + \begin{bmatrix} [x]_1 \\ [x]_1 \\ [x]_1 \\ [x]_1 \\ \vdots \\ [x]_1 \\ [x]_1 \end{bmatrix} . \tag{20}
$$

This equation generates the following simple representation-conversion algorithm(Table 4) of a field element from circular dual basis to its standard basis:

Table 4. Conversion to the standard based representation

INPUT : $\bar{\mathbf{x}} = ([x]_0, [x]_1, \ldots, [x]_m)$ over Cir.Dual Basis.
OUTPUT : $\mathbf{x} = (x_0, x_1, \ldots, x_{m-1}, 0)$ over Stand.Basis.
1. $\mathbf{x} \leftarrow$ rotate $\bar{\mathbf{x}}$ by one bit to the left;
2.   if $([x]_1 \neq 0)$ $\mathbf{x} \leftarrow$ negation of $\mathbf{x}$;
3. $\mathbf{x} \leftarrow$ take the reciprocal of $\mathbf{x}$;

But, simply, we need only the line 1 and 2 for the inversion algorithm in the following subsection.

3.4   Field Inversion

We point out that, from the previous results, we can construct inversion algorithm by use of the hereto made multiplication and squaring algorithms and Fermat's Theorem like as the optimized one in [10][9][7]. But here we construct it by some more fast inversion algorithm using *almost inverse algorithm*[14] and its advantage in our circular dual basis.

Let $p(t) = 1 + t + \cdots + t^m$ be a circular polynomial, i.e. irreducible polynomial and $p(\alpha) = 0$ in $GF(2^m)$, then $p(t)$ is a self-reciprocal, i.e. $t^m p(\frac{1}{t}) = p(t)$ and $\alpha^{m+1} = 1$. Let $\alpha^{-1} = u$ and let

$$
\begin{aligned}
A &= a_0 + a_1\alpha + a_2\alpha^2 + \cdots + a_{m-1}\alpha^{m-1} := A(\alpha) \in GF(2^m) \\
&= \alpha^{m-1}(a_{m-1} + a_{m-2}u + a_{m-3}u^2 + \cdots + a_0 u^{m-1}) \\
&= \alpha^{m-1} A(u) \in GF(2^m).
\end{aligned}
$$

Then the two coefficient strings, $A(\alpha)$ and $A(u)$ represented in the powers of α and u respectively, are reciprocal to each other. We can apply the *almost inverse* algorithm to $A(u)$ with the reduction polynomial $p(u) \in GF(2)[u]$. That is, We can find a polynomial in u, $B(u)$, such that

$$
A(u)B(u) = u^k \mod p(u) \tag{21}
$$

for some integer k, $0 \le k \le 2(m-1)$. And so $B(\alpha) = \alpha^{m-1} B(u)$ is an almost inverse of $A(\alpha)$ with reduction polynomial $p(\alpha)$. Now the exact inverse of $A(\alpha)$ comes to the following(by multiplying $\alpha^{2(m-1)}$ to both sides of equation(21));

$$
A(\alpha)^{-1} = \alpha^{m-1} B(u)(u^k \alpha^{2(m-1)})^{-1}
$$
$$
= B(\alpha)\alpha^{(k-2(m-1)) \bmod m+1} \tag{22}
$$

Note that, following the above notations, first, to convert the circular based element $\mathbf{x}$ into the u-polynomial type of $A(u)$ is very simple and easy(see the section §3.3) and second, α^j, $j = 1, 2, \ldots, m$, corresponds to the circular dual based element, δ_{m-j+1}, of which all components are zero except only the $(m - j + 1)_{th}$ component. The later tells us that the product of a circular dual based element $\mathbf{x}$ and α^j in the circular dual based form can be easily achieved only by one vector rotation of $\mathbf{x}$ to the right by $m - j + 1$ positions(see section §3.1).

Therefore we can describe the inversion algorithm(Table 5) for the circular dual based representation by the following pseudo-code (in the code, $ROTL_s(*, i)$ denotes the vector rotation of $*$ to the right by i bit positions in the total size of s bits, and so does $ROTR_s(*, i)$ except the rotating direction converted):

In the algorithm(Table 5), the lines indexed 11-12 in table-5 carry out the co-efficient conversion process of circular dual basis to the reciprocal(u-polynomial) of the standard basis, the lines indexed 21-26 in table-5 carry out the *almost inverse* algorithm, and, finally, the lines 31-36 carry out the coefficient conversion process of the u-polynomial to the circular dual basis. Note that, in the lines 22, 32, the division by u and the multiplication by u are simply accomplished by the left and right shift operations respectively. From this we see that, in the above inverse calculating algorithm, the representation converting part has very negligible implementation complexity comparing with just the *almost inverse* algorithm.

In this section we did not mentioned the algorithm to solve a quadratic equation, since its performance do not have an influence on the performance or efficiency of the whole elliptic curve arithmetic. But even in that case our circular dual based representation gives a very efficient resolution routine with very high (recursive)regularity and without any basis conversion and any table memory.

Table 5. Field inversion algorithm

INPUT : **x** in circular dual based form;
OUTPUT : $\mathbf{x}^{-1}$ in circular dual based form;
11. $A(u) \leftarrow ROTL_{m+1}(\mathbf{x}, 2)$;
12.   if $(A(u)_m \neq 0)$ negate $A(u)$ in the first $m + 1$ bits;

21.   set: $k = 0, B(u) = 1, C(u) = 0, F(u) = A(u), G(u) = p(u)$;
22.   While$(F(0) = 0)$ do $F = F/u$, $C = C * u$, $k = k + 1$;
23.   if ($F = 1$) goto 31;
24.   if ($\deg(F) < \deg(G)$), exchange F, G and B, C;
25. $F = F \oplus G$, $B = B \oplus C$;
26.   goto 22;

31. $t \leftarrow$ XOR sum of all coefficients in $B(u)$;
32.   if $(t \neq 0)$ $B = \neg B + t * u^m$; /* $\neg B$: negation of $B(m$ bits) */
33. $\mathbf{x}^{-1} \leftarrow ROTR_{m+1}(B, 2)$;
34. $k \leftarrow (k - 2 * (m - 1))$ mod $m + 1$;
35.   if $(k = 0)$ return $\mathbf{x}^{-1}$;
36.   return $\mathbf{x}^{-1} = ROTR_{m+1}(\mathbf{x}^{-1}, m - k + 1)$;

---

4   Attributes and advantages of the techniques

4.1   Advantages over other representation methods

There are many advantages of this representation method for field arithmetic. With hereto presented results, its advantages are described as the following.

1. There is not required any basis changing process for field multiplication, which is the extra work in the case of the conventional dual basis.
2. The field multiplication can be implemented only by vector rotations and vector XOR operations, and so its code is much simpler and its performance is much better than those over optimized normal bases.
3. The squaring of field element is just a simple bit-by-bit permutation and has a very high regularity.
4. The field inversion using *almost inverse*[14] algorithm can be implemented to calculate the exact inverse element with almost the same cost of just the *almost inverse* algorithm process, since the work to compute the production of the factor x^{-k} is reduced into only one vector rotating operation.

4.2   Limitations of the method

As said in the previous sections, §1 and §2, the circular dual basis exists only for the finite field in which the first type of optimal normal basis exists. This, however, is not a severe limitation for the cryptographic system, since there are sufficiently many suitable fields which has circular dual basis for cryptographic goals.

Notes and Comments.

- In the practical implementation of the circular dual based field arithmetic for ECC(Elliptic Curve Cryptosystem) over $GF(2^m)$, the binary representation of a field element takes the reversed order of the previously written form for one's easy comprehension, i.e.

$$a = (a_0, a_1, \ldots, a_{m-1}, a_m = s[a]) \to (a_m = s[a], a_{m-1}, \ldots, a_1, a_0).$$

And the additional dummy bit, $s[a]$, should be appeared just during the inner ECC arithmetic process.

- Following the above representation form, one would become aware of the following two facts.

  a. multiplicative identity in $GF(2^m)$ is $(\overbrace{1, 1, \ldots, 1}^{m}, 0)$
  b. For $a = (a_m, a_{m-1}, \ldots, a_1, a_0) \in GF(2^m)$, $Tr(a) = a_0$

5 Performance

5.1 Algorithm Analysis

The table-6 shows the algorithm complexities to compute one field multiplication and one field inversion(using *almost inverse* algorithm) in the three types of vector(field element in $GF(2^m)$) representation methods. In the table, the abbreviations CDB, ONB, and TPB mean the *Circular Dual Basis*, *Optimal Normal Basis*, and *Trinomial Polynomial Basis*, respectively. And AIP denotes the *Almost Inverse Process*(The measurement was roughly estimated in average sense).

Table 6. Estimations for the Algorithm Complexities

in $GF(2^m)$	CDB	ONB	TPB
field multiplication	• $m+1$ vector rotat. • $\frac{m}{2}$ vector XORs • $m+1$ bit-scannings	• $2m$ vector rotat. • $2m$ vector XORs • m vector ANDs	• $\frac{m}{2}$ vector shift operat. • $m + \frac{m}{2}$ vector XORs • m bit-scannings • $\frac{m}{2}$ table look-ups
field Inversion	• 1 AIP • 2 vector rotations	• 1 AIP • 2 basis changes • 1 field multiplication	• 1 AIP • 1 field multiplication
static memory	• 1 Kbytes	• 8 Kbytes	• 8 Kbytes

5.2 Performance of a Reference Implementation

In the table 7, the process timings of our methods for various field operations in $GF(2^{178})$ are presented, wherein they are compared with other efficient software implementations[17][18] for field arithmetic in $GF((2^{16})^{11})$ by use of composite Galois Fields and by use of the multiplication table for $GF(2^{16})$ and trinomial standard basis. The present circular dual based implementation of our method,

Table 7. Timings comparison for various field operations

	Our Method in $GF(2^{178})$	Method in [18] in $GF(2^{177})$	Method in [18] in $GF(2^{176})$	Method in [17] in $GF(2^{176})$
Field Repres. Type	Circular Dual Basis over $GF(2)$	Trinomial Stand.Basis over $GF(2)$	Trinomial Stand.Basis over $GF(2^{16})$	Trinomial Stand.Basis over $GF(2^{16})$
Total Table Memory	$\leq$ 1Kbytes	$\leq$ 1Kbytes	$\geq$ 256Kbytes	$\geq$ 256Kbytes
Plat-forms	Pentium 133MHz V.C++comp.	Pentium 133MHz Watcom 10.6 ANSI-C comp.	Pentium 133MHz Watcom 10.6 ANSI-C comp.	DEC alpha 3000, 175MHz 64-bit word
Square	$1.76\mu s$	$2.7\mu s$	$5.9\mu s$	$4.23\mu s$
Mult.	$50\mu s$	$71.8\mu s$	$62.7\mu s$	$38.6\mu s$
Invers.	$160\mu s$	$225\mu s$	$160\mu s$	$158.7\mu s$

as one sees in the above table, shows that it is very efficient in its software implementation(as well as hardware implementation) and by noting that the platform, DEC alpha 3000, has a very efficient RISC architecture for parallel processing of multi-instructions and that the simple processing structure of our circular dual based field arithmetic has a good parallelism, we see that it would be more faster than the others on the same platforms, DEC alpha 3000.

6 Conclusion

In this paper, we present a newly proposed implementation technique for an effective field arithmetic by using a special type of dual basis, named *circular dual basis*, and considered its efficiency in the field arithmetic operations. The proposed circular dual based implementation of various field operations seems to be more efficient both than those software implementations by trinomial standard bases(and other bases, but consider the notion that trinomial standard based representation is believed to be the most efficient method for the software implementation of field operations) and than those hardware implementations by optimal normal bases(,this part was dealt in our another article). Finally we point out that our method is also available and efficient on such composite

Galois fields, $GF((2^n)^m)$, that $gcd(m, n) = 1$ and m is one of the numbers in theorem 5. This would be comprehended by intuition.

References

1. N. Koblitz, *Elliptic curve cryptosystems*, Math. Comp., 48 (1987), 203-209.
2. V. Miller, *Uses of elliptic curves in cryptography*, Advances in Cryptology: Proceedings of Crypto'85, Lecture Notes in Computer Science 218 (1986), Springer-Verlag, 417-426.
3. E.R. Berlekamp, *Bit-serial Reed-Solomon encoder*, IEEE Trans. Information Theory, vol. IT-28, pp.869-874, Nov.1982.
4. C.C. Wang, T.K. Truong, H.M. Shao, L.J. Deutsch, J.K. Omura, and I.S. Reed, *VLSI architecture for computing multiplications and inversions in $GF(2^m)$*, IEEE Trans. Comput., vol. C-34, pp.1230-1234, Aug. 1985.
5. Sebastian T.J. Fenn, Mohammed Benaissa, and David Taylor, *$GF(2^m)$ Multiplication and Division Over the Dual Basis*, IEEE Trans. Comput., vol.45, pp.319-327, March 1996.
6. J.L. Massey and J.K. Omura, *Computational Method and Apparatus for Finite Field Arithmetic*, U.S. Patent Application, submitted 1981.
7. G.B. Agnew, R.C. Mullin and S.A. Vanstone, *An implementation of elliptic curve cryptosystems over $F_{2^{155}}$*, IEEE Journal on Selected Areas in Communications, Vol.11, no.5(June 1993), pp.804-813.
8. D.W. Ash, I.F. Blake, and S. Vanstone, *Low complexity normal bases*, Discrete Applied Math. 25(1989), pp.191-210.
9. T. Itoh, S. Tsujii, *A fast algorithm for computing multiplicative inverses in $GF(2^m)$ using normal bases*, Information and Computation, 78:171-177, 1988.
10. R.C. Mullin, I.M. Onyszchuk, S.A. Vanstone, and R.M. Wilson, *Optimal Normal Bases in $GF(p^n)$*, Discrete Applied Maths., pp.142-169, 1988/1989.
11. A. Lempel and M.J. Weinberger, *Self complementary normal bases in finite fields*, SIAM J. Disc. Math., 1 (1988), 193-198.
12. R. Lidl and H. Niederreiter, *An Introduction to Finite Fields and Their Applications*, Cambridge Univ. Press, 1986.
13. Alfred J. Menezes, *Applications of Finite Fields*, Kluwer Academic Publishers, 1993.
14. R. Schroepel, H. Orman, S. O'Malley and O. Spatscheck, *Fast key exchange with elliptic curve systems*, Advances in Cryptology, Proc. Crypto'95, LNCS963, D. Coppersmith, ED., Springer-Verlag, 1995, pp.43-56.
15. P.K.S. Wah and M.Z. Wang, *Realization and application of the Massey-Omura lock*, in Proc. Int. Zurich Sem., Mar.1984.
16. S.T.J. Fenn and M. Benaissa, and D. Taylor, *Finite Field Inversion Over the Dual Basis*, IEEE Trans. on VLSI Systems, vol.4, No.1, March 1996.
17. J. Guajardo and C. Paar, *Efficient Algorithms for Elliptic Curve Cryptosystems*, Advances in Cryptology, CRYPTO'97, pp.342-356, 1997.
18. Erik De Win, Antoon Bosselaers, and Servaas Vandenberghe, *A Fast Software Implementation for Arithmetic Operations in $GF(2^n)$*, Advances in Cryptology, ASIACRYPT'96, pp.65-76, 1996.

On the Security of Random Sources

Jean-Sébastien Coron

Ecole Normale Supérieure
45 rue d'Ulm
Paris, F-75230, France
coron@clipper.ens.fr

Gemplus Card International
34 rue Guynemer
Issy-les-Moulineaux, F-92447, France
coron@gemplus.com

Abstract. Many applications rely on the security of their random number generator. It is therefore essential that such devices be extensively tested for malfunction. The purpose of a statistical test is to detect *specific* weaknesses in random sources.

Maurer's universal test is a very common randomness test, capable of detecting a wide range of statistical defects. The test is based on the computation of a function which is asymptotically related to the source's entropy, which measures the effective key-size of block ciphers keyed by the source's output.

In this work we develop a variant of Maurer's test where the test function is in theory *exactly* equal to the source's entropy, thereby enabling a better detection of defects in the tested source.

1 Introduction

Random number generators are probably the most basic cryptographic primitives. They are widely used for block cipher, public-key (*e.g.* RSA-moduli), keystream generation and as passwords sources. In some algorithms (*e.g.* DSA) or protocols (*e.g.* zero-knowledge), random numbers are intrinsic to the computation. In all these applications, security tightly depends on the randomness of the source.

A *pseudo-random* generator is a deterministic polynomial time algorithm that expands short seeds into longer bit sequences, which distribution is polynomially-indistinguishable from the uniform probability distribution. In other words, the output bits must appear to be statistically independent and uniformly distributed. The first pseudo-random generator was constructed and proved by Blum and Micali, under the assumption that the discrete logarithm problem is intractable on a non-negligible fraction of instances [2]. In the light of their practical and theoretical value, constructing pseudo-random generators is a major concern. Procedures for ensuring the security of random number generators are becoming of great importance with the increased usage of electronic communication [4].

It is nevertheless difficult to give a general and reliable measure of the cryptographic quality of a pseudo-random sequence. In practice, many different tests are carried on sequences generated by the random source to evaluate its performance. These practical tests are divided into two groups : complexity tests and statistical tests. Complexity tests evaluate how much of a generated string is required to reconstruct the whole string [8] while statistical tests evaluate whether the generator's behaviour matches a specific probabilistic model. We refer the reader to [5] for a general treatment of randomness tests.

Maurer's universal test is based on the stationary ergodic source with finite memory statistical model [6]. This model allows the computation of the source's entropy, which, in turn, measures the number of bits of "unpredictability". Failure to provide such unpredictability can weaken severely the security of a cryptosystem, as an attacker could use the reduction in entropy to speed-up exhaustive search on an otherwise secure encryption algorithm.

However, Maurer's universal test only provides an asymptotic measure of the source's entropy. In this paper, we show that with a simple transformation, Maurer's test function can yield *the source's entropy*. Therefore the new test enables a more accurate detection of defects in the tested source.

The paper is organized as follows: we first recall the basic definitions of the stationary ergodic source model and the asymptotic relation between Maurer's test function and the source's entropy. Then we propose a simple transformation of Maurer's test so that the test function yields the source's entropy. Then we study the distribution of the modified test and give a sample program. Finally, we compare the performance of the two tests with respect to different random sources.

2 Statistical model for a random source

2.1 Definition

Consider an information source S emitting a sequence $U_1, U_2, U_3, \ldots$ of binary random variables. S is a *finite memory source* if there exists a positive integer M such that the conditional probability distribution of U_n, given $U_1, \ldots, U_{n-1}$, only depends on the last M bits emitted [6]:

$$P_{U_n|U_1\ldots U_{n-1}}(u_n|u_1\ldots u_{n-1}) = P_{U_n|U_{n-M}\ldots U_{n-1}}(u_n|u_{n-M}\ldots u_{n-1})$$

for $n > M$ and for every binary sequence $[u_1, \ldots, u_n] \in \{0,1\}^n$. The smallest M is called the *memory* of the source. The probability distribution of U_n is thus determined by the source's *state* $\Sigma_n = [U_{n-M}, \ldots, U_{n-1}]$ at step n.

The source is *stationary* if it satisfies :

$$P_{U_n|\Sigma_n}(u|\sigma) = P_{U_1|\Sigma_1}(u|\sigma)$$

for all $n > M$, for $u \in \{0,1\}$ and $\sigma \in \{0,1\}^M$.

The state-sequence of a stationary source with memory M forms a finite Markov chain : the source can be in a finite number (actually 2^M) of states σ_i, $0 \le i \le 2^M - 1$, and there is a set of transition probabilities $\Pr(\sigma_j|\sigma_i)$, expressing the odds that if the system is in state σ_i it will next go to state σ_j. For a general treatment of Markov chains, the reader is referred to [1].

For a general Markov chain with r states, let $P_i^{(n)}$ be the probability of being in state σ_i at time $t = n$ and let $P^{(n)}$ be the "state distribution vector" at time n, i.e., $P^{(n)} = [P_1^{(n)}, \ldots, P_r^{(n)}]$.

Let Π be the transition matrix of the chain, i.e., $\Pi_{i,j} = \Pr(\sigma_j|\sigma_i)$ where $\Pi_{i,j}$ is the element in row i and column j of Π.

For state σ_j at time n the source may originate from any state σ_i at time $n - 1$ and thus :

$$P_j^{(n)} = \Pr(\sigma_j|\sigma_1)P_1^{(n-1)} + \ldots + \Pr(\sigma_j|\sigma_r)P_r^{(n-1)}$$

which becomes in matrix notations :

$$P^{(n)} = P^{(n-1)}\Pi$$

For the class of *ergodic* Markov processes the probabilities $P_j^{(n)}$ of being in state σ_j after n emitted bits, approach (as $n \to \infty$) an equilibrium P_j which must satisfy the system of r linear equations :

$$\begin{cases} \sum_{j=1}^{r} P_j = 1 \\ \\ P_j = \sum_{i=1}^{r} P_i \Pr(\sigma_j|\sigma_i) \quad \text{for } 1 \leq j \leq r - 1 \end{cases}$$

In the case of a source with memory M, each of the 2^M states has at most two successor states with non-zero probability, depending on whether a zero or a one is emitted. The transition probabilities are thus determined by the set of conditional probabilities $p_i = \Pr(1|\sigma_i)$, $0 \leq i \leq 2^M - 1$ of emitting a one from each state σ_i. The transition matrix Π is thus defined by :

$$\Pi_{i,j} = \begin{cases} p_i & \text{if } j = 2i + 1 \bmod 2^M \\ 1 - p_i & \text{if } j = 2i \quad \bmod 2^M \\ 0 & \text{otherwise} \end{cases}$$

The entropy of state σ_i is then $H_i = H(p_i)$, where H is the binary entropy function :

$$H(x) = -x \log_2 x - (1 - x) \log_2(1 - x)$$

The source's entropy is then the average of the entropies H_i (of states σ_i) weighted with the state-probabilities P_i :

$$H_S = \sum_i P_i H_i$$

Let us now assume that the random source is used to generate the N-bit key of a block cipher and let $n(q)$ be the number of N-bit keys that must be tested (in decreasing probability order) in order to reach an overall success probability of q. Shannon proved (see [7], theorem 4) that for $q \neq 0$ and $q \neq 1$:

$$\lim_{N \to \infty} \frac{\log_2 n(q)}{N} = H_S$$

This shows that when an ergodic stationary source is used to key a block cipher, the entropy H_S is closely related to the number of keys an attacker has to try in order to find the right key. In other words, the entropy measures the effective key-size of a cryptosystem keyed by the source's output.

2.2   Probability of a bit sequence

In this section we compute the probability of emitting a bit sequence, which will be used in section 7.2. Starting from a state distribution vector $W = [W_1, \ldots, W_r]$, the probability of emitting a bit $b \in \{0, 1\}$ is :

$$\Pr[b|W] = \sum W_i \Pi_{i,j} \tag{1}$$

where the sum is taken over the couples $\{i, j\}$ for which b is emitted during the transition from σ_i to σ_j.

Let $\Pi(b)$ be the transition matrix corresponding to an emitted bit b :

$$\Pi(b)_{i,j} = \begin{cases} \Pi_{i,j} & \text{if bit } b \text{ is emitted from } \sigma_i \text{ to } \sigma_j \\ 0 & \text{otherwise} \end{cases}$$

It follows that $\Pi = \Pi(0) + \Pi(1)$ and equation (1) becomes :

$$\Pr[b|W] = W \Pi(b) U \quad \text{where} \quad U = \begin{bmatrix} 1 \\ \vdots \\ 1 \end{bmatrix}$$

By iteration, the probability of emitting the sequence $b = [b_0, \ldots, b_n]$ from the state distribution vector W is :

$$\Pr[b|W] = W \Pi(b_0) \Pi(b_1) \ldots \Pi(b_n) U$$

and with $\Pi(b) = \Pi(b_0) \Pi(b_1) \ldots \Pi(b_n)$ the probability of appearance of sequence b is :

$$\Pr[b] = P \Pi(b) U$$

3 Maurer's universal test and the source's entropy

3.1 Maurer's test

Maurer's universal test [6] takes as input three integers $\{L, Q, K\}$ and a $(Q+K)\times L = N$-bit sample $s^N = [s_1, \ldots, s_N]$ generated by the tested source. The parameter L is chosen from the interval $[6, 16]$. The sequence s^N is partitioned into non-overlapping L-bit blocks. For $1 \leq n \leq Q + K$, let $b_n(s^N) = [s_{L(n-1)+1}, \ldots, s_{Ln}]$ denote the n-th L-bit block of s^N.

The first Q blocks of the sequence are used to initialize the test; Q should be chosen to be at least 10×2^L in order to have a high likelihood that each of the 2^L blocks of L bits occurs at least once in the first Q blocks. The remaining K blocks are used to compute the test function $f_{T_U} : B^N \to \mathbb{R}$:

$$f_{T_U}(s^N) = \frac{1}{K} \sum_{n=Q+1}^{Q+K} \log_2 A_n(s^N) \tag{2}$$

where B denotes the set $\{0, 1\}$ and $A_n(s^N)$ the minimum distance between the n-th block and any similar preceding block :

$$A_n(s^N) = \begin{cases} n & \text{if } \forall i < n, b_{n-i}(s^N) \neq b_n(s^N) \\ \min\{i : i \geq 1, b_n(s^N) = b_{n-i}(s^N)\} & \text{otherwise.} \end{cases} \tag{3}$$

3.2 Asymptotic entropy relation

As will be justified later, Maurer's test function is closely related to the source's entropy. It follows that Maurer's universal test is able to detect any of the statistical defects that can be modeled by an ergodic stationary source with finite memory.

Let K_L be the entropy of L-bit blocks, G_L the per-bit entropy of blocks of L bits and F_L the entropy of the L-th order approximation of the source (see Shannon [7]) :

$$K_L = - \sum_{b \in B^L} \Pr[b] \log_2 \Pr[b] \tag{4}$$

$$F_L = - \sum_{b \in B^{L-1}, j \in B} \Pr[b, j] \log_2 \Pr[j|b] \tag{5}$$

$$G_L = \frac{K_L}{L} = \frac{1}{L} \sum_{i=1}^{L} F_i \tag{6}$$

In [3] we proved the following asymptotic relation between the expectation of Maurer's test function for a stationary ergodic source S outputting a sequence U_S^N of random binary variables and the entropy of L-bit blocks of S :

$$\lim_{L\to\infty} \left[E[f_{T_U}(U_S^N)] - K_L \right] = C \triangleq \int_0^\infty e^{-\xi} \log_2 \xi \, d\xi \cong -0.8327462 \qquad (7)$$

In the next section we improve the performance of Maurer's test by modifying the test function so that its expectation yields the source's entropy, instead of having an asymptotical relation.

4 Improving Maurer's universal test

Maurer's test function is defined as the average of the logarithm to the base two of the minimum distances between two similar blocks. Here we generalize the definition of the test parameter to any function $g : \mathbb{N} \to \mathbb{R}$ of the minimum distance between two similar blocks :

$$f_{T_U}^g(s^N) = \frac{1}{K} \sum_{n=Q+1}^{Q+K} g(A_n(s^N))$$

The mean of $f_{T_U}^g(U_S^N)$ for S is given by :

$$E[f_{T_U}^g(U_S^N)] = \sum_{i \geq 1} \Pr[A_n(U_S^N) = i] g(i)$$

with

$$\Pr[A_n(U_S^N) = i] = \sum_{b \in B^L} \Pr[b_n = b, b_{n-1} \neq b, \ldots, b_{n-i+1} \neq b, b_{n-i} = b] \qquad (8)$$

If we assume that the L-bit blocks are statistically independent, the above probability factors into :

$$\Pr[A_n(U_S^N) = i] = \sum_{b \in B^L} \Pr[b]^2 \times (1 - \Pr[b])^{i-1}$$

and we get :

$$E[f_{T_U}(U_S^N)] = \sum_{b \in B^L} \Pr[b] \times \gamma_g(\Pr[b]) \qquad (9)$$

where :

$$\gamma_g(x) = x \sum_{i=1}^\infty (1 - x)^{i-1} g(i)$$

Equation (9) shows that the mean value of the generalized test may be interpreted as the expectation of a random variable $W = W(X)$ which hits the value

$\gamma_g(\Pr[b])$ with probability $\Pr[b]$. However, the entropy of L-bit blocks K_L (equation (4)) can be viewed as the expectation of a random variable $W' = W'(X)$ which takes the value $- \log_2(\Pr[b])$ with probability $\Pr[b]$.

In order to determine the expectation of the test with the entropy of L-bit blocks, we have to solve the following equation :

$$\gamma_g(x) = - \log_2(x) \tag{10}$$

Letting $t = 1 - x$, equation (10) yields :

$$(1 - t) \sum_{i=1}^{\infty} t^{i-1} g(i) = - \log_2(1 - t) = \frac{1}{\log(2)} \sum_{i=1}^{\infty} \frac{t^i}{i}$$

and we get :

$$\begin{cases} g(1) = 0 \\ g(i + 1) - g(i) = \frac{1}{i \log(2)} & \text{for } i \geq 1, \end{cases}$$

Hence we can define a modified version of Maurer's test which test parameter $f_{T_U}^H(s^N)$ is computed using :

$$f_{T_U}^H(s^N) = \frac{1}{K} \sum_{n=Q+1}^{Q+K} g(A_n(s^N)) \tag{11}$$

$$g(i) = \frac{1}{\log(2)} \sum_{k=1}^{i-1} \frac{1}{k} \tag{12}$$

and equation (3) for the definition of $A_n(s^N)$.

The mean value of this new test function taking as input a sequence U_S^N generated by an ergodic stationary source S is equal to the entropy of L-bit blocks of S :

$$E[f_{T_U}^H(U_S^N)] = K_L \tag{13}$$

5 Distribution of the modified test parameter

To tune the test's rejection rate, one must first know the distribution of $f_{T_U}^H(R^N)$, where R^N denotes a sequence of N bits emitted by a binary symmetric source (BSS, $i.e.$ a truly random source). A sample s^N would then be rejected if the number of standard deviations separating its $f_{T_U}^H(s^N)$ from $E[f_{T_U}^H(R^N)]$ exceeds a reasonable constant.

In this section we compute the mean and standard deviation of the modified test parameter for a BSS under the reasonable assumption that $Q \to \infty$ (in practice, Q should be larger than 10×2^L).

From equations (11 and 12) the expected value $E[f_{T_U}^H(R^N)]$ of the test parameter $f_{T_U}^H$ for a BSS is given by :

$$E[f_{T_U}^H(R^N)] = \frac{1}{\log(2)} \sum_{i=2}^{\infty} \Pr[A_n(R^N) = i] \sum_{k=1}^{i-1} \frac{1}{k} \tag{14}$$

Using equation (8) we have for a BSS :

$$\Pr[A_n(R^N) = i] = 2^{-L}(1 - 2^{-L})^{i-1} \quad \text{for } i \geq 1 \tag{15}$$

and with equation (14) :

$$E[f_{T_U}^H(R^N)] = \frac{2^{-L}}{\log(2)} \sum_{i=2}^{\infty} (1 - 2^{-L})^{i-1} \sum_{k=1}^{i-1} \frac{1}{k} = L$$

Thus the mean of the test parameter for a truly random source is simply equal to L, the length of the blocks in the tested sequence. Note that this result is straightforward considering equation (13) since the entropy K_L of L-bit blocks is equal to L for a truly random source.

For statistically independent random variables the variance of a sum is the sum of variances but the A_n-terms in (11) are heavily inter-dependent; of course, the same holds for Maurer's original test function (2). Consequently, Maurer introduced in [6] a corrective factor $c(L, K)$ by which the standard deviation of f_{T_U} is reduced compared to what it would have been if the A_n-terms were independent :

$$\text{Var}[f_{T_U}(R^N)] = c(L, K)^2 \times \frac{\text{Var}[\log_2 A_n(R^N)]}{K}$$

Similarly, we can define $c^H(L, K)$ to be the corrective factor by which the standard deviation of the modified test parameter $f_{T_U}^H$ is reduced compared to what it would have been if the A_n-terms were independent :

$$\text{Var}[f_{T_U}^H(R^N)] = c^H(L, K)^2 \times \frac{\text{Var}[g(A_n(R^N))]}{K}$$

The variance of the A_n-terms can be easily computed using equation (15) :

$$\text{Var}[g(A_n(R^N))] = E[(g(A_n(R^N)))^2] - \left(E[g(A_n(R^N))]\right)^2$$

$$= 2^{-L} \sum_{i=2}^{\infty} (1 - 2^{-L})^{i-1} \left(\sum_{k=1}^{i-1} \frac{1}{k \log(2)}\right)^2 - L^2$$

In [3] we have computed the exact value of the factor $c(L, K)$, while only a heuristic estimate of $c(L, K)$ was given in [6].

The expression of $c^H(L, K)$ is very similar to the one of $c(L, K)$ given in [3] as one should simply replace the terms in the formulae containing $\log_2 i$ by :

$$g(i) = \frac{1}{\log(2)} \sum_{k=1}^{i-1} \frac{1}{k}.$$

As in [3], the factor $c^H(L, K)$ can be approximated for $K \geq 33 \times 2^L$ by :

$$c^H(L, K)^2 = d(L) + \frac{e(L) \times 2^L}{K}$$

and $\text{Var}[g(A_n(R^N))]$, $d(L)$ and $e(L)$ are listed in table 1 for $3 \leq L \leq 16$ and $L \to \infty$.

This approximation is sufficient because the test must be performed with $K \geq 1000 \times 2^L$.

To summarize, the distribution of $f_{T_U}^H(R^N)$ can be approximated by the normal distribution of mean $E[f_{T_U}^H(R^N)] = L$ and standard deviation :

$$\sigma = c(L, K)\sqrt{\text{Var}[g(A_n(R^N))]/K}$$

L	$\text{Var}[g(A_n(R^N))]$	$d(L)$	$e(L)$
3	2.5769918	0.3313257	0.4381809
4	2.9191004	0.3516506	0.4050170
5	3.1291382	0.3660832	0.3856668
6	3.2547450	0.3758725	0.3743782
7	3.3282150	0.3822459	0.3678269
8	3.3704039	0.3862500	0.3640569
9	3.3942629	0.3886906	0.3619091
10	3.4075860	0.3901408	0.3606982
11	3.4149476	0.3909846	0.3600222
12	3.4189794	0.3914671	0.3596484
13	3.4211711	0.3917390	0.3594433
14	3.4223549	0.3918905	0.3593316
15	3.4229908	0.3919740	0.3592712
16	3.4233308	0.3920198	0.3592384
∞	3.4237147	0.3920729	0.3592016

Table 1. $\text{Var}[g(A_n(R^N))]$, $d(L)$ and $e(L)$ for $3 \leq L \leq 16$ and $L \to \infty$

A source is then rejected if and only if either $f_{T_U}^H(s^N) < t_1$ or $f_{T_U}^H(s^N) > t_2$ where the thresholds t_1 and t_2 are defined by :

$$t_1 = L - y\sigma \quad \text{and} \quad t_2 = L + y\sigma,$$

where y is the number of standard deviations σ from the mean allowed for $f_{T_U}^H(s^N)$. The parameter y must be chosen such that $\mathcal{N}(-y) = \rho/2$, where ρ is the rejection rate expressing the probability that a sequence emitted by a truly random source will be rejected. $\mathcal{N}(x)$ is the integral of the normal density function :

$$\mathcal{N}(x) = \frac{1}{\sqrt{2\pi}} \int_{-\infty}^{x} e^{-\xi^2/2} d\xi$$

[6] recommends to choose the parameters L between 6 and 16, $Q \simeq 10 \times 2^L$ and $K \simeq 1000 \times 2^L$, and to take a rejection rate $\rho \simeq 0.01, \ldots, 0.001$, obtained by setting $y = 2.58$ or $y = 3.30$ respectively. We suggest to keep these bounds for the new test.

6 A sample program

As pointed out in [6], the test can be implemented efficiently by using a table tab of size $V = 2^L$ that stores for each L-bit block the time index of its most recent occurrence. At step n the program gets the L-bit block $b_n(s^N)$ from the random source, computes the minimum distance $A_n(s^N) \leftarrow n - \text{tab}[b_n(s^N)]$, adds $g(A_n(s^N))$ to an accumulator and updates the most recent occurrence table with $\text{tab}[b_n(s^N)] \leftarrow n$.

To improve efficiency, the coefficients computed by the function $g(i)$ are approximated for large i using (16). For $i \geq 23$ the error is smaller than 10^{-8}.

$$\sum_{i=1}^{n} \frac{1}{i} = \log n + \gamma + \frac{1}{2n} - \frac{1}{12n^2} + \mathcal{O}(\frac{1}{n^4}) \tag{16}$$

where γ is Euler's constant :

$$\gamma = -\int_{0}^{\infty} e^{-x} \log x \, dx \simeq 0.577216$$

The sample program calls the function fsource(L) which returns an L-bit integer produced by the random source.

```
double fcoef(int i)
{
      double l=log(2),s=0,C=-0.8327462;
      int k,j=i-1,limit=23;
      if(i<limit) {
            for(k=1;k<i;k++) { s=s+1./k; }
            return s/l;
      }
      return log(j)/l-C+(1./(2*j)-1./(12.*j*j))/l;
}

double NewUniversalTest(int L,int Q, int K)
{
      int V=(1 << L),i,n,k;
      int *tab=new int[V];
```

```
        double sum=0;

        for(i=0;i<V;i++) {
                tab[i]=0;
        }
        for(n=1;n<=Q;n++) {
                tab[fsource(L)]=n;
        }
        for(n=Q+1;n<=(Q+K);n++) {
                k=fsource(L);
                sum=sum+fcoef(n-tab[k]);
                tab[k]=n;
        }
        delete tab;
        return sum/K;
}
```

7 A comparative analysis of the two tests

In section 4 we assumed the block sequences of length L to be statistically independent, *i.e.* that the probability of appearance of a block does not depend on the preceding ones. But this assumption is valid only if the tested source is a binary memoryless source BMS_p (random binary source which emits ones with probability p and zeroes with probability $1 - p$). In section 7.1 we compare the performance of Maurer's test and the modified test for a BMS_p.

In the general case of a source with finite (non-zero) memory, the blocks are not statistically independent and the expectation of the modified test function is not equal to the source's entropy of L-bit blocks. However, if the statistics of the tested random source differ from the statistics of a truly random source, the tested source will be rejected with high probability. Only random sources with small statistical bias will pass the test. As shown in section 7.2, this small bias will still make the difference between the expectation of the modified test function and the source's entropy negligible.

7.1 Comparison with respect to a BMS_p

In this section we compute the expectation of Maurer's test function for a BMS_p and compare it with the expectation of the modified test function and with the actual source's entropy. The expectation of Maurer's test function for a BMS_p with output sequence $U^N_{BMS_p}$ is given by :

$$E[f_{T_U}(U^N_{BMS_p})] = \sum_{i=1}^{\infty} \Pr[A_n(U^N_{BMS_p}) = i] \log_2(i)$$

while equation (8) and :

$$\Pr[b_n(U^N_{\text{BMS}_p}) = b] = p^{w(b)}(1-p)^{L-w(b)}$$

(where $w(b)$ denotes the Hamming weight of $b \in \{0,1\}^L$) yield :

$$E[f_{T_U}(U^N_{\text{BMS}_p})] = \sum_{k=0}^{L} \binom{L}{k} p^k (1-p)^{L-k} \alpha(p^k(1-p)^{L-k}) \tag{17}$$

where

$$\alpha(x) = x \sum_{i=1}^{\infty} (1-x)^{i-1} \log_2 i$$

One can show that :

$$\lim_{x \to 0} [\alpha(x) + \log_2 x] = -\frac{\gamma}{\log 2} \triangleq C \tag{18}$$

where γ is Euler's constant.
From equations (17 and 18) we recover the result given in [6] :

$$\lim_{L \to \infty} E[f_{T_U}(U^N_{\text{BMS}_p}) - L \times H(p)] = C$$

Note that this result is straightforward using equation (7) as $K_L = L \times H(p)$ for a BMS_p.

In the case of a BMS_p the assumption of statistical independence between the blocks in section 4 is valid and thus equation (13) leads to :

$$E[f^H_{T_U}(U^N_{\text{BMS}_p})] = L \times H(p) \tag{19}$$

Equation (19) shows that the modified test is more accurate than the original one, as it measures the entropy of a BMS_p whereas the relation is only asymptotical in the original one. This is illustrated in table 2, which summarizes the expectation of Maurer's test function, the expectation of the modified test function, and the entropy of a BMS_p, for $L = 4$, $L = 8$, $L = 16$ and several values of p.

7.2 Comparison in the general case

The mean of the modified test for an ergodic stationary source S is given by :

$$E[f^H_{T_U}(U^N_S)] = \sum_{b \in B^L} \sum_{i \geq 2} \Pr[b(\neg b)^{i-1} b] \sum_{k=1}^{i-1} \frac{1}{k \log(2)}$$

where $\Pr[b(\neg b)^{i-1}b]$ denotes $\Pr[b_n = b, b_{n-1} \neq b, \ldots, b_{n-i+1} \neq b, b_{n-i} = b]$. Using the fact that $\Pr[b(\neg b)^i] = \Pr[b(\neg b)^i b] + \Pr[b(\neg b)^{i+1}]$, we get :

$$E[f^H_{T_U}(U^N_S)] = \sum_{b \in B^L} \sum_{i \geq 1} \Pr[b(\neg b)^i] \frac{1}{i \log(2)}$$

L	p	$E[f_{T_U}(U^N_{\mathrm{BMS}_p})] - C$	$E[f^H_{T_U}(U^N_{\mathrm{BMS}_p})]$	$L \times H(p)$
4	0.5	4.14397	4.00000	4.00000
4	0.4	4.04187	3.88380	3.88380
4	0.3	3.73034	3.52516	3.52516
8	0.5	8.01641	8.00000	8.00000
8	0.4	7.78833	7.76760	7.76760
8	0.3	7.08957	7.05033	7.05033
16	0.5	16.00012	16.00000	16.00000
16	0.4	15.53542	15.53521	15.53521
16	0.3	14.10161	14.10065	14.10065

Table 2. Comparison between the expectation of Maurer's test $E[f_{T_U}(U^N_{\mathrm{BMS}_p})]$, the expectation of the modified test $E[f^H_{T_U}(U^N_{\mathrm{BMS}_p})]$ and the L-bit block entropy of a BMS_p.

From section 2.2 we obtain the expectation of the modified function in the general case of an ergodic stationary source S with finite memory :

$$E[f^H_{T_U}(U^N_S)] = \sum_{b \in \{0,1\}^L} \sum_{i \geq 1} P\Pi(b) \left(\Pi^L - \Pi(b)\right)^i U \frac{1}{i \log(2)}$$

where Π is the transition matrix of S and $\Pi(b)$ the transition matrix associated to sequence b as defined in section 2.2.

Table 3 gives $E[f^H_{T_U}(U^N_S)]$ for an STP_p, a random binary source for which a bit is followed by its complement with probability p. An STP_p is thus a source with one bit of memory and two equally-probable states. It follows (5 and 6) that $F_1 = H(1/2) = 1$, $H_S = H(p)$, and $K_L = 1 + (L-1)H(p)$. Table 3 compares the mean of Maurer's function, the mean of the modified function and the entropy of L-bit block of an STP_p for $L = 4$ and $L = 8$ and various values of p. As expected, the new test is closer to the source's entropy than the original one.

Moreover, the difference between the expectation of the modified test function and the source's entropy becomes negligible when p is close to 0.5. This is due to the fact that the L-bit blocks become statistically independent as the source's bias disappears. Extensive experiments performed with random sources with memory bigger than one all led the same result.

8   Conclusion and further research

We have introduced a modification in Maurer's universal test that improves its performance. The modification is very simple to implement (a few lines of code) and does not increase the computation time. The new test is more closely related to the source's entropy and therefore enables a more accurate detection of the possible defects in the tested source.

L	p	$E[f_{T_U}(U^N_{\text{STP}_p}] - C$	$E[f^H_{T_U}(U^N_{\text{STP}_p})]$	$(L-1)H(p)+1$
4	0.5	4.14397	4.00000	4.00000
4	0.49	4.14321	3.99914	3.99913
4	0.45	4.12488	3.97831	3.97832
4	0.4	4.06677	3.91196	3.91285
4	0.3	3.82175	3.62743	3.64387
8	0.5	8.01641	8.00000	8.00000
8	0.49	8.01443	7.99798	7.99798
8	0.45	7.96671	7.94942	7.94942
8	0.4	7.81679	7.79665	7.79665
8	0.3	7.20403	7.16848	7.16904

Table 3. Numerical comparison between the expected value of Maurer's original test $E[f_{T_U}(U^N_{\text{STP}_p}]$, the expected value of the modified test $E[f^H_{T_U}(U^N_{\text{STP}_p}]$ and the L-bit block entropy of an STP_p.

We have not found an analytic expression of the modified test's variance, although the expectation for a truly random source is simply equal to the block length. In addition, an interesting generalization would consist of extending the exact correspondence between the modified test function and the source's entropy to the general class of stationary ergodic random sources with finite (non necessarily zero) memory.

References

1. R. Ash, *Information theory*, Dover publications, New-York, 1965.
2. M. Blum, S. Micali, *How to generate cryptographically strong sequences of pseudo-random bits*. SIAM J. Comput., vol. 13, no. 4, pp. 850-864, 1984
3. J.-S. Coron, D. Naccache, *An accurate evalutation of Maurer's universal test*. Proceedings of SAC'98, Lecture notes in computer science, springer-verlag, 1998. To appear. Available at http://www.eleves.ens.fr:8080/home/coron/index.html
4. FIPS 140-1, *Security requirements for cryptographic modules*, Federal Information Processing Standards Publication 140-1, U.S. Department of Commerce / N.I.S.T., National Technical Information Service, Springfield, Virginia, 1994.
5. D. Knuth, *The art of computer programming, Seminumerical algorithms*, vol. 2, Addison-Wesley publishing company, Reading, pp. 2–160, 1969.
6. U. Maurer, *A universal statistical test for random bit generators*, Journal of cryptology, vol. 5, no. 2, pp. 89–105, 1992.
7. C. Shannon, *A mathematical theory of communication*, The Bell system technical journal, vol. 27, pp. 379–423, 623–656, July-October, 1948.
8. J. Ziv, *Compression tests for randomness and estimating the statistical model of an individual sequence*, Sequences, pp. 366-373, 1990.

Anonymous Fingerprinting Based on Committed Oblivious Transfer *

Josep Domingo-Ferrer
Universitat Rovira i Virgili,
Department of Computer Science,
Autovia de Salou s/n, E-43006 Tarragona, Catalonia, Spain
e-mail jdomingo@etse.urv.es

No Institute Given

Abstract. Thwarting unlawful redistribution of information sold electronically is a major problem of information-based electronic commerce. Anonymous fingerprinting has appeared as a technique for copyright protection which is compatible with buyer anonymity in electronic transactions. However, the complexity of known algorithms for anonymous fingerprinting deters their practical implementation, since they rely either on secure multiparty computation or on general zero-knowledge proofs. A scheme for anonymous fingerprinting based on committed oblivious transfer is presented in this paper where all computations can be performed efficiently.

Keywords: Secure electronic commerce, Intellectual property protection, Anonymous fingerprinting, Committed oblivious transfer.

1 Introduction

In information-based electronic commerce, copyright protection of the information being sold is a key problem to be solved, together with secure payment. Fingerprinting is a technique which allows to track redistributors of electronic information. Given an original item of information, an l-uple of *marks* is probabilistically selected. A mark is a piece of the information item of which two slightly different versions exist. At the moment of selling a copy of the item, the merchant selects one of the two versions for each mark; in other words, she hides an l-bit word in the information, where the i-th bit indicates which version of the data is being used for the i-th mark. Usually, it is assumed that two or more dishonest buyers can only locate and delete marks by comparing their copies (Marking Assumption, [Bone95]).

Classical fingerprinting schemes [Blak86][Bone95] are symmetrical in the sense that both the merchant and the buyer know the fingerprinted copy. Even if the merchant succeeds in identifying a dishonest buyer, her previous knowledge of

---

* This work is partly supported by the Spanish CICYT under grant no. TEL98-0699-C02-02.

the fingerprinted copies prevents her from using them as a proof of redistribution in front of third parties. In [Pfit96], asymmetric fingerprinting was proposed, whereby only the buyer knows the fingerprinted copy; the drawback of this solution is that the merchant knows the buyer's identity even if the buyer is honest. Later ([Pfit97]) the concept of anonymous fingerprinting was introduced; the idea is that the merchant does not know the fingerprinted copy nor the buyer's identity. Upon finding a fingerprinted copy, the merchant needs the help of a registration authority to identify a redistributor. In [Domi98a], a scheme for anonymous fingerprinting is presented where redistributors can be identified by the merchant without help from the authority. The problem with the constructions [Pfit97][Domi98a] is that, being based on secure multiparty computation ([Chau88a]), their complexity is much too high to be implementable in practice. In [Domi98b], an anonymous fingerprinting algorithm is proposed which avoids secure multi-party computation and is based on Rabin's one-out-of-two oblivious transfer; however, this approach also relies on a (unspecified) general zero-knowledge proof whereby the buyer Bob shows to the merchant Mary that a hash value was correctly computed by the buyer.

1.1 Our result

We present in this paper a scheme for anonymous fingerprinting which is efficiently and completely specified from a computational point of view. The basic primitive used is committed oblivious transfer (see [Crép95]).

Section 2 contains some background on committed oblivious transfer. Section 3 describes the new construction. Section 4 contains a complexity evaluation. Section 5 is a security analysis. Section 6 is a conclusion.

2 Background

In Subsection 2.1, bit commitment with XOR is recalled. This special kind of bit commitment has been shown to be useful for efficient implementation of committed oblivious transfer, which is a concept reviewed in Subsection 2.2.

2.1 Bit commitment with XOR

In a bit commitment (BC), Mary sends a committed bit $\boxed{a}$ to Bob in such a way that she is able to reveal it later in a *unique* way (a) but Bob is *not able to find* the value a by himself. Mary cannot change her mind and open $\boxed{a}$ as $\bar{a}$.

In [Crép95], bit commitment with XOR was introduced. If a special kind of bit commitments (BCX) is used, then it is possible to prove that some commitments satisfy an XOR-relation, without giving away any other information about the contents of the commitments. In particular, it is possible to prove that two BCXs $\boxed{a}$ and $\boxed{b}$ are equal simply by proving $\boxed{a} \oplus \boxed{b} = 0$; the verifier learns nothing about the bits contained in the commitments, except that they are equal or different.

Call BCX operations the following: creation of a BCX, opening of a BCX and proof that a constant number of BCXs satisfy a given linear relation. Then, if m is the security parameter, it is argued in [Crép95] that each BCX operation can be implemented using $O(m)$ BC operations, where BC denotes plain bit commitment. Unless otherwise specified, all commitments mentioned in the rest of this paper are BCX commitments.

2.2 Committed oblivious transfer

Oblivious transfer was originally invented by Rabin [Rabi81]. Mary has one secret; the protocol allows Bob to learn the secret with probability 1/2; whatever they do, Mary and Bob cannot modify the probability of Bob learning the secret; moreover, Mary cannot infer from the protocol whether Bob learned the secret or not. A slight variation of the above yields Rabin's one-out-of-two oblivious transfer, whereby Mary has two secrets and the protocol allows Bob to learn one of them; the probability of Bob learning either secret is 1/2; whatever they do, Mary and Bob cannot modify that probability; moreover, Mary cannot infer from the protocol which was the secret learned by Bob. A provably secure protocol for implementing Rabin's oblivious transfers can be found in [Berg85].

In a one-out-of-two oblivious transfer (OT), Bob has to choose between learning bit a_0 or a_1 prepared by Mary but she does not learn his choice b. If m is the security parameter, it is well known ([Crép88]) that OT can be constructed using $O(m)$ of Rabin's oblivious transfers.

Now let us turn to committed oblivious transfer (COT). Suppose that Mary is committed to bits $\boxed{a_0}$, $\boxed{a_1}$ and Bob is committed to bit $\boxed{b}$. After running COT($\boxed{a_0}$, $\boxed{a_1}$)($\boxed{b}$) Bob knows a_b and is committed to $\boxed{a_b}$. Mary, whatever she does, cannot use the protocol to learn information on b and Bob, whatever he does, cannot use the protocol to learn information on $a_{\bar{b}}$.

COT was introduced in [Crép90] under the label "Verifiable Oblivious Transfer"; unfortunately, that first protocol used $O(m^3)$ OTs. In [Gold91], a more efficient protocol for COT was presented as "Preprocess-Oblivious-Transfer". In the best case, such a proposal requires $O(m^2)$ OTs. In [Crép95], a protocol for COT was proposed that used $O(m)$ OTs and $O(m)$ BCX operations (the latter can be replaced by $O(m^2)$ BC operations).

3 Anonymous fingerprinting based on committed oblivious transfer

In this section, a fingerprinting scheme is presented which provides anonymity and has the advantage of being efficient and completely specified from a computational point of view. This was not the case for previous asymmetric and anonymous fingerprinting schemes.

3.1 Merchandise initialization

Let the information *item* to be fingerprinted be n bits long. For $i = 1$ to n, the merchant Mary creates two versions $item_i^0$ and $item_i^1$ of the i-th bit $item_i$. Both versions differ only for bit positions containing one mark (in the sense of Section 1).

Now, for $i = 1$ to n, Mary commits, using BCXs, to $item_i^0$ and to $item_i^1$ to get $\boxed{item_i^0}$ and $\boxed{item_i^1}$. The $2n$ BCXs are stored by Mary for later use.

Mary sends to the registration authority Ron a signed and time-stamped message containing a short description of *item* (but not the full *item*) as well as a list of the $l < n$ bit positions in *item* containing a mark.

Note 1. The only reason to use BCXs for $item_i^0$ and $item_i^1$ instead of plain BCs is that $\boxed{item_i^0}$ and $\boxed{item_i^1}$ are used as inputs to a COT in the fingerprinting protocol of Subsection 3.3. As mentioned above and justified in [Crép95], using BCXs allows an efficient construction for COT (the XOR property is used only inside the COT construction).

3.2 Buyer registration

Let p be a large prime such that $q = (p-1)/2$ is also prime. Let G be a group of order p, and let g be a generator of G such that computing discrete logarithms to the base g is difficult. Assume that both the buyer Bob and the registration authority Ron have ElGamal-like public-key pairs ([ElGa85]). Bob's secret key is x_B and his public key is $y_B = g^{x_B}$. The registration authority Ron uses his secret key to issue certificates which can be verified using Ron's public key. The public keys of Ron and all buyers are assumed to be known and certified.

Protocol 1

1. *Ron chooses a random nonce $x_r \in \mathbf{Z}_p$ and sends $y_r = g^{x_r}$ to B.*
2. *Bob chooses secret random s_1 and s_2 in $\mathbf{Z}_p$ such that $s_1 + s_2 = x_B \pmod{p}$ and sends $S_1 = y_r^{s_1}$ and $S_2 = y_r^{s_2}$ to Ron. Bob convinces Ron in zero-knowledge of possession of s_1 and s_2. The proof given in [Chau88b] for showing possession of discrete logarithms may be used here. The buyer Bob computes an ElGamal public key $y_1 = g^{s_1} \pmod{p}$ and sends it to Ron.*
3. *Ron checks that $S_1 S_2 = y_B^{x_r}$ and $y_1^{x_r} = S_1$. Ron returns to Bob a certificate $Cert(y_1)$. The certificate states the correctness of y_1.*

By going through the registration procedure above several times, Bob can obtain several different certified keys y_1.

Note 2. If Bob is represented by his smart card, then the private key x_B is the smart card's private key, which is recorded in PROM by the card manufacturer or issuer. Having Bob represented by a tamper-proof smart card has several advantages, as will be discussed in Notes 3, 4 and 6 below.

3.3 Fingerprinting

If we denote by *item** the fingerprinted copy of the original information *item* being sold, the fingerprinting protocol can be specified as follows:

Protocol 2

1. For $i = 1$ to n, the merchant Mary shuffles the pairs $(item_i^0, item_i^1)$ to obtain $(item_i^{(0)}, item_i^{(1)})$. Mary records the result of the shuffling in the purchase record.

2. For $i = 1$ to n, Mary and Bob run $\mathrm{COT}(\boxed{item_i^{(0)}}, \boxed{item_i^{(1)}})(\boxed{b_i})$, where b_i is a bit value chosen by Bob and $\boxed{b_i}$ is a BCX. In this way, Bob obtains $item_i^*$ and returns to Mary a signed commitment $\boxed{item_i^*}$ on it. This commitment is signed using the private key s_1 corresponding to the public key y_1 registered in Protocol 1.

Note 3 (Collusion-resistance). The information embedded in the fingerprinted copy is formed by bits b_i, for which $item_i^0 \neq item_i^1$. Assume that there are l such bits b_i, with $l \leq n$. If Bob takes part in the fingerprinting process through a tamper-proof device such as a smart card, then assumptions about the structure of the embedded information can be made. A possibility is for Mary to provide Bob's card with information on which are the l bit positions containing a mark; such information should be encrypted under the card's pseudonymous public key y_1. Then the card could be programmed to choose the l embedded bits as a random codeword of a c-secure code ([Bone95]), which would provide protection against buyer collusions. Bob should not learn the codeword chosen by his card. It is worth mentioning that this way of using smart cards to counter buyer collusion also applies to the scheme described in [Domi98b] if OTs or COTs are used in that scheme instead of Rabin's oblivious transfers (*i.e.* if the buyer's card is allowed to input its choice to oblivious transfers).

Note 4. A second advantage of Bob taking part in the fingerprinting process through a tamper-proof smart card is that Step 1 of Protocol 2 is not needed. However, if the choice of b_i is known and controlled by Bob personally (instead of a smart card), shuffling is necessary because otherwise Bob could go twice through the fingerprinting protocol (perhaps under different pseudonyms), first with $b_i = 0$ and then with $b_i = 1$, which with probability 1 would allow him to discover whether $item_i$ contains a mark, *i.e.* whether $item_i^0 \neq item_i^1$. This would be against the marking assumption stated in Section 1.

3.4 Identification

Following [Pfit96], it only makes sense to try to identify a redistributor if the redistributed copy $item^{red}$ is not too different from the original *item*:

Definition 1. *Let sim be an arbitrary relation where $sim(item^{red}, item)$ means that a redistributed illegal copy $item^{red}$ is still so close to item that the merchant Mary wants to identify the original buyer.*

If $sim(item^{red}, item)$ holds, then it is reasonable to assume that $item^{red}$ contains a substantial number of bits which are (perhaps modified) copies of $item_1^*, \cdots, item_n^*$, for some fingerprinted version $item^*$ of item.

Protocol 3

1. *Upon detecting a redistributed $item^{red}$, Mary determines whether*

$$sim(item^{red}, item)$$

   holds for some information item on sale. If not, Mary quits the protocol.
2. *Mary looks in her purchase record for all entries corresponding to sales of item. Each entry contains the buyer-signed BCX bit commitments for the fingerprinted copy $\boxed{item_1^*}$, $\cdots$, $\boxed{item_n^*}$.*
3. *Mary sends a signed and time-stamped copy of $item^{red}$ to the authority Ron and all (pseudonymous) buyers having bought a copy of item. Requiring Mary to give away $item^{red}$ for free to the suspect buyers is meant to thwart her from systematically and unjustly accusing all buyers of false redistributions. In other words, $item^{red}$ represents no gift only for those buyers having purchased something similar to $item^{red}$.*
4. *Take all suspect pseudonymous buyers in turn and do the following until a redistributor is found or all buyers have been examined:*
   (a) *Using a coin-flipping protocol, Mary and the pseudonymous buyer agree on $l_1 \leq l < n$ bit positions. If the resulting positions contain less than $l_2 \leq l_1$ marks, then Mary requests the buyer to start again the coin flipping protocol to agree on a new set of positions. The procedure is repeated until the resulting positions contain l_3 marks, with $l_2 \leq l_3 \leq l_1$.*
   (b) *The pseudonymous buyer opens his BCX bit commitments corresponding to the l_1 agreed bit positions.*
   (c) *If all l_3 opened commitments agree with the corresponding bit values in $item^{red}$, then Mary takes this as a proof of redistribution (see Note 6 below). Otherwise the suspect pseudonymous buyer is declared innocent and will be given by Mary a new fingerprinted copy (this is necessary because the buyer has been forced to reveal l_3 out of the l commitments in his fingerprinted copy; an honest buyer who is declared suspect several times might end up with virtually all his commitments opened).*
5. *Mary presents the opened signed commitments to the authority Ron asking for identification of the dishonest buyer. The opened commitments constitute a proof of redistribution, together with the signed $item^{red}$ sent to Ron at Step 2 and the list of mark positions in item sent to Ron during merchandise initialization.*

Note 5. If Ron refuses to collaborate in Protocol 3, his role can be performed by an arbiter except buyer identification and mark recognition. Replace "identify buyer" by "declare Ron guilty". If a suspect pseudonymous buyer refuses to collaborate, then the transcript of the protocol is sent to Ron, asking for identification. If the parameter l_2 is tuned properly, the risk of unjustly accusing a buyer is sufficiently low not to deter suspect buyers from proving their innocence (see Section 5).

Note 6. A third advantage of having buyers use tamper-proof smart cards during fingerprinting is that the embedded information (i.e. the set of marks) can be assumed to be a codeword of an error-correcting code with minimal distance $d > 1$. In this case, finding $l_3 - d + 1$ matches in Substep 4c of Protocol 3 suffices to declare a buyer guilty.

4 Complexity analysis

The complexity of the construction of Section 3 is next assessed.

Merchandise initialization involves a digital signature and $2n$ BCX commitments, where n is the bitlength of the information *item* to be fingerprinted. If m is the security parameter, each BCX commitment requires $O(m)$ plain bit commitments BC, as mentioned in Subsection 2.1. Thus merchandise initialization requires $O(nm)$ BCs. However, notice that merchandise initialization is an off-line procedure that *is only run once* for each information *item* on sale.

The buyer registration protocol requires five exponentiations and a zero-knowledge proof for showing possession of discrete logarithms (an efficient protocol for such a proof can be found in [Chau88b]).

The fingerprinting protocol basically involves n committed oblivious transfers and n signatures (on the commitments resulting from the COTs). From Section 2.2, the n COTs are equivalent to $O(nm)$ plain oblivious transfers OT and $O(nm^2)$ plain bit commitments BC.

The identification protocol requires opening $O(n)$ BCX commitments. This is equivalent to opening $O(nm)$ plain BCs. In addition, one instance of the fingerprinting protocol should be run for each suspect buyer who cannot be found guilty.

Note 7. Previously proposed anonymous fingerprinting protocols rely on computationally unspecified *black boxes*: secure multiparty computation in the case of [Pfit97] and [Domi98a] or a generic zero-knowledge proof in the case of [Domi98b]. Therefore, implementation of such protocols is far from obvious. The construction in this paper does not suffer from this problem, because it is based on well-known primitives.

5 Security analysis

We analyze in this section the security of the construction of Section 3.

Proposition 1 (Registration security). *Protocol 1 provides buyer authentication without compromising the private key x_B of the buyer.*

Proof. In registration, the authority Ron sees S_1, S_2, y_1 and a zero-knowledge proof. The latter leaks no information. Without considering the zero-knowledge proof, Ron needs no knowledge of x_B to find values S_1', S_2' and y_1' which are related in the same way as S_1, S_2 and y_1. Take a random s_1', then compute $y_1' = g^{s_1'}$ and $S_1' = y_r^{s_1'}$. Finally, $S_2' = y_B^{x_r}/S_1'$.

Now consider the zero-knowledge proofs; imagine that an impersonator not knowing x_B can compute S_1, S_2 such that he/she can demonstrate possession of $\log_{y_r} S_1$ and $\log_{y_r} S_2$ and $S_1 S_2 = y_r^{x_B}$ holds. Then the impersonator can compute the discrete logarithm x_B. In general, if impersonation is feasible, so is computing discrete logarithms. ◊

Proposition 2 (Buyer anonymity). *Let l_2 be the minimal number of marks to be opened by a suspect buyer in the identification protocol. Then the probability that the merchant identifies an honest buyer who correctly followed Protocol 2 is upper-bounded by 2^{-l_2}.*

Proof. In the fingerprinting protocol, Mary sees a pseudonym y_1, which is related to y_B by the equation $y_1^{x_r} S_2 = y_B^{x_r}$. Even knowledge of $\log_g y_r = x_r$ would not suffice to uniquely determine y_B from y_1, since S_2 is unknown to Mary.

Thus Mary must rely on Protocol 3 to unduly identify an honest buyer. Suspect but honest buyers are not especially vulnerable since they are given a new fingerprinted copy if they cannot be proven guilty. So the only strategy is for Mary to fabricate an $item^{red}$ with the hope that the $l_3 \geq l_2$ bit positions agreed upon by coin-flipping will contain the same values than the l_3 commitments opened by the buyer. Since the n COTs performed by Mary and the buyer during fingerprinting do not allow Mary to learn anything about the buyer's choices b_i (see [Crép95]), the probability of unlawful identification is $2^{-l_3} \leq 2^{-l_2}$. ◊

Merchant security depends on the marks being preserved. The next proposition shows that, for a non-colluding redistributor to remain undetected, the fingerprinted copy must be modified substantially and randomly.

Proposition 3 (Merchant security). *In order to remain undiscovered after the identification protocol, a non-colluding redistributor must modify on average n/l_2 randomly chosen bits of the fingerprinted copy. This number can be made large by choosing $l_2 \ll n$.*

Proof. Since the redistributor does not know where the marks are, his only possibility is random search. The probability that modification of one bit of the fingerprinted copy results in modification of one of the l_2 marks opened during the identification protocol is l_2/n. Thus, to ensure modification of one mark, n/l_2 randomly chosen bits of the fingerprinted copy must be modified on average. ◊

Collusion is another strategy for buyers to delete marks. In Note 3, the use of tamper-proof smart cards was sketched as a way to obtain collusion-secure fingerprinting. If no smart cards are used, then we can only state the following:

Proposition 4. *The expected percent of marks that can be deleted by a collusion of c buyers is* $100(1 - 1/2^{c-1})$.

Proof. By the marking assumption, if the i-th bit position of *item* contains a mark, c colluding buyers can locate (and delete) this mark if and only if they can pool two bit versions $item_i^0$ and $item_i^1$ such that $item_i^0 \neq item_i^1$. Thanks to the shuffling step in Protocol 2, buyers cannot control which version of the i-th bit is delivered to them. Thus, the probability that all c buyers were given the same version is $1/2^{c-1}$. Therefore, the probability that they can pool both versions is $1 - 1/2^{c-1}$. $\diamond$

Merchant security also depends on the kind of similarity relation *sim* used (see Subsection 3.4). If *sim* is very loose, this means that Mary wishes to identify the original buyer of any redistributed item that vaguely resembles an item on sale; of course, identification may often fail in such cases (the authority Ron is likely to deny identification).

6 Conclusion and future directions

To our best knowledge, we have presented the first construction for anonymous fingerprinting which is completely specified from a computational point of view and is thus readily implementable. Unlike previous proposals, the proposed construction relies only on computationally well-defined primitives. By properly tuning its security parameters, good buyer and merchant protection can be attained. In addition, if combined with smart cards for fingerprinting on the buyer's side, the construction also provides protection against collusions.

Future research should be directed to:

- Implementing all buyer functionality on a smart card. This may require further efficiency improvements.
- Speeding up the whole process. A possible way to speed up the fingerprinting protocol is to modify the protocol for COT proposed in [Crép95] so that what is transferred is not a single bit but an r-bit string. In the protocol described in [Crép95] a privacy amplification function $h : \{0,1\}^m \to \{0,1\}$ is used; to achieve the desired speed-up, one could replace h with another privacy amplification function $h' : \{0,1\}^m \to \{0,1\}^r$.

References

[Berg85] R. Berger, R. Peralta and T. Tedrick, "A provably secure oblivious transfer protocol", in *Advances in Cryptology-EUROCRYPT'84*, LNCS 209. Berlin: Springer-Verlag, 1985, pp. 408-416.

[Blak86] G. R. Blakley, C. Meadows and G. B. Purdy, "Fingerprinting long forgiving messages", in *Advances in Cryptology-CRYPTO'85*, LNCS 218. Berlin: Springer-Verlag, 1986, pp. 180-189.

[Bone95] D. Boneh and J. Shaw, "Collusion-secure fingerprinting for digital data", in *Advances in Cryptology-CRYPTO'95*, LNCS 963. Berlin: Springer-Verlag, 1995, pp. 452-465.

[Chau88a] D. Chaum, I. B. Damgaard and J. van de Graaf, "Multiparty computations ensuring privacy of each party's input and correctness of the result", in *Advances in Cryptology - CRYPTO'87*, LNCS 293. Berlin: Springer-Verlag, 1988, pp. 87-119.

[Chau88b] D. Chaum, J.-H. Evertse and J. van de Graaf, "An improved protocol for demonstrating possession of discrete logarithms and some generalizations", in *Advances in Cryptology- EUROCRYPT'87*, LNCS 304. Berlin: Springer-Verlag, 1988, pp. 127-141.

[Crép88] C. Crépeau, "Equivalence between two flavours of oblivious transfer", in *Advances in Cryptology-CRYPTO'87*, LNCS 293. Berlin: Springer-Verlag, 1988, pp. 350-354.

[Crép90] C. Crépeau, "Verifiable disclosure of secrets and applications", in *Advances in Cryptology-EUROCRYPT'89*, LNCS 434. Berlin: Springer-Verlag, 1990, pp. 181-191.

[Crép95] C. Crépeau, J. van de Graaf and A. Tapp, "Committed oblivious transfer and private multi-party computation", in *Advances in Cryptology-CRYPTO'95*, LNCS 963. Berlin: Springer-Verlag, 1995, pp. 110-123.

[Domi98a] J. Domingo-Ferrer, "Anonymous fingerprinting of electronic information with automatic identification of redistributors", *Electronics Letters*, vol. 34, no. 13, June 1998.

[Domi98b] J. Domingo-Ferrer and J. Herrera-Joancomartí, "Efficient smart-card based anonymous fingerprinting", in *Preproceedings of CARDIS'98*. Louvain-la-Neuve: Université Catholique de Louvain, 1998.

[ElGa85] T. ElGamal, "A public-key cryptosystem and a signature scheme based on discrete logarithms", *IEEE Transactions on Information Theory*, vol. IT-31, July 1985, pp. 469-472.

[Gold91] S. Goldwasser and L. Levin, "Fair computation of general functions in presence of moral majority", in *Advances in Cryptology-CRYPTO'90*, LNCS 537. Berlin: Springer-Verlag, 1991, pp. 77-93.

[Pfit96] B. Pfitzmann and M. Schunter, "Asymmetric fingerprinting", in *Advances in Cryptology-EUROCRYPT'96*, LNCS 1070. Berlin: Springer-Verlag, 1996, pp. 84-95.

[Pfit97] B. Pfitzmann and M. Waidner, "Anonymous fingerprinting", in *Advances in Cryptology-EUROCRYPT'97*, LNCS 1233. Berlin: Springer-Verlag, 1997, pp. 88-102.

[Rabi81] M. Rabin, *How to Exchange Secrets by Oblivious Transfer*, Technical Report TR-81, Aitken Computation Laboratory, Harvard University, 1981.

How to Enhance the Security of Public-Key Encryption at Minimum Cost

Eiichiro FUJISAKI and Tatsuaki OKAMOTO

NTT Laboratories,
1-1 Hikarinooka, Yokosuka-shi, 239-0847 **JAPAN**
Email: {fujisaki, okamoto}@sucaba.isl.ntt.co.jp

Abstract. This paper presents a simple and efficient conversion from a semantically secure public-key encryption scheme against *passive adversaries* to a non-malleable (or semantically secure) public-key encryption scheme against *adaptive chosen-ciphertext attacks (active adversaries)* in the random oracle model. Since our conversion requires only one random (hash) function operation, the converted scheme is almost as efficient as the original one, when the random function is replaced by a practical hash function such as SHA-1 and MD5. We also give a concrete analysis of the reduction for proving its security, and show that our security reduction is (almost) optimally efficient. Finally this paper gives some practical examples of applying this conversion to some practical and semantically secure encryption schemes such as the ElGamal, Blum-Goldwasser and Okamoto-Uchiyama schemes [4, 7, 9].

1 Introduction

1.1 Background

One of the most important topics in cryptography is to propose a practical and provably secure public-key encryption scheme. The strongest security notion in the public-key encryption is that of non-malleability or semantical security against adaptive chosen-ciphertext attacks. In [3], Bellare, Desai, Pointcheval and Rogaway show that semantical security against adaptive chosen-ciphertext attacks (IND-CCA2) is equivalent to (or sufficient for) the strongest security notion (NM-CCA2).

A promising way to construct a practical public-key encryption scheme semantically secure against adaptive chosen-ciphertext attacks (IND-CCA2) is to convert from a primitive trap-door one-way function (such as RSA or ElGamal) by using *random functions*. Here, an ideally random function, the "random oracle", is assumed when proving the security, and the random function is replaced by a practical random-like function such as a one-way hash function (e.g., SHA-1 and MD5, etc.) when realizing it in practice. This approach was initiated by Bellare and Rogaway, and is called the *random oracle model* [2].

Although security in the random oracle model cannot be guaranteed formally when a practical random-like function is used in place of the random oracle, this paradigm often yields much more efficient schemes than those in the *standard model* and gives an informal security guarantee of the schemes.

Two typical primitives of the trap-door one-way function are RSA and ElGamal. The RSA function is a trap-door one-way permutation, and the ElGamal function is a probabilistic trap-door one-way function.

Bellare and Rogaway presented a generic and efficient way to convert a trap-door one-way permutation to an IND-CCA2 secure scheme in the random oracle model (The scheme created in this way from the RSA function is called OAEP).

However, their method cannot be applied to a probabilistic trap-door one-way function such as ElGamal. Therefore, a new measure to convert a probabilistic trap-door one-way function to an IND-CCA2 secure scheme (in the random oracle model) should be very valuable.

This paper will present such a generic and efficient measure. It converts a probabilistic trap-door one-way function to an IND-CCA2 secure scheme in the random oracle model provided that the trap-door one-way function is semantically secure (IND-CPA).

Since our conversion requires only one random (hash) function operation, the converted scheme is almost as efficient as the original scheme, when the random function is replaced by a practical hash function such as SHA-1 and MD5. Therefore, we can construct practical IND-CCA2 secure schemes (in the random oracle model) based on several practical IND-CPA secure schemes (under some reasonable assumptions) such as the (elliptic curve) ElGamal, Blum-Goldwasser and Okamoto-Uchiyama schemes [4, 7, 9, 11].

We begin by examining the notions of public-key encryption security.

1.2 Classification of Encryption Scheme Security

We can define the security levels of public-key encryption schemes, using the pairs of *goals* and *adversary models* (We saw this classification first in the paper of [3], which stated that the viewpoint was suggested to the authors by Naor).

The goals are one-wayness (OW), indistinguishability (IND) [8],and non-malleability (NM) [6] of encryption. One-wayness (OW) is defined by the adversary's inability, given a challenge ciphertext y, to decrypt y and get the whole plaintext x. Indistinguishability (IND) is defined by the adversary's inability, given a challenge ciphertext y, to learn any information about the plaintext x. Non-malleability (NM) is defined by the adversary's inability, given a challenge ciphertext y, to get a different ciphertext y' such that the corresponding plaintexts, x and x', are *meaningfully* related. Here a *meaningful* relation is, for instance, $x = x' + 1$.

The three adversary models are called chosen plaintext attack model (CPA), non-adaptive chosen-ciphertext attack model (CCA1), and adaptive chosen ciphertext attack model (CCA2). In CPA, the adversary is given only the public key. Of course, she can get the ciphertext of any plaintext chosen by her. Clearly, in public-key encryption schemes, this attack cannot be avoided. In CCA1, in addition to the public key, the adversary can access to the decryption oracle although she is only allowed to access to the oracle before given a challenge ciphertext. In CCA2, the adversary can access to the decryption oracle anytime (before or after given a challenge ciphertext). She is only prohibited from asking for the decryption of the challenge ciphertext itself.

Furthermore, we separate public-key encryption schemes into the random oracle (RO) model or the standard model. In the random oracle model, every adversary, independent of the adversary models, can be allowed to access to the random oracle anytime,

We say, for the security of public-key encryption scheme Π, that Π is secure in the sense of GOAL-ATK in the RO (or standard) model, where GOAL = {OW, IND, NM} and ATK = {CPA, CCA1,CCA2}. Here one can think of pairs of *goals* and *attacks*; OW-CPA, ..., OW-CCA2, IND-CPA, ..., NM-CCA2. According to [3], the relations among each notion of security are as follows: [1]

$$
\begin{array}{ccccc}
\text{NM-CPA} & \longleftarrow & \text{NM-CCA1} & \longleftarrow & \text{NM-CCA2} \\
& & & \not\longrightarrow & \\
\downarrow \quad \times \; \nwarrow & & \downarrow & & \downarrow\uparrow \\
\text{IND-CPA} & \longleftarrow & \text{IND-CCA1} & \longleftarrow & \text{IND-CCA2} \\
\downarrow & & \downarrow & & \downarrow \\
\text{OW-CPA} & \longleftarrow & \text{OW-CCA1} & \longleftarrow & \text{OW-CCA2}
\end{array}
$$

Here, for $\mathbb{A}, \mathbb{B} \in$ GOAL-ATK "$\mathbb{A} \to \mathbb{B}$" (say, $\mathbb{A}$ implies $\mathbb{B}$) denotes that encryption scheme $\Pi := (\mathcal{K}, \mathcal{E}, \mathcal{D})$ being secure in the sense of $\mathbb{A}$ is also secure in the sense of $\mathbb{B}$, while "$\mathbb{A} \not\to \mathbb{B}$" (say, $\mathbb{A}$ doesn't imply $\mathbb{B}$) denotes Π being secure in the sense of $\mathbb{A}$ is not always secure in the sense of $\mathbb{B}$.

We will provide precise definitions of these notations in Sec.2 (Due to the space limitation, one-wayness is not discussed).

1.3 Our Results

This paper shows a simple and efficient conversion from an IND-CPA secure public-key encryption scheme to an NM-CCA2 (or IND-CCA2) secure public-key encryption scheme in the random oracle model.

Suppose $\Pi := (\mathcal{K}, \mathcal{E}, \mathcal{D})$ is an IND-CPA secure public-key encryption scheme and $\mathcal{E}_{pk}(X, R)$ is encryption function in it, where pk is a public-key, X is a message with $k + k_0$ bits and R is a random string with l bits. The conversion is

$$\bar{\mathcal{E}}_{pk}(x, r) := \mathcal{E}_{pk}(x\|r, H(x\|r)), \tag{1}$$

where H is a random function of $\{0,1\}^{k+k_0} \longrightarrow \{0,1\}^l$, x is a message of the converted public-key encryption scheme $\bar{\Pi} := (\bar{\mathcal{K}}, \bar{\mathcal{E}}, \bar{\mathcal{D}})$, r is a random string with k_0 bits, and $\|$ denotes concatenation.

Main Theorem (Theorem 3)

---

[1] Although one-wayness is not described in [3], the relations among OW and other goals in the diagram are clear.

Suppose that $\Pi(1^{k+k_0})$ is the original IND-CPA secure scheme and $\bar{\Pi}$ is the converted scheme. If there exists a (t, q_H, q_D, ϵ)-breaker A for $\bar{\Pi}(1^k)$ in the sense of IND-CCA2 in the random oracle model, then there exist constants, c and $(t', 0, 0, \epsilon')$-breaker A' for $\Pi(1^{k+k_0})$ where

$$t' = t + q_H \cdot (T_\mathcal{E}(k) + c \cdot k), \ and$$
$$\epsilon' = (\epsilon - q_H \cdot 2^{-(k_0-1)}) \cdot (1 - 2^{-l_0})^{q_D}.$$

Here, (t, q_H, q_D, ϵ)-breaker A, informally, means that A stops within t steps, succeeds with probability $\geq \epsilon$, makes at most q_H queries to random oracle H, and makes at most q_D queries to decryption oracle $\mathcal{D}_{sk}$ (see Sec. 2 for the formal definition). $T_\mathcal{E}(k)$ denotes the computational time of the encryption algorithm $\mathcal{E}_{pk}(\cdot)$, and c_0 and c_1 depend on details of the underlying model of computation.

This theorem implies that if the original scheme Π is IND-CPA secure, the converted scheme $\bar{\Pi}$ is IND-CCA2 secure (and NM-CCA2 secure as well) in the random oracle model, provided that k, k_0 and l are in proportion to system size.

1.4   Merits and Related Works

As mentioned above, Bellare-Rogaway conversion [2] is a generic scheme to be applied to trap-door one-way permutations (such as RSA) while our conversion is a generic one to be applied to probabilistic trap-door one-way functions (such as ElGamal).

Since our conversion starts from an IND-CPA secure scheme, which is more secure than Bellare-Rogaway conversion does, our conversion is simpler and more efficient than theirs, i.e., our conversion requires only one random function operation, while Bellare-Rogaway conversion requires two random function operations. In addition, the security reduction of our conversion is more efficient (tight) than that of Bellare-Rogaway's, since we need no additional reduction for semantical security.

Recently, Cramer and Shoup presented a new public-key encryption scheme based on the ElGamal, which is the first practical IND-CCA2 secure scheme in the standard model [5]. Compared with theirs, our converted version of the ElGamal scheme has a disadvantage in terms of the assumptions (ours in the random oracle model and under the decision Diffie-Hellman assumption, while the Cramer-Shoup scheme under the universal one-way hash assumption and the decision Diffie-Hellman assumption), but ours still has better efficiency, at least twice that of theirs. In addition, since our approach is generic, unlike the Cramer-Shoup scheme, it can be adopted by other IND-CPA secure schemes such as Blum-Goldwasser and Okamoto-Uchiyama schemes [4, 9].

Compared with the converted ElGamal scheme presented by Tsiounis and Yung [11], which is secure in the IND-CCA2 (i.e. NM-CCA2) sense, our converted one is at least twice as efficient as theirs under the same assumptions, the random oracle model and the decision Diffie-Hellman assumption.

2 Definitions and Security Models

In this section, we give some definitions about encryption scheme security. Basically, we follow the terminology in [2,3].

Definition 1. *Let A be a probabilistic algorithm and let $A(x_1, \ldots, x_n; r)$ be the result of A on input $(x_1, \ldots, x_n)$ and coins r. We define by $y \leftarrow A(x_1, \ldots, x_n)$ the experiment of picking r at random and letting y be $A(x_1, \ldots, x_n; r)$. If S is a finite set, let $y \leftarrow_R S$ be the operation of picking y at random and uniformly from finite set S. ε denote the null symbol and, for list τ, $\tau \leftarrow \varepsilon$ denote the operation of letting list τ be empty. Moreover, let $\|$ denote the concatenation operator and, for n-bit string x, $[x]^k$ and $[x]_k$ denote the first and last k-bit strings of x respectively ($k \leq n$).*

Definition 2. **[Public-Key Encryption]** *We say that a triple of algorithm $\Pi := (\mathcal{K}, \mathcal{E}, \mathcal{D})$ is a public-key encryption scheme if*

- *$\mathcal{K}$, the key-generation algorithm, is a probabilistic algorithm which on input 1^k ($k \in \mathbb{N}$) outputs, in polynomial-time in k, a pair (pk, sk) of matching public and secret keys.*
- *$\mathcal{E}$, the encryption algorithm, is a probabilistic algorithm which on input public-key pk and plaintext $x \in \{0,1\}^k$ outputs ciphertext y in polynomial-time in k. We denote by $\mathcal{E}_{pk} : \{0,1\}^k \times \{0,1\}^{l(k)} \to \{0,1\}^{n(k)}$ the map from the product of k-bit message and $l(k)$-bit coin-flipping spaces to $n(k)$-bit cipher space, where functions, $l(\cdot)$ and $n(\cdot)$, are positive integer valued functions bounded in some polynomial, namely $l(k), n(k) < \exists poly(k)$ for enough large k.*
- *$\mathcal{D}$, the decryption algorithm, is a deterministic algorithm which on input secret-key sk and ciphertext y outputs $\mathcal{D}_{sk}(y)$ such that*

$$\mathcal{D}_{sk}(y) := \begin{cases} x \in \{0,1\}^k & \text{if there exists } x \text{ such that } y = \mathcal{E}_{pk}(x) \\ \varepsilon \text{ (null)} & \text{otherwise.} \end{cases}$$

We say that ciphertext y is valid if there exists a plaintext x such that $y = \mathcal{E}_{pk}(x)$. We insist that in a public-key encryption scheme the map from the plaintext space to the ciphertext space should be one-to-one (injective): the decryption of each ciphertext should be unique.

Definition 3. **[Random Oracle Model]** *We define by Ω the set of all maps from the set $\{0,1\}^*$ of finite strings to the set $\{0,1\}^\infty$ of infinite strings. $H \leftarrow \Omega$ means that we chose map H from a set of an appropriate finite length (say $: \{0,1\}^a$) to a set of an appropriate finite length (say $\{0,1\}^b$), from Ω at random and uniformly, restricting the domain to $\{0,1\}^a$ and the range to the first b bits of output. If $\mathcal{E}$ and $\mathcal{D}$ in public-key encryption scheme Π are allowed to access such identical map H, we say that the scheme is defined in the random oracle model. If we insist on the fact, then we will denote $\Pi := (\mathcal{K}, \mathcal{E}^H, \mathcal{D}^H)$.*

Below, we give the precise definitions of GOAL-ATK described in Sec.1.2. Due to the space limitations, one-wayness is not described.

Definition 4. **[IND-ATK]** *Let $\Pi := (\mathcal{K}, \mathcal{E}, \mathcal{D})$ be a public-key encryption scheme and let $A := (A_1, A_2)$ be a pair of probabilistic algorithms (say Adversary). For $atk \in \{cpa, cca1, cca2\}$ and $k \in \mathbb{N}$, let define*

$$Adv_{A,\Pi}^{ind\text{-}atk}(k) := 2\Pr[H \leftarrow \Omega; (pk, sk) \leftarrow \mathcal{K}(1^k); (x_0, x_1, s) \leftarrow A_1^{O_1, H}(pk);$$
$$b \leftarrow_R \{0, 1\}; y \leftarrow \mathcal{E}_{pk}(x_b) : A_2^{O_2, H}(x_0, x_1, s, y) = b] - 1.$$

Here, $O_1(\cdot)$, $O_2(\cdot)$ are defined as follows:

- *If atk=cpa then $O_1(\cdot) = \varepsilon$ and $O_2(\cdot) = \varepsilon$*
- *If atk=cca1 then $O_1(\cdot) = \mathcal{D}_{sk}(\cdot)$ and $O_2(\cdot) = \varepsilon$*
- *If atk=cca2 then $O_1(\cdot) = \mathcal{D}_{sk}(\cdot)$ and $O_2(\cdot) = \mathcal{D}_{sk}(\cdot)$*

In addition we define that A_1 outputs x_0, x_1 with $|x_0| = |x_1|$ and, in the case of IND-CCA2, A_2 does not ask its oracle to decrypt y.

We say that Π is secure in the sense of IND-ATK if for any adversary A being polynomial-time in k $Adv_{A,\Pi}^{ind\text{-}atk}(k)$ is negligible in k.

We insist that $A := (A_1, A_2)$ is not allowed to access to H in the standard model. When we insist on that, we write $A_1^{O_1}$ and $A_2^{O_2}$ instead of $A_1^{O_1, H}$ and $A_2^{O_2, H}$, respectively. On the other hand, when we insist on the random oracle model, we write $\mathcal{E}_{pk}^H(\cdot)$ and $\mathcal{D}_{sk}^H(\cdot)$ instead of $\mathcal{E}_{pk}(\cdot)$ and $\mathcal{D}_{sk}(\cdot)$, respectively.

Definition 5. **[NM-ATK]** *Let $\Pi := (\mathcal{K}, \mathcal{E}, \mathcal{D})$ be a public-key encryption scheme and let $A := (A_1, A_2)$ be a pair of probabilistic algorithms (say Adversary). For $atk \in \{cpa, cca1, cca2\}$ and $k \in \mathbb{N}$, let define*

$$Adv_{A,\Pi}^{nm\text{-}atk}(k) := |Succ_{A,\Pi}^{nm\text{-}atk}(k) - Succ_{A,\Pi,\$}^{nm\text{-}atk}(k)|$$

where $Succ_{A,\Pi}^{nm\text{-}atk}(k) :=$

$$\Pr[H \leftarrow \Omega; (pk, sk) \leftarrow \mathcal{K}(1^k); (M, s) \leftarrow A_1^{O_1, H}(pk); x, x' \leftarrow M; y \leftarrow \mathcal{E}_{pk}(x);$$
$$(R, \boldsymbol{y}) \leftarrow A_2^{O_2, H}(M, s, y); \boldsymbol{x} \leftarrow \mathcal{D}_{sk}(\boldsymbol{y}) : (\boldsymbol{y} \notin y) \wedge (\varepsilon(null) \notin \boldsymbol{x}) \wedge R(x, \boldsymbol{x})]$$

and $Succ_{A,\Pi,\$}^{nm\text{-}atk}(k) :=$

$$\Pr[H \leftarrow \Omega; (pk, sk) \leftarrow \mathcal{K}(1^k); (M, s) \leftarrow A_1^{O_1, H}(pk); x, x' \leftarrow M; y \leftarrow \mathcal{E}_{pk}(x);$$
$$(R, \boldsymbol{y}) \leftarrow A_2^{O_2, H}(M, s, y); \boldsymbol{x} \leftarrow \mathcal{D}_{sk}(\boldsymbol{y}) : (\boldsymbol{y} \notin y) \wedge (\varepsilon(null) \notin \boldsymbol{x}) \wedge R(x', \boldsymbol{x})]$$

Here, $O_1(\cdot)$, $O_2(\cdot)$ are defined as before. In the case of IND-CCA2, A_2 does not ask its oracle to decrypt y.

We say that M is valid if $|x| = |x'|$ for any x, x' that are given non-zero probability in the message space M.

We say that Π is secure in the sense of NM-ATK if any adversary A being polynomial-time in k outputs a valid message space M samplable in polynomial in k and a relation R computable in polynomial in k, then $Adv_{A,\Pi}^{nm\text{-}atk}(k)$ is negligible in k.

We insist that $A := (A_1, A_2)$ is not allowed to access to H in the standard model. When we insist on that, we write $A_1^{O_1}$ and $A_2^{O_2}$ instead of $A_1^{O_1,H}$ and $A_2^{O_2,H}$, respectively. On the other hand, when we insist on the random oracle model, we write $\mathcal{E}_{pk}^H(\cdot)$ and $\mathcal{D}_{sk}^H(\cdot)$ instead of $\mathcal{E}_{pk}(\cdot)$ and $\mathcal{D}_{sk}(\cdot)$, respectively.

We review some important results proven in [3] below. Here, as mentioned above, for $\mathbb{A}, \mathbb{B} \in$ GOAL-ATK "$\mathbb{A} \to \mathbb{B}$" (say, $\mathbb{A}$ implies $\mathbb{B}$) denotes that encryption scheme $\Pi := (\mathcal{K}, \mathcal{E}, \mathcal{D})$ being secure in the sense of $\mathbb{A}$ is also secure in the sense of $\mathbb{B}$, while "$\mathbb{A} \nrightarrow \mathbb{B}$" (say, $\mathbb{A}$ doesn't imply $\mathbb{B}$) denotes Π being secure in the sense of $\mathbb{A}$ is not always secure in the sense of $\mathbb{B}$.

Proposition 1. *IND-CCA2 $\to$ NM-CCA2.*

From this proposition, it is clear that

Corollary 1. *IND-CCA2 $\longleftrightarrow$ NM-CCA2.*

Proposition 2. *IND-CCA1 $\nrightarrow$ NM-CCA2.*

The following definition is utilized to discuss security more exactly (exact security).

Definition 6. [Breaking Algorithm] *Let $\Pi := (\mathcal{K}, \mathcal{E}, \mathcal{D})$ be a public-key encryption scheme. We say that an adversary A is a (t, q_H, q_D, ϵ)-breaker for $\Pi(1^k)$ in GOAL-ATK if $Adv_{A,\Pi}^{goal-atk}(k) \geq \epsilon$ and, moreover, A runs within at most running time t, asking at most q_H queries to $H(\cdot)$ and at most q_D queries to $\mathcal{D}_{sk}(\cdot)$. In addition, q_H denotes the number of queries A asks to random function $H(\cdot)$, and similarly, q_D denotes the number of queries A asks to decryption oracle $\mathcal{D}_{sk}(\cdot)$. In the case of atk = cpa, then $q_D = 0$. In the case of the standard model, then $q_H = 0$.*

In the following, we will recall the notion of Plaintext Awareness and the main results.

Definition 7. [Plaintext Awareness (PA)] *Let $\Pi := (\mathcal{K}, \mathcal{E}, \mathcal{D})$ be a public-key encryption scheme, let B be an adversary, and let K be an polynomial-time algorithm (say knowledge extractor) . For any $k \in \mathbb{N}$ let*

$$Succ_{K,B,\Pi}^{pa}(k) := \Pr[H \leftarrow \Omega; (pk, sk) \leftarrow \mathcal{K}(1^k);$$

$$(\tau, \eta, y) \leftarrow runB^{H,\mathcal{E}_{pk}}(pk) : K(\tau, \eta, y, pk) = \mathcal{D}_{sk}(y)],$$

where $\tau := \{(h_1, H_1), \ldots, (h_{q_H}, H_{q_H})\}$, $\eta := \{y_1, \ldots, y_{q_E}\}$, and $y \notin \eta$. We describe a supplementary explanation: By $(\tau, \eta, y) \leftarrow runB^{H,\mathcal{E}_{pk}}(pk)$ we mean the following. Run B on input pk and oracles $H(\cdot)$ and $\mathcal{E}_{pk}(\cdot)$ and record (τ, η, y) from B's interaction with its oracles. τ denotes the set of all B's queries and the corresponding answers of $H(\cdot)$. η denotes the set of all the answers (ciphertexts) received as the result of $\mathcal{E}_{pk}$. Here we insist that η doesn't include the corresponding queries (plaintexts) from B. y denotes the output of B.

We say that K is a $(t, \lambda(k))$-knowledge extractor if $Succ^{pa}_{K,B,\Pi}(k) \geq \lambda(k)$ and K runs within at most running time t (or t steps).

We say that Π is secure in the sense of PA if Π is secure in the sense of IND-CPA and there exists a $(t, \lambda(k))$-knowledge extractor K where t is polynomial in k and $(1 - \lambda(k))$ is negligible in k.

The following results proven in [3] is important.

Proposition 3. *PA $\rightarrow$ IND-CCA2 in the random oracle model.*

Corollary 2. *PA $\rightarrow$ NM-CCA2 in the random oracle model.*

3 Basic Scheme

Suppose a public-key encryption scheme, $\Pi := (\mathcal{K}, \mathcal{E}, \mathcal{D})$, exists which is semantically secure against every chosen-plaintext (passive) attack (IND-CPA). Let $k_0(\cdot)$, $l_0(\cdot)$, $l(\cdot)$ and $n(\cdot)$ be positive integer valued functions bounded in some polynomial, namely $k_0(k), l_0(k), l(k), n(k) < \exists poly(k)$ for enough large k. We denote by $\Pi(1^{k+k_0}) = (\mathcal{K}, \mathcal{E}, \mathcal{D})$ a public-key encryption scheme with $(k + k_0(k))$-bit length plaintext space, $l(k + k_0(k))$-bit length random value space and $n(k + k_0(k))$-bit length ciphertext space:

$$\mathcal{E}_{pk} : \{0,1\}^{k+k_0} \times \{0,1\}^l \to \{0,1\}^n \text{ and } \mathcal{D}_{sk} : \{0,1\}^n \to \{0,1\}^{k+k_0},$$

where we write k_0, l, and n for $k_0(k)$, $l(k + k_0(k))$ and $n(k + k_0(k))$. In public-key encryption scheme Π, the (encryption) map from the plaintext space to the ciphertext space is one-to-one (injective). In addition, we define by

$$l_0(k + k_0) := \log_2(\min_{x \in \{0,1\}^{k+k_0}} [\#\{\mathcal{E}_{pk}(x, r) | r \in \{0,1\}^l\}])$$

the minimum number of the cardinality of encrypted values for fixed plaintext x. We often write l_0 for $l_0(k + k_0)$ for simplicity. Furthermore, we define by $H : \{0,1\}^{k+k_0} \to \{0,1\}^{l(k+k_0)}$ an ideal hash function.

We introduce a new public-key encryption scheme, $\bar{\Pi} := (\bar{\mathcal{K}}, \bar{\mathcal{E}}, \bar{\mathcal{D}})$ which is derived from Π and hash function H as follows:

Basic Scheme $\bar{\Pi} := (\bar{\mathcal{K}}, \bar{\mathcal{E}}, \bar{\mathcal{D}})$

- $\bar{\mathcal{K}}(1^k) := \mathcal{K}(1^{k+k_0})$ where k_0 denotes $k_0(k)$ for simplicity.
- $\bar{\mathcal{E}}_{pk} : \{0,1\}^k \times \{0,1\}^{k_0} \to \{0,1\}^n$ is defined by

$$\bar{\mathcal{E}}_{pk}(x, r) := \mathcal{E}_{pk}(x \| r, H(x \| r)),$$

  where $|x| = k$, $|r| = k_0$, and $n := n(k + k_0(k))$.
- $\bar{\mathcal{D}}_{sk}(y) : \{0,1\}^n \to \{0,1\}^k$ is defined by

$$\bar{\mathcal{D}}_{sk}(y) := \begin{cases} [\mathcal{D}_{sk}(y)]^k & \text{if } y = \mathcal{E}_{pk}(\mathcal{D}_{sk}(y), H(\mathcal{D}_{sk}(y))) \\ \varepsilon \text{ (null)} & \text{otherwise} \end{cases}$$

  where $[\mathcal{D}_{sk}(y)]^k$ denotes the first k-bit of $\mathcal{D}_{sk}(y)$.

Hereafter we will show that $\bar{\Pi}$ is semantically secure against every adaptive chosen-ciphertext attack.

4 Security

In this section, our goal is to prove Theorem 3. This theorem doesn't only show that if Π is IND-CPA secure then $\bar{\Pi}$ is IND-CCA2, but also show the exact reduction cost from $\bar{\Pi}$ to Π. The proof of Theorem 3 is derived from Theorems, 1 and 2.

We begin by showing Theorem 1. Recall that $k_0(\cdot)$, $l_0(\cdot)$, $l(\cdot)$ and $n(\cdot)$ are functions bounded in some polynomial, namely $k_0(k), l(k), n(k) < \exists poly(k)$ for enough large k and, for simplicity, we often use k_0, l_0, l, and n for $k_0(k)$, $l_0(k + k_0(k))$, $l(k + k_0(k))$ and $n(k + k_0(k))$.

Theorem 1. [Knowledge extractor K of $\bar{\Pi}$] *If there exists a (t, q_H)-adversary B, then there exist a constant c_0 and a $(t', \lambda(k))$-knowledge extractor K such that*

$$t' = t + q_H(T_{\mathcal{E}}(k) + c_0 \cdot k) \text{ and}$$
$$\lambda(k) = 1 - 2^{-l_0}.$$

Here $T_{\mathcal{E}}(k)$ denotes the computational running time of the encryption algorithm $\mathcal{E}_{pk}(\cdot)$ and $l_0 := \log_2(\min_{x \in \{0,1\}^{k+k_0}}[\#\{\mathcal{E}_{pk}(x,r)|r \in \{0,1\}^l\}])$.

Proof. The specification of knowledge extractor K is as follows:

Extractor: $K(\tau, \eta, y, pk)$
        for q_H times do
            if $y == \mathcal{E}_{pk}(h_i, H_i)$;
                then $x \leftarrow [h_i]^k$ and break
            else $x \leftarrow \varepsilon$ (null)
        return x
End.

Here note that $\tau := \{(h_1, H_1), \dots, (h_{q_H}, H_{q_H})\}$.

Now we define c_0 as corresponding to the computation time of comparing a bit to a bit plus some overhead, which depends on details of the underlying model of computation of K. Then, from the specification, K runs within $t + q_H(T_{\mathcal{E}}(k) + c_0 \cdot k)$ time.

Next we think of the probability that K outputs the plaintext, x, correctly, namely $x = \bar{\mathcal{D}}_{sk}(y)$. Here let $Fail$ be an event assigned to be true iff $x \neq \bar{\mathcal{D}}_{sk}(y)$ and let $AskH$ be an event assigned to be true iff there exists (h_i, H_i) in the list τ such that $y = \mathcal{E}_{pk}(h_i, H_i)$. Then it follows that

$$\Pr[Fail] = \Pr[Fail|AskH] \cdot \Pr[AskH] + \Pr[Fail|\neg AskH] \cdot \Pr[\neg AskH]$$
$$\leq \Pr[Fail|AskH] + \Pr[Fail|\neg AskH] \leq 0 + 2^{-l_0} = 2^{-l_0}.$$

If $AskH$ is true then K never fail to guess the plaintext x and hence it is clear that $\Pr[Fail|AskH] = 0$.

Next in the case that $\neg AskH$ is true, K outputs ε: K guess y as *invalid*. Therefore, the probability of K's failure is that of B outputting *valid* y. We explain that $\Pr[Fail|\neg AskH]$ is at most 2^{-l_0} in the following.

Let us define event *good y* by being true iff $\mathcal{D}_{sk}(y) \neq \varepsilon$. Don't confuse it with *valid y*: *valid y* is defined to be true iff $\bar{\mathcal{D}}_{sk}(y) \neq \varepsilon$. Then note that

$$\Pr[P] := \Pr[Fail|\neg AskH] = \Pr[P| \text{ good } y] \cdot \Pr[good\ y]$$
$$+ \Pr[P|\neg good\ y] \cdot \Pr[\neg good\ y] \leq \Pr[P|good\ y].$$

Therefore, it is enough to think of $\Pr[P| \text{ good } y]$.

Recall that $l_0 := \log_2(\min_{x \in \{0,1\}^{k+k_0}} [\#\{\mathcal{E}_{pk}(x,r)|r \in \{0,1\}^l\}])$. For *good y*, let define by $\mathcal{H}_y$ the set of $(h, \hat{H}_j)$'s such that $y = \mathcal{E}_{pk}(h, \hat{H}_j)$. Here $j \in \{1, \ldots, s\}$ and $s \leq 2^{l-l_0}$. Then since $\eta := \{y_1, \ldots, y_{q_E}\}$ and $y \notin \eta$, it follows that $h \neq \mathcal{D}_{sk}(y_i)$ for every $y_i \in \eta$. Therefore, for fixed *good y* (and h), since B doesn't ask query h to oracle $H(\cdot)$,

$$\Pr[P| \text{ good } y] = \Pr_{H \leftarrow \Omega}[H(h) \in \mathcal{H}_y] = s \cdot 2^{-l} \leq 2^{-l_0}.$$

This means that

$$\Pr[P] := \Pr[Fail|\neg AskH] \leq \Pr[P|good\ y] \leq 2^{-l_0}.$$

Hence, $\lambda(k) = 1 - \Pr[Fail] = 1 - 2^{-l_0}$.

Theorem 2. [$\bar{\Pi}$: **IND-CPA secure**] *If there exists a* $(t, q_H, 0, \epsilon)$*-breaker* $A := (A_1, A_2)$ *for* $\bar{\Pi}(1^k)$ *in the sense of IND-CPA in the RO model, then there exist a constant* c_1 *and a* $(t', 0, 0, \epsilon')$*-breaker* $A' := (A'_1, A'_2)$ *for* $\Pi(1^{k+k_0})$ *in the sense of IND-CPA (in the standard model) where*

$$t' = t + c_1 \cdot q_H \cdot k, \quad and \quad \epsilon' = \epsilon - q_H \cdot 2^{-(k_0-1)}.$$

Proof. We run $A' := (A'_1, A'_2)$ in the IND-CPA and standard model setting, using $A := (A_1, A_2)$ as oracles respectively.

Basically, when A_i asks query h, A'_i works as follows: If h has not been entered in list τ, A'_i, choosing l-bit random string H, makes an entry of (h, H) in τ and answers A_i with H. If (h, H) is already in list τ, A'_i answers A_i with the corresponding H. The list τ is empty at first. When A_1 outputs (x_0, x_1, s), A'_1 outputs $(x_0\|r_0, x_1\|r_1, s)$ where r_0, r_1 are k_0-bit random strings generated by A'_1. Then, outside A', $y := \mathcal{E}_{pk}(X_b, R)$ is computed using a random bit $b \in \{0,1\}$ and l-bit random string R, where $X_0 := (x_0\|r_0)$ and $X_1 := (x_1\|r_1)$. y is inputted on A'_2 as well as (X_0, X_1, s).

If A_2 asks either X_0 or X_1 as a query, A'_2 makes A_2 stop and outputs the corresponding $b \in \{0,1\}$ as an answer, otherwise A'_2 follows the basic rule mentioned above. When A_2 asks neither of them, A'_2 outputs b that A_2 output as an answer.

The argument behind the proof is as follows: If A_2 asks a query to A'_2, which coincides with either $(x_0\|r_0)$ or $(x_1\|r_1)$, it is almost equivalent to $\mathcal{D}_{sk}(y)$, because (even unbounded powerful) A_2 has no clue to k_0-bit random string $r_{\bar{b}}$, where $\bar{b}$ is the complement of bit b. Therefore, if A_2 asks either of them, the corresponding b is expected to be *valid*. On the other hand, if A_2 asks neither of them, A_2 is expected to output *valid* b because A_2 cannot distinguish y from a correct ciphertext for A_2.

The specification of adversary $A' := (A_1', A_2')$ is as follows:

Adversary: $A_1'(pk)$

$\quad\quad \tau \leftarrow \varepsilon;$

$\quad\quad$ run $A_1(pk)$

$\quad\quad\quad\quad$ do while A_1 does not make H-query h.

$\quad\quad\quad\quad\quad\quad$ if $h \notin \tau_h$, where τ_h is the list of h's in τ

$\quad\quad\quad\quad\quad\quad\quad\quad H \leftarrow_R \{0,1\}^l;$

$\quad\quad\quad\quad\quad\quad\quad\quad$ put (h, H) on the list τ;

$\quad\quad\quad\quad\quad\quad\quad\quad$ answer A_1 with H;

$\quad\quad\quad\quad\quad\quad$ else $h \in \tau_h$

$\quad\quad\quad\quad\quad\quad\quad\quad$ answer A_1 with H such that $(h, H) \in \tau$

$\quad\quad\quad\quad A_1$ outputs (x_0, x_1, s)

$\quad\quad\quad\quad r_0, r_1 \leftarrow_R \{0,1\}^{k_0};$

$\quad\quad\quad\quad$ return $(x_0\|r_0, x_1\|r_1, s)$

End.

Adversary: $A_2'(x_0\|r_0, x_1\|r_1, s, y)$

$\quad\quad$ run $A_2(x_0, x_1, s, y)$

$\quad\quad\quad\quad$ do while A_1 does not make H-query h.

$\quad\quad\quad\quad\quad\quad$ if $h == (x_b\|r_b)$ for $b \in \{0,1\}$

$\quad\quad\quad\quad\quad\quad\quad\quad$ stop A_2 and output b

$\quad\quad\quad\quad\quad\quad$ else if $h \notin \tau_h$, where τ_h is the list of h's in τ

$\quad\quad\quad\quad\quad\quad\quad\quad H \leftarrow_R \{0,1\}^l;$

$\quad\quad\quad\quad\quad\quad\quad\quad$ put (h, H) on the list τ;

$\quad\quad\quad\quad\quad\quad\quad\quad$ answer A_1 with H;

$\quad\quad\quad\quad\quad\quad$ else $h \in \tau_h$

$\quad\quad\quad\quad\quad\quad\quad\quad$ answer A_1 with H such that $(h, H) \in \tau$

$\quad\quad\quad\quad A_2$ outputs b

$\quad\quad$ return b

End.

Here, from Definition 4, b is chosen from $\{0,1\}$ with probability $1/2$, R is an l-bit random string, and $y = \mathcal{E}_{pk}(x_b\|r_b, R)$.

c_1 corresponds to the computational time of comparing a bit to a bit, coin-flipping, and some overhead, depending on details of the underlying model of computation of A'. Then, from the specification of A', it runs within at most running time $(t + c_1 \cdot q_H \cdot k)$.

We now analyze the success probability of adversary $A' := (A_1', A_2')$. First we define the following events:

$$SuccA := [H \leftarrow \Omega; (pk, sk) \leftarrow \mathcal{K}(1^{k+k_0}); (x_0, x_1, s) \leftarrow A_1^H(pk); b \leftarrow_R \{0,1\};$$
$$r_b, r_{\bar{b}} \leftarrow_R \{0,1\}^{k_0}; y \leftarrow \mathcal{E}_{pk}((x_b\|r_b), H(x_b\|r_b)) : A_2^H(x_0, x_1, s, y) = b],$$
$$SuccA' := [(pk, sk) \leftarrow \mathcal{K}(1^{k+k_0}); (X_0, X_1, s) \leftarrow A_1'(pk'); b \leftarrow_R \{0,1\};$$
$$R_b, R_{\bar{b}} \leftarrow_R \{0,1\}^{k_0}; y \leftarrow \mathcal{E}_{pk}(X_b, R_b) : A_2'(X_0, X_1, s, y) = b],$$

where $\bar{b}$ denotes the complement of b.

We can define the advantages of A and A', without loss of generality, as $Adv_{A,\Pi}^{\text{ind-atk}}(k+k_0) := 2 \cdot \Pr[SuccA] - 1$, and $Adv_{A',\Pi}^{\text{ind-atk}}(k) := 2 \cdot \Pr[SuccA'] - 1$.

Next, let us define by $Ask0$ an event assigned to be true iff a query of A_2 coincides with $(x_b \| r_b)$ and by $Ask1$ an event assigned to be true iff a query of A_2 coincides with $(x_{\bar{b}} \| r_{\bar{b}})$. Then,

$$\begin{aligned} \Pr[SuccA] &= \Pr[SuccA|Ask0] \cdot \Pr[Ask0] + \Pr[SuccA|(\neg Ask0) \wedge Ask1] \\ &\quad \cdot \Pr[(\neg Ask0) \wedge Ask1] + \Pr[SuccA|(\neg Ask0) \wedge (\neg Ask1)] \\ &\quad \cdot \Pr[(\neg Ask0) \wedge (\neg Ask1)] \text{ and} \\ \Pr[SuccA'] &= \Pr[SuccA'|Ask0] \cdot \Pr[Ask0] + \Pr[SuccA'|(\neg Ask0) \wedge Ask1] \\ &\quad \cdot \Pr[(\neg Ask0) \wedge Ask1] + \Pr[SuccA'|(\neg Ask0) \wedge (\neg Ask1)] \\ &\quad \cdot \Pr[(\neg Ask0) \wedge (\neg Ask1)]. \end{aligned}$$

From the specification of A', it is clear that $\Pr[SuccA'|Ask0] = 1$, $\Pr[SuccA'|(\neg Ask0) \wedge Ask1] = 0$ and $\Pr[SuccA|(\neg Ask0) \wedge (\neg Ask1)] = \Pr[SuccA'|(\neg Ask0) \wedge (\neg Ask1)]$. Hence, $\Pr[SuccA']$ is at most $\Pr[(\neg Ask0) \wedge Ask1])$ less than $\Pr[SuccA]$ because

$$\begin{aligned} \Pr[SuccA'] - \Pr[SuccA] &= (1 - \Pr[SuccA|Ask0]) \cdot \Pr[Ask0] \\ &\quad - \Pr[SuccA|(\neg Ask0) \wedge Ask1] \cdot \Pr[(\neg Ask0) \wedge Ask1] \\ &\geq - \Pr[(\neg Ask0) \wedge Ask1]. \end{aligned}$$

Finally, we have

$$\Pr[SuccA'] \geq \frac{\epsilon + 1}{2} - \frac{q_H}{2^{k_0}},$$

since we infer that $\Pr[(\neg Ask0) \wedge Ask1] \leq \frac{q_H}{2^{k_0}}$,

Therefore, we have that $\epsilon' = \epsilon - \frac{q_H}{2^{k_0-1}}$.

From Definition 7 and Theorems, 1 and 2, Π is secure in the sense of PA, and hence, by Proposition 3, secure in the sense of IND-CCA2. Thus, our interest in the following theorem is focused on the efficiency of the reduction.

Theorem 3. [$\bar{\Pi}$: **IND-CCA2 secure**] *If there exists a (t, q_H, q_D, ϵ)-breaker $A := (A_1, A_2)$ for $\bar{\Pi}(1^k)$ in the sense of IND-CCA2 in the RO model, then there exist constants, c, and $(t', 0, 0, \epsilon')$-breaker $A' := (A_1', A_2')$ for $\Pi(1^{k+k_0})$ in the sense of IND-CPA (in the standard model) where*

$$t' = t + q_H \cdot (T_{\mathcal{E}}(k) + c \cdot k), \text{ and}$$
$$\epsilon' = (\epsilon - q_H \cdot 2^{-(k_0-1)}) \cdot (1 - 2^{-l_0})^{q_D}.$$

$T_{\mathcal{E}}(k)$ *denotes the computational running time of the encryption algorithm $\mathcal{E}_{pk}(\cdot)$ and $l_0 := \log_2(\min_{x \in \{0,1\}^{k+k_0}}[\#\{\mathcal{E}_{pk}(x,r)|r \in \{0,1\}^l\}])$.*

c corresponds to $c_0 + c_1$. We omit the proof because it is straightforward from the following specification of adversary A':

Adversary: $A_1'(pk)$
  $\tau \leftarrow \varepsilon$;
  $\eta \leftarrow \varepsilon$;
  run $A_1^{\mathcal{D}_{sk},H}(pk)$
    do while A_1 makes neither H-query h nor D-query y'
      if A_1 makes H-query h.
        if $h \notin \tau_h$
          $H \leftarrow_R \{0,1\}^l$;
          put (h,H) on the list τ;
          answer A_1 with H;
        else $h \in \tau_h$
          answer A_1 with H such that $(h,H) \in \tau$
      else if A_1 makes D-query y'.
        run $K(\tau,\eta,y',pk)$
          K outputs x'
          answer A_1 with x'
    A_1 outputs (x_0,x_1,s)
    $r_0, r_1 \leftarrow_R \{0,1\}^{k_0}$;
    return $(x_0\|r_0, x_1\|r_1, s)$
End.

Adversary: $A_2'(x_0\|r_0, x_1\|r_1, s, y)$
  $\eta \leftarrow y$;
  run $A_2^{\mathcal{D}_{sk},H}(x_0,x_1,s,y)$
    do while A_1 makes neither H-query h nor D-query y'
      if A_1 makes H-query h
        if $[h]_{k_0} == r_b$, where $[h]_{k_0}$ the last k_0-bit of h
          stop A_1 and output b
        else if $h \notin \tau_h$
          $H \leftarrow_R \{0,1\}^l$;
          put (h,H) on the list τ;
          answer A_1 with H;
        else $h \in \tau_h$
          answer A_1 with H such that $(h,H) \in \tau$
      else if A_1 makes D-query y'
        run $K(\tau,\eta,y',pk)$
          K outputs x'
          answer A_1 with x'
    A_1 outputs b
    return b
End.

5 Examples: Enhanced Probabilistic Encryptions

In this section, we convert IND-CPA secure ones to IND-CCA2 (or NM-CCA2) secure ones. The ElGamal, Okamoto-Uchiyama, and Blum-Goldwasser encryption schemes [4, 7, 9] are candidates, since they are practical and secure in the IND-CPA sense under some reasonable assumptions; the decision Diffie-Hellman [2], p-subgroup, and factoring assumptions, respectively.

[Enhanced ElGamal scheme]

- Key-generator $\bar{\mathcal{K}}$: $(pk, sk) \leftarrow \bar{\mathcal{K}}(1^k) := \mathcal{K}(1^{k+k_0(k)})$
- $pk := (p, q, g, y)$ and $sk := (p, q, g, s)$ where $y = g^s \bmod p$, $|p| = k + k_0$, $s \in \mathbb{Z}/q\mathbb{Z}$, $q|p-1$, and $\# <g> = q$.
- Hash function $H: \{0,1\}^{k+k_0} \longrightarrow \mathbb{Z}/q\mathbb{Z}$.
- Encryption $\bar{\mathcal{E}}$:

$$(y_1, y_2) := \bar{\mathcal{E}}_{pk}(x, r) := (g^{H(x||r)} \bmod p, (x||r) \oplus (y^{H(x||r)} \bmod p)),$$

where message $x \in \{0,1\}^k$ and $r \leftarrow_R \{0,1\}^{k_0}$.
- Decryption $\bar{\mathcal{D}}$:

$$\bar{\mathcal{D}}_{sk}(y_1, y_2) := \begin{cases} [y_2 \oplus (y_1^s \bmod p)]^k & \text{if } y_1 = g^{H(y_2 \oplus (y_1^s \bmod p))} \bmod p \\ \varepsilon \text{ (null)} & \text{otherwise} \end{cases}$$

where $[y_2 \oplus (y_1^s \bmod p)]^k$ denotes the first k-bit of $y_2 \oplus (y_1^s \bmod p)$.

Lemma 1. *In the random oracle model, the Enhanced ElGamal encryption scheme is secure in the sense of NM-CCA2 (or IND-CCA2) if the decision Diffie-Hellman problem is intractable.*

[Enhanced Okamoto-Uchiyama scheme]

- Key-generator $\bar{\mathcal{K}}$: $(pk, sk) \leftarrow \bar{\mathcal{K}}(1^k) := \mathcal{K}(1^{k+k_0(k)})$
- $pk := (n, g, h, k)$ and $sk := (p, q)$ where $n = p^2 q$, $|p| = |q| = k + k_0$, $g \in (\mathbb{Z}/n\mathbb{Z})^*$ such that the order of $g_p := g^{p-1} \bmod p^2$ is p, and $h = g^n \bmod n$.
- Hash function $H: \{0,1\}^{k+k_0-1} \longrightarrow \mathbb{Z}/n\mathbb{Z}$.
- Encryption $\bar{\mathcal{E}}$:

$$y := \bar{\mathcal{E}}_{pk}(x, r) := g^{(x||r)} h^{H(x||r)} \bmod n,$$

where message $x \in \{0,1\}^k$ and $r \leftarrow_R \{0,1\}^{k_0-1}$.
- Decryption $\mathcal{D}$:

$$\bar{\mathcal{D}}_{sk}(y) := \begin{cases} [\frac{L(y_p)}{L(g_p)} \bmod p]^k & \text{if } y = g^X h^{H(X)} \bmod n \\ \varepsilon \text{ (null)} & \text{otherwise} \end{cases}$$

where $y_p := y^{p-1} \bmod p^2$, $L(x) := \frac{x-1}{p}$, and $X := \frac{L(y_p)}{L(g_p)} \bmod p$.

---

[2] To our knowledge, Tsiounis and Yung first proved in [11] that the ElGamal encryption scheme is as secure as the decision Diffie-Hellman problem. In addition, they also presented a converted ElGamal scheme which is NM-CCA2 secure in the random oracle model. However, our converted one is more efficient than theirs.

Lemma 2. *In the random oracle model, the Enhanced Okamoto-Uchiyama encryption scheme is secure in the sense of NM-CCA2 (or IND-CCA2) if the p-subgroup problem (see [9]) is intractable.*

[Enhanced Blum-Goldwasser scheme]

- Key-generator $\bar{\mathcal{K}}$: $(pk, sk) \leftarrow \bar{\mathcal{K}}(1^k) := \mathcal{K}(1^{k+k_0(k)})$
- $pk := (n)$ and $sk := (n, p, q)$ where $n = pq$, $|p| = |q| = k/2$, and p, q are William integers (i.e. $p, q \equiv 7 \pmod 8$ and primes).
- Hash function $H: \{0, 1\}^{k+k_0} \longrightarrow \mathbb{Z}/n\mathbb{Z}$.
- Encryption $\bar{\mathcal{E}}$:

$$(y_1, y_2) := \bar{\mathcal{E}}_{pk}(x, r) := (H(x\|r)^{2^{k+1}} \bmod n, \ x \oplus R).$$

where message $x \in \{0, 1\}^k$, $r \leftarrow_R \{0, 1\}^{k_0}$, and $R := LSB[H(x\|r)^2] \| LSB[H(x\|r)^{2^2}] \| \cdots \| LSB[H(x\|r)^{2^k}]$.
- Decryption $\bar{\mathcal{D}}$:

$$\bar{\mathcal{D}}_{sk}(y_1, y_2) := \begin{cases} [y_2 \oplus \hat{R}]^k & \text{if } y_1 = H(y_2 \oplus \bar{R})^{2^{k+1}} \bmod n \\ \varepsilon \ (\text{null}) & \text{otherwise} \end{cases}$$

where $\hat{R} := LSB[y_1^{2^{-k}}] \| \cdots \| LSB[y_1^{2^{-1}}]$.

Lemma 3. *In the random oracle model, the Enhanced Blum-Goldwasser encryption scheme is secure in the sense of NM-CCA2 (or IND-CCA2) if the factoring problem is intractable.*

6 Conclusion

This paper presented a simple and efficient conversion from a semantically secure public-key encryption scheme against *passive adversaries* to a non-malleable (or semantically secure) public-key encryption scheme against *chosen-ciphertext attacks* (*active adversaries*) in the random oracle model. Our conversion incurs minimum cost, i.e., only one random (hash) function operation. We also showed that our security reduction is (almost) optimally efficient, or exact security. Finally this paper presented some practical examples, the enhanced ElGamal, Blum-Goldwasser and Okamoto-Uchiyama schemes.

Acknowledgment

The second author would like to thank Phillip Rogaway for useful discussions.

References

1. M. Bellare and P. Rogaway, "Random Oracles are Practical: A Paradigm for Designing Efficient Protocols," Proc. of the First ACM Conference on Computer and Communications Security, pp.62–73.
2. M. Bellare and P. Rogaway, "Optimal Asymmetric Encryption—How to encrypt with RSA" Advances in Cryptology –EUROCRYPT'94.
3. M. Bellare, A. Desai, D. Pointcheval, and P. Rogaway, "Relations Among Notions of Security for Public-Key Encryption Schemes" Advances in Cryptology –CRYPTO'98.
4. M. Blum, and S. Goldwasser, "An efficient probabilistic public-key encryption scheme which hides all partial information", Proceeding of Crypto'84, LNCS 196, Springer-Verlag, pp.289-299 (1985).
5. R. Cramer and V. Shoup, "A practical public key cryptosystem provably secure against adaptive chosen message attack", Advances in Cryptology –CRYPTO'98, Springer-Verlag, 1998.
6. D. Dolev and C. Dwork and M. Naor, "Non-malleable cryptography", Proceeding of STOC91, pp 542–552.
7. T. ElGamal, "A Public Key Cryptosystem and a Signature Scheme Based on Discrete Logarithms," IEEE Transactions on Information Theory, IT-31, 4, pp.469–472, 1985.
8. S. Goldwasser, and S. Micali, "Probabilistic Encryption", JCSS, vol.28, pp.270–299, 1984.
9. T. Okamoto, and S. Uchiyama, "A New Public-Key Cryptosystem as Secure as Factoring", Advances in Cryptology –EUROCRYPT'98, Springer-Verlag, 1998.
10. R. Rivest, A. Shamir and L. Adleman, "A Method for Obtaining Digital Signatures and Public Key Cryptosystems", Communications of ACM, 21, 2, pp.120-126, 1978.
11. Y. Tsiounis and M. Yung, "On the Security of ElGamal based Encryption", PKC'98, January, 1998.

Encrypted Message Authentication by Firewalls

Chandana Gamage, Jussipekka Leiwo, and Yuliang Zheng

Peninsula School of Computing and Information Technology
Monash University, McMahons Road, Frankston, Vic 3199, Australia
{chandag,skylark,yuliang}@pscit.monash.edu.au

Abstract. Firewalls typically filter network traffic at several different layers. At application layer, filtering is based on various security relevant information encapsulated into protocol messages. The major obstacle for efficient verification of authenticity of messages at application layer is the difficulty of verifying digital signatures without disclosure of content protected by encryption. This is due to a traditional paradigm of generating a digital signature of a message and then encrypting the signature together with the message to preserve confidentiality, integrity, non-repudiation and authenticity. To overcome this limitation, a scheme shall be proposed for enabling signature verification without disclosing the content of messages. To provide maximum efficiency, the scheme is based on digital signcryption.

Keywords. Encryption, Digital Signatures, Firewalls, Confidentiality, Authenticity, Network Security, Signcryption, Public Key Cryptography

1 Introduction

Firewalls are one of the most useful and versatile tools available for securing a LAN and other applications such as constructing secure private virtual networks [21]. They are typically operated as a filtering gateway [2, 6] at the LAN-WAN interface, usually a router. Firewalls operating at data link level perform a primitive level of filtering based on frame level addressing. The network level firewalls work at a step higher and filter packets based on a set of rules including packet addresses, port addresses and possibly packet header authentication as supported by new IPv6 extensions. The most comprehensive filtering is done at the application layer with end-user level authentication of messages.

For secure communication using public key cryptography, the standard practice is for a sender to sign a message (or its hash) using her secret key and then encrypt the message *and* the signature using receivers public key. The signature is used to provide sender authenticity, message integrity and message origin non-repudiation while encryption provide message confidentiality. Other redundant information such as time-stamps or sequence numbers in messages can be used against replay and existential forgery attacks. When this cipher text message reaches its intended recipient, he first decrypts the cryptogram using his secret key. Then the signature is verified using senders public key.

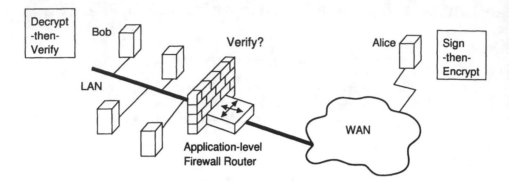

Fig. 1. Application-level firewall used for inward message authentication in a LAN

1.1 The Problem

In a LAN secured with a firewall, this standard use of public key cryptographic techniques for secure communication causes serious difficulties in filtering. As both the signed message and the signature is encrypted, the filtering process at the firewall cannot authenticate the message independent of the end-point receiver. The firewall cannot access the signature as the cryptogram cannot be decrypted without receivers secret key. This scenario is illustrated in figure 1 for communication between external user Alice and LAN user Bob.

Another problem from the users view point is that they may want to maintain the confidentiality of their communication while allowing the firewall to verify the message origin for filtering. Most widely used digital signature schemes require access to the signed text for signature verification (schemes with appendix such as DSA [17], ElGamal [11, 12] or Schnorr [27, 28]) or recover the message as part of the verification step (such as RSA [26], Rabin [25] or Nyberg-Rueppel [18, 19]).

1.2 Research Contribution

This problem of authentication of secure messages by a firewall is common to all widely used public key cryptosystems that use standard sign-then-encrypt mode of operation. We suggest that following properties should be satisfied by any practical scheme which aim to solve the problem:

Property 1. Preserve the semantics of signature-then-verification.
Property 2. Signature verified without access to the plain text.
Property 3. Should not increase the original computational and transmission costs incurred by end-user signer or verifier.
Property 4. Cost of signature verification by the firewall, measured in terms of computational and transmission effort, should not be greater than that for the end-user verifier.

In section 3 we present a complete solution to this problem which is more efficient than standard sign-then-encrypt schemes.

1.3 Structure of the Paper

There are seemingly straightforward ways to achieve authenticity without disclosure of messages in a public key cryptographic setting. These alternative mechanisms shall be summarized in section 2 and reasons pointed out why they are not capable of adequate security and objectives of this research. The proposed mechanism shall be established in section 3 and informal arguments shall be provided for security and performance of the proposal. The informal discussion shall be enhanced and a formal proof of security of the proposed scheme shall be given in section 4. Section 5 shall conclude with remarks highlighting important issues related to the proof mechanism used in this paper.

2 Related Work

We will first discuss two straightforward solutions to the problem outlined above and resulting security implications for those schemes.

Reordering If the cryptographic operations are reordered so that encryption is followed by signing, anyone can verify the signature while not compromising the confidentiality of the encrypted message. However, reordering is not a desirable option as an adversary could replace an original signature with his own in particular situations to obtain some advantage even without knowledge of the actual message content.

Chen and Hughes in [9] discuss the security protocol failures due to reordering when RSA encryption is used. Their work is an extension of the general attack presented by Anderson and Needham in [1] for protocols that sign after encryption. Apart from the apparent insecurity, this mode of operation does not satisfy the first and second properties listed earlier.

Signcryption with public key only signature verification The original signcryption primitive proposed in [30] by Zheng combines the sign-then-encrypt two-step process to create a secure authenticated message into a single logical step with significant savings in both computational and transmission costs. A disadvantage for some applications such as firewall authentication is that only the intended recipient can verify the message. A modified signcryption scheme was proposed in [3] by Bao and Deng to overcome this limitation at the cost of increased computational cost while still preserving the transmission cost savings achieved by the original scheme. Two disadvantages of this modified signcryption scheme are:

1. The signature verification only mode of operation can be used only after the original recipient has recovered the plain text message.
2. The plain text message must be forwarded to a third party for signature verification and the message confidentiality is lost.

Therefore, this scheme is unusable by a firewall as a message must be recovered by the end-user prior to firewall verification which violate the second property listed earlier. Hao Zheng and Robert Blakley [29] have also proposed a similar scheme called *Authenticryption* based on ElGamal signature scheme and its variants. This scheme is also unusable for implementing fire-wall message authentication as it does not satisfy the last three properties we have stated.

3 Signcryption for Third-Party Verification

In this section, we show that with a small change to the original signcryption scheme it is possible to modify the Bao-Deng scheme to carry out signature verification without accessing the plain text. The advantages of this new mode of operation for signcryption are:

1. The cipher text only signature verification that preserves confidentiality of the original message without altering sign-then-encrypt paradigm (first and second properties).
2. The computational cost is higher than in original scheme of Zheng [30] but lower than Bao-Deng modified scheme and thus standard sign-then-encrypt schemes (third and fourth properties).
3. The transmission cost saving of the original signcryption scheme is preserved (third property).

The main parameters used in the signcryption scheme are p : a large prime number, q : a large prime factor of $p-1$, g : an integer in $[1, \ldots, p-1]$ with order $q \bmod p$, $hash$: a cryptographically strong one-way hash function of the form $\{0, 1\}^* \rightarrow \{0, 1\}^l$ where l is a security parameter, (E, D) : the encryption and decryption algorithms of a private key cipher such as DES, x_a : Secret key of Alice, a randomly chosen integer, y_a : Public key of Alice ($y_a = g^{x_a} \bmod p$), x_b : Secret key of Bob, a randomly chosen integer, y_b : Public key of Bob ($y_b = g^{x_b} \bmod p$) and m : a message.

3.1 Scheme for Single Prover - Single Verifier

Signcryption Choose an integer x randomly from $[1, \ldots, q-1]$ and compute $k = hash(y_b^x \bmod p)$ and $y = g^x \bmod p$. The signcrypted cryptogram (c, r, s) is computed by Alice as

$c = E_k(m)$

$r = hash(y, c)$

$s = \frac{x}{r + x_a} \bmod q$

Remark 1. We compute r by taking the hash value of c instead of m as in the original scheme. This change results in a corresponding change for the unsigncryption step. Also, we do not hash the value of y as in Bao-Deng scheme as that hashing operation is redundant. Note that we have delib-erately put y before c. Here, y can be pre-computed, and hence $hash(y, c)$ can be partially pre-hashed, as every hash works in a block-by-block fashion. Otherwise if c is in front of y, then nothing can be pre-hashed until we get c.

Unsigncryption For full unsigncryption with message recovery, Bob will compute from (c, r, s)

$y = (y_a g^r)^s \bmod p$

$k = hash(y^{x_b} \bmod p)$

$m = D_k(c)$

Accept signature if and only if $hash(y, c) \overset{?}{=} r$

Signature Verification For partial unsigncryption with signature verification only, any verifier will compute from (c, r, s)

$y = (y_a g^r)^s \bmod p$

Accept signature if and only if $hash(y, c) \overset{?}{=} r$

This signature verification does not require access to the plain text message.

Use of signcryption paradigm has already satisfied our first property and the verification without message recovery shown above satisfies second property. In next section we give relative estimations of computational and transmission costs to show that third and fourth properties are also satisfied.

3.2 Discussion on Security and Performance

A question that arises due to our modification of the original signcryption scheme is whether the use of cipher text c (a public value) for computing r instead of m (a private value) weakens the resulting scheme. The value r, when viewed as corresponding to the commitment value in a three-move zero-knowledge identification scheme, only need to be a random value. For a signature scheme, this random value must also be bound to the message m. As we have used a hash function to compute r from y and c, both these conditions are satisfied. Therefore, in an *informal* analysis, the modification does not seem to reduce the security of the original signcryption scheme. However, given the major weaknesses that arise due to even minor changes to cryptographic protocols (see [1, 9]), it is essential to perform a *formal* security analysis of the proposed scheme.

Furthermore, we cannot directly use the security arguments given in the original signcryption scheme [30] as the modified schemes (both [3] and [29]) are fundamentally different due to the two step computation of the commitment value using a secret random integer. In Zheng's scheme [30], the security of the single computed value $y_b^x \bmod p$ is guaranteed by its equivalence to the *computational Diffie-Hellman problem* [10]. In Bao-Deng scheme, the computation of two values, $y_b^x \bmod p$ and $g^x \bmod p$ using the same secret random integer x does not provide such a straightforward security argument. In section 4 we give a formal proof of security based on the random oracle model [4] and show the pseudo-independence of the two computed values as an adequate guarantee of security for the signature scheme.

In digital signature generation and verification, the computational effort is dominated by the exponentiation modulo p. Other computational costs due to modular multiplication, addition, inversion and also hashing and symmetric key encryption constitute only a small fraction of the overall cost. Therefore, when

Table 1. Comparison of number of exponentiations modulo p

Operation	Signcryption	Modified Signcryption	DSA sign + ElGamal encrypt
Signcrypt	1 EXP	2 EXP	1 + 2 EXP
Unsigncrypt	2 EXP (1.17)	3 EXP (2.17)	1 + 2 EXP (1 + 1.17)
Verify only	n/a	2 EXP (1.17)	n/a

we try to improve the performance of digital signature schemes, the main aim is to reduce the number of modular exponentiations in the scheme. In table 1 we show that Bao-Deng scheme modified by us can verify a signature at the cost of 4 modular exponentiations as against 5 for the original Bao-Deng method. The values within parenthesis show the instances where 2 modular exponentiations can be done for the cost of 1.17 modular exponentiations using the algorithm for simultaneous multiple exponentiations [16, page 618]. In table 2 we show that the modified signcryption scheme in signature verification only mode can achieve nearly a 40% saving in computational cost over a standard DSA-ElGamal style scheme for secure and authenticated message transmission.

Table 2. Computational cost savings for modified signcryption over DSA-ElGamal

Operating mode of the modified scheme	Cost saving
Signcryption with message recovery	5/6 (4.17/5.17) 17% (19%)
Signcryption with verification only	4/6 (3.17/5.17) 33% (39%)

4 Formal Proof of Security for Verification only Mode

The security of a cryptographic protocol such as an encryption scheme or a signature scheme can be informally established through its resistance to cryptanalytic attacks. However, a more desirable guarantee of security is a formal proof that provides arguments for the strength of a particular scheme in a given computational model. Currently, there are two main techniques to achieve this goal of provable security: (1) *complexity theoretic arguments* that provide computational reductions to well-known presumably hard problems such as the discrete logarithm problem, the RSA problem, Diffie-Hellman problem, etc. (2) *random oracle technique* described by Bellare and Rogaway [4] which provide a new paradigm for security analysis through replacement of hash functions in protocols by an ideally random oracle.

To analyze the security of the verification only signcryption mode, we apply the security arguments developed by Pointcheval and Stern for digital signature schemes [23, 22, 24] using random oracle technique of Bellare and Rogaway. The main result of Pointcheval and Stern is the *Forking Lemma* which gives a probability of finding a forking pair of signatures in the random oracle model giving an asymptotic reduction to a hard problem.

4.1 Security of a Digital Signature Scheme

There are two main classes of attacks on digital signature schemes and we will briefly describe the attacks and their consequences based on the definitions by Goldwasser, Micali and Rivest [15]:

1. *Key only* or *no message* attacks in which an attacker A has access only to public parameters and public keys.
2. Message attacks in which A has access to pairs of message texts and corresponding signatures. These known message attacks can be further categorized to four modes depending on the power A has on selecting messages signed by the legitimate signer Σ.
   (a) *Known-messages* in which A does not choose messages signed by Σ.
   (b) *Generic chosen-messages* in which A choose a set of messages to be signed before knowing the actual Σ targeted for attack.
   (c) *Directed chosen-messages* in which A choose a set of messages to be signed after selecting a specific Σ but before the actual attack.
   (d) *Adaptive chosen-messages* in which A choose messages for signing dynamically after inspecting signatures he obtained for previous messages.

The no message attack is the weakest type of attack on a digital signature scheme while the adaptive chosen-message attack is the strongest. The outcome of attacks on signature schemes are forgeries. There are four main types of forgeries:

1. *Total break* in which A recovers the secret key of Σ under attack.
2. *Universal forgery* in which A does not obtain the secret key of Σ but gains the ability to generate valid signatures for any message.
3. *Selective forgery* in which A does not obtain the secret key of Σ but gains the ability to generate valid signatures for any set of preselected messages.
4. *Existential forgery* in which A is able to create at least one new message and signature pair without knowing the secret key. However, the messages are only arbitrary bit strings and A does not have any power over their composition.

The total break is the hardest type of forgery to make while existential forgery is the easiest type of subversion of a digital signature scheme.

Therefore, a proverbly secure digital signature schemes is defined as one that could withstand an adaptive chosen-message attack (strongest) to create an existential forgery (easiest). Here the attacker is assumed to run in probabilistic polynomial time and the success of a forgery to have a non-negligible probability. The attacker A, oracle O and signer Σ are all modeled as probabilistic polynomial time Turing machines in the security analysis to follow. The chosen message attack is modeled by allowing A to query Σ as an oracle. We summarize the discussion on digital signature security in the random oracle model with the following two definitions.

Definition 1. *A signature scheme is (T, Q, ϵ)-secure if an attacker A who is limited to Q queries from the random oracle O over a period of time T can create an existentially forged signature with probability at most ϵ after a no-message attack. The probability is taken over the coin flips of A and O.*

Definition 2. *A signature scheme is (T, Q, R, ϵ)-secure if an attacker A who is limited to Q queries from the random oracle O and R queries from the signing oracle Σ over a period of time T can create an existentially forged signature with probability at most ϵ after a chosen-message attack. The probability is taken over the coin flips of A, O and Σ.*

4.2 Signature Schemes from ZK Identification Schemes

Fiat and Shamir in [14] have described a three-move identification protocol between a prover and a verifier that is perfect zero-knowledge against an honest-verifier. They have also used a general technique to derive a provably secure signature scheme from the ZK identification protocol and an improved version of this signature scheme was presented by Feige, Fiat and Shamir in [13] which we recall below.

The setup phase of the signature scheme chooses two distinct primes p and q randomly and compute the composite integer $n = pq$. The two primes p and q are kept secret while n is the public modulus. For a security parameter k which is a positive integer, distinct integers $s_1, \ldots, s_k \in \mathbb{Z}_n^*$ are chosen randomly. A public key K_p which is a tuple $(v_1, \ldots, v_k)$ is computed as $v_j = s_j^{-2} \bmod n$, $1 \leq j \leq k$ and the corresponding private key K_s is the tuple $(s_1, \ldots, s_k)$. The scheme uses a one-way hash function $hash : \{0, 1\}^* \to \{0, 1\}^k$ where the security parameter k is chosen to prevent off-line attacks on the hash function.

1. Prover chooses a random value (commitment) r, $1 \leq r \leq n - 1$, and compute the value (witness) $u = r^2 \bmod n$.
2. Prover computes the random value (challenge) $e = (e_1, \ldots, e_k)$ where each $e_i \in \{0, 1\}$ as $e = hash(m \| u)$ for a message $m \in \{0, 1\}^*$.
3. Prover computes the value (response) $s = r \cdot \prod_{j=1}^{k} s_j^{e_j} \bmod n$.
4. Prover sends the signature (e, s) and message m to verifier.
5. Verifier computes the value $w = s^2 \cdot \prod_{j=1}^{k} v_j^{e_j} \bmod n$ and $e' = hash(m \| w)$. The signature is accepted if and only if $e' = e$. This step is the signature verification test.

Remark 2. We make following observation on the necessary attributes of signature schemes that belong to the class derived from ZK identification protocols. The transmitted signed message consists of the tuple (challenge, response, message), where:

1. The witness value is a random permutation from a very large set.
2. The challenge is simply a one-way hash of the message being signed and the witness value.
3. The response is bound only to witness, challenge, message and private key K_s.

4.3 Properties of Modified Signcryption Scheme

Drawing from the above observations, we now show that the signature verification only mode has the necessary attributes that make the modified scheme to be within the class of signatures derived from ZK identification schemes.

1. The commitment value is the random integer x and the witness value is y. If the length of the output of hash function is sufficiently large, then y is a random permutation from a large set of size $\lceil \log_2 p \rceil$ for a given x.
2. The challenge r is a one-way hash of the cipher text c and the witness y. As our intention is to authenticate the cipher message at the input to the firewall, use of c instead of the plain text m does not affect the security of the scheme.
3. The response is computed from commitment x (therefore, equivalently the witness), challenge r (therefore, including the cipher message c) and private key of signer x_a.

4.4 Security Results

Arguments for a (T, Q, ϵ)-secure Scheme. We assume a no message attack by $\mathcal{A}$ with access to $\mathcal{O}$ and public key of Σ with security parameter l. If $\mathcal{A}$ is successful in an existential forgery within a time bound T and random oracle query bound Q with probability of success $\epsilon \geq 7Q/2^l$, then the Forking Lemma of Pointcheval and Stern [24, Theorem 10] states that DLP in sub groups of prime order can be solved in expected time less than $84480QT/\epsilon$.

The proof of above claim can be directly shown by using the same approach in [24] for the Schnorr signature scheme: After a polynomial replay of $\mathcal{A}$, we obtain two valid signatures, (c, r, s) from signing oracle σ and (c, r', s') from random oracle $\mathcal{O}$ with $r \neq r'$, for the same cipher message using modified signcryption scheme. Then we have the following two equalities as part of the signature verification test: $y = (y_a g^r)^s \bmod p$ and $y = (y_a g^{r'})^{s'} \bmod p$. By solving the two equations we can compute the secret key x_a of Σ as $\log_g y_a = \frac{(rs - r's')}{(s' - s)} \bmod q$. That is, if a signature can be successfully forged for any message then the DLP can be efficiently solved to reveal the secret values. It is important to note that the reduction is to the basic discrete logarithm problem although the security of the signcryption scheme is based on computational Diffie-Hellman problem which is argued to be less secure [7].

Arguments for a (T, Q, R, ϵ)-secure Scheme. We assume an adaptive chosen-message attack by $\mathcal{A}$ with access to $\mathcal{O}$ and public key of Σ with security parameter l. Furthermore $\mathcal{A}$ can query Σ as an oracle. If $\mathcal{A}$ is successful in an existential forgery within a time bound T, random oracle query bound Q and signing oracle query bound R with probability of success $\epsilon \geq 10(R+1)(R+Q)/2^l$, then the Forking Lemma of Pointcheval and Stern [24, Theorem 13] states that DLP in sub groups of prime order can be solved in expected time less than $120686QT/\epsilon$.

Similar to the proof in the original paper we only need to show that two signatures can be forked without using the secret value of Σ. This is done by showing the signatures σ due to Σ and signatures σ' due to $\mathcal{O}$ have the same probability distribution.

$$
\sigma = \left\{ (c,r,s) \left| \begin{array}{l} x \in_R (\mathbb{Z}/q\mathbb{Z})^* \\ k = hash(y_b^x \bmod p) \\ y = g^x \bmod p \\ c = E_k(m) \\ r = hash(y,c) \\ s = x/(r+x_a) \bmod q \end{array} \right. \right\} \text{ and } \sigma' = \left\{ (c,r,s) \left| \begin{array}{l} x \in_R \mathbb{Z}/q\mathbb{Z} \\ r \in_R \mathbb{Z}/q\mathbb{Z} \\ s = x \\ c \in \{0,1\}^* \\ t = (y_a g^r)^s \bmod p \\ y = hash(t) \\ t \neq 1 \bmod p \end{array} \right. \right\}
$$

The probabilities of obtaining a signature σ with r computed by Σ and σ' with r obtained from $\mathcal{O}$ such that $y = hash((y_a g^r)^s \bmod p) \neq 1 \bmod p$ are

$$
\Pr_\sigma [c,r,s] = \Pr_{x \neq 0,r} [c,r,s] = \frac{1}{(q-1)2^l} \text{ and } \Pr_{\sigma'} [c,r,s] = \Pr_{y,r} [c,r,s] = \frac{1}{(q-1)2^l}
$$

Finally, if Σ chooses the integer x uniformly and randomly, then the two values $t = y_b^x \bmod p$ and $y = g^x \bmod p$ are (pseudo) independent as both g and $y_b = g^{x_b} \bmod p$ are generators in $\mathbb{Z}_p^*$ of order q where q is a prime. This ensures that the signature verification and partial recovery of bits at the firewall does not leak information that can be used in an attack on breaking message confidentiality or signature forgery.

5 Conclusions

The security proof given in section 4 provide only an asymptotic security analysis (compared to the notion of exact security [5]). However, it is possible to give the exact security of the proposed scheme using the concrete security analysis methodology of Ohta and Okamoto [20] based on the ID reduction technique.

As a concluding remark, we observe that Canetti, Goldreich and Halevi [8] have given counter-examples for protocols proverbly secure in the random oracle model but found to be insecure in practical implantation using cryptographic hash functions. More importantly, the specific counter-example they have provided, *correlation intractability*, is at the core of the three-move ZK identification scheme to signature scheme conversion technique of Fiat-Shamir that we have used for constructing our proof. However, as yet we have not found any security weaknesses in the proposed scheme for authentication of encrypted messages by a network firewall due to the findings in [8].

References

[1] R. Anderson and R. Needham. Robustness principles for public key protocols. In D. Coppersmith, editor, *Advances in Cryptology - CRYPTO'95*, volume 963 of *Lecture Notes in Computer Science*, pages 236–247. Springer-Verlag, 1995.

[2] F. M. Avolio and M. J. Ranum. A network perimeter with secure external access. In *Proceedings of the 3rd Annual System Administration, Networking and Security Conference (SANS III)*, pages 1–14. Open Systems Conference Board, 1994.

[3] F. Bao and R. H. Deng. A signcryption scheme with signature directly verifiable by public key. In H. Imai and Y. Zheng, editors, *Public Key Cryptography - PKC'98*, volume 1431 of *Lecture Notes in Computer Science*, pages 55–59. Springer-Verlag, 1998.

[4] M. Bellare and P. Rogaway. Random oracles are practical: A paradigm for designing efficient protocols. In *Proceedings of the 1st ACM Conference on Computer and Communications Security*, pages 62–73. ACM Press, 1993.

[5] M. Bellare and P. Rogaway. The exact security of digital signatures - how to sign with RSA and Rabin. In U. M. Maurer, editor, *Advances in Cryptology - EUROCRYPT'96*, volume 1070 of *Lecture Notes in Computer Science*, pages 399–416. Springer-Verlag, 1996.

[6] S. M. Bellowin and W. R. Cheswick. *Firewalls and Internet Security*. Addison-Wesley, 1994.

[7] D. Boneh. The decision Diffie-Hellman problem. In x, editor, *Proceedings of the 3rd Algorithmic Number Theory Symposium*, volume 1423 of *Lecture Notes in Computer Science*, pages 48–63. Springer-Verlag, 1998.

[8] R. Canetti, O. Goldreich, and S. Halevi. The random oracle methodology, revisited. In *Proceedings of the 30th Annual ACM Symposium on Theory of Computing*, pages 9–9. ACM Press, 1998. (to appear).

[9] M. Chen and E. Hughes. Protocol failures related to order of encryption and signature - computation of discrete logarithms in RSA groups. In C. Boyd and E. Dawson, editors, *Information Security and Privacy - ACISP'98*, volume 1438 of *Lecture Notes in Computer Science*, pages 238–249. Springer-Verlag, 1998.

[10] W. Diffie and M. Hellman. New directions in cryptography. *IEEE Transactions on Information Theory*, IT-22(6):644–654, November 1976.

[11] T. ElGamal. A public key cryptosystem and a signature scheme based on discrete logarithms. In G. R. Blakley and D. Chaum, editors, *Advances in Cryptology - CRYPTO'84*, volume 196 of *Lecture Notes in Computer Science*, pages 10–18. Springer-Verlag, 1985.

[12] T. ElGamal. A public-key cryptosystem and a signature scheme based on discrete logarithms. *IEEE Transactions on Information Theory*, IT-31(4):469–472, July 1985.

[13] U. Feige, A. Fiat, and A. Shamir. Zero-knowledge proofs of identity. *Journal of Cryptology*, 1:77–94, 1988.

[14] A. Fiat and A. Shamir. How to prove yourself: Practical solutions to identification and signature problems. In A. M. Odlyzko, editor, *Advances in Cryptology - CRYPTO'86*, volume 263 of *Lecture Notes in Computer Science*, pages 186–194. Springer-Verlag, 1987.

[15] S. Goldwasser, S. Micali, and R. L. Rivest. A digital signature scheme secure against adaptive chosen-message attacks. *SIAM Journal of Computing*, 17(2):281–308, April 1988.

[16] A. J. Menezes, P. C. van Oorschot, and S. A. Vanstone. *Handbook of Applied Cryptography*. CRC Press, 1996.

[17] National Institute of Standards and Technology, U.S. Department of Commerce. *Digital Signature Standard. Federal Information Processing Standards Publication (FIPS PUB) 186*, 1994.

[18] K. Nyberg and R. A. Rueppel. A new signature scheme based on the DSA giving message recovery. In *Proceedings of the 1st ACM Conference on Computer and Communications Security*, pages 58–61. ACM Press, 1993.

[19] K. Nyberg and R. A. Rueppel. Message recovery for signature schemes based on the discrete logarithm problem. *Designs, Codes and Cryptography*, 7:61–81, 1996.

[20] K. Ohta and T. Okamoto. On concrete security treatment of signatures derived from identification. In H. Krawczyk, editor, *Advances in Cryptology - CRYPTO'98*, volume 1462 of *Lecture Notes in Computer Science*, pages 354–369. Springer-Verlag, 1998.

[21] R. Oppliger. Internet security: Firewalls and beyond. *Communications of the ACM*, 40(5):92–102, May 1997.

[22] D. Pointcheval and J. Stern. Provably secure blind signature schemes. In U. M. Maurer, editor, *Advances in Cryptology - ASIACRYPT'96*, volume 1070 of *Lecture Notes in Computer Science*, pages 387–398. Springer-Verlag, 1996.

[23] D. Pointcheval and J. Stern. Security proofs for signature schemes. In U. M. Maurer, editor, *Advances in Cryptology - EUROCRYPT'96*, volume 1070 of *Lecture Notes in Computer Science*, pages 387–398. Springer-Verlag, 1996.

[24] D. Pointcheval and J. Stern. Security arguments for digital signatures and blind signatures. *Journal of Cryptology*, 9:9–9, 1999.

[25] M. O. Rabin. Digitalized signatures and public key functions as intractable as factorization. Technical Report MIT/LCS/TR-212, MIT Laboratory for Computer Science, January 1979.

[26] R. L. Rivest, A. Shamir, and L. M. Adleman. A method for obtaining digital signatures and public-key cryptosystems. *Communications of the ACM*, 21(2):120–126, February 1978.

[27] C.-P. Schnorr. Efficient identification and signatures for smart cards. In G. Brassard, editor, *Advances in Cryptology - CRYPTO'89*, volume 435 of *Lecture Notes in Computer Science*, pages 239–252. Springer-Verlag, 1990.

[28] C.-P. Schnorr. Efficient signature generation by smart cards. *Journal of Cryptology*, 4(3):161–174, 1991.

[29] H. Zheng and G. R. Blakley. Authenticryption: Secrecy with authentication. Manuscript, 1998.

[30] Y. Zheng. Digital signcryption or how to achieve cost(signature & encryption) ≪ cost(signature) + cost(encryption). In B. S. Kaliski, editor, *Advances in Cryptology - CRYPTO'97*, volume 1294 of *Lecture Notes in Computer Science*, pages 165–179. Springer-Verlag, 1997.

A Relationship between
One-Wayness and Correlation Intractability

Satoshi Hada[1] and Toshiaki Tanaka[2]

[1] KDD R&D Laboratories,
2-1-15 Ohara, Kamifukuoka, Saitama 356-8502, Japan
hada@lab.kdd.co.jp
[2] KDD,
2-3-2 Nishishinjuku, Shinjuku-ku, Tokyo 163-8003, Japan
tl-tanaka@kdd.co.jp

Abstract. Correlation intractable function ensembles were introduced in an attempt to capture the "unpredictability" property of a random oracle: It is assumed that if R is a random oracle then it is infeasible to find an input x such that the input-output pair $(x, R(x))$ has some desired property. Since this property is often useful to design many cryptographic applications in the random oracle model, it is desirable that a plausible construction of correlation intractable function ensembles will be provided. However, no plausibility result has been proposed. In this paper, we show that proving the implication, "if one-way functions exist then correlation intractable function ensembles exist", is as hard as proving that "3-round auxiliary-input zero-knowledge Arthur-Merlin proofs exist only for trivial languages such as $\mathcal{BPP}$ languages." As far as we know, proving the latter claim is a fundamental open problem in the theory of zero-knowledge proofs. Therefore, our result can be viewed as strong evidence that the construction based solely on one-way functions will be *impossible*, i.e., that any plausibility result will require stronger cryptographic primitives.

Keywords: One-way functions, correlation intractability, zero-knowledge, interactive proofs, round complexity, random oracle.

1 Introduction

In this paper, we investigate the relationship between one-wayness and correlation intractability.

1.1 Realizing Random Oracles

The random oracle model formulated in [BeRo93] is a very useful for designing cryptographic schemes such as public key encryption and digital signature since the schemes in this model are often very simple and efficient; Moreover, the security analysis is often clearer than in real life. However, we do not have a general mechanism for transforming schemes that are secure in the random oracle model into schemes that are secure in real life. For the purpose of realizing such transformations, Canetti started a research program aimed at identifying, defining and realizing the special-purpose properties of a random oracle [Ca97]. He roughly sketched its two properties. One is "total secrecy": It is assumed that if $F(\cdot)$ is a random oracle, $F(x)$ gives no information on x. The other property is "unpredictability": It is assumed to be infeasible to find an input x such that the input-output pair $(x, F(x))$ has some desired property.

Canetti introduced a new primitive called "oracle hashing" (renamed "perfectly one-way functions" in [CMR98]) in an attempt to capture the total secrecy [Ca97]. Recently, it was shown that perfectly one-way functions can be constructed based on any one-way permutation [CMR98]. On the other hand, Canetti, Goldreich and Halevi introduced another new primitive called "correlation intractable function ensembles" in order to capture the unpredictability [CGH98]. They showed that there exist no correlation intractable function ensembles. However, their result leaves open the question of the existence of *restricted* correlation intractable function ensembles, where "restricted" means that each function will only be applied to inputs of pre-specified length. They described that it is interesting to either provide a negative result even for this special case or provide a plausible construction based on general complexity assumptions. In light of the above, it is important to investigate the relationships among restricted correlation intractable function ensembles and other cryptographic primitives such as one-way functions.

This paper addresses the question of whether one can prove the implication that

> *If one-way functions exist,*
> *then restricted correlation intractable function ensembles exist.*

Our answer is a negative one: It seems difficult to prove it. This negative relationship between one-wayness and restricted correlation intractability is obtained by investigating the lower bounds for the round complexity of auxiliary-input zero-knowledge proofs.

1.2   The Round Complexity of Auxiliary-Input Zero-Knowledge

Zero-knowledge (ZK) protocols [GMR85] play a central role in modern cryptography. The round complexity, the number of messages exchanged, is a standard complexity measure for the efficiency of ZK protocols. The lower bounds for the round complexity have been investigated from the practical and theoretical viewpoint so far. Goldreich and Oren showed that only languages in $\mathcal{BPP}$ have 1-round GMR-ZK protocols [GoOr94], where GMR-ZK is the original definition of ZK [GMR85]. They also showed that only languages in $\mathcal{BPP}$ have 2-round auxiliary-input ZK (AIZK) protocols [GoOr94]. Furthermore, Goldreich and Krawczyk showed that only languages in $\mathcal{BPP}$ have 3-round blackboxsimultion ZK (BSZK) protocols [GoKr96] [1]. Since the proof in [GoKr96] uses the notion of blackbox-simulation in an essential way, their result does not apply to the notion of GMR-ZK and AIZK. In fact, it is an interesting open problem whether there exists a 3-round ZK protocol for a non-trivial language with respect to GMR-ZK and AIZK [2].

In this paper, we focus on *Arthur-Merlin* (AM) protocols. Recall that in AM protocols, the (honest) verifier chooses all its messages at random, that is, all the messages sent by the verifier are *public* random coins [BaMo88]. We consider the question of whether one can prove that

there exist 3-round ZK (GMR-ZK or AIZK) AM proofs
only for trivial languages such as $\mathcal{BPP}$ languages.

We believe that proving it *unconditionally* is a fundamental open problem in the theory of ZK proofs. However, it may be possible to prove it *under some complexity assumptions*.

In 3-round AM protocols, a cheating verifier may choose its public-coin message (challenge message) as a cryptographic hash function value of the first message sent by the prover. Many researchers consider that the simulation for such a cheating verifier is difficult to do. Therefore, we naturally conjecture that assuming the existence of cryptographic hash functions, only trivial languages have 3-round ZK protocols [3]. What can we show if we use restricted correlation intractable function ensembles as cryptographic hash functions ? We show that assuming the existence of restricted correlation intractable function ensembles, 3-round AIZK AM proofs exist only for *easy-to-approximate* languages: We say that a language is easy to approximate if it can be recognized in probabilistic polynomial-time on average when the instance is generated from any polynomial samplable distribution. This triviality result is our main technical contribution. Furthermore, we show that, under a stronger assumption that there exist *non-uniform* restricted correlation intractable function ensembles, 3-round AIZK AM proofs exist only for $\mathcal{BPP}$ languages. We also argue that our results extend to both the argument model and the constant round case. Therefore, we may say that our results complement the results of [GoKr96] in the case of the AM protocols although the complexity assumptions are required.

1.3   Our Result and Related Works

We show that proving the implication, "if one-way functions exist then correlation intractable function ensembles exist", is as hard as proving that "3-round

---

[1] It is known that $Cl(BSZK) \subseteq Cl(AIZK) \subset Cl(GMR-ZK)$ where $Cl(def)$ denotes the class of all ZK protocols satisfying the requirements of definition def [GoOr94].

[2] This problem was partially solved in [HT98]

[3] Nevertheless, Goldreich and Krawczyk showed that only languages in $\mathcal{BPP}$ have 3-round BSZK protocols without making any assumptions [GoKr96]. Their proof uses the blackbox-smulation of a (deterministic) cheating verifier which behaves as a random oracle.

AIZK AM proofs exist only for trivial languages." As described above, whether one can prove the latter claim unconditionally is an open problem. Therefore, this can be viewed as strong evidence that it will be difficult to construct restricted correlation intractable function ensembles assuming only that one-way functions exist, i.e., that any plausibility result will require stronger cryptographic primitives. It is easily obtained by combining our triviality result of 3-round AIZK AM proofs with the result of Ostrovsky and Wigderson [OW93] which shows that one-way functions are essential for non-trivial zero-knowledge proofs.

The limits on the provable consequences of one-way functions were studied in [ImRu89]. Impagliazzo and Rudich showed that constructing a secure secret-key agreement protocol using any one-way permutation as a "blackbox" is as hard as proving $\mathcal{P} \neq \mathcal{NP}$. That is, it is highly unlikely that secret-key agreement protocols can be constructed based on any one-way permutation. Recently, Simon showed that there is no "blackbox" reduction from one-way permutations to collision intractable hash functions [Si98]. We note that both results leave open the possibility of the existence of *non-relativizing* reduction from one-way permutations to secret-key agreement protocols or collision intractable hash functions. In non-relativizing reductions, one can not only use a one-way permutation as a blackbox, but also use the actual programs for it. Our result can be viewed as a stronger type of limit since our result says that there can not seem to exist even a non-relativizing reduction from one-way functions to restricted correlation intractable function ensembles.

1.4 Organization

In Section 2, we give the definitions of interactive proofs, auxiliary-input zero-knowledge, restricted correlation intractability and the class of trivial languages. In Section 3, we show the triviality of 3-round auxiliary-input zero-knowledge AM proofs. Section 4 presents the negative relationship between one-way functions and restricted correlation intractable function ensembles using the triviality result in Section 3. We conclude with some remarks in Section 5.

2 Preliminaries

We say that a function $\nu(\cdot) : \mathsf{N} \to \mathsf{R}$ is negligible in n if for every polynomial $poly(\cdot)$ and all sufficiently large n's, it holds that $\nu(n) < 1/poly(n)$. Also, we say that a function $f(\cdot) : \mathsf{N} \to \mathsf{R}$ is overwhelming in n if $f(\cdot) = 1 - \nu(\cdot)$ for some negligible function $\nu(\cdot)$. We often omit the expression "in n" when the definition of n will be clear by the context.

If S is any probability distribution then $x \leftarrow S$ denotes the operation of selecting an element uniformly at random according to S. If S is a set then we use the same notation to denote the operation of picking an element x uniformly from S. If A is a probabilistic machine then $A(x_1, x_2, \cdots, x_k)$ denotes the output distribution of A on inputs $(x_1, x_2, \cdots, x_k)$. Let $\Pr[R_1; R_2; \cdots; R_k : E]$ denote the probability of the event E after the random or deterministic processes $R_1, R_2, \cdots, R_k$ are performed in order.

2.1 Interactive Proofs and Arguments

We consider two probabilistic interactive machines called the prover and the verifier. The verifier is always a probabilistic polynomial-time machine. Initially both machines have access to a common input tape which includes x of length n. The prover and the verifier send messages to one another through two communication tapes. After exchanging a polynomial number of messages, the verifier stops in an accept state or in a reject state. Each machine only sees its own tapes, namely, the common input tape, the random tape, the auxiliary-input tape and the communication tapes. Let $A(x, y, m)$ denote the next message of the machine A, where x is the common input, y the auxiliary-input and m the messages so far. Let $\mathsf{Acc}(P_x^y, V_x)$ denote the probability that V accepts the common input x when interacting with P which takes an auxiliary-input y. The probability is taken over the random tapes of both machines.

We deal with two kinds of interactive protocols. One is "interactive proof" and the other is "interactive argument". The former requires that even a computationally unrestricted prover should be unable to make the verifier accept $x \notin L$, except with negligible probability [GMR85]. On the other hand, the latter requires that any cheating prover restricted to probabilistic polynomial-time should be unable to make the verifier accept $x \notin L$, except with negligible probability [BrCr86][BCC88]. Clearly, the notion of interactive arguments is a generalization of the notion of interactive proofs.

Definition 1 (interactive proofs [GMR85]). *Let P, V be two probabilistic interactive machines. We say that (P, V) is an* interactive proof *for L if V is a probabilistic polynomial-time machine and the following two conditions hold:*

- Completeness: *For every polynomial $poly(\cdot)$, all sufficiently long $x \in L$,*

$$\mathsf{Acc}(P_x, V_x) > 1 - 1/poly(|x|).$$

- Statistical Soundness: *For every machine $\hat{P}$ (the computationally unrestricted cheating prover), every polynomial $poly(\cdot)$, all sufficiently long $x \notin L$,*

$$\mathsf{Acc}(\hat{P}_x, V_x) < 1/poly(|x|).$$

Since the prover P is computationally unrestricted, the auxiliary-input to P is omitted.

Definition 2 (interactive arguments [Go98]). *Let P, V be two probabilistic polynomial-time interactive machines. We say that (P, V) is an* interactive argument *for L if the following two conditions hold:*

- Completeness: *For every polynomial $poly(\cdot)$, all sufficiently long $x \in L$, there exists an auxiliary-input y such that*

$$\mathsf{Acc}(P_x^y, V_x) > 1 - 1/poly(|x|).$$

- Computational Soundness: *For every probabilistic polynomial-time machine $\hat{P}$ (the polynomial-time bounded cheating prover), every polynomial $poly(\cdot)$, all sufficiently long $x \notin L$ and every auxiliary-input y,*

$$\mathsf{Acc}(\hat{P}_x^y, V_x) < 1/poly(|x|).$$

2.2 Auxiliary-Input Zero-Knowledge

We recall the definition of auxiliary-input zero-knowledge. A *view* of the verifier is a distribution ensemble which consists of the common input, the verifier's auxiliary input, the verifier's random coins and the sequence of messages sent by the prover and the verifier during the interaction. Let $\text{View}(P_x, V_x^y) = [x, y, r, m]$ denote V's view after interacting with P, where x is the common input, y the auxiliary input to V, r the random coins of V and m the sequence of messages sent by P and V.

Definition 3 (auxiliary-input zero-knowledge [GoOr94]). *Let P, V be two probabilistic interactive machines. We say that (P, V) is an auxiliary-input zero-knowledge for L if for every probabilistic polynomial-time machine $\hat{V}$ (the cheating verifier), there exists a probabilistic polynomial-time machine $S_{\hat{V}}$ (the simulator) such that the following two distribution ensembles are computationally indistinguishable:*

$$\{S_{\hat{V}}(x,y)\}_{x \in L, y \in \{0,1\}^*} \text{ and } \{\text{View}(P_x, \hat{V}_x^y)\}_{x \in L, y \in \{0,1\}^*}.$$

Namely, for every polynomial-size circuit family $D = \{D_{x,y}\}_{x \in L, y \in \{0,1\}^*}$, every polynomial $poly(\cdot)$, all sufficiently long $x \in L$ and all $y \in \{0,1\}^*$,

$$|\Pr[v \leftarrow S_{\hat{V}}(x,y) : D_{x,y}(v) = 1] - \Pr[v \leftarrow \text{View}(P_x, \hat{V}_x^y) : D_{x,y}(v) = 1]| < \frac{1}{poly(|x|)}.$$

GMR-ZK is defined in the same way, except that the verifier is not allowed to take an auxiliary-input y. We denote by $\mathcal{ZK}$ (resp. $\mathcal{AIZK}$) the class of languages that have a GMR-ZK (resp. AIZK) interactive proof. Also, we denote by $\mathcal{3R}$-$\mathcal{AIZK}$-$\mathcal{AM}$ the class of languages that have 3-round AIZK AM interactive proofs.

2.3 Restricted Correlation Intractable Function Ensembles

We review the definition of *restricted* correlation intractable function ensembles introduced in [CGH98]. At the same time, we give its non-uniform variant. Let $l_{in}, l_{out} : \mathbb{N} \to \mathbb{N}$ be length functions.

Definition 4 (function ensembles). *An l_{out}-function ensemble is a sequence $\mathcal{F} = \{F_k\}_{k \in \mathbb{N}}$ of function family $F_k = \{f_s : \{0,1\}^* \to \{0,1\}^{l_{out}(k)}\}_{s \in \{0,1\}^k}$, so that the following two conditions hold:*

Length requirement. *For every $s \in \{0,1\}^k$ and every $x \in \{0,1\}^*$, $|f_s(x)| = l_{out}(k)$.*

Efficiency. *There exists a polynomial-time algorithm Eval so that for all $s \in \{0,1\}^k$ and $x \in \{0,1\}^*$, $Eval(s, x) = f_s(x)$. In the sequel, we call s the seed of the function f_s.*

A machine M is called l_{in}-respectful if $|M(s)| = l_{in}(|s|)$ for all $s \in \{0,1\}^*$. A uniform (l_{in}, l_{out})-function ensemble $\mathcal{U}_{l_{in}, l_{out}}$ is a sequence $\{U_{l_{in}(k), l_{out}(k)}\}_{k \in \mathbb{N}}$, where $U_{l_{in}(k), l_{out}(k)}$ is a set of all functions $f : \{0,1\}^{l_{in}(k)} \to \{0,1\}^{l_{out}(k)}$.

We say that a relation R is *evasive* if it is hard to find an input-output pair satisfying R under a truly random function (in the random oracle model). Note that there is a relation which is easy to satisfy even in the random oracle model.

Definition 5 (evasive relations). *A binary relation R is* evasive *with respect to (l_{in}, l_{out}) if for every l_{in}-respectful probabilistic polynomial-time machine M, every polynomial $poly(\cdot)$ and all sufficiently large k's,*

$$\Pr[\mathcal{O} \leftarrow U_{l_{in}(k), l_{out}(k)}; x \leftarrow M^{\mathcal{O}}(1^k) : (x, \mathcal{O}(x)) \in R] < \frac{1}{poly(k)}.$$

Also, we say that R is non-uniformly evasive *with respect to (l_{in}, l_{out}) if the above condition holds for every l_{in}-respectful polynomial-size circuit family M.*

A special case of evasive relations consists of R's for which for every polynomial $poly(\cdot)$ and all sufficiently large k's,

$$\max_{x \in \{0,1\}^{l_{in}(k)}} \{\Pr[y \leftarrow \{0,1\}^{l_{out}(k)} : (x, y) \in R]\} < \frac{1}{poly(k)}.$$

We say that a function ensemble $\mathcal{F}$ is *correlation intractable* if, given any evasive relation R and a randomly chosen description of function f_s, it is hard to find an input-output pair satisfying R under f_s.

Definition 6 (restricted correlation intractability). *We say that an l_{out}-function ensemble $\mathcal{F}$ is (l_{in}, l_{out})-restricted correlation intractable if for every l_{in}-respectful probabilistic polynomial-time machine M and every evasive relation R with respect to (l_{in}, l_{out}), every polynomial $poly(\cdot)$ and all sufficiently large k's,*

$$\Pr[s \leftarrow \{0,1\}^k; x \leftarrow M(s) : (x, f_s(x)) \in R] < \frac{1}{poly(k)}.$$

Also, we say that an l_{out}-function ensemble $\mathcal{F}$ is (l_{in}, l_{out})-restricted non-uniform correlation intractable if the above condition holds for every l_{in}-respectful polynomial-size circuit family M and every non-uniformly evasive relation R.

Note that if $l_{out}(k) = O(\log k)$, there exist no (l_{in}, l_{out})-restricted correlation intractable function ensembles. In the sequel, we always assume that $\omega(\log k) \leq l_{out}(k) \leq poly(k)$. Canetti, Goldreich and Halevi showed that if $l_{in}(k) \geq k - O(\log k)$ for infinitely many k's or if $l_{in}(k) + l_{out}(k) \geq k + \omega(\log k)$ for infinitely many k's, then there exist no (l_{in}, l_{out})-restricted correlation intractable function ensembles [CGH98]. However, their results leave open the question of the existence of restricted correlation intractable function ensembles, for the case $l_{in}(k) + l_{out}(k) < k + O(\log k)$. Therefore, when we say that *there exist restricted correlation intractable function ensembles*, we mean that for any pair of length functions (l_{in}, l_{out}) such that $l_{in}(k) + l_{out}(k) < k + O(\log k)$, there exists a (l_{in}, l_{out})-restricted correlation intractable function ensemble.

Remark 1 ([CGH98]). Definition 6 quantifies over all evasive relations. A weaker notion, called restricted *weak* correlation intractability, is obtained by quantifying only over all *polynomial-time recognizable* evasive relations.

2.4 The Class of Trivial Languages

For any language L, we denote by χ_L the characteristic function of the language L, that is, $\chi_L(x) = \text{ACC}$ if $x \in L$ and $\chi_L(x) = \text{REJ}$ otherwise. $\mathcal{BPP}$ is a typical class of "trivial" languages.

Definition 7 ($\mathcal{BPP}$). *We say that a language L is in $\mathcal{BPP}$ if there exists a probabilistic polynomial-time machine A such that every polynomial $poly(\cdot)$ and all sufficiently long x's, $\Pr[b \leftarrow A(x) : b = \chi_L(x)] > 1 - \frac{1}{poly(|x|)}$.*

The class of trivial languages is not only $\mathcal{BPP}$. We define the class of easy-to-approximate languages which is a variant of the class of hard-to-approximate languages defined in [Go98, Definition 4.5.3 on p.180].

Definition 8 ($\mathcal{ETA}$). *We say that a language L is easy to approximate if for every probabilistic polynomial-time machine S, there exists a probabilistic polynomial-time machine A such that every polynomial $poly(\cdot)$ and all sufficiently large n's, $\Pr[x \leftarrow S(1^n); b \leftarrow A(x) : b = \chi_L(x)] > 1 - \frac{1}{poly(n)}$, where $S(1^n)$ ranges over $\{0,1\}^n$. We denote by $\mathcal{ETA}$ the class of languages which are easy to approximate.*

$\mathcal{BPP}$ requires that every instances in the language is easy to recognize. On the other hand, $\mathcal{ETA}$ only requires that it is infeasible to find an instance which is hard to recognize. Therefore, it holds that $\mathcal{BPP} \subseteq \mathcal{ETA}$.

3 The Complexity of 3-Round AIZK AM Proofs

In this section, we prove that 3-round AIZK AM proofs exist only for trivial languages in $\mathcal{ETA}$ or $\mathcal{BPP}$.

Theorem 1 ($\mathcal{ETA}$ Version). *Assume that there exist restricted correlation intractable function ensembles. Then $3\mathcal{R}\text{-}\mathcal{AIZK}\text{-}\mathcal{AM} \subseteq \mathcal{ETA}$.*

Proof. We assume that a language L has an AIZK AM interactive proof (P, V). In order to complete the proof, we have to show that L is easy to approximate.

We use the following notation. Denote by x the common input for the protocol (P, V) and by n the length of x. The first message α is sent by the prover P. In the second round, the verifier V sends a challenge message β. The third message γ is sent from the prover. We denote by $l_\alpha(n)$ and $l_\beta(n)$ the length of α and β, respectively. Without loss of generality, we assume that the honest verifier chooses β uniformly at random in $\{0,1\}^{l_\beta(n)}$. The predicate computed by the verifier in order to decide whether to accept or reject is denoted by $\rho_V(x, \alpha, \beta, \gamma)$. That is, V accepts x if and only if $\rho_V(x, \alpha, \beta, \gamma) = \text{ACC}$. We note that ρ_V may be a randomized function.

Firstly, we select an (l_{in}, l_{out})-restricted correlation intractable function ensemble $\mathcal{F} = \{F_k\}_{k \in \mathbb{N}}$ and the seed length k such that $l_{in}(k) = l_\alpha(n)$ and $l_{out}(k) = l_\beta(n)$. We note that the length functions (l_{in}, l_{out}) must be selected so that they satisfy the condition $k + O(\log k) > l_{in}(k) + l_{out}(k)$. Since the verifier is a polynomial-time machine, there exist constants c, d such that $l_\alpha(n) + l_\beta(n) < cn^d$. We set $k = cn^d$ and select (l_{in}, l_{out}) such that $l_{in}(k) = l_\alpha((k/c)^{1/d})$ and $l_{out}(k) = l_\beta((k/c)^{1/d})$. As a result, the desired condition $k + O(\log k) > k > l_{in}(k) + l_{out}(k)$ is satisfied. We note that a function is negligible and overwhelming "in n" if and only if it is negligible and overwhelming "in k", respectively. Therefore, even if we omit the expressions "in n" and "in k", there is no ambiguity.

Next, we consider a (deterministic) cheating verifier $\hat{V}$ which uses the selected (l_{in}, l_{out})-restricted correlation intractable function ensemble $\mathcal{F} = \{F_k\}_{k \in \mathbb{N}}$ ($F_k = \{f_s\}_{s \in \{0,1\}^k}$) in order to compute the second message β from the first message α. The key idea is to let $\hat{V}$ use its auxiliary-input as a seed of $\mathcal{F}$.

Machine: The cheating verifier $\hat{V}$.
Input: The common input x of length n, the auxiliary-input y and the first message α.
Output: The second message $\beta = \hat{V}(x, y, \alpha)$.
CV1: $\hat{V}$ checks if y is of length $k = cn^d$. If this is false then $\hat{V}$ aborts.
CV2: $\hat{V}$ computes $\beta = f_y(\alpha)$ and outputs β.

Except for the computation of β, $\hat{V}$ behaves in the same way as the honest verifier V.

Since the language L has an AIZK interactive proof, there exists a simulator $S_{\hat{V}}$ for the cheating verifier $\hat{V}$. We construct a probabilistic polynomial-time machine A which uses $S_{\hat{V}}$ to recognize L.

Machine: A which tries to recognize L.
Input: The common input x of length n generated by a probabilistic polynomial-time machine S on input 1^n.
Output: ACC or REJ.
Step1: A generates a seed s uniformly at random in $\{0,1\}^k$, where $k = cn^d$.
Step2: A runs $S_{\hat{V}}(x, s)$ to get a view $[x, s, -, (\alpha, \beta, \gamma)]$, where the random coins in the view of $\hat{V}$ are empty since it is deterministic.
Step3: A outputs $\rho_V(x, \alpha, \beta, \gamma)$.

To complete the proof, we need to show that if $x \in L$ then A outputs ACC with overwhelming probability, otherwise A outputs REJ with overwhelming probability. That is, we need to show that for every probabilistic polynomial-time machine S,

$$\Pr\left[x \leftarrow S(1^n); b \leftarrow A(x) : b = \chi_L(x)\right]$$
$$= \Pr\left[\begin{array}{l} x \leftarrow S(1^n); s \leftarrow \{0,1\}^k; \\ [x, s, -, (\alpha, \beta, \gamma)] \leftarrow S_{\hat{V}}(x, s); b \leftarrow \rho_V(x, \alpha, \beta, \gamma) \end{array} : b = \chi_L(x)\right]$$

is overwhelming. Note that ρ_V may be a randomized function.

The case of $x \notin L$. This part of the proof uses the soundness of the protocol (P, V) and the correlation intractability of $\mathcal{F}$.

We consider a relation R_1 defined as follows: $(\alpha, \beta) \in R_1$ if and only if there exists γ such that $\Pr[b \leftarrow \rho_V(x, \alpha, \beta, \gamma) : b = \text{ACC}]$ is overwhelming. Roughly speaking, $(\alpha, \beta) \in R_1$ is a prefix of an accepting conversation on $x \notin L$. We claim that R_1 is evasive with respect to (l_{in}, l_{out}). It follows from the soundness. The soundness requires that for every polynomial $poly(\cdot)$ and all sufficiently large n's,

$$\max_{\alpha \in \{0,1\}^{l_\alpha(n)}} \{\Pr[\beta \leftarrow \{0,1\}^{l_\beta(n)} : (\alpha, \beta) \in R_1]\} < \frac{1}{poly(n)}.$$

Since $k = cn^d$, for every polynomial $poly(\cdot)$ and all sufficiently large k's, we have

$$\max_{\alpha \in \{0,1\}^{l_{in}(k)}} \{\Pr[\beta \leftarrow \{0,1\}^{l_{out}(k)} : (\alpha, \beta) \in R_1]\} < \frac{1}{poly(k)}.$$

This means that R_1 is evasive.

Next, we claim that the probability

$$\Pr[x \leftarrow S(1^n); s \leftarrow \{0,1\}^k; [x, s, -, (\alpha, \beta, \gamma)] \leftarrow S_{\hat{V}}(x, s) : (\alpha, \beta) \in R_1]$$

is negligible. This means that the view output by $S_{\hat{V}}$ in Step2 is accepting with negligible probability. Assume that the above probability is not negligible. Then we can construct a probabilistic polynomial-time machine M which violates the correlation intractability of $\mathcal{F}$.

Machine: M which violates the correlation intractability of $\mathcal{F}$.
Input: The seed s chosen uniformly at random in $\{0,1\}^k$.
Output: (α, β)
M1: M runs $S(1^n)$ in order to generate x, where $n = (k/c)^{1/d}$.
M2: M runs $S_{\hat{V}}(x, s)$ in order to get a view $[x, s, -, (\alpha, \beta, \gamma)]$.
M3: M outputs (α, β).

Clearly, the probability that M outputs $(\alpha, \beta) \in R_1$ is not negligible. This contradicts the correlation intractability of $\mathcal{F}$ since R_1 is evasive. Therefore, we conclude that A outputs REJ with overwhelming probability.

The case of $x \in L$. This part of the proof uses the completeness, the zero-knowledge property of the protocol (P, V) and the correlation intractability of $\mathcal{F}$.

We consider a relation R_2 defined as follows: $(\alpha, \beta) \in R_2$ if and only if α is a possible first message of the prescribed prover and for every γ, $\Pr[b \leftarrow \rho_V(x, \alpha, \beta, \gamma) : b = \text{REJ}]$ is overwhelming. Roughly speaking, $(\alpha, \beta) \in R_2$ is a prefix of a rejecting conversation on $x \in L$. We claim that R_2 is evasive with respect to (l_{in}, l_{out}). It follows from the completeness. The completeness requires that for every polynomial $poly(\cdot)$ and all sufficiently large n's,

$$\max_{\alpha \in \{0,1\}^{l_\alpha(n)}} \{\Pr[\beta \leftarrow \{0,1\}^{l_\beta(n)} : (\alpha, \beta) \in R_2] < \frac{1}{poly(n)}\}.$$

Since $k = cn^d$, for every polynomial $poly(\cdot)$ and all sufficiently large k's,

$$\max_{\alpha \in \{0,1\}_{l_{in}(k)}} \{ \Pr[\beta \leftarrow \{0,1\}^{l_{out}(k)} : (\alpha, \beta) \in R_2] < \frac{1}{poly(k)} \}.$$

This means that R_2 is evasive. We remark that if R_2 does not require that α is a possible first message of the prescribed prover, R_2 is not necessarily evasive.

Next, we claim that the view of $\hat{V}$ interacting with the honest prover P is accepting with overwhelming probability (or rejecting with negligible probability) when x is generated by $S(1^n)$ and y is randomly chosen from $\{0,1\}^k$. Assume that the probability

$$\Pr \left[\begin{matrix} x \leftarrow S(1^n); y \leftarrow \{0,1\}^k; \\ [x, y, -, (\alpha, \beta, \gamma)] \leftarrow \mathsf{View}(P_x, \hat{V}_x^y); b \leftarrow \rho_V(x, \alpha, \beta, \gamma) \end{matrix} : b = \mathrm{REJ} \right] \quad (1)$$

is not negligible. By the definition of R_2, this assumption means that the probability

$$\Pr \left[\begin{matrix} x \leftarrow S(1^n); y \leftarrow \{0,1\}^k; \\ [x, y, -, (\alpha, \beta, \gamma)] \leftarrow \mathsf{View}(P_x, \hat{V}_x^y) \end{matrix} : (\alpha, \beta) \in R_2 \right]$$

is not negligible. Then we can construct a probabilistic polynomial-time machine M which violates the correlation intractability of $\mathcal{F}$.

Machine: M which violates the correlation intractability of $\mathcal{F}$.
Input: The seed s chosen uniformly at random in $\{0,1\}^k$.
Output: (α, β)
M1: M runs $S(1^n)$ in order to generate x, where $n = (k/c)^{1/d}$.
M2: M runs the simulator $S_{\hat{V}}(x, s)$ in order to get the first message α.
M3: M runs the cheating verifier $\hat{V}(x, s, \alpha)$ in order to get the second message β.
M4: M outputs (α, β).

Since the zero-knowledge property of (P, V) guarantees that the first message α output by $S_{\hat{V}}$ in M2 is computationally indistinguishable from a real first message sent by P, the output distribution of M is computationally indistinguishable from the (α, β) distribution of $\mathsf{View}(P_x, \hat{V}_x^y)$. This means that the probability that M outputs $(\alpha, \beta) \in R_2$ is not negligible. Therefore, this contradicts the correlation intractability of $\mathcal{F}$ since R_2 is evasive.

Now we know that when the input x is generated by $S(1^n)$ and y is randomly chosen from $\{0,1\}^k$, the view of $\hat{V}$ interacting with P is accepting with overwhelming probability. That is, the probability of equation (1) is negligible. Since the zero-knowledge property guarantees that the view output by $S_{\hat{V}}$ is computationally indistinguishable from $\mathsf{View}(P_x, \hat{V}_x^y)$, it holds that

$$\Pr \left[\begin{matrix} x \leftarrow S(1^n); y \leftarrow \{0,1\}^k; \\ [x, y, -, (\alpha, \beta, \gamma)] \leftarrow S_{\hat{V}}(x, y); b \leftarrow \rho_V(x, \alpha, \beta, \gamma) \end{matrix} : b = \mathrm{REJ} \right] \quad (2)$$

is negligible. Therefore, we conclude that A outputs ACC with overwhelming probability.

Theorem 1 follows from the claims in two cases. □

In Section 4, we need the special case of Theorem 1. We denote by $3\mathcal{R}$-$\mathcal{AIZK}$-$\mathcal{AM}[l_\alpha, l_\beta]$ the class of languages that have 3-round AIZK AM proofs in which the first and second messages are of length $l_\alpha(n)$ and $l_\beta(n)$, respectively.

Theorem 2. *Assume that there exist (l_α, l_β)-restricted correlation intractable function ensembles. Then $3\mathcal{R}$-$\mathcal{AIZK}$-$\mathcal{AM}[l_\alpha, l_\beta] \subseteq \mathcal{ETA}$.*

Proof. In the proof of Theorem 1, consider the special case in which the length functions (l_α, l_β) satisfy the condition $n + O(\log n) > l_\alpha(n) + l_\alpha(n)$. Since it is sufficient to set $k = n, l_{in} = l_\alpha$ and $l_{out} = l_\beta$, it follows. □

Next, we strengthen Theorem 1 using the assumption of the existence of restricted *non-uniform* correlation intractable function ensembles.

Theorem 3 ($\mathcal{BPP}$ Version). *Assume that there exist restricted non-uniform correlation intractable function ensembles. Then $3\mathcal{R}$-$\mathcal{AIZK}$-$\mathcal{AM}=\mathcal{BPP}$.*

Proof. It is clear that $\mathcal{BPP} \subseteq 3\mathcal{R}$-$\mathcal{AIZK}$-$\mathcal{AM}$. The proof of $3\mathcal{R}$-$\mathcal{AIZK}$-$\mathcal{AM}$ $\subseteq \mathcal{BPP}$ is essentially equivalent to the proof of Theorem 1, except that the input x is given non-uniformly. However, this non-uniformly given input can be dealt with by the non-uniformity in the definition of the non-uniform correlation intractability. □

Remark 2. Both R_1 and R_2 can not be recognized in probabilistic polynomial-time. Therefore, assuming the existence of restricted *weak* correlation intractable function ensembles is not sufficient for Theorem 1, 2 and 3.

Remark 3 (Interactive Arguments). We show how to generalize the proof of Theorem 1 and 3 in order to obtain the same results in the argument model. R_2 remains evasive in the setting of interactive arguments since the evasiveness of R_2 relies on the completeness, but not on the soundness. Therefore, the proof of the part $x \in L$ automatically holds for interactive arguments. On the other hand, R_1 is not always evasive in the setting of interactive arguments since the evasiveness of R_1 relies on the statistical soundness. Therefore, we need to modify R_1 as follows: $(\alpha, \beta) \in R_1$ if and only if for every probabilistic polynomial-time machine $\hat{P}$ and every y, the probability

$$\Pr[\gamma \leftarrow \hat{P}_x^y(\alpha, \beta); b \leftarrow \rho_V(x, \alpha, \beta, \gamma) : b = \text{ACC}]$$

is overwhelming. If we use this evasive relation R_1, the proof of the part $x \notin L$ holds for interactive arguments.

Remark 4 (Constant Round Case). Our results extend to the constant-round case. But we need to generalize the evasiveness and the correlation intractability to deal with multiple input-output pairs rather than a single pair. We omit the details here.

4 One-Wayness and Restricted Correlation Intractability

In this section, we show the negative relationship between one-way functions and restricted correlation intractable function ensembles. We start by reviewing the result of Ostrovsky and Wigderson [OW93].

It is well-known that assuming the existence of non-uniform one-way functions, it holds that $\mathcal{NP} \subseteq \mathcal{ZK}$ [GMW91] [4]. Ostrovsky and Wigderson considered the question of whether this sufficient condition is also necessary. They showed that the existence of zero-knowledge interactive proofs for languages outside $\mathcal{ETA}$ implies the existence of one-way functions (but not of non-uniform one-way functions).

Definition 9 (one-way functions). *A function $f : \{0,1\}^* \to \{0,1\}^*$ is one-way if the following two conditions hold:*

Easy to compute   *There exists a (deterministic) polynomial-time machine A so that on input x, A outputs $f(x)$.*

Hard to invert   *For every probabilistic polynomial-time machine A', every polynomial $poly(\cdot)$ and all sufficient large n's, $\Pr[x \leftarrow \{0,1\}^n; y = f(x); x' \leftarrow A'(y) : y = f(x')] < \frac{1}{poly(n)}$.*

Theorem 4 ([OW93]). *Assume that there exists a $\mathcal{ZK}$ language outside $\mathcal{ETA}$. Then there exist one-way functions.*

Now we show that the negative relationship is obtaind by combining Theorem 2 and Theorem 4.

Theorem 5. *For any pair of length functions (l_{in}, l_{out}), proving the implication, "if one-way functions exist then (l_{in}, l_{out})-restricted correlation intractable function ensembles exist", is as hard as proving $3\mathcal{R}\text{-}\mathcal{AIZK}\text{-}\mathcal{AM}[l_{in}, l_{out}] \subseteq \mathcal{ETA}$.*

Proof. Let (l_{in}, l_{out}) be any pair of length functions. Recall that $3\mathcal{R}\text{-}\mathcal{AIZK}\text{-}\mathcal{AM}[l_{in}, l_{out}] \subseteq \mathcal{AIZK} \subseteq \mathcal{ZK}$. Therefore, Theorem 4 says that assuming that there exists a $3\mathcal{R}\text{-}\mathcal{AIZK}\text{-}\mathcal{AM}[l_{in}, l_{out}]$ language outside $\mathcal{ETA}$, one-way functions exist. On the other hand, Theorem 2 says that if there exist (l_{in}, l_{out})-restricted correlation intractable function ensembles, it holds that $3\mathcal{R}\text{-}\mathcal{AIZK}\text{-}\mathcal{AM}[l_{in}, l_{out}] \subseteq \mathcal{ETA}$.

Assume that if one-way functions exist then (l_{in}, l_{out})-restricted correlation intractable function ensembles exist. Then, it follows that if there exists a $3\mathcal{R}\text{-}\mathcal{AIZK}\text{-}\mathcal{AM}[l_{in}, l_{out}]$ language outside $\mathcal{ETA}$, then $3\mathcal{R}\text{-}\mathcal{AIZK}\text{-}\mathcal{AM}[l_{in}, l_{out}] \subseteq \mathcal{ETA}$. This means that it unconditionally holds that $3\mathcal{R}\text{-}\mathcal{AIZK}\text{-}\mathcal{AM}[l_{in}, l_{out}] \subseteq \mathcal{ETA}$. □

Theorem 5 does not imply the non-existence of restricted correlation intractable function ensembles. There may exist one-way functions and restricted correlation intractable function ensembles, simultaneously.

---

[4] Furthermore, it is well-known that $\mathcal{IP}=\mathcal{ZK}=\mathcal{PSPACE}$ assuming the existence of non-uniform one-way functions [BGG+88][Sh92]

As mentioned above, the assumption of the existence of restricted *weak* correlation intractable function ensembles is not sufficient for the triviality of 3-round AIZK AM proofs. Therefore, Theorem 5 does not extend to restricted *weak* correlation intractable function ensembles.

5 Concluding Remarks

In this paper, we have shown that assuming the existence of restricted correlation intractable function ensembles, 3-round AIZK AM protocols exist only for trivial languages. Our proof uses the verifier's auxiliary-input in an essential way: The auxiliary-input of the cheating verifier is used as the seed of restricted correlation intractable function ensembles. Therefore, our result does not apply to the notion of GMR-ZK. One may think that if we define the restricted correlation intractability in a single-function model, we can prove an analogous result with respect to GMR-ZK. However, as described in [CGH98], such functions do not exist.

Using the above triviality result, we have shown that, for any pair of length functions (l_{in}, l_{out}), proving the implication, "if one-way functions exist then (l_{in}, l_{out})-restricted correlation intractable function ensembles exist", is as hard as proving $3\mathcal{R}\text{-}\mathcal{AIZK}\text{-}\mathcal{AM}[l_{in}, l_{out}] \subseteq \mathcal{BPP}$. We believe that proving the latter claim unconditionally is a fundamental open problem in the theory of ZK proofs. Therefore, this can be viewed as strong evidence that it will be difficult to construct restricted correlation intractable function ensembles assuming only that one-way functions exist. It is interesting to investigate how hard it is to prove that $3\mathcal{R}\text{-}\mathcal{AIZK}\text{-}\mathcal{AM}[l_{in}, l_{out}] \subseteq \mathcal{BPP}$ without making any assumptions.

Acknowledgments

We would like to thank Shai Halevi for pointing out a mistake in an earlier version. We also thank Masahiro Wada and Kenji Suzuki for their encouragement.

References

[BaMo88] L. Babai and S. Moran, "Arthur-Merlin Games: A Randomized Proof System, and a Hierarchy of Complexity Classes," J. Comput. System Sci., 36, pp.254-276, 1988.

[BeRo93] M. Bellare and P. Rogaway, "Random Oracles are Practical: a paradigm for designing efficient protocols, " Proceedings of the 1st ACM Conference on Computer and Communications Security, pp. 62-73, 1993.

[BGG+88] M. Ben-Or, O. Goldreich, S. Goldwasser, J. Håstad, J. Kilian, S. Micali and P. Rogaway, "Everything Provable is Provable in Zero-Knowledge," Proceedings of Crypto'88, 1990.

[BCC88] G. Brassard, D. Chaum and C. Crépeau, "Minimum Disclosure Proofs of Knowledge, " Journal of Computer and System Sciences, Vol. 37, No. 2, pp. 156-189, 1988.

[BrCr86]   G. Brassard and C. Crépeau, "Non-Transitive Transfer of Confidence : A
           Perfect Zero-Knowledge Interactive Protocol for SAT and Beyond, " Pro-
           ceedings of 27th FOCS, 1986.

[Ca97]   R. Canetti, "Towards Realizing Random Oracles: Hash Functions that Hide
           All Partial Information," Proceedings of Crypto'97, pp.455-469, 1997.

[CGH98]   R. Canetti, O. Goldreich and S. Halevi, "The Random Oracle Model, Re-
           visited," Proceedings of 30th STOC, 1998.

[CMR98]   R. Canetti, D. Micciancio and O. Reingold, "Perfectly One-Way Probabilis-
           tic Hash Functions," Proceedings of 30th STOC, 1998.

[Go98]   O. Goldreich, "Foundations of Cryptography (Fragments of a Book - Version
           2.03)," February 27, 1998.

[GoKr96]   O. Goldreich and H. Krawczyk, "On the Composition of Zero-Knowledge
           Proof Systems," SIAM Journal on Computing, Vol.25, No.1, pp.169-192,
           1996.

[GMW91]   O. Goldreich, S. Micali, and A. Wigderson, "Proofs that Yield Nothing
           But Their Validity or All Languages in NP Have Zero-Knowledge Proof
           Systems," Journal of the ACM, Vol.38, No.1, pp.691-729, 1991.

[GoOr94]   O. Goldreich and Y. Oren, "Definitions and Properties of Zero-Knowledge
           Proof Systems," Journal of Cryptology, Vol.7, No. 1, pp.1-32, 1994.

[GMR85]   S. Goldwasser, S. Micali, and C. Rackoff, "The Knowledge Complexity of
           Interactive Proofs," Proceedings of 17th STOC, pp.291-304, 1985.

[HT98]   S. Hada and T. Tanaka, "On the Existence of 3-Round Zero-Knowledge
           Protocols, " , Proceedings of Crypto'98, pp. 408-423, 1998.

[ImRu89]   R. Impagliazzo and S. Rudich, "Limits on the provable consequences of
           one-way permutations," Proceedings of 21st STOC, 1989.

[OW93]   R. Ostrovsky and A. Wigderson, "One-Way Functions are Essential for Non-
           Trivial Zero-Knowledge," Technical Report in ICSI, TR-93-073, 1993.

[Sh92]   A. Shamir, "IP=PSPACE, " Journal of ACM, Vol. 39, No. 4, pp. 869-877,
           1992.

[Si98]   D. R. Simon, "Finding Collisions on a One-Way Street: Can Secure Hash
           Functions Be Based on General Assumptions," Proceedings of Eurocrypt'98,
           pp.334-345, 1998.

Message Recovery Fair Blind Signature

Hyung-Woo Lee and Tai-Yun Kim

Dept. of Computer Science & Engineering, Korea University,
1, 5-ga, Anam-dong, Seongbuk-ku, Seoul, 136-701, Korea
{hwlee, tykim}@netlab.korea.ac.kr
http://netlab.korea.ac.kr/~hwlee/index.html

Abstract. As the blind signature introduced by *Chaum*[10] does not reveal any information about the message or its signature, it has been used for providing the anonymity in secure electronic payment systems. Unfortunately, this perfect anonymity could be misused by criminals as blind signatures prevent linking the withdrawal of money and the payment made by the same customer. Therefore, we should provide publicly verifiable mechanism if it is required for the judge to trace the blackmailed messages. In this study, we propose a *modified fair blind signature*, which additionally provides the role of *message recovery*. After analyzing the existing *meta-ElGamal* scheme[12] suggested by *Horster*, the model of message recovery blind signature is considered at first. And we suggest *a new fair blind signature* based on the oblivious transfer protocol, with which a judge can verify its fairness. Proposed scheme can be advanced into the blind multi-signature and it is also applicable to the diverse payment applications.

1 Introduction

Both the anonymity and prevention of double spending must be considered for implementing secure electronic cash based on public key cryptosystem[1,2]. Since the existing proposals of electronic payment systems such as *Chaum*[3] and *Brands*[4,5] provide perfect anonymity, they could be misused by criminals. Concretely, as a blind signature scheme introduced by *Chaum*[10] provides perfect unlinkability, it can be used for providing anonymity in electronic payment systems. However, as a blind signature prevents linking the withdrawal of money and the payment made by the same customer, this anonymity could be misused by criminals[6,7]. Provided perfect unlinkability, double spending problem can be happen as a *"side-effect"*.

Therefore, it would be useful if the anonymity could be removed with the help of a trusted entity, when this is required for legal reasons. A judge as a trusted entity can verify the message-signature pair if necessary. We must pursue a similar mechanism for electronic payment system by considering a new publicly verifiable type of *fair cryptosystem*. By running the link-recovery protocol, the signer obtains information from the judge and he can recognize the corresponding protocol view and message-signature pair. Using this *fair blind signature*[18], both the confidence and the fairness can be enhanced in the signed message of electronic payment system.

In this study, we propose a new fair blind signature with the investigation of the essential blind signature for implementing electronic payment systems. The model of message recovery blind signature scheme is suggested by the transformation of existing *Horster* scheme[11,12,13,14]. And it is also modified into a fair blind signature scheme using the properties of *oblivious transfer protocol*[15,16]. Proposed scheme does the pre-registration processes for providing fairness on each entities with the relations of the trusted entity. Proposed scheme can be advanced into the blind multi-signature and it is also applicable to the diverse applications.

We first present the *Horster*'s scheme with common concepts of blind signature and review the existing fair blind signature in section 2 and 3 respectively. We then propose message recovery fair blind signature that is to make the most of the characteristics of oblivious transfer protocol in section 4. Furthermore, we compare suggested scheme with existing one in section 5 and conclude this study with the consideration of the future works in final section.

2 Message Recovery Blind Signature

2.1 Definition of Blind Signature

Blind signature scheme, first introduced by *Chaum*[10], is a protocol for obtaining a signature from a signer such that the signer's view of the protocol cannot be linked to the resulting message-signature pair. Unlinkability means that we can't find any relations for linking the message and its signature between the signer and the sender by whom transaction of blind signature is done. In other words, blind signature scheme is an important cryptographic tool for realizing systems with which the signer B can issue such a credential without obtaining any useful information about neither the pseudonym of sender A nor the issued credential.

Sender A receives a signature of B as a blinded message. From this, A compute B's signature on a message m chosen a priori by A. B has no knowledge of m nor the signature associated with m. B's RSA public and private key are (n,e) and d respectively. k is a random secret integer chosen by A satisfying $0 \leq k \leq n - 1$ and $\gcd(n, k) = 1$. Blind signature can be applicable to the diverse applications. In electronic payment systems, message m means the A's electronic cash. This may be important in electronic cash applications where a message m might represent a monetary value which A can spend. When m^* and are presented to B for payment, B is unable to deduce which party was originally given the signed value. This allows A to remain anonymous so that spending patterns cannot be monitored.

The *Horster*'s *meta-ElGamal* scheme[12] has developed existing blind signature with *ElGamal*[9]-type cryptosystem, which provides secure blind scheme based on the difficulty of primitive discrete logarithm problem. In this study, we propose the message recovery blind signature based on the *Horster*'s scheme and generalize it into customized model. Furthermore, we can develop this scheme to the modified fair blind signature scheme by analyzing this model.

2.2 Model of Message Recovery Blind Signature

The definition of blind signature that provides message recovery is as follows. Although the key generation algorithm is similar with common blind signature, the interactive protocol provides additional message recovery functions itself.

Definition 1. Message recovery blind signature $(SKG,\ IP_{MR},\ Ver_{MR})$.

- SKG: A signature key generation algorithm for public/private key pair (x,y).
- IP_{MR}: An interactive blind signature protocol $(sender(m,y),\ signer(x))$ which provides message recovery between the sender and the signer. On sender's input of message m and signer's public key y, signer inputs his pricate key x. Signer transfers blind signature $s = sender(m,y)_{signer(x)}$ to the sender.
- Ver_{MR}: A signature verification algorithm which outputs *accept* on input a public key y, a signature s, if s is a valid signature of the message m with respect to the public key y, and otherwise outputs *reject*.

Model of message recovery blind signature is as follow Fig. 1.

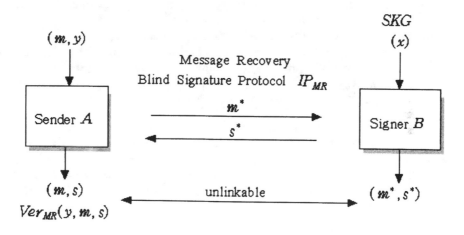

Fig. 1. Model of blind signature protocol providing message recovery.

Based on this generalized model, we will review a new blind signature providing verification by public entity and enhance it into fair signature scheme.

3 Fair Blind Signature

3.1 Model of *Stadler*'s Fair Blind Signature[18]

A fair blind signature scheme introduced by *Stadler* is a blind signature scheme with an additional algorithm which publicly verifies blinded message and also makes it possible to selectively revoke the *"blindness"* of the scheme. On the message-signature pair generated between the sender A and the signer B, trusted entity J can associate those blinded information. Model of *Stadler*'s fair blind signature defines the revocation key generation algorithm RKG and the secret key generation algorithm SKG. And it also suggest the blind signature protocol IP between the sender and the signer and the verification protocol Ver. For extracting the linkability, revocation algorithm R is defined. Concrete model of *Stadler*'s fair blind signature is as follow definition.

Definition 2. *Stadler*'s fair blind signature (RKG, SKG, IP, Ver, R).

- RKG: A probabilistic revocation key generation algorithm. It outputs a random secret/public revocation key pair.
- $(SKG(y_R), IP, Ver)$: A protocol of fair blind signature. It does the blind signature on y_R if the corresponding secret revocation key is not known.
- $R(x_R, \ldots)$: A revocation algorithm with one or both of the following properties.
  - $type_I$: Given the signer's view of the protocol, the judge delivers information that enables the signer to efficiently recognize the corresponding message-signature pair. On input the secret revocation key and the signer's view $View(Signer(x)_{sender(m,y)}$, R outputs a linkable value to the corresponding message-signature pair *(m,s)*.
  - $type_{II}$: Given the sender's view of the protocol, the judge delivers information that enables the sender to efficiently recognize the corresponding message-signature pair. On input the secret revocation key and a message-signature pair *(m,s)*, R outputs a linkable value to the corresponding the signer's view $View(Signer(x)_{sender(m,y)}$.

Using this link revocation protocol, the judge can associate the signer's signature according to the sender's message. There are two type of revocations in proposed protocol, $type_I$ and $type_{II}$. Judge can extract the illegal withdrawal and perceive the double spending using those revocations respectively in electronic payment systems. Concrete model of *Stadler*'s scheme is as follow Fig. 2.

3.2 *Stadler*'s Fair Blind Schemes

Stadler had proposed both a fair blind signature scheme based on *Chaum*'s blind signature[10] with the well-known cut-and-choose method and a variation of the *Fiat-Shamir* signature scheme[8]. We define the former as a Stadler-CC and the latter as a Stadler-FS scheme.

First of all, the Stadler-CC scheme applies the *Chaum*'s blind signature with RSA methods using cut-and-choose. Unfortunately, this fair blind signature scheme is inefficient as a large amount of data is exchanged during the signing protocol and the resulting signature is long for providing $type_I$ and $type_{II}$ verification processes. More efficient implementation is the Stadler-FS.

Stadler-FS scheme is based on the concept of *fair one-out-of-two oblivious transfer* f-OT$_2^1$, which uses the property of quadratic residue in the generation

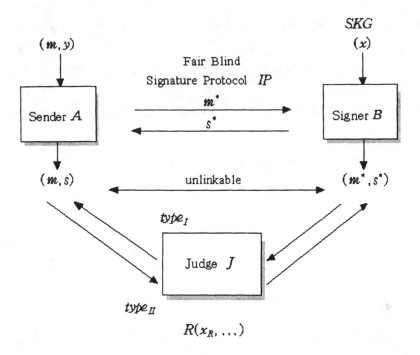

Fig. 2. Model of *Stadler*'s fair blind signature.

step of blind signature with a variation of the *Fiat-Shamir* signature scheme[8]. However, *Stadler*'s scheme does not provide the message recovery facility. In this study, publicly verifiable fair blind signature is proposed based on the model of message recovery signature scheme.

4 Proposed Message Recovery Fair Blind Signature

Suggested fair blind signature scheme provides publicly verifiable process on signed message if the trusted entity want to certificate blind signature. The concrete processes of registration protocol and the message recovery fair blind signature is as follows.

4.1 Model of Registration for Fair Blindness

For providing fairness, publicly verifiable functions must be provided by the trusted entity. Therefore, the sender A does the pre-registration processes to the trusted entity and receive the secrets used for fair blind signature. The signer performs blind signature on sender's message and returns this signed message to the sender. We can define the registration protocol.

Definition 3. Registration protocol for fair blind signature RP.

- RP: An interactive registration protocol *(sender(δ,y),judge(x))* which provides the secrets required for blind signature between the sender and trusted entity.

The sender inputs his own random secret δ and trusted entity's public key y. Trusted entity returns registration results $v' = sender(\delta, y)_{judge(w,x)}$ on input of the secret key x. From the response v', the sender gets the secret v that can be used in fair blind signature. Both the sender's δ, v and the trusted entity's c, v' come under the basic information for confirming their fairness. The value c contains the publicly verifiable information of the trusted entity. We can depict the registration protocol as follow Fig. 3.

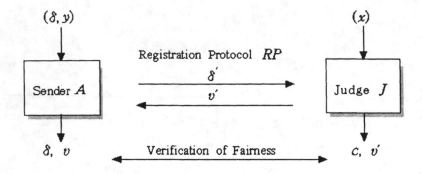

Fig. 3. Pre-registration protocol model for fair blind signature.

4.2 Model of Message Recovery Fair Blind Signature

We can enhance the existing fair blind signature into the message recovery scheme based on the *Horster*'s mechanism. Using pre-registration protocol, the trusted entity allocates the secrets for fairness to the sender. And by the key generation algorithm, the signer receives his secret key. Additionally, a verifiable fair blind function can be defined by this suggested interactive signature protocol with message recovering facility. The Fig. 4 shows the model of fair blind signature providing message recovery.

Definition 4. Message recovery fair blind signature (RP, SKG, FIP_{MR}, R, $FVer_{MR}$).

- SKG: Public/secret key generation algorithm based on the registration protocol RP.
- FIP_{MR}: An interactive fair blind signature issuing protocol involving a sender and a signer for message recovery. The sender's inputs are a value v generated in registration process and a message m and a public key y. The

signer's inputs are the information c for fair protocol and a corresponding secret key x. The signer sends his blinded message $s = sender(v, m, y)_{signer(c,x)}$ to the sender.

- R: A revocation algorithm on blind signature with one or both of the following properties, r_I on $type_I$ and r_{II} on $type_{II}$.

  - r_I: From the signer's signature (m^*, s^*), the trusted entity J can associate the sender's message (m, s).

  - r_{II}: From the sender's signature (m, s), the trusted judge J can associate the signer's message (m^*, s^*).

- $FVer_{MR}(r, y, m, s)$: A fairness verification algorithm that confirms the overall blinded signature if s is a valid signature of the message m with respect to the revocation information r and the public key y.

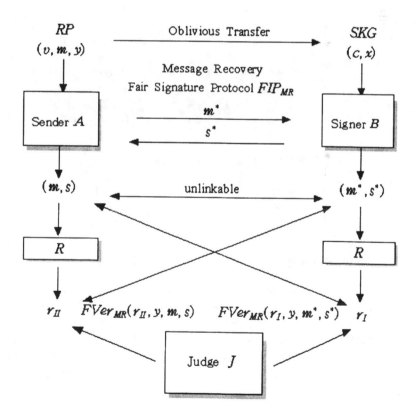

Fig. 4. Proposed model of message recovery fair blind signature.

4.3 Registration Steps for Fair Blindness

In this study, proposed signature scheme based on *Horster*'s protocol does the registration steps at first for generating fair signature. The sender A performs the registration with the trusted entity J as follow sequences.

Step 1: Request for registration.
 - The sender A generates random secret $s_A \in Z_q$.
 - A sends both a $\delta \equiv g^{s_A} \bmod p$ and identity information ID_A to the trusted entity J for requesting his registration.

Step 2: Registration.
 - Trusted entity J generates both a $v_j, v_{1-j} \in Z_q$ used for fair signature process and random $w_J \in Z_q$, which satisfies $t_j \bmod g^{w_J} \bmod p$.
 - J stores the A's ID_A, δ and revocation keys v_j, v_{1-j} in his database.
 - J computes $c = h(\delta \cdot v_j \parallel \delta \cdot v_{1-j} \parallel t_J)$ using hash function on the keys v_j, v_{1-j}.
 - Trusted entity generates s_J based ont eh *Schnorr* signature scheme and sends the message $(\delta \cdot v_j, \delta \cdot v_{1-j}, s_j, c)$ to A.

Step 3: Verification of registration.
 - A verifies J's message using his own random δ and gets the revocation keys v_j, v_{1-j} on it.
 - As the value c will be used in the β_j, β_{1-j} of oblivious transfer protocol, we can fairly verify the message-signature pair in the end.

The Fig. 5 shows the detailed registration steps of our proposed scheme.

(Proof) Verification of $u_J \equiv g^{s_J} y^{-c} \bmod p$.

$$u_J \equiv g^{s_J} y^{-c} \equiv g^{x_J \cdot c + w_J} g^{x_J - c} \equiv t_J \bmod p$$

$$c' = h(\delta \cdot v_j \parallel \delta \cdot v_{1-j} \parallel u_J) = h(\delta \cdot v_j \parallel \delta \cdot v_{1-j} \parallel t_J) = c$$

4.4 Modified Message Recovery Fair Blind Signature(Mo-MR-FBS)

Both a sender and a signer interact for generating fair blind signature after those registration processes. In this study, we apply the concept of *oblivious transfer* to the blind signature for providing fairness on signed message. The concept of an oblivious transfer was introduced by *Rabin*[15]. As A send m bits in a message to B in 50% probability, The A does not know which bits were sent. A has two string s_0, s_1. A encrypts one of his strings and message m with B's public key P_B. And A sends this to B. B decrypts it and extracts one out of the strings s_0 or s_1 using his private key. However, A will not know which one out of the two B got. In this study, we use this as an intermediation for providing fair verification by trusted entity. Proposed message recovery fair blind signature scheme uses the secrets v_j, v_{1-j} received from the trusted entity for doing its oblivious transfer protocol. Detail processes are as follows with Fig. 6.

Sender (A)		Judge (J)

$y_j \equiv g^{x_j} \bmod p$ x_j

$s_A \in Z_q$

$ID_A , \; \delta \equiv g^{s_A} \bmod p$

$$\xrightarrow{\quad request(ID_A, \delta) \quad}$$

$$ID_A , \delta$$
$$v_j , v_{1-j} \in Z_q$$
$$w_j \in G(q) , \; t_j \equiv g^{w_j} \bmod p$$
$$c = h(\delta \cdot v_j \| \delta \cdot v_{1-j} \| t_j)$$
$$s_j = x_j \cdot c + w_j \bmod q$$
$$(\delta \cdot v_j, \delta \cdot v_{1-j}, s_j, c)$$

$(\delta \cdot v_j, \delta \cdot v_{1-j}, s_j, c) \quad \xleftarrow{\quad (\delta \cdot v_j, \delta \cdot v_{1-j}, s_j, c) \quad}$

$u_j \equiv g^{s_j} y_j^{-c} \bmod p$

$c' = h(\delta \cdot v_j \| \delta \cdot v_{1-j} \| u_j)$

$c = c'$

(δ, v_j, v_{1-j}) (w_j, s_j, c)

Fig. 5. Registration protocol on trusted judge J.

Step 1: Initial oblivious transfer.
- The sender A generates β_j, β_{1-j} using the revocation keys v_j, v_{1-j}.

$$\beta_j \equiv g^{v_j + v_{1-j}} \bmod p, \quad \beta_{1-j} \equiv c \cdot (g^{v_j + v_{1-j}})^{-1} \bmod p$$

- A sends the β_j, β_{1-j} to the signer B.

Step 2: Generation of fair blind parameters.
- The signer B verifies received values $c \equiv \beta_j \cdot \beta_{1-j} \bmod p$ and checks whether it is same with that value stored in trusted entity's database.
- The signer generates his own random secrets $z_j^*, z_{1-j}^* \in Z_q$.
- B sends the blind parameters λ_0^*, λ_1^* and γ_0, γ_1 to A.

$$\lambda_j^* \equiv g^{z_j^*} \bmod p, \quad \lambda_{1-j}^* \equiv g^{z_{1-j}^*} \bmod p$$

$$\gamma_j \equiv \beta_j^{z_j^*} \bmod p, \quad \gamma_{1-j} \equiv \beta_{1-j}^{z_{1-j}^*} \bmod p$$

Step 3: Sending of blinded message.
- The sender A generates r_j and m_j^* on his own message m.

$$r_j \equiv m^{-1} (\lambda_j^*)^{v_j} y^{v_{1-j}} \bmod p, \quad m_j^* \equiv v_j^{-1} \cdot (r_j - v_{1-j}) - \lambda_j^* \bmod q$$

- A sends m_j^* to the signer B.

Step 4: Generation of blinded signature.
- The signer B generates blind signature s_j^* on the m_j^*.

$$s_j^* \equiv x \cdot (m_j^* + \lambda_j^*) - z_j^* \bmod q$$

– B sends it to the sender A.

Step 5: Verification of fair blind signature with message recovery.

– Sender A computes s_j for recovering the message from the signer's s_j^*.

$$s_j \equiv v_j \cdot s_j^* \bmod q$$

– A calculates $m \equiv g^{-s_j} y^{r_j} r_j^{-1} \bmod p$ for verifying its signature.

Sender (A)   *Signer* (B)

$m,\; y \equiv g^x \bmod p$ x

$j \in \{0,1\},\; v_j,\, v_{1-j} \in Z_q$

$\beta_j \equiv g^{v_j + v_{1-j}} \bmod p,\quad \beta_{1-j} \equiv c \cdot (g^{v_j + v_{1-j}})^{-1} \bmod p$

$$\xrightarrow{\quad \beta_j,\, \beta_{1-j} \quad}$$

$$\beta_j,\, \beta_{1-j}$$
$$c \equiv \beta_j \cdot \beta_{1-j} \bmod p$$
$$z_j^*,\, z_{1-j}^* \in Z_q$$
$$\lambda_j^* \equiv g^{z_j^*} \bmod p,\quad \lambda_{1-j}^* \equiv g^{z_{1-j}^*} \bmod p$$
$$\gamma_j \equiv \beta_j^{z_j^*} \bmod p,\quad \gamma_{1-j} \equiv \beta_{1-j}^{z_{1-j}^*} \bmod p$$

$\lambda_0^*,\, \lambda_1^*,\, \gamma_0,\, \gamma_1$ $\xleftarrow{\quad \lambda_0^*,\, \lambda_1^*,\, \gamma_0,\, \gamma_1 \quad}$

$\lambda_j^{*v_j} \equiv \gamma_j \bmod p$

$r_j \equiv m^{-1}(\lambda_j^*)^{v_j} y^{v_{1-j}} \bmod p$

$m_j^* \equiv v_j^{-1} \cdot (r_j - v_{1-j}) - \lambda_j^* \bmod q$

$$\xrightarrow{\quad m_j^* \quad}$$

$$m_j^*$$
$$s_j^* \equiv x \cdot (m_j^* + \lambda_j^*) - z_j^* \bmod q$$

s_j^* $\xleftarrow{\quad s_j^* \quad}$

$s_j \equiv v_j \cdot s_j^* \bmod q$

$m \equiv g^{-s_j} y^{r_j} r_j^{-1} \bmod p$

$(m, (r_j, s_j))$ $(\lambda_j^*, m_j^*, z_j^*, s_j^*)$

Fig. 6. Modified *Horster*-type message recovery fair blind signature(Mo-MR-FBS).

(Proof) Verification of $m \equiv g^{-s_j} y^{r_j} r_j^{-1} \bmod p$.

$$g^{-s_j} y^{r_j} r_j^{-1} \equiv g^{-(v_j \cdot s_j^*)} \cdot g^{(x \cdot r_j)} \cdot m \cdot g^{-(z_j^* \cdot v_j)} \cdot g^{-(x \cdot v_{1-j})}$$

$$\equiv m \cdot g^{-v_j \cdot s_j^*} \cdot g^{x \cdot r_j} \cdot g^{-z_j^* \cdot v_j - x \cdot v_{1-j}}$$

$$\equiv m \cdot g^{-v_j \cdot (x \cdot (m_j^* + \lambda_j^*) - z_j^*)} \cdot g^{x \cdot r_j} \cdot g^{-z_j^* \cdot v_j - x \cdot v_{1-j}}$$

$$\equiv m \cdot g^{-v_j \cdot x \cdot (m_j^* + \lambda_j^*)} \cdot g^{x \cdot r_j - x \cdot v_{1-j}}$$

$$\equiv m \cdot g^{-v_j \cdot x \cdot v_j^{-1} \cdot (r_j - v_{1-j})} \cdot g^{x \cdot (r_j - v_{1-j})}$$

$$\equiv m \bmod p$$

5 Analysis of the Proposed Schemes

5.1 Fairness of the Proposed Schemes

Verifying the fairness of proposed scheme, we overview each revocation types of r_I on $type_I$ and r_{II} on $type_{II}$. Trusted entity J can associate the signer's signature (m^*, s^*) with the signer's message (m, s) by using revocation function r_I. And J can do it in reverse order by the r_{II} function. As s_j^* and s_j have relation of $s_j \equiv v_j \cdot s_j^* \bmod q$ with follow equations, we can associate signer's message (m^*, s^*) with its correspondence.

$$r_j \equiv m^{-1} \cdot (\lambda_j^*)^{v_j} \cdot y^{v_1-j} \bmod p, \ r_j \equiv v_j \cdot (m_j^* + \lambda_j^*) + v_{1-j} \bmod q$$

$$m \equiv (v_j \cdot (m_j^* + \lambda_j^*) + v_{1-j})^{-1} (\lambda_j^*)^{v_j} y^{v_1-j} \bmod p$$

$$s_j \equiv v_j \cdot s_j^* \bmod q$$
$$\equiv v_j \cdot (x \cdot (m_j^* + \lambda_j^*) - z_j^*) \bmod q$$
$$\equiv v_j \cdot (x \cdot (v_j^{-1} \cdot (r_j - v_{1-j})) - z_j^*) \bmod q$$
$$\equiv x \cdot (r_j - v_{1-j}) - v_j \cdot z_j^* \bmod q$$

Moreover, the trusted entity can link the sender's message (m, s) with m_j^* and s_j^* using his own secrets as follows. The trusted entity can publicly verify the blinded signature s_j^* using the signer's secret x and his random variable z_j^*. However, this $type_{II}$ verification can be provided by the additional pre-processing between the trusted entity and the signer.

$$m_j^* + \lambda_j^* \equiv v_j^{-1} \cdot (r_j - v_{1-j}) \bmod q, \ s_j^* \equiv x \cdot v_j^{-1} \cdot (r_j - v_{1-j}) - z_j^* \bmod q$$

5.2 Security of the Proposed Schemes

The registration protocol is secure as *Schnorr* signature scheme. Trusted judge J uses hash function on the keys v_i, v_{1-j} for sending revocation keys based on the discrete logarithm problems. As the sender generates his own random number $s_A \in Z_q$, a forger can't get any information about δ without knowing s_A. Thus the calculation of s_A seems to be as difficult as the computation of the discrete logarithm $log_g(\delta)$. Additionally, as the value c in registration protocol is used in the initial parameters of oblivious transfer protocol, we can fairly verify its correctness in message-signature pair by calculating $c \equiv \beta_j \cdot \beta_{1-j} \bmod p$.

We can assume that the security of the proposed message recovery fair blind signature(Mo-MR-FBS) is similar to the meta-ElGamal signature scheme. The security analysis for a total break of the signature scheme and universal forgery of messages can also be adapted from the meta-ElGamal scheme. Proposed scheme uses oblivious transfer protocol and generates fair blind parameters. An attacker can choose signature parameters at random and calculate the corresponding values. To aviod a total break of the proposed scheme, the forger can randomly choose the secrets z_j^*, z_{1-j}^*, then attempts to find γ_j, γ_{1-j}. In this method, the forger must solve the discrete logarithm of $\gamma_j \equiv \lambda_j^{v_j} \bmod p$. These computations are extremely difficult and it's still an open question whether it is more difficult than solving the discrete logarithm problem.

5.3 Extensions of the Proposed Schemes

We can extend the proposed scheme into message recovery fair blind multisignature (Mo-MR-FBMS). As the Mo-MR-FBMS provides message recovery facility on the signatures of multiple users, the registration step of this scheme is similar with that of the Mo-MR-FBS. The sender merely generates message with additional hash function and multiple signers sign on it. Finally, the sender verifies those multisignature with rehashing function.

Using secret v_j, v_{1-j} from the trusted entity, the sender A sends β_j, β_{1-j} to the k number of B_j. Each signer B_j verifies $c \equiv \beta_j \cdot \beta_{1-j} \bmod p$ whether it is equal to the value generated by the trusted entity. And then each B_j generates their own secrets $z_{B_j j}^*, z_{B_j 1-j}^* \in Z_q$. The sender computes $m_i (1 \le i \le k)$ for each signer B_i, which satisfies the equation $m = h(m_i \parallel i)$. On the signer's signature $s_{B_i j}^*$, the sender A calculates m_i and applies hash function on it as follow equation. If m' is equal to m, we can accept overall multisignature as correct one.

$$m' = h(m_i' \parallel i)(1 \le i \le k), \prod_{i=1}^{k} m_i' \equiv \prod_{i=1}^{k} g^{-s_{B_i j}} (y_{B_i j})^{r_{B_i j}} (r_{B_i j})^{-1} \bmod p$$

Message recovery fair blind signature generates precise blindness without leaking any information on the sender's message such as digital cash when it is used for electronic payment systems. In verification steps on signed message, the sender regenerates same message with his own one. Therefore, this message recovery scheme has an advantage in managing the amount of electronic cash on the payment systems such as micropayment frameworks.

5.4 Performance Analysis of Proposed Schemes

Stadler-CC and Stadler-FS schemes are fair blind signature based on the security of RSA[2] and *Fiat-Shamir*[8] respectively with the difficulty of factoring problem. Stadler-FS provides *type$_I$* verification on its fairness, although it also can be modified into message recovery scheme.

Proposed Mo-MR-FBS scheme has its security on the difficulty of discrete logarithm problem such as *ElGamal*[9]. Mo-MR-FBS also secures as *meta-ElGamal* [12] scheme. However, suggested scheme applies oblivious transfer protocol to both the key generation and blind signature transactions only once after the registration steps on its preprocessing with trusted entity. Therefore, proposed scheme has efficiency in the amount of computations and communication bandwidth than existing Stadler-FS protocol, which repeatedly applies oblivious transfer scheme in overall blind signature processes. Mo-MR-FBS provides both the

$type_I$ and the $type_{II}$ verification with trusted entity. We can compare the performance of fair blind signature as follow Table 1.

Table 1. Property comparision of fair blind signature.

Items/Methods	Stadler-CC	Stadler-FS	Mo-MR-FBS	Mo-MR-FBMS
Primitive Problem	*RSA* Factoring	*Fiat-Shamir* Factoring	*ElGamal* Dis. Log.	*ElGamal* Dis. Log.
Message Recovery	×	△	○	○
Fair Blind Multisignature	◇	△	△	○
Fair Cryptosystem	◇	△	△	△
Additional Cryptosystem for Fairness	Cut and Choose	Oblivious Transfer	Oblivious Transfer	Oblivious Transfer
Applying Step of Fairness	Signature Step	Signature Step	Initial Step	Initial Step
Secret Sharing	×	△	△	△
Types of Fairness	I/II	I	I/II	I/II

×: impossible, ◇: unable to decide, △: possible after modification, ○: providing

Suggested scheme has similar properties with the secret sharing[22]. The partitioned signatures s_i are sent to each verifyers B_i. Required to certificate the signature, they can verify it using their shared secrets. Proposed Mo-MR-FBMS scheme also has the similar properties with the secret sharing. We can analyze the performance of fair blind signature as follow Table 2.

Table 2. Performance analysis of fair blind signature.

Methods Items	Stadler-CC	Stadler-FS $(|c| = k')$	Mo-MR-FBS	Mo-MR-FBMS $(M = k)$
Iteration Number	4	$1 + 2k'$	4	$4k$
Preprocessing	○	×	△	△
On-line Processing(Sender) 1024-bits Mod. Multi.	$300 + \alpha$	$550,000 + \alpha$	$300 + \alpha$	$(300 + \alpha)k$
Processing of Signature(Signer) 1024-bits Mod. Multi.	$1,650 + \alpha$	$830,000 + \alpha$	$300 + \alpha$	$(300 + \alpha)k$
Processing of Signature(Sender) 1024-bits Mod. Multi.	$60 + \alpha$	$90 + \alpha$	$300 + \alpha$	$(300 + \alpha)k$

6 Conclusions

In this paper, we modify existing *meta-ElGamal* schemes introduced by *Horster*, which is based on the difficulty of discrete logarithm problems, for improving the "side-effects" of *Chaum*'s blind signature[10]. As a result of it, the message recovery fair blind signature scheme is also proposed using the properties of oblivious transfer protocol. We first have analyzed the model of blind signature that is providing the function of message recovery. Proposed fair blind signature scheme applies additional oblivious transfer protocol in the first stage of blind signature, which rise the overall performance even than the existing fair blind schemes[18,19]. Judge can publicly verify the two types of fairness on signed message if it is required.

We can combine this proposed scheme with the off-line electronic payment system using additional concepts such as counter based micropayment framework keeping an accurate account based on the ability of suggested message recovery function. As the recovered message will be generate the electronic cash in itself, we can apply countering methods on the balance in its account. As a results, message recovery scheme can be provide advanced electronic payment systems on the aspect of its computation and complexity especially in smart card based micropayment system.

References

1. W. Diffie, M. Hellman: New Directions in Cryptography, IEEE Transactions on Information Theory, Vol. IT-22, No. 6, (1976) 472–492
2. R. L. Rivest, A. Shamir, L. Adleman: A Method for Obtaining Digital Signatures and Public-Key Cryptosystems, Communication of the ACM, Vol. 21, No. 2, (1978) 120–126
3. D. Chaum, A. Fiat, M. Noar: Untraceable Electronic Cash, Advances in Cryptology - Crypto'88, Lecture Notes in Computer Science, Springer-Verlag, (1990) 319–327
4. S. Brands: An Efficient Off-line Electronic Cash System Based on the Representation Problem, Technical Report CS-R9323, CWI, (1993)
5. S. Brands.: Untraceable Off-line Cash in Wallets with Observers, Advances in Cryptology - Cryptology'93, Lecture Notes in Computer Science, Vol. 773, Springer-Verlag, (1994)
6. B. von Solms, D. Naccache: On Blind Signatures and Perfect Crimes, Computers ans Security, Vol. 11, No. 6, (1992) 581–583
7. E. F. Brickell, P. Gemmell, D. Kravitz: Trustee-based Tracing Extensions to Anonymous Cash and the Making of Anonymous Change, Symposium of Distributed Algorithms (SODA), (1995)
8. A. Fiat, A. Shamir: How to Prove Yourself: Practical Solutions of Identification and Signature Problems, Advances in Cryptology - Crypto'86, Lecture Notes in Computer Science, Vol. 263, Springer-Verlag, (1987)
9. T. ElGamal: A Public Key Cryptosystem and a Signature Scheme based on Discrete Logarithm, IEEE Transactions on Information Theory, Vol. IT-30, No. 4, (1985) 469–472
10. D. Chaum: Blind Signature for Untraceable Payments, Advances in Cryptology - Crypto'82, Lecture Notes in Computer Science, Springer-Verlag, (1982) 199-203

11. Patrick Horster, Holger Petersen: Meta Message Recovery and Meta Blind Signature Scheme Based on the Discrete Logarithm Problem and Their Applications, Advances in Cryptology - Asiacrypt'94, Lecture Notes in Computer Science, Springer-Verlag, (1994)
12. Patrick Horster, Markus Michels, Holger Petersen: Meta-ElGamal Signature Schemes, Proc. 2nd ACM Conference on Computer and Communications Security, Fairfax, Virginia, (1994)
13. Patrick Horster, Markus Michels, Holger Petersen: Efficient Blind Signature Scheme based on the Discrete Logarithm Problem, Technical Report TR-94-6-D, University of Technology Chemnitz-Zwichau, Dept. of Computer Science, (1994)
14. Patrick Horster, Markus Michels, Holger Petersen: Meta-Multisignature Scheme based on the Discrete Logarithm Problem, Technical Report TR-94-12-F, University of Technology Chemnitz-Zwichau, Dept. of Computer Science, (1994)
15. M. Rabin: How to Exchange Secrets by Oblivious Transfer, Technical Reports TR-81, Harvard Aiken Computation Laboratory, (1981)
16. Mihir Bellare, Silvio Micali: Non-Interactive Oblivious Transfer and Applications, Advances in Cryptology - Crypto'89, Lecture Notes in Computer Science, Vol. 435, Springer-Verlag, (1989)
17. S. Micali: Fair Cryptosystems, Technical Reports MIT/LCS/TR-579-b, (1993)
18. Markus Stadler, Jean-Marc Piveteau, Jan Camenisch: Fair Blind Signature, Advances in Cryptology - Eurocrypt'95, Lecture Notes in Computer Science, Vol. 921, Springer-Verlag, (1995)
19. Jan Camenisch, Jean-Marc Piveteau, Markus Stadler: An Efficient Electronic Payment System Protecting Privacy, Advances in Cryptology - Eurocrypt'94, Lecture Notes in Computer Science, Vol. 875, Springer-Verlag, (1994)
20. N. Asokan, Victor shoup, Michael Waidner: Optimistic Fair Exchange of Digital Signature, IBM Technical Report RZ 2973. (1997)
21. Holger Petersen, Guillaume Poupard: Efficient Scalable Fair Cash with Off-line Extortion Prevention, Technical Report LIENS-97-7, (1997)
22. Markus Stadler: Publicly Verifiable Secret Sharing, Advances in Cryptology - Eurocrypt'96, Lecture Notes in Computer Science, Springer-Verlag, (1995) 190–199
23. Alfred J. Menezed, Paul C. van Oorschot, Scott A. Vanstone (ed.): Handbook of Applied Cryptography, CRC Press. (1996)

On Quorum Controlled Asymmetric Proxy Re-encryption

Markus Jakobsson

Information Sciences Research Center, Bell Laboratories
Murray Hill, NJ 07974
markusj@research.bell-labs.com

Abstract. We present a scheme for quorum controlled asymmetric proxy re-encryption, with uses ranging from efficient key distribution for pay-tv to email applications. We prove that the scheme, which is based on El-Gamal encryption, leaks no information as long as there is no dishonest quorum of proxy servers. Of potential independent interest is a method providing publicly verifiable *translation certificates*, proving that the input and output encryptions correspond to the same plaintext message, without leaking any information about the plaintext to either the verifier or a subset of the servers of the prover. The size of the certificate is small, and independent of the number of prover servers.

Keywords: asymmetric proxy re-encryption, translation certificate, El Gamal encryption, quorum control, robustness, privacy.

1 Introduction

With an increasing importance of encryption methods for privacy and protection of business secrets, and with an increasing need for a flexible infrastrucure, we foresee the need for many new secure and flexible primitives extending the basic communication and encryption capabilities available today. One such primitive is *proxy re-encryption*, which was recently introduced by Blaze, Bleumer and Strauss [2]. Proxy re-encryption is a translation between ciphertexts from one encryption key to another encryption key. It can be used to forward encrypted messages without having to expose the cleartexts to the participants involved, a primitive with many potential commercial uses.

In *symmetric* proxy encryption, which was exhibited by Blaze, Bleumer and Strauss, the proxy (who is the entity performing the translation, and who is typically not a distributed entity) needs to know a function of the secret keys associated with both the incoming and outgoing transcripts. The proxy needs to be trusted not to collude with one of the participants holding these secret keys, or the other secret key can be derived. (This characterization has the same meaning as that of [2], in which no trust has to be placed in the proxy, but the two other participants need to trust each other.)

On the other hand, in *asymmetric* proxy re-encryption, it is not necessary for the proxy to any function of the secret key corresponding to the produced ciphertext, which is advantageous given that we often want to forward encrypted messages to parties who do not trust us with their secret key. In a quorum control setting, the proxy only needs to know the secret key corresponding to the incoming ciphertext. It is natural that the party whom the incoming ciphertext is for needs to trust the proxy to some extent, since the proxy controls how incoming messages are re-encrypted and forwarded. However, if the proxy is quorum controlled and the re-encryption is robust, then this party only needs to trust that there is no dishonest quorum of proxy servers.

In this paper, we demonstrate how to implement asymmetric proxy re-encryption, which was posed as an open problem in [2]. For security, the transformation is performed under quorum control: This guarantees that if there is no dishonest quorum, then the plaintext message whose encryption is being transformed is not revealed to the proxy servers. Our solution is efficient; allows tight control over actions (by the use of quorum cryptography); does not require any pre-computation phase to set up shared keys; and has a trust model appropriate for a variety of settings. We believe that such a mechanism may be very useful in many applications:

- It allows the proxy to transform encrypted messages to encryptions with a variety of different recipient public keys, to allow for categorization of the encryptions. The categorization may be performed either as a function of the transcripts and their origins, randomly (e.g., assigning an examiner to an electronically submitted patent), or as a function of time, and may be used to sort the encrypted messages according to priority or security clearance. A practical and concrete example is that you want somebody to be able to read your email while you are on vacation, but you do not want to force the senders of the messages to have to know that the messages are being re-routed. In a situation like this, a symmetric model is inappropriate. Also, some form of control is desirable, guaranteeing that the messages are being handled according to the instructions.
- It allows more efficient communication to a large number of recipients that are physically clustered around the proxy; the sender would only need to send *one* encryption, along with an authenticated list of recipients. This may prove very useful for pay-tv, general multi-cast, and related applications.
- Last but not least, we believe that asymmetric proxy encryption may become a useful building block in the design of secure and efficient multi-party protocols.

A partial result of potential independent interest is a non-interactive proof that the correct translation between encryptions was performed, i.e., that the incoming and outgoing encryptions indeed encrypt the same message. The transcript, which we call a *translation certificate* is publicly verifiable, is compact (using standard[1] security parameters, it is a mere 396 bytes long, independently of the number of provers), and does not leak any information about the plaintext to verifiers or to a subset of the provers.

---

[1] We use $|p| = 1024$, $|q| = 160$.

Our techniques draw on ideas used in the work on proactive security (e.g, [7, 9, 10]), on methods for undeniable signatures (e.g., [3, 4]), Schnorr signatures [14], and methods for information-theoretical secret sharing [12].

Outline: We start in section 2 by reviewing related work. We then discuss the requirements on our scheme in section 3. In section 4, we then present our basic scheme for proxy re-encryption, followed in section 5 by a protocol for generating translation certificates. We end by stating and proving claims in section 7.

2 Review

Public and Secret Information: Let p, q be primes such that $p = 2q + 1$, and g be a generator of G_p. The proxy servers share a secret key x_1 using a (k, n) threshold scheme (see [15, 11]); their corresponding public key is $y_1 = g^{x_1} \bmod p$. (Onwards, we assume all arithmetic to be modulo p where applicable, unless otherwise stated.) Likewise, the recipient has a secret key x_2 with a corresponding public key $y_2 = g^{x_2}$.

ElGamal: Our protocol uses ElGamal encryption [6]: To encrypt a value[2] m using the public key y, a value $\gamma \in_u Z_q$ is picked uniformly at random, and the pair $(a, b) = (my^\gamma, g^\gamma)$ calculated. Thus, (a, b) is the encryption of m. In order to decrypt this and obtain m, $m = a/b^x$ is calculated.

The Decision Diffie-Hellman Assumption: Let $p = 2q + 1$, for primes p and q, and let m, g be generators of a subgroup of order q. Then, the pairs (m, m^x, g, g^x) and (m, m^r, g, g^x) are indistinguishable, for random and unknown values $r, x \in Z_q$, $m, g \in G_p$.

3 Preliminaries

An entity with public key y_1 assigns a proxy, agrees with the proxy on rules for re-encryption, and distributes shares of his secret key x_1 to the servers of the proxy. Later, the proxy receives a transcript E_1, which is an ElGamal encryption of a message m using public key y_1. The proxy produces and outputs a transcript E_2, which is an ElGamal encryption of the same message m, but using a given public key y_2, which is chosen according to the rules set by the entity associated with y_1. We note the re-encryption method can be extended to long messages by replacing m by a symmetric key used for encryption of a long message m_{long} whose ciphertext is passed along unaltered to the entity associated with y_2.

The transformation is controlled by the use of quorum actions. Informally, the requirements on our scheme are:

1. *Correctness:* Any quorum Q of proxy servers, sharing a secret key x_1, will be able to perform the above re-encryption.

---

[2] Here, $m = (\frac{M}{p})M$ for an original message $M \in [1 \dots \frac{p-1}{2}]$, where $(\frac{M}{p})$ is the Jacobi symbol of M.

2. *Robustness:* If any participant in the transformation protocol would output incorrect transcripts, then this will be detected by all honest participants. The protocol will allow the honest participants to determine what participants cheated, and to substitute these.

3. *Public Verifiability:* Anybody must be able to verify that the correct transformation was performed, without having or recieving knowledge of any secret information. The corresponding proof, the *translation certificate*, must be compact and be verifiable without interaction.

4. *Asymmetry:* The proxy servers must need no information about the secret key x_2 corresponding to the receiver's public key y_2 in order to perform the computation, and the receiver will need no information about x_1 or y_1 in order to decrypt E_2.

5. *Privacy:* The proxy re-encryption (including the generation of the translation certificate, and other robustness mechanisms) does not leak any information about m to any set of proxy servers smaller than a quorum.

In section 7, we formalize these requirements and prove that our proposed scheme satisfies the same.

4 Gradual and Simultaneous Proxy Re-Encryption

The concept of our solution is to use *gradual* and *simultaneous* translation of transcripts. The translation is called gradual, since it is performed by quorum action, and each server's contribution to the computation is only a partial translation. We call it simultaneous since each server performs one partial decryption *and* one partial encryption, outputting such gradual re-encryptions without the cleartext ever being exposed. This approach makes all the partial translations simultaneous in the sense that no result is obtained until all the portions are accounted for.

We first consider a non-robust version of the proxy re-encryption, and then add on a proof to guarantee robustness.

Let (a_1, b_1) be an ElGamal encryption of a message m w.r.t. a public key y_1, and let x_1 be the corresponding secret key, which is shared by the proxy servers using a threshold scheme. The proxy servers wish to compute the ElGamal encryption (a_2, b_2) of m w.r.t. the public key y_2. They wish not to expose m to any set of dishonest proxy servers (or any other set of servers); according to our assumptions, they do not know the secret key x_2 of y_2.

For simplicity of denotation, we assume that x_{1j} is the Lagrange-weighted secret key (using the methods in [11]) of proxy server j w.r.t. a given active quorum Q; $y_{1j} = g^{x_{1j}}$ is the corresponding public key share. The servers in the quorum perform the following computation:

1. Server j selects a random value δ_j uniformly at random from Z_q, and computes $(c_j, d_j) = (b_1^{-x_{1j}} y_2^{\delta_j}, g^{\delta_j})$. This pair is sent to the other proxy servers.

2. The servers (or alternatively, a non-trusted gateway) compute the pair $(a_2, b_2) = (a_1 \prod_{j \in Q} c_j, \prod_{j \in Q} d_j)$. The pair (a_2, b_2) is output.

The above protocol for proxy re-encryption is made robust by use of translation certificates.

5 Generating the Translation Certificate

We want to produce a translation certificate, i.e., a non-interactive proof that $a_1/b_1{}^{x_1} = a_2/b_2{}^{x_2}$, or in other words, a proof that (a_1, b_1) and (a_2, b_2) are encryptions of the same message, for secret decryption keys x_1 resp. x_2 of the two encryptions. The certificate must not leak any information to the verifier or to any non-quorum of prover servers. Also, it must not require knowledge of the second secret key, x_2, since this is not assumed to be known by the prover. Finally, it must be publicly verifiable. Our solution will produce such certificates that are short, and whose length does not depend on the number of provers.

More specifically, we need to prove that $(a_2, b_2) = (a_1 b_1{}^{-x_1} y_2{}^\delta, g^\delta)$, for $y_1 = g^{x_1}$. In the proof, we will use a new generator, h, whose discrete log w.r.t. g is not known to any set of parties. We will also use a hash function $hash$, which is assumed to be collision free, and whose output is in Z_q. The proof has two components: One proving knowledge of the secret keys corresponding to two "public keys", the other proving that the output has the claimed relation to these two public keys. The version we show first is, for clarity, the single-prover version. We then explain how this is extended to a distributed prover, and how cheating provers are detected and traced.

In order to increase the readability of the protocol, we will rename certain variables to obtain a more uniform naming. To this extent, we will use the variable names $(z_1, z_2, w_1, w_2, \sigma, \mu_1, \mu_2)$ to mean $(y_1, b_2{}^{-1}, x_1, -\delta, a_2/a_1, b_1, y_2)$. Thus, wanting to prove that $a_2 = a_1 b_1{}^{-x_1} y_2{}^\delta$, for $(y_1, b_2) = (g^{x_1}, g^\delta)$ is the same as wanting to prove that $\sigma = \mu_1{}^{w_1} \mu_2{}^{w_2}$ for $(z_1, z_2) = (g^{w_1}, g^{w_2})$.

Initialization:
P computes and outputs $(\bar{z}_1, \bar{z}_2) = (h^{w_1}, h^{w_2})$.

Part I:

1. P selects $\alpha \in_u Z_q$, and computes $(\mathcal{G}, \mathcal{H}) = (hash([g^\alpha]_p), hash([h^\alpha]_p))$.
2. P computes a pair of challenges $(\epsilon_1, \epsilon_2) = (hash(\mathcal{G}, \mathcal{H}, 1), hash(\mathcal{G}, \mathcal{H}, 2))$.
3. P computes the response $\delta = [\alpha - \epsilon_1 w_1 - \epsilon_2 w_2]_q$. He outputs $(\mathcal{G}, \mathcal{H}, \delta)$.

Part II:

1. P selects $\beta_1, \beta_2 \in_u Z_q$, and computes $(\mathcal{F}, \mathcal{M}) = (hash([g^{\beta_1} h^{\beta_2}]_p), hash([\mu_1{}^{\beta_1} \mu_2{}^{\beta_2}]_p))$.
2. P computes a challenge $e = hash(\mathcal{F}, \mathcal{M})$.
3. P computes the response $(d_1, d_2) = ([\beta_1 - ew_1]_q, [\beta_2 - ew_2]_q)$. He outputs $(\mathcal{F}, \mathcal{M}, d_1, d_2)$.

The translation certificate is the transcript $(\bar{z}_1, \bar{z}_2, \mathcal{G}, \mathcal{H}, \delta, \mathcal{F}, \mathcal{M}, d_1, d_2)$. The proof can be distributively generated, with tracing of dishonest provers, as shown in the Appendix. It is verified by the verifier V as follows:

Verification:

1. V computes $(\epsilon_1, \epsilon_2) = (hash(\mathcal{G}, \mathcal{H}, 1), hash(\mathcal{G}, \mathcal{H}, 2))$, and accepts part I iff $\mathcal{G} = hash([g^{\delta} z_1{}^{\epsilon_1} z_2{}^{\epsilon_2}]_p)$ and $\mathcal{H} = hash([h^{\delta} \bar{z}_1{}^{\epsilon_1} \bar{z}_2{}^{\epsilon_2}]_p)$.
2. V computes $e = hash(\mathcal{F}, \mathcal{M})$, and accepts part II iff $\mathcal{F} = hash([g^{d_1} h^{d_2} (z_1 \bar{z}_2)^e]_p)$ and $\mathcal{M} = hash([\mu_1{}^{d_1} \mu_2{}^{d_2} \sigma^e]_p)$.
3. If V accepted both part I and part II, then he outputs accept, otherwise he rejects.

6 Claims

The protocol for generation of translation certificates is *correct* (lemma 1,) *sound* (lemma 2,) and *zero-knowledge in the random oracle model* (lemma 3.)

The protocol for robust proxy re-encryption satisfies the previously stated requirements: it satisfies *correctness* (theorem 1,) *robustness* (theorem 2,) *asymmetry* (theorem 3,) and *privacy* (theorem 4.)

These lemmae and theorems are proven in section 7.

7 Proofs of Claims

Lemma 1: The protocol generating translation certificates is *correct*, i.e., if the prover is honest, then the verifier will accept with an overwhelming probability.

Proof of Lemma 1:
We assume that the prover is honest. Four equations have to be satisfied in order for the verifier to accept.
1: $g^{\delta} z_1{}^{\epsilon_1} z_2{}^{\epsilon_2} = g^{\alpha - \epsilon_1 w_1 - \epsilon_2 w_2} g^{w_1 \epsilon_1} g^{w_2 \epsilon_2} = g^{\alpha} = hash^{-1}(\mathcal{G})$.
2: $h^{\delta} \bar{z}_1{}^{\epsilon_1} \bar{z}_2{}^{\epsilon_2} = h^{\alpha - \epsilon_1 w_1 - \epsilon_2 w_2} h^{w_1 \epsilon_1} h^{w_2 \epsilon_2} = h^{\alpha} = hash^{-1}(\mathcal{H})$.
3: $g^{d_1} h^{d_2} (z_1 \bar{z}_2)^e = g^{\beta_1 - e w_1} h^{\beta_2 - e w_2} (g^{w_1} h^{w_2})^e = g^{\beta_1} h^{\beta_2} = hash^{-1}(\mathcal{F})$.
4: $\mu_1{}^{d_1} \mu_2{}^{d_2} \sigma^e = \mu_1{}^{\beta_1 - e w_1} \mu_2{}^{\beta_2 - e w_2} (\mu_1{}^{w_1} \mu_2{}^{w_2})^e = \mu_1{}^{\beta_1} \mu_2{}^{\beta_2} = hash^{-1}(\mathcal{M})$.
By the definition of $\mathcal{G}, \mathcal{H}, \mathcal{F}, \mathcal{M}$, these relations hold. □

It can easily be seen that the robust and distributed version of the protocol for generating translation certificates is correct if the single-server version is.

Lemma 2: The protocol for generating translation certificates is *sound*: If a participant has a non-negligible probability of answering three[3] or more challenges

---

[3] Normally, soundness is defined as the claimed relationship must hold if the prover can answer *two* queries with a non-negligible probability. However, since this is only to bound the probability of a verifier accepting an incorrect proof, any polynomial number works.

correctly, then this participant can be used as a black-box to extract the secret key for decryption.

Proof of Lemma 2: *(Sketch)*
In this proof, we assume that it is not feasible to find hash collisions. Then, the only time the verifier will acccept is if $g^\alpha = g^\delta z_1{}^{\epsilon_1} z_2{}^{\epsilon_2}$ and $h^\alpha = h^\delta \overline{z}_1{}^{\epsilon_1} \overline{z}_2{}^{\epsilon_2}$. We now further assume that the challenges are randomly generated. We consider the two parts of the proof independently:

Part I: Let (ϵ_1, ϵ_2), $(\epsilon_1', \epsilon_2')$ and $(\epsilon_1'', \epsilon_2'')$ be three different pairs of challenges, and let δ, δ', and δ'' be the corresponding correct responses. Then, given that we have three equations for these, with common choices of α, and we only have two unknowns (w_1 and w_2), we can solve the equations for these. Therefore, if the prover can answer three or more challenges with a non-negligible probability, he must know w_1 and w_2.

Part II: Using a similar argumant to that above, we see that if the prover can answer two different challenges e and e', then he can solve the response equations for w_1 and w_2.

For these two cases, therefore, being able to answer three or more possible challenges out of all possible challenges can be used to compute the secret key w_1, which corresponds to the secret key for decryption. $\square$

Lemma 3: The interactive scheme for proving valid exponentiation is *zero-knowledge in the random oracle model.*

This can be seen using a standard argument, by turning the protocol into an interactive procol, where the challenges are randomly chosen instead of chosen as functions of previously seen transcripts. If the challenges are committed to at the beginning of the protocol, then a rewinding technique will allow a simulator to produce the expected outputs after having seen the challenges.

Theorem 1: The transformation scheme scheme satisfies *correctness*, i.e., if E_1 is an encryption of m w.r.t. y_1, then the output of the scheme will be E_2, an encryption of m w.r.t. y_2, for a value y_2 chosen by the proxy.

Proof of Theorem 1: *(Sketch)*
Assume that $(a_1, b_1) = (my_1{}^\gamma, g^\gamma)$, i.e., (a_1, b_1) is a valid ElGamal encryption of a message m w.r.t. the proxy's public key y_1. We have that $(c_j, d_j) = (b_1{}^{-x_{1j}} y_2{}^{\delta_j}, g^{\delta_j})$, for an already Lagrange-weighted (w.r.t the quorum Q) secret key share x_{1j} of proxy server j, and a random number δ_j. Then, we have that $(a_2, b_2) = (a_1 \prod_{j \in Q} c_j, \prod_{j \in Q} d_j)$. We therefore have that $a_2 = a_1 b_1{}^{-x_1} y_2{}^\delta$, for $\delta = \sum_{j \in Q} \delta_j \, mod \, q$, and $x_1 = \sum_{j \in Q} x_{1j} \, mod \, q$. Recall that $y_1 = g^{x_1}$ and that $a_1/b_1{}^{x_1}$ is the plaintext m corresponding to the ciphertext (a_1, b_1) w.r.t. the public key y_1. Thus, $a_2 = my_2{}^\delta$, according to the decryption algorithm for ElGamal encryption. Since $b_2 = \prod_{j \in Q} d_j = g^\delta$, we have that (a_2, b_2) is a valid ElGamal encryption of the message m w.r.t. the public key y_2, and thus, the transformation protocol is correct. $\square$

It follows automatically that the protocol that is made robust by the added use of translation certificates must be correct if the non-robust version is correct.

Theorem 2: The scheme satisfies *robustness*, i.e., if any participating proxy server outputs a transcript that would result in an incorrect end result, then the honest participants will detect this, and will be able to determine the cheating server's identity.

This follows from the soundness of the translation certificates, which was shown in Lemma 2: Only correct outputs (corresponding to valid re-encryptions) will have correct translation certificate. If an invalid translation certificate is found, the individual portions of this certificate can be verified for validity. This can be done without interaction. An invalid portion (w.r.t. the public key of the participant generating it) corresponds to a cheater.

Theorem 3: The scheme satisfies *asymmetry*.

This is obvious given the specification of the protocol; the proxy servers never need any secret information corresponding to the public key y_2 of the intended recipient, nor does the recipient need any secret information apart from this secret key in order to decrypt the received transcript.

Theorem 4: The scheme satisfies *privacy*: Let A be a set of proxy servers not containing a quorum. A can simulate transcripts such that these cannot be distinguished by A from transcripts of the transformation protocol, other than with a negligible probability.

Proof of Theorem 4: *(Sketch)*
We consider the interactive version of the translation certificate herein, to make the argument simple. Let E_2 be a value that cannot be distinguished by A from a valid re-encryption (according to the given public keys) of the input E_1. (For ElGamal encryption, it is commonly believed that any pair of randomly chosen elements from G_p may be chosen as such a value E_2, given no partial knowledge of the corresponding decryption key x_2.) Let us assume that the secret key x_2 needed to decrypt the transformed encryption is not known by any proxy servers. Focusing on the non-robust transformation protocol only, one can then show that the view of a set of proxy servers not containing a quorum can be simulated, following the (somewhat space-consuming) method used in [10] for proving the simulability of two related protocols, namely those for proactive key update and for distributed signature generation. The same result will be obtained when such a protocol is interleaved (a constant and low number of times) with a protocol that is zero-knowledge. Therefore, the robust transformation protocol has the property that a partial view (corresponding to the views of a set of proxy servers not containing a quorum) is simulable in p-time, and the simulated transcripts cannot be distinguished (by the same set of proxy servers) from real transcripts. This argument holds for a serial concatenation of protocol executions (following the proof method in [10],) and so, is valid also when cheating servers corrupt the protocol and force a restart of the same.
In more detail, the simulator will compute transcripts according to the inputs given by A, and select transcripts for the appropriate distributions from the proxy servers not controlled by A. This is done so that the resulting output is E_2.

The simulator then simulates the zero-knowledge proofs for the honest servers (i.e., those not controlled by A), giving transcripts showing that these transcripts are valid and correspond to the previously set outputs of these servers. We note that it will not be possible for A to distinguish transcripts in a simulation where a *false* statement is "proven" from transcripts from a simulation of a *true statement* (and therefore also not from real transcripts.) If this were not the case, then it would not be hard to decide whether a given input is valid or not, without the interaction of the prover, which in turn would violate our computational assumption. □

Acknowledgements

Many thanks to Matt Blaze and Daniel Bleichenbacher for helpful comments.

References

1. M. Bellare, P. Rogaway, "Random Oracles are Practical: a paradigm for designing efficient protocols," 1st ACM Conference on Computer and Communications Security, pp. 62–73, 1993.
2. M. Blaze, G. Bleumer, M. Strauss, "Divertible Protocols and Atomic Proxy Cryptography," Eurocrypt '98, pp. 127–144
3. D. Chaum, H. Van Antwerpen, "Undeniable Signatures," Crypto '89, pp. 212–216
4. D. Chaum, "Zero-Knowledge Undeniable Signatures," Eurocrypt '90, pp. 458-464
5. A. De Santis, Y. Desmedt, Y. Frankel, and M. Yung, "How to Share a Function Securely," STOC '94, pp. 522-533
6. T. ElGamal "A Public-Key Cryptosystem and a Signature Scheme Based on Discrete Logarithms," Crypto '84, pp. 10-18
7. Y. Frankel, P. Gemmell, P. MacKenzie, M. Yung, "Proactive RSA," Proc. of CRYPTO '97, pp. 440-454
8. S. Goldwasser and S. Micali, "Probabilistic Encryption," J. Comp. Sys. Sci. 28, pp 270-299, 1984.
9. A. Herzberg, S. Jarecki, H. Krawczyk, M. Yung, "Proactive Secret Sharing, or How to Cope with Perpetual Leakage," Crypto '95, pp. 339-352
10. A. Herzberg, M. Jakobsson, S. Jarecki, H. Krawczyk, M. Yung, "Proactive Public Key and Signature Systems," Proceedings of the 4th ACM Conference on Computer and Communications Security, 1997, pp. 100-110
11. T. P. Pedersen. A threshold cryptosystem without a trusted party. In D. W. Davies, editor, *Advances in Cryptology — EUROCRYPT '91*, volume 547 of *Lecture Notes in Computer Science*, pp. 522 – 526. Springer-Verlag, 1991.
12. T. P. Pedersen. "Non-interactive and information-theoretic secure verifiable secret sharing," Crypto '91, pp. 129–140
13. D. Pointcheval, J. Stern, "Security Proofs for Signature Schemes," Eurocrypt '96, pp. 387–398
14. C. P. Schnorr, "Efficient Signature Generation for Smart Cards," Advances in Cryptology - Proceedings of Crypto '89, pp. 239-252
15. A. Shamir, "How to Share a Secret," Communications of the ACM, Vol. 22, 1979, pp. 612-613

16. D. Tygar, B. Yee, "Strongbox: A System for Self Securing Programs," CMU Computer Science: 25th Anniversary Commemorative, Addison-Wesley, 1991
17. B. Yee, D. Tygar, "Secure Coprocessors in Electronic Commerce Applications," Proceedings of the First USENIX Workshop on Electronic Commerce, New York, New York, July, 1995
18. B. Yee, "Using Secure Coprocessors," Ph.D. Thesis, Carnegie Mellon University, CMU-CS-94-149, 1994

A Distributed Generation of Translation Certificates

Initialization:

$P_i, i \in Q$ has a (already Lagrange weighted w.r.t. Q) pair (w_{1i}, w_{2i}). P_i computes and outputs $(\overline{z}_{1i}, \overline{z}_{2i}) = (h^{w_{1i}}, h^{w_{2i}})$.

Part I:

1. $P_i, i \in Q$ selects $\alpha_i \in_u Z_q$, computes and publishes $(G_i, H_i) = (g^{\alpha_i}, h^{\alpha_i})$. P_i computes $(G, H) = (\prod_{j \in Q} G_j, \prod_{j \in Q} H_j)$, and $(\mathcal{G}, \mathcal{H}) = (hash(G), hash(H))$.
2. $P_i, i \in Q$ computes a pair of challenges $(\epsilon_1, \epsilon_2) = (hash(\mathcal{G}, \mathcal{H}, 1), hash(\mathcal{G}, \mathcal{H}, 2))$.
3. $P_i, i \in Q$ computes and outputs $\delta_i = [\alpha_i - \epsilon_1 w_{1i} - \epsilon_2 w_{2i}]_q$. P_i computes $\delta = \sum_{j \in Q} \delta_j$. The triple $(\mathcal{G}, \mathcal{H}, \delta)$ is output.

Part II:

1. $P_i i \in Q$ selects $\beta_{1i}, \beta_{2i} \in_u Z_q$, computes and outputs $(F_i, M_i) = (g^{\beta_1} h^{\beta_2}, \mu_1^{\beta_1} \mu_2^{\beta_2})$. P_i computes $(F, M) = (\prod_{j \in Q} F_j, \prod_{j \in Q} M_j)$, and $(\mathcal{F}, \mathcal{M}) = (hash(F), hash(M))$.
2. $P_i, i \in Q$ computes a challenge $e = hash(\mathcal{F}, \mathcal{M})$.
3. $P_i, i \in Q$ computes and outputs $(d_{1i}, d_{2i}) = ([\beta_{1i} - ew_{1i}]_q, [\beta_{2i} - ew_{2i}]_q)$. P_i computes $(d_1, d_2) = (\sum_{j \in Q} d_{1j}, \sum_{j \in Q} d_{2j})$. The quadruple $(\mathcal{F}, \mathcal{M}, d_1, d_2)$ is output.

Verification and Tracing (by provers):

1. P_i verifies that $\mathcal{G} = hash([g^\delta z_1^{\epsilon_1} z_2^{\epsilon_2}]_p)$, $\mathcal{H} = hash([h^\delta \overline{z}_1^{\epsilon_1} \overline{z}_2^{\epsilon_2}]_p)$, $\mathcal{F} = hash([g^{d_1} h^{d_2} (z_1 \overline{z}_2)^e]_p)$ and $\mathcal{M} = hash([\mu_1^{d_1} \mu_2^{d_2} \sigma^e]_p)$. If this holds, P_i accepts the transcript, otherwise he proceeds:
2. For all $j \in Q$, P_j is replaced if one of the following equations is not satisfied: $G_j = g^{\delta_j} z_{1j}^{\epsilon_1} z_{2j}^{\epsilon_2}$, $H_j = h^{\delta_j} \overline{z}_{1j}^{\epsilon_1} \overline{z}_{2j}^{\epsilon_2}$, $F_j = g^{d_{1j}} h^{d_{2j}} (z_{1j} \overline{z}_{2j})^e$, $M_j = \mu_1^{d_{1j}} \mu_2^{d_{2j}} \sigma^e$.

The generated transcripts are identical to those of the single-server case, and thus, the verification (by the verifier) is identical to what was previously presented.

Mini-Cash: A Minimalistic Approach to E-Commerce

Markus Jakobsson

Information Sciences Research Center, Bell Laboratories
Murray Hill, NJ 07974
markusj@research.bell-labs.com

Abstract. By introducing a new e-commerce paradigm - that of *disposable anonymous accounts* - we are able to reduce storage requirements, while protecting against strong attacks on the system, and keeping computaional requirements low. Our proposed scheme reduces storage costs of payers and merchants to the lowest theoretically possible, offers users computational (but not revokable) privacy, and protects against the bank robbery attack. Furthermore, by being practically implementable as a smart card payment scheme, it avoids the threats of viral attacks on users. The scheme allows the notion of "pre-paid" cards by not requiring a link to the identity of the card owner.

1 Introduction

Current research in the area of electronic commerce pushes the knowledge frontier forward in two important directions, which to some extent represent the *theory* and *practice* of payment schemes. The first direction increases the protection against attacks on the system, thereby protecting users against monetary losses and losses of system properties such as privacy. The second direction decreases the hardware and communication costs of maintaining and running the system. General-purpose computers are powerful enough to accomodate as well highly efficient as very *in*efficient schemes. Still, this second direction of finding efficiency improvements is of significance, especially so since the risk of viral attacks makes special-purpose computers (such as smart cards) more attractive than traditional computer systems as payment platforms.

With the considerable attention given to electronic commerce, both of these frontiers have moved considerably since Chaum, Fiat and Naor [8] introduced the first cryptographic payment protocol in 1988. Lately, any attempt on improvement has turned into a very delicate balancing act in order not to cause the loss of some desireable properties with the advancement of others.

In this paper, we introduce a scheme that protects against the strongest known attack (namely the *bank robbery attack*, in which an attacker obtains the secret key of the currency issuing agency). At the same time, our scheme drastically reduces the hardware costs compared to previously proposed schemes. Although our scheme does require payments to be cleared using an on-line technique, which is less beneficial in terms of communication than an off-line scheme, we argue that *practically* it is, in fact, not a step backwards. This is the case given the current trend in banking, suggesting that only on-line payment schemes (and hybrid schemes such as [20, 39], which are on-line with a certain probability) will be considered by banks, in order to minimize the potential losses made possible by global and instantaneous commerce capabilities[1].

Previously, the bank robbery attack has only been possible to prevent in schemes with revokable anonymity. The system we introduce demonstrates that the same level of system security in fact can be achieved without the ability for some entities to revoke anonymity. Positive aspects of not implementing revokability are an increased level of comfort for some users, and a lowering of computational and storage costs. On the negative side, the lack of revokability potentially opens up for attacks such as blackmail and money laundry. These attacks, however, are to some extent socially unacceptable versions of otherwise legal payment transactions, which makes them difficult to avoid at any rate. Such attacks may therefore require other outside mechanisms to detect and avoid.

As a result of not requiring revokability to protect against the system attacks, our system *allows* the distribution of entities, such as the bank, but does not *require* it. Yet another advantage of our scheme is its very simple construction, making it easy to analyze and to prove secure. Furthermore, our scheme is fairly flexible in that it can be implemented using a wide variety of security primitives, which is an advantage in that its security – and therefore also existence – does not rely on the availability and soundness of a small number of components.

What we believe is the biggest advantage of our scheme, though, is its minimal storage requirements. Our proposed scheme drastically reduces the storage requirements of users (both payers and merchants) to the theoretically lowest possible, namely to a constant size storage of a secret key (except for the temporary storage needed to perform the transactions). A payment scheme with smaller memory complexity is not feasible, since such a scheme would not allow the distinction of different parties from each other. For practical reasons, we add a logarithmic-sized storage indicating the amount of money held by the device; we note, however, that this is not necessary for the scheme to work. We also add storage to implement access control, e.g., PIN control. Our low memory requirements allow the affordable employment of specialized devices, such as smart cards, and their distribution to the masses. Such devices also have the definitive advantage of not being easy targets of viruses, which pose a significant threat to the security of any system running on a multi-purpose computer.

By not being linked to the identity of the owner, the payment devices can be sold as "pre-paid" cards, much like phone cards are. This is likely to increase

---

[1] The ability to drastically overspend coins during very short periods of time, whereas not necessarily appealing to the average user (who knows that the bank will detect the overspending and identify him/her as the overspender), is still not a desireable property of a payment scheme. The reason is that it makes the scheme vulnerable to terrorist attacks (causing inflation by agressive overspending) and makes the monetary losses incurred by the loss (and claimed loss) of payment devices unnecessarily high.

the user acceptance of the payment scheme, and open up a bigger market by providing for wider distribution channels.

Outline. After presenting related work (section 2), we introduce the model (section 3), briefly state some definitions (section 4), after which we state our requirements on the scheme (section 5). We then explain our architecture (section 6) and introduce our solution (section 7). We prove our scheme to satisfy the listed requirements in the Appendix.

2 Related Work

Our scheme is conceptally related to the coin paradigm, as introduced by Chaum, Fiat and Naor [8], and later used in several other schemes. It is also related to account-based schemes, such as [16]. In fact, it is probably best described as being a hybrid of the two: The coins, which are stored by the bank and accessed by users to perform transfers, can be seen as "disposable anonymous accounts". When a coin is spent, the corresponding account is removed, and a new account is created (corresponding to a new coin). The payee is given access rights to this new anonymous account, and the payment has been completed. Using this amount of detail, our scheme is therefore very similar to the work by Simon [30], where the underlying idea of bank-kept coins was introduced.

Just as in the pioneering work of Chaum et al., we work in the *on-line* payment model. This model has been abandoned for a long period of time, and much effort has been spent in developing off-line payment schemes, but now, the on-line paradigm is seeing a renaissance again, given the commercial preference for it.

We also to some degree revisit these early schemes in terms of privacy, as privacy cannot be revoked in our scheme. We offer what we call *chain privacy*. Think of the beginning of a chain as the point where a user identifies himself to the bank and transfers money from a traditional account into our scheme. The end of the same chain corresponds to the point where a user in our scheme transfers funds out to a traditional account. Chain privacy means that the bank will know the length of the chain, where each payment corresponds to one link of the chain, and will know the identities of the end-points, but will not be able to correlate the identities of the users to payments that are in between the endpoints. If the transfers are done from or to cash, we think of this as a chain with anonymous end-points, in which case the bank will know even less. Practically, and for chains of sufficient length, this type of privacy will appear to users as very similar to the privacy offered by early schemes, i.e., perfect privacy. This is the case since, like all early schemes, our protocol offers users privacy even against a collusion of all other entities (to the extent that other users can limit the number of possible guesses a bank has to make in order to learn how a payment was made, by revealing all their private informaton to the bank). Again, this is very similar to the scheme by Simon [30], although he did not analyze the privacy properties in detail.

A strong reason why perfect privacy had to give way to revokable privacy in recent work (e.g., [4, 6, 17, 18, 19, 16]) is that the latter model allowed the strengthening of the attack model. In a setting with revokable privacy, it is possible to render attacks such as blackmail and bank robbery meaningless, by allowing privacy and funds to be revoked. (This is not possible for the early work granting perfect privacy.) In the bank robbery attack, introduced in [17], the attacker obtains the secret key of the bank and trustee, allowing him to mint money himself. This attack was prevented against in [17, 19] by ascertaining that all coins can *always* be identified, no matter how they were produced. In [16], a different approach was taken, in which knowledge of the secret keys does not allow the attacker to produce funds – only trace them. In our scheme, we prevent against the bank robbery attack in a way that is similar to that of [16], in the sense that we are making knowledge of the bank secret keys useless to an attacker.

One main difference between our method and previous work is where the coin representation is being kept. In all work of this genre, except for [30, 16], a significant portion of the transcripts equaling funds were kept by the users (as a secret key for an unspent coin, and as a signature for a spent coin). In [16], the users only store a secret key needed to sign encrypted purchase orders, and the bank kept the other data. We take a similar approach in this work. We let the bank store information corresponding to funds, leaving the users with only having to store a secret key needed to access the data stored by the bank. Shifting the storage requirements in this manner not only eases the load on the user devices, but also allows for the much stronger attack model that we implement. Our result differs from [16] structurally by not requiring distributed control of the bank functionality, and functionally by crediting the account of the merchants immediately a payment has been performed. This also allows the introduction of new functionality by the use of challenge semantics.

As previously mentioned, our scheme is a very close relative to the scheme by Simon [30]. One difference is that we do not assume a secure communication channel. In Simon's scheme, there is a brief moment, inbetween the debiting and crediting of accounts, when a coin reverts to the bank and does not belong to either payer or payee. In principle, this makes the scheme susceptible to fraud, embezzlement and system failures. Also, we allow for evidence of transactions to be provided (in our construction, the secret access key is not known by the bank), and we elaborate more carefully what privacy is obtained from the scheme. More importantly, we investigate methods to compress the data to be kept by the payment devices, allowing these to hold only a constant sized (in the numbers of coins) secret seed, although for convenience, balance information would probably be desireable to be kept as well. In comparison, Simon's scheme uses a representation of each coin to be stored by its owner. Moreover, our scheme is contrasted to Simon's, which, by not using signatures, limits computational costs, but at the same time also reduces the functionality of the resulting scheme.

Technically, our work bears some resemblance to micro-payment schemes (e.g., [20, 21, 29, 35]). These allow a user to spend a coin representation in small steps by sending the merchant transcripts that are computed as incremental hashes of a seed. Similarly, we maintain low storage costs for user devices by letting these store only a seed and counters, from which payment transcripts can be computed during a transaction. However, our scheme differs conceptually from published micro-payment schemes in that we require the bank to be on-line, and that we offer increased versatility and security.

During the intensive period of research on payment schemes over the last ten years, a multitude of properties have been proposed. One of these is divisibility (e.g., [26, 17]). In our setting, we do not provide for divisibility of coins. However, this property was mainly required to battle the considerable costs of a large and diverse wallet in the original coin model. As we significantly limit storage requirements, we also limit the need for coin divisibility. However, coin divisibility also has the advantage of reduced communication requirements. We suggest *another* possible method to reduce the communication requirements of several simultaneous coins. An advantage of not allowing divisibility is a slight improvement of privacy related issues, which suffer both with divisibility and the related notion of k-spendability [2, 10] (the notion of being able to spend a coin up to a fix k number of times).

3 Model

Users. We have three main types of protocol participants, *payers*, *merchants*, and banks. One entity may first act as a payer (when making a payment) and later act as a merchant (when receiving a payment). For simplicity, we call anybody making a payment a payer, and anybody receiving a payment a merchant. The bank keeps account information and transfer funds between accounts. A fourth type of entity is the *issuer*, who manufactures and/or distributes the computational devices corresponding to the payers and the merchants. The last type of participant is the *interface*, which shows the sum to be added or subtracted from the card connected, and is used for human identification to the payment device. The interface may be part of the user payment device.

Trust. All users trust the bank not to steal, i.e., trusts the bank not to cancel or fail to create accounts that should be active according to the protocol description. All users trust the issuer to produce payment devices that follow the protocol. If the device is sold to the user with a seed installed, then the user trusts the issuer (for his privacy and security) not to use this seed in any computation, but to forget it after installing it. Similarly, if the card is sold to the user with funds on it, the user trusts the issuer not to steal, i.e., he trusts the issuer that the payment device indeed has access rights to the claimed sum. Finally, if an interface is used, the users trust the interface not to move a different sum from the payment device than the human user agreed to. The interface is also trusted not to store or use the PIN, or any other identifying information used for human access control to the payment device.

4   Definitions

A *payment chain* is a sequence of links, each one of them corresponding to a *transaction*, or a group of transactions that are known or very likely to be made by one particular device (i.e., intentionally linked together or made at the same time from the same IP address). A transaction is one of the following: (1) a transfer of funds to a payment device from a source outside the payment scheme (such as a normal bank account), (2) a transfer between payment devices, or (3) a transfer from a payment device to a destination outside the payment scheme. The *beginning* of a chain corresponds to a transaction of the first type, and the *end* of a chain corresponds to a transaction of the third type.

By (computational) *chain privacy* we mean that it is infeasible for any collusion of parties to determine the origin or destination of a payment corresponding to a link where they are not themselves the origin or destination, even if all previously seen transactions can be matched to the identities of their respective participants.

Let us clarify this with an example: In our scheme, the bank will know the identity of the user associated with the first link in a chain. It will not know the identity of the merchant of the second link, but will know who paid this person. Similarly, for the third link, it will know who *paid the payer* of this merchant – this corresponds to the identity of the user associated with the first link. Finally, it will know the identity of the user who becomes the final link of the chain.

5   Requirements

Privacy. We require our system to satisfy *chain privacy*. Furthermore, we require that it be impossible for a payer or merchant to prove to a third party what the identity of the other participant of the transaction was.

Access Rights. First, our scheme must satisfy the standard requirement of *unforgeability*, i.e., that it is not possible for an attacker to create a transcript that corresponds to a transfer of funds he is not entitled to.

Secondly, we require that the system is secure against *bank robbery*. In a bank robbery attack, we have an attacker, who gains read access to all the secret information of the bank, and who has write access to main memory (but not the backup tapes) of the bank in a limited time interval. We wish to prevent him from performing payments not corresponding to funds that are obtained following the specified protocols.

Finally, we require that a user can *block access* to the funds of a lost device, and to recover these funds.

In the appendix, we prove that our proposed scheme satisfies the above listed requirements.

6   Architecture

We now discuss the general architechure of our scheme. We begin by briefly describing two common architectures from the literature, namely coin-based and account-based schemes:

In coin-based schemes, payers store information corresponding to certificates and secret keys, which are used to produce payment transcripts. The payment transcripts correspond closely to certificates, one by the bank, and one by the payer. These are later stored by the bank until the expiration date of the coin, after which they can be erased.

In an account-based scheme, the storage requirements are shifted towards the bank. The user typically only stores a secret key, which is used to produce certificates corresponding to an account that the bank maintains. The merchant deposits certificates with the bank, who keeps a record of the remaining balance. Often, the same secret key is used for an extended amount of time.

Disposable Anonymous Accounts. Our scheme draws on both of the above concepts. Funds can be thought of as coins kept by the bank and accessed by users. Alternatively, we can think of funds as one-time accounts. We use the term *disposable anomymous account* to describe the representation of funds, in order to highlight two of its most distinguishing properties. The first is that an account corresponds to a fixed amount, much like a coin does, and can only be spent in its entirety, after which it is cancelled. The second property corresponds to the fact that accounts are not associated with the identities of the owners. For brevity, we also use the term *coin* for such an account in its different representations.

Bank Representation. For each account, the bank stores an account description. This is either a public key or a function of a public key, such as a hash. Accounts can be created by users transferring funds to the bank, who then registers public keys given to it by the user in question. Accounts can also be created by performing a payment. During a payment, a new account is created and an old one cancelled, with the funds previously associated with the first account becoming associated with the second account.

More specifically, the payer signs a public key provided by the merchant using a secret key whose public counterpart is stored by the bank and associated with a certain amount. Signing the document transfers the access rights to the holder of a second secret key, corresponding to the public key signed. When the bank receives such a payment order, it verifies the validity of the payer's account, erases the latter, and then creates a new account labelled by the public key signed by the payer.

User Representation. In order to obtain a compact representation of funds, the payment devices will have the following structure: Each device contains a seed, from which secret keys can be generated by the application of a pseudo-random generator to the seed and a serial number describing the coin. Two counters will be maintained, one corresponding to the next coin to be spent, another corrsponding to the last coin that can be spent. A payment is performed by the merchant creating a secret key using the merchant's "max coin" position, computing the corresponding public key, and having the payer sign this using the secret key indicated by the payer's "next coin" position. At the end of the transaction, involving the cancellation of the payer's account and the creation of the merchant's account, the payer increases his "next coin" counter, and the merchant his "max coin" pointer in order to keep track of their balances. (Notice that the use of counters is only for the users' own benefit, and it would not constitute an attack to update the counters in another manner.)

7   Solution

Denotation. We let p and q be large primes such that $p - 1$ is a multiple of q. We let f be a one-way function, modeled by a random oracle, with an output in Z_q.

Bank Database. The Bank has a secret key with a corresponding public key associated with himself. The keys are used only to authenticate acknowledgements of funds transfers. The Bank keeps a database of all valid accounts. For each valid account y the Bank stores an identifier, such as a hash of y. When an account becomes invalid, its identifier is erased from the Bank database; when a new account is generated, the corresponding identifier is added to the Bank database. Additionally, when an account is created by a transfer from a source outside our payment scheme, the bank labels the corresponding account identifier by a description of the source.

Payment Device Setup. When a new user joins, he obtains a payment device, such as a smart card. During an initiation phase, he sets a PIN (or initiates some other identification scheme, such as a biometric scheme). He then selects a random seed σ, also to be stored on the payment device. He sets the counters $next = 1$, $max = 0$. (A device carries funds when $max \geq next$.) The first indicates what payment is to be performed next; the latter indicates the last valid payment that can be made. The setup is done using a trusted device, such as a home computer with a smart card reader/writer.

Performing a Backup. A PIN-protected backup[2] can be made at any time by copying the counters, *next* and *max* to a secure backup device, such as a home computer. The first time such a backup is made, or during *payment device setup*, the seed σ is copied as well. For advanced devices, other information may be kept,

---

[2] We note that performing backups to a multi-tasking computer opens up the scheme to possible virus attacks that are otherwise not possible for smart card only schemes. Also, making backups limits the protection given by the PIN, unless similar protection mechanisms are employed for the computer. These problems can be avoided by encrypting all backup data on the smart card, using the banks public key.

such as information about what is purchased, and when; such information may also be copied during a backup. Additionally, the values of the counters may be sent to the bank during a transfer of money to or from the payment device.

Transfering Money to/from the Payment Device. A user transfers money *to* a payment device by paying the bank the sum to be added, and creating new disposable anonymous accounts (the number of which corresponds to the amount to be added to the card). A user transfers money *from* a payment device by paying the bank the corresponding sum. In order to transfer the sum to a standard bank account, the user may indicate in his payment the designation of the payment. In *performing a payment* below, it is explained how a payment is performed, and how an account is selected and created. (We later discuss the designation of accounts as well.)

Performing a Payment.

1. The Payer P verifies the availability of funds by checking that the balance is sufficient for the desired transfer. Using appropriate access control mechanisms (such as a PIN) it verifies that only users allowed access can perform the transaction.
2. The Merchant M with a secret seed σ_M and a max-counter max_M computes a key $x_M = f(\sigma_M, max_M + 1, 1)$. He computes $y_M = g^{x_M} \bmod p$ and sends y_M to the Payer P.
3. The Payer P with a secret seed σ_P and a next-counter $next_P$ computes a keypair $(x_P, k) = (f(\sigma_P, next_P, 1), f(\sigma_P, next_P, 2))$. He then computes a pair $(y_P, r) = (g^{x_P}, g^k)$, where the operations are modulo p. He finally computes a Schnorr[3] signature s on y_M: $s = k - x_P H(y_M, r)$, where H is an appropriate hash function.
4. The quadruple[4] (y_P, y_M, r, s) is sent to the Bank B. The Bank verifies that y_P is a valid account, and that (r, s) is a valid signature on y_M using the public key y_P. For Schnorr signatures, this amounts to verifying that $r = g^s y_P^{H(y_M, r)}$. If the account exists and the signature is valid, then the Bank cancels y_P and stores the new account y_M, after which it acknowledges the transaction by returning a Bank signature on (y_P, y_M).
5. If a Bank acknowledgement is received, the Payer P increases the counter $next_P$ by one, and the Merchant M increases the counter max_M by one. The payment has now been performed.

Blocking a Lost Payment Device. All the payments from a payment device can be blocked using the backup device by attempting to perform payments, starting at the position indicated by $next_P$, and with increasing values for the counter from the first successful payment until the first failed attempt. The payments

---

[3] A variety of other schemes may be used in place of Schnorr signatures.

[4] The public signing key y_P does not have to be sent if the signature scheme allows y_P to be computed from (y_M, r, s). Schnorr signatures allows this shorter format to be employed.

are done to a new device which is controlled by P. Performing the payments effectively empties the lost payment device.

8 Extensions and Remarks

Preprocessing. We note that the modular exponentiations can be performed using pre-processing, since they do not depend on the transaction specifics.

Batch payments. It is possible to perform a payment involving several coins at the same time by creating a signature using all the corresponding secret keys. As an example, a Schnorr signature on n merchant public keys $y_{M1}, \ldots, y_{Mn}$, using n payer secret keys $x_{P1}, \ldots, x_{Pn}$ could be computed as $s = k - XH(\mu, r)$, for $r = g^k$. Here, the message $\mu = (\mu_M, \mu_P) = ((y_{M1}, \ldots, y_{Mn}), (y_{P1}, \ldots, y_{Pn}))$, indicates the public keys of the accounts to be created and those to be debited, where $(y_{P1} \ldots y_{Pn})$ correspond to the secret keys $(x_{P1}, \ldots x_{Pn})$ used to perform the payment. Finally, the secret signing key X is a weighted version of all the involved signing keys, computed as $X = \sum_{i=1}^{n} w_i x_i \bmod q$, where w_i is a weight that can be computed as $hash(\mu_P, i)$. The corresponding signature would be verified by checking that $r = g^s Y^{H(\mu, r)}$, where $Y = \prod_{i=1}^{n} y_{Pi}^{w_i} \bmod p$, using the same w_i as above.

Fungibility. Several different denominations are possible, in which case the bank keeps one account database for each such denomination. It is possible to "make change" by transferring a high-denomination coin to several low-denomination coins (by signing a list of public keys and a description of the wanted denominations), some of which can be given to the merchant, and others kept by the payer. Likewise, it is possible to get rid of change by using several low-denomination coins simultaneously to create one high-denomination coin (by signing one public key only, using several secret keys).

Added functionality. Using challenge semantics [17], it is possible to introduce functionality such as fairness. This is done by letting the payer sign a pair (y_M, c) instead of merely y_M, where c is an arbitrary contract. This can also be used to designate the payments for a certain account or purpose. Similarly, it is possible to transfer funds to other payment schemes or account types, by signing an identifyer of the recipient account (such as a credit card number) instead of signing y_M. It is also possible to implement agent-based commerce using the same principle. We refer to [17, 15] for a more thorough discusion of these ideas.

Using prepaid cards. For prepaid cards, parts of the *payment device setup* may be performed by a trusted card manufacturer or distributor, whose tasks may include to select the random seed and set the counters appropriately. If the card is used only for low-cost payments, e.g., to hold subway tokens or to be used as a phone card, it may not require a PIN. Alternatively, a prepaid card may require a PIN to be entered (using a trusted interface) the first time it is used, or may (as is common for phone cards) have the PIN printed on a piece of paper that can only be read once the card is unwrapped.

A remark on counters: In the above we have ignored the problem of wrap-around of counters; however, this problem can easily be addressed. We also see that the actual value of the counters is not important for the sake of security, i.e., if a user would alter his counter, then this would not enable him to gain access to more funds (as there would be no corresponding accounts stored by the bank).

A Counter-free system. It is theoretically possible to reduce the storage requirements to a constant by removing the use of the counters. Instead, we will keep two seeds, one corresponding to the *next* pointer, one corresponding to the *max* counter. For each payment made, the *next* seed would be updated as $\sigma_{next} := f(\sigma_{next})$; for each payment received, we would have $\sigma_{max} := f(\sigma_{max})$. Here, the relation between the two seeds is such that $\sigma_{max} = f^B(\sigma_{next})$ for a balance B (that is not stored by the device.) If $\sigma_{max} = \sigma_{next}$, there is no money on the storage device. It appears advantageous, though, to keep the balance stored, making a system using counters superior.

A remark on privacy: We have assumed that no identifying information, such as an IP-address, is leaked when a device connects to the Bank. Should this not be the case, then we can let the payer connect to the bank for every other payment of the chain, and the merchant for every other payment. Note that this requires a one-bit state to be stored by the user for each unit of funds, indicating whether the transcript will be sent by him or the merchant. This efficiently disassociates every second holder of a portion of funds to the bank, thereby making any association between payer and merchant impossible for the bank to perform.

Acknowledgements

Many thanks to Daniel Bleichenbacher, Ari Juels, Phil MacKenzie, Elizabeth Shriver, and Julien Stern for helpful discussions and valuable feedback.

References

1. M. Bellare, J. Garay, R. Hauser, A. Herzberg, H. Krawczyk, M. Steiner, G. Tsudik and M. Waidner, "iKP - A Family of Secure Electronic Payment Protocols', Proceedings of the First USENIX Workshop on Electronic Commerce, New York, July 1995, pp. 89–106.
2. S. Brands, "Untraceable Off-line Cash in Wallets with Observers," Advances in Cryptology - Proceedings of Crypto '93, pp. 302–318.
3. S. Brands, "An Efficient Off-line Electronic Cash Systems Based on the Representation Problem," C.W.I. Technical Report CS-T9323, The Netherlands
4. E. Brickell, P. Gemmell and D. Kravitz, "Trustee-based Tracing Extensions to Anonymous Cash and the Making of Anonymous Change," Proc. 6th Annual ACM-SIAM Symposium on Discrete Algorithms (SODA), 1995, pp. 457–466.
5. J. Camenisch, U. Maurer and M. Stadler, "Digital Payment Systems with Passive Anonymity-Revoking Trustees," Computer Security - ESORICS 96, volume 1146, pp. 33–43.

6. J. Camenisch, J-M. Piveteau and M. Stadler, "An Efficient Fair Payment System," Proceedings of the 3rd ACM Conference on Computer and Communications Security, 1996, pp. 88–94.

7. D. Chaum, "Blind Signatures for Untraceable Payments," Advances in Cryptology - Proceedings of Crypto '82, 1983, pp. 199–203.

8. D. Chaum, A. Fiat and M. Naor, "Untraceable Electronic Cash," Advances in Cryptology - Proceedings of Crypto '88, pp. 319–327.

9. G.I. Davida, Y. Frankel, Y. Tsiounis, and M. Yung, "Anonymity Control in E-Cash Systems," Financial Cryptography 97.

10. N. Ferguson, "Extensions of Single-term Coins," Advances in Cryptology - Proceedings of Crypto '93, pp. 292–301.

11. Y. Frankel, Y. Tsiounis, and M. Yung, "Indirect Discourse Proofs: Achieving Efficient Fair Off-Line E-Cash," Advances in Cryptology - Proceedings of Asiacrypt 96, pp. 286–300.

12. M. Franklin and M. Yung, "Blind Weak Signatures and its Applications: Putting Non-Cryptographic Secure Computation to Work," Advances in Cryptology - Proceedings of Eurocrypt '94, pp. 67–76.

13. E. Fujisaki, T. Okamoto, "Practical Escrow Cash System", LNCS 1189, Proceedings of 1996 Cambridge Workshop on Security Protocols, Springer, pp. 33–48.

14. M. Jakobsson, "Ripping Coins for a Fair Exchange," Advances in Cryptology - Proceedings of Eurocrypt '95, pp. 220–230.

15. M. Jakobsson, A. Juels, "X-Cash: Executable Digital Cash," Financial Cryptography '98.

16. M. Jakobsson, D. M'Raihi, "Mix-Based Electronic Payments," SAC '98.

17. M. Jakobsson and M. Yung, "Revokable and Versatile Electronic Money," 3rd ACM Conference on Computer and Communications Security, 1996, pp. 76–87.

18. M. Jakobsson and M. Yung, "Distributed 'Magic Ink' Signatures," Advances in Cryptology - Proceedings of Eurocrypt '97, pp. 450–464.

19. M. Jakobsson and M. Yung, "Applying Anti-Trust Policies to Increase Trust in a Versatile E-Money System," Advances in Cryptology - Proceedings of Financial Cryptography '97.

20. S. Jarecki and A. Odlyzko, "An efficient micropayment system based on probabilistic polling," Advances in Cryptology - Proceedings of Financial Cryptography '97.

21. C. Jutla and M. Yung, "Paytree: 'amortized signature' for flexible micropayments," 2nd USENIX Workshop on Electronic Commerce, November 1996.

22. S. H. Low, N. F. Maxemchuk and S. Paul, "Anonymous Credit Cards," Proceedings of the Second ACM Conference on Computer and Communications Security, Nov. 1994, pp. 108–117.

23. G. Medvinsky and B. C. Neuman, "Netcash: A design for practical electronic currency on the internet," Proceedings of the First ACM Conference on Computer and Communications Security, Nov. 1993, pp. 102–106.

24. D. M'Raihi, "Cost-Effective Payment Schemes with Privacy Regulation," Advances in Cryptology - Proceedings of Asiacrypt '96.

25. B. C. Neuman and G. Medvinsky, "Requirements for Network Payment: The NetCheque^{TM} Perspective," Compcon '95, pp. 32–36.

26. T. Okamoto, "An Efficient Divisible Electronic Cash Scheme," Advances in Cryptology - Proceedings of Crypto '95, pp. 438–451.

27. T. Okamoto and K. Ohta, "Disposable Zero-Knowledge Authentication and Their Applications to Untraceable Electronic Cash," Advances in Cryptology - Proceedings of Crypto '89, pp. 481–496.
28. T. Okamoto and K. Ohta, "Universal Electronic Cash," Advances in Cryptology - Proceedings of Crypto '91, pp. 324–337.
29. R. Rivest and A. Shamir, "PayWord and MicroMint: two simple micropayment schemes," Cryptobytes, vol. 2, num. 1, 1996, pp. 7–11.
30. D. Simon, "Anonymous Communication and Anonymous Cash," Crypto '96, pp. 61–73.
31. M. Sirbu and J. D. Tygar, "NetBill: An Internet Commerce System Optimized for Network Delivered Services," Compcon '95, pp. 20–25.
32. S. von Solms and D. Naccache, "On Blind Signatures and Perfect Crimes," Computers and Security, 11 (1992) pp. 581–583.
33. C. P. Schnorr, "Efficient Signature Generation for Smart Cards," Advances in Cryptology - Proceedings of Crypto '89, pp. 239–252.
34. M. Stadler, J-M. Piveteau and J. Camenisch, "Fair Blind Signatures," Advances in Cryptology - Proceedings of Eurocrypt '95, pp. 209–219.
35. J. Stern and S. Vaudenay, "SVP: a Flexible Micropayment Scheme," Advances in Cryptology - Proceedings of Financial Cryptography '97.
36. J. M. Tenenbaum, C. Medich, A. M. Schiffman, and W. T. Wong, "CommerceNet: Spontaneous Electronic Commerce on the Internet," Compcon '95, pp. 38–43.
37. B. Witter, "The Dark Side of Digital Cash," Legal Times, January 30, 1995.
38. Y. Yacobi, "Efficient Electronic Money," Advances of Cryptology - Proceedings of Asiacrypt '94, pp. 153–164.
39. Y. Yacobi, "On the continuum between on-line and off-line e-cash systems - I," Advances in Cryptology - Proceedings of Financial Cryptography '97.

A Proofs

Theorem 1: Given that it is infeasible to invert the one-way function used for the PRG, the scheme satisfies chain privacy. Moreover, it prevents a merchant from proving the identity of a payer to a third party.

Proof of Theorem 1: *(Sketch)*
We prove the theorem by reducing a successful predicting adversarial strategy to an algorithm for inverting a one-way function. First, there cannot exist a p-time distinguisher that decides whether an output comes from a first or second PRG, or this could be used to distinguish a pseudo-random sequence from a truly random sequence. (This argument uses a hybrid argument in which one random sequence is gradually replaced with a pseud-random sequence and for each step compared to another pseudo-random sequence.)

We now assume that a third party is able to correlate to a transaction (which does not constitute an end-point of the payment chain) the identity of a party involved in the transaction. Without loss of generality, we assume that this adversary is able to determine with some probability (non-negligibly exceeding that of a guess among all potential parties whom he does not control) the identity of a merchant corresponding to a given link of the chain, such that this link is not the end point of the chain. In order to do so, the adversary needs to be able to successfully match the public key y generated by the merchant to a previous transaction of the same merchant (since valid transactions not involving said merchant are independent of the merchant's seed). Given the previous argument, this is not possible for two potential merchants. The argument trivially extends to multiple parties.

The second part of the theorem trivially holds since there is no proof of identity in the payment protocol, and so, there exists no transferable proof of identity of neither the merchant nor the payer. □

Theorem 2: The scheme satisfies unforgeability, i.e., it infeasible for an adversary to perform a payment unless he (or a collaborator) generated the secret key correponding to the account originating the payment, or he knows the secret key of the bank.

This follows directly from the soundness of the signature schemes used, and the fact that it is not possible to predict the value of the secret key even if all previously generated secret keys were known (as shown in Theorem 1).

Theorem 3: The scheme protects against bank robbery, i.e., it is infeasible for an adversary who forces the bank to give him temporary but unrestricted read and write access to the bank's storage to gain access to funds he is not entitled to, without allowing the immediate tracing of the corresponding transactions and the replacement of the bank keys.

Unrestricted read access to the bank storage does not allow the adversary to produce represention of funds, since this can only be done by entering new public keys in the bank database. The only way an attacker can produce new representations of funds is to enter new public keys in the bank's database, or increasing the balance of a standard account, both of which can be undone once the bank regains control. The only time the bank uses its secret key is when it acknowledges a transaction. Being able to acknowledge transactions (real and forged) does not allow the adversary access to funds *per se*, although it may allow the adversary to perform (detectable) transactions that he is not entitled to.

Preserving Privacy
in Distributed Delegation
with Fast Certificates

Pekka Nikander[†], Yki Kortesniemi[‡], Jonna Partanen[‡]

[†] Ericsson Research
FIN-02420 Jorvas, Kirkkonummi, Finland
pekka.nikander@ericsson.com

[‡] Helsinki University of Technology, Department of Computer Science,[1]
FIN-02015 TKK, Espoo, Finland
yki.kortesniemi@hut.fi, jonna.partanen@hut.fi

Abstract. In a distributed system, dynamically dividing execution between nodes is essential for service robustness. However, when all of the nodes cannot be equally trusted, and when some users are more honest than others, controlling where code may be executed and by whom resources may be consumed is a non-trivial problem. In this paper we describe a generic authorisation certificate architecture that allows dynamic control of resource consumption and code execution in an untrusted distributed network. That is, the architecture allows the users to specify which network nodes are trusted to execute code on their behalf and the servers to verify the users' authority to consume resources, while still allowing the execution to span dynamically from node to node, creating delegations on the fly as needed. The architecture scales well, fully supports mobile code and execution migration, and allows users to remain anonymous.

We are implementing a prototype of the architecture using SPKI certificates and ECDSA signatures in Java 1.2. In the prototype, agents are represented as Java JAR packages.

1   Introduction

There are several proposals for distributed systems security architectures, including the Kerberos [14], the CORBA security architecture [23], and the ICE-TEL project proposal [6], to mention but a few. These, as well as others, differ greatly in the extent they support scalability, agent mobility, and agent anonymity, among other things. Most of these differences are clearly visible in the trust models of the systems, when analyzed.

In this paper we describe a Simple Public Key Infrastructure (SPKI) [7] [8] [9] based distributed systems security architecture that is scalable and supports agent mobility, migration and anonymity. Furthermore, all trust relationships in our architecture are explicitly visible and can be easily analyzed. The architecture allows various secu-

---

[1] This work was partially funded by the TeSSA research project at Helsinki University of Technology under a grant from TEKES.

rity policies to be explicitly specified, and in this way, e.g., to specify where an agent may securely execute [27].

Our main idea is to use dynamically created SPKI authorisation certificates to delegate permissions from an agent running on one host to another agent running on another host. With SPKI certificates, we are able to delegate only the minimum rights the receiving agent needs to perform the operations that the sending agent wants it to carry out. The architecture allows permissions to be further delegated as long as the generic trust relationships, also presented in the form of SPKI certificates, are preserved.

A typical application could be a mobile host, such as a PDA. Characteristic to such devises are limited computational power, memory constraints and an intermittent, low bandwidth access to the network. These pose some limitations on the cryptographic system used. Favourable characteristics would be short key length and fast operation with limited processing power.

In order to be able to distinguish running agents, and delegate rights to them, new cryptographic key pairs need to be created, and new certificates need to be created and verified. To make this happen with an acceptable speed, we have implemented the relevant public key functions with Elliptic Curve based DSA (ECDSA), yielding reasonable performance.

In our architecture, cryptographic key pairs are created dynamically to represent running agents. This also has a desirable side effect of making anonymous operations possible while still preserving strong authorisation. In practical terms, some of the certificates that are used to verify agent authority may be encrypted to protect privacy. This hinders third parties, and even the verifying host, from determining the identity of the principal that is responsible for originally initiating an operation. This allows users' actions to remain in relative privacy, while still allowing strong assurance on whether an attempted operation is authorised or not.

We are in the process of implementing a practical prototype of our architecture. The prototype is based on distributed Java Virtual Machines (JVM) running JDK 1.2, but the same principles could be applied to any distributed system. The main parts of the prototype architecture are already implemented, as described in [15], [21], and [25], while others are under way.

The rest of this paper is organized as follows. In Sect. 2 we describe the idea of authorisation certificates, their relation to trust relationships and certificate loops, and the security relevant components of the SPKI certificates. Sect. 3 summarizes the dynamic nature of the SPKI enhanced JDK 1.2 security architecture. Next, in Sect. 4, we describe how our ECDSA implementation complements the Java cryptography architecture. In Sect. 5, we define the main ideas of our architecture, and show how SKPI certificates and dynamically generated key pairs can be used to anonymously, but securely, delegate permissions from one JVM to another. Sect. 6 describes the current implementation status, and Sect. 7 includes our conclusions from this research.

2   Authorisation and Delegation

The basic idea of authorisation, as opposed to simple (identity) authentication, is to attest that a party, or an agent, is authorised to perform a certain action, rather than merely confirm that the party has a claimed identity. If we consider a simple real life example, the driver's licence, this distinction becomes evident. The primary function of a driver's licence is to certify that its holder is entitled, or authorised, to operate vehicles belonging to certain classes. In this sense, it is a device of authorisation. However, this aspect is often overseen, as it seems obvious, even self-evident, for most people.

The secondary function of a driver's licence, the possibility of using it as an evidence of identity, is more apparent. Yet, when a police officer checks a driver's licence, the identity checking is *only* a necessary side step in assuring that the operator of a vehicle is on legal business.

The same distinction can and should be applied to computer systems. Instead of using X.509 type identity certificates for authenticating a principal's identity, one should use authorisation certificates, or signed credentials, to gain assurance about a principal's permission to execute actions. In addition to a direct authorisation, as depicted in the driver's licence example, in a distributed computer system it is often necessary to delegate authority from a party to a next one. The length of such delegation chains can be pretty long on occasions. [17]

2.1   Trust and Security Policy

Trust can be defined as a belief that an agent or a person behaves in a certain way. Trust to a machinery is usually a belief that it works as specified. Trust to a person means that even if that person has the possibility to harm us, we believe that he or she chooses not to. The trust requirements of a system form the system's trust model. For example, we may need to have some kind of trust to the implementor of a software whose source code is not public, or trust to the person with whom we communicate over a network.

Closely related to the concept of trust is the concept of policy. A security policy is a manifestation of laws, rules and practices that regulate how sensitive information and other resources are managed, protected and distributed. Its purpose is to ensure that the handled information remains confidential, integral and available, as specified by the policy. Every agent may be seen to function under its own policy rules.

In many cases today, the policy rules are very informal, often left unwritten. However, security policies can be meaningful not only as internal regulations and rules, but as a published document which defines some security-related practices. This could be important information when some outsider is trying to decide whether an organization can be trusted in some respect. In this kind of situation it is useful to define the policy in a systematic manner, i.e., to have a formal policy model.

Another and a more important reason for having a formally specified policy is that most, or maybe even all, of the policy information should be directly accessible by the computer systems. Having a policy control enforced in software (or firmware) rather than relying on the users to follow some memorized rules is essential if the policy is to be followed. A lot of policy rules are already implicitly present in the operating systems, protocols, and applications, and explicitly in their configuration files. Our mission includes the desire to make this policy information more explicit, and make it possible to manage it in a distributed way.

2.2 Certificates, Certificate Chains, and Certificate Loops

A certificate is a signed statement about the properties of some entity. A certificate has an issuer and a subject. Typically, the issuer has attested, by signing the certificate, its belief that the information stated in the certificate is true. If a certificate states something about the issuer him or herself, it is called a self-signed certificate or an auto-certificate, in distinction from other certificates whose subject is not the issuer.

Certificates are usually divied in two categories: Identity certificates and authorisation certificates. An identity certificate usually binds a cryptographic key to a name. An authorisation certificate, on the other hand, can make a more specific statement; for example, it can state that the subject entity is authorised to have access to a specified service. Furthermore, an authorisation certificate does not necessarily need to carry any explicit, human understandable information about the identity of the subject. That is, the subject does not need to have a name. The subject can prove its title to the certificate by proving that it possesses the private key corresponding to the certified public key; indeed, that is the only way a subject can be trusted to be the (a) legitimate owner of the certificate.

Certificates and trust relationships are very closely connected. The meaning of a certificate is to make a reliable statement concerning some trust relationship. Certificates form chains, where a subject of a certificate is the issuer of the next one. In a chain the trust propagates transitively from an entity to another. These chains can be closed into loops, as described in [17].

The idea of certificate loops is a central one in analyzing trust. The source of trust is almost always the checking party itself. A chain of certificates, typically starting at the verifying party and ending at the party claiming authority, forms an open arc. This arc is closed into loop by the online authentication protocol where the claimant proves possession of its private key to the verifying party.

2.3 Authorisation and Anonymity

In an access control context, an authorisation certificate chain binds a key to an operation, effectively stating that the holder of the key is authorised to perform the operation. A run time challenge operates between the owner of operation (the reference monitor) and the key, thus closing the certification loop. These two bindings, i.e., the certificate chain and the run time authentication protocol, are based on cryptography and can be made strong.

In an authorisation certificate, a person-key binding is different from the person-name binding used in the identity certificates. By definition, the keyholder of a key has sole possession of the private key. Therefore, the corresponding public key can be used as an identifier (a name) of the keyholder. For any public key cryptosystem to work, it is essential that a principal will keep its private key to itself. So, the person is the only one having access to the private key and the key has enough entropy so that nobody else has the same key. Thus, the identifying key is bound tightly to the person that controls it and all bindings are strong. The same cannot be claimed about human understandable names, which are relative and ambiguous [10].

However, having a strong binding between a key and a person does not directly help the provider of a controlled service much. The provider does not know if it can trust the holder of the key. Such a trust can only be acquired through a valid certificate chain that starts at the provider itself. The whole idea of our architecture centres around the concept of creating such certificate chains when needed, dynamically providing agents the permissions they need.

The feature of not having to bind keys to names is especially convenient in systems that include anonymity as a security requirement. It is easy for a user to create new keys for such applications, while creating an authorised false identity is (hopefully) not possible.

2.4 SPKI Certificates

The Simple Public Key Infrastructure (SPKI) is an authorisation certificate infrastructure being standardized by the IETF. The intention is that it will support a range of trust models. [7] [8] [9]

In the SPKI world, principals are keys. Delegations are made to a key, not to a keyholder or a global name. Thus, an SPKI certificate is closer to a "capability" as defined by [16] than to an identity certificate. There is the difference that in a traditional capability system the capability itself is a secret ticket, the possession of which grants some authority. An SPKI certificate identifies the specific key to which it grants authority. Therefore the mere ability to read (or copy) the certificate grants no authority. The certificate itself does not need to be as tightly controlled.

In SPKI terms, a certificate is basically a signed five tuple (I,S,D,A,V) where
- I is the Issuer's (signers) public key, or a secure hash of the public key,
- S is the Subject of the certificate, typically a public key, a secure hash of a public key, a SDSI name, or a secure hash of some other object such as a Java class,
- D is a Delegation bit,
- A is the Authorisation field, describing the permissions or other information that the certificate's Issuer grants to or attests of the Subject,
- V is a Validation field, describing the conditions (such as a time range) under which the certificate can be considered valid.

The meaning of an SPKI certificate can be stated as follows:
Based on the assumption that I has the control over the rights or other information described in A, I grants S the rights/property A whenever V is valid. Furthermore, if D is true and S is a public key (or hash of a public key), S may further delegate the rights A or any subset of them.

2.5 Access control revisited

The traditional way of implementing access control in a distributed system has been based on authentication and Access Control Lists (ACLs). In such a system, when execution is transferred from one node to another, the originating node authenticates itself to the responding node. Based on the identity information transferred during the authentication protocol, the responding node attaches a local identifier, i.e., an user account, to the secured connection or passed execution request (e.g., an RPC call). The actual access control is performed locally by determining the user's rights based on the local identifier and local ACLs.

In an authorisation based system everything works differently. Instead of basing access control decisions on locally stored identity or ACL information, decisions are based on explicit access control information, carried from node to node. The access rights are represented as authorisation delegations, e.g., in the authorisation field of an SPKI certificate. Because the certificates form certificate loops, the interpreter of this access control information is always the same party that has initially issued it. The rights may, though, have been restricted along the delegation path.

In Sect. 5 we show how this kind of an infrastructure can be effectively extended to an environment of mobile agents, represented as downloadable code, that is run on a network of trusted and untrusted execution nodes.

3 An SPKI based Dynamic Security Architecture for JDK 1.2

As described in more detail in [25], we have extended the JDK 1.2 security architecture with SPKI certificates. This makes it possible to dynamically modify the current security policy rules applied at a specific Java Virtual Machine (JVM). This dynamic modification allows an agent running on one trusted JVM to delegate permissions to another agent running on another trusted JVM.

The components of the basic and SPKI extended access control architecture are enumerated in Table 1 and discussed in more detail in Sections 3.1-3.2. The most relevant changes needed to the basic architecture are described in Sect. 3.2.

Table 1: The parts of the JDK 1.2 access control Architecture

Class or classes	The role of the class or classes
Permission and its subclasses	Represent different "tickets" or access rights.
ProtectionDomain	Connects the Permission objects to classes.
Policy and its subclasses	Decide what permissions each class gets.
AccessController	The reference monitor. [1]

3.1 Access Control in JDK 1.2

The JDK 1.2 has a new, capability based access control architecture. Java capabilities are objects called permissions. Each protected resource in the system has a corresponding permission object that represents access to the resource. There are typically many instances of a given permission, possessed by and thus granting access for different classes.

Permissions are divided into several subtypes that extend the Permission class. Each resource type or category, such as files or network connections, has its own Permission subclass. Inside the category, different instances of the Permission class correspond to different instances of the resource. In addition, the programmers may provide their own Permission subclasses if they create protected resources of their own.

Just as in any capability-based access control system, the Java classes must be prevented from creating permissions for themselves and thus gaining unauthorised access. This is done by assigning the classes to protection domains. Each class belongs to one and only one protection domain. Each ProtectionDomain object has a PermissionCollection object that holds the permissions of that domain. Only these permissions can be used to gain access to resources. The classes cannot change their protection domain nor the PermissionCollection of the domain. Thus, the classes are free to create any Permission objects they like, but they cannot affect the access control decisions and gain unauthorised access.

The actual access control is done by an object called AccessController. When a thread of execution requests access to a protected resource such as a file, the AccessController object is asked whether the access is granted or not. To determine this, the AccessController checks the execution context to see if the caller and all the previous classes in the call chain have the Permission object corresponding to the resource. The previous classes in the call chain are checked to ensure that a class does not bypass the access control simply by calling another class with more permissions.

3.2 Policy Management

A security policy defines the rules that mandate which actions the agents in the system are allowed or disallowed to do [1]. Java security policy defines what permissions each

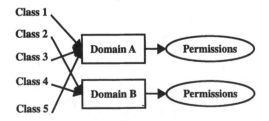

Fig. 1. Classes, domains and permissions

protection domain gets. The objects implementing the security policy management in JDK are subclasses of the Policy class. The implementation can be changed easily by just creating and installing a new Policy subclass.

The default policy implementation of JDK 1.2 uses a set of configuration files to define the security policy. This system has several small defects discussed in [21] and [25]. Furthermore, this approach makes delegating permissions from a class in one JVM to another class in some other JVM virtually impossible, as the delegating party should be able to edit the configuration file of the other JVM. We have solved these problems by replacing the configuration files with a capability-based policy definition that uses SPKI certificates to represent capabilities.

In our model, the policy manager and the dynamic permission evaluation are slightly more complex than in the basic implementation. In the SPKI extended system, the main task of the policy manager is to attempt to reduce a set of SPKI certificates to form a valid chain from its own key, called the Self key, to the hash of the classes composing a protection domain, and to interpret the authorisation given by the chain into Java Permission objects. This chain reduction includes checking the validity of the certificates, checking that all but the last certificate have the delegation bit set, and intersecting the authorisation fields to get the final authorisation given by the chain.

In the default JDK implementation, the ProtectionDomains get the permissions when they are initialized, and the permissions are not revised after that. We have made the policy evaluation more dynamic. When a class tries to access a protected resource, the reference monitor asks the protection domain whether it contains the specific permission required, and the protection domain in turn asks the Policy for the permission. The Policy will try to produce a certificate chain reduction that would imply the permission in question. If it fails, the access is not granted.

The SPKI drafts propose that the Prover (i.e. the class) is responsible of presenting a valid certificate chain to the Verifier (i.e. the Policy) at the time of access request or authentication [7]. We argue that this approach does not work with mobile agents. Requiring that each mobile agent includes the logic for locating all certificates needed to access resources is infeasible and counterproductive. Instead, we think that the Policy will need to locate the relevant certificates as well as to reduce the certificate chains.

4   Adding Elliptic Curve based Certificates to Java

Java defines and partially implements security related functionality as part of its core API. This functionality is collected in the `java.security` package and its subpackages. To facilitate and co-ordinate the use of cryptographic services, JDK 1.1 introduced the Java Cryptography Architecture (JCA). It is a framework for both accessing and developing new cryptographic functionality for the Java platform. JDK 1.1 itself included the necessary APIs for digital signatures and message digests.[7]

In Java 1.2, JCA has been significantly extended. It now encompasses the cryptography related parts of the Java Security API, as well as a set of conventions and specifications. Further, the basic API has been complemented with the Java Cryptography Extension (JCE), which includes further implementations of encryption and key exchange functionality. This extension, however, is subject to the US export restrictions and is therefore not available to the rest of the world. To fully utilise Java as a platform for secure applications, the necessary cryptographic functionality has to be developed outside the US.

4.1 The Java Cryptography Architecture

One of the key concepts of the JCA is the provider architecture. The key idea is that all different implementations of a particular cryptographic service conform to a common interface. This makes these implementations interchangeable; the user of any cryptographic service can choose whichever implementation is available and be assured that his application will still function.

To achieve true interoperability, Java 1.2 defines cryptographic services in an abstract fashion as engine classes. The following engine classes, among others, have been defined in Java 1.2:

- MessageDigest – used to calculate the message digest (hash) of given data
- Signature – used to sign data and verify digital signatures
- KeyPairGenerator – used to generate a pair of public and private keys suitable for a specific algorithm
- CertificateFactory – used to create public key certificates and Certificate Revocation Lists (CRLs)
- AlgorithmParameterGenerator – used to generate a set of parameters to be used with a certain algorithm

A generator is used to create objects with brand-new contents, whereas a factory creates objects from existing material.

To implement the functionality of an engine class, the developer has to create classes that inherit the corresponding abstract Service Provider Interface (SPI) class and implement the methods defined in it. This implementation then has to be installed in the Java Runtime Environment (JRE), after which it is available for use.[7] [8]

4.2 Implementing an Elliptic Curve Cryptography Provider in Java 1.2

In our project we implemented the Elliptic Curve Digital Signature Algorithm (ECDSA). The signature algorithm and all the necessary operations are defined in IEEE P1363 and ANSI X9.62 drafts. To facilitate the interoperability of different implementations, Java 1.2 includes standard names for several algorithms in each engine class together with their definitions. ECDSA, however, is not among them. We therefore propose that ECDSA should be adopted in Java 1.2 as a standard algorithm for signatures.

Similarrly with the DSA implementation in JDK 1.2, we have defined interfaces for the keys, algorithm parameters (curves) and points. These are used to facilitate the use of different co-ordinate representations and arithmetics. Our implementation of ECDSA uses prime fields and affine co-ordinates. The mathematics have been implemented using the BigInteger-class. The BigInteger class is easy to use and flexible as it implements several operations necessary for modular arithmetic and provides arbitrary precision. The down side is that performance is not optimal. If the key length could be kept small enough, the arithmetic could be based on the `long` type. The necessary operations could be based on using a few `long` type variables for each value. With regular elliptic curves, which require a key length of at least 160 bits, this approach might be inconvenient, but if hyperelliptic curves were used, the approach could prove feasible.

Even further improvements in performance could be achieved by implementing the key mathematic operation in the hardware, e.g., in a mobile host. With the small key size of (hyper)elliptic curves, this would not pose unreasonable demands on the processor design or memory.

5 Extending Java Protection Domains into Distributed Agents

The dynamic and distributed nature of the SPKI based Java protection domains, described in Sect. 3, opens up new possibilities for their use. In particular, it is possible to dynamically delegate a permission from one domain, executing on one Java virtual machine, to another domain, executing on another Java virtual machine. For example, when a distributed application requests a service from a server, it might want to allow a certain class, an agent, in the server to execute as if it were the user that started the application in the first hand. This ability allows us to view the protection domains not just as internal Java properties, but they can be considered to represent active agents that are created and executed in the network.

In order to be able to perform these kinds of functions, the domains (or agents) involved must have local access to some private keys, and a number of trust conditions must be met. The requirement of having access to a private key can be easily accomplished by creating a temporary key pair for each policy domain, i.e., for each incarnation of an agent. This is acceptable from a security point of view, because the underlying JVM must be trusted anyway, and so it can be trusted to provide temporary keys as well. The public temporary key can be signed by the local machine key, denoting it as belonging to the domain involved.

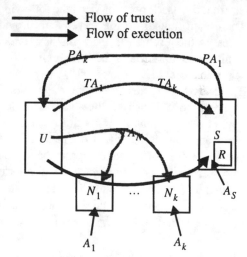

Fig. 2. The user U requests for a service needing the resource R through intermediate nodes $N_1, ..., N_k$.

To analyze the trust conditions, let us consider the situation depicted in Fig. 2. The user U wants to use a protected resource R, located on the server S. However, we assume that it is not possible or feasible that the user U would have a direct secured connection with S. As an example application, the user may be using a mobile terminal whose connectivity cannot be guaranteed. So, instead of a direct connection the user's actions are carried out by one or more intermediate nodes N_i, each acting on the user's behalf.

The setting is still slightly more complicated by the assumption that the code that actually executes at the server S and the intermediate nodes N_i consist of independent agents, which are dynamically loaded as needed. In practical terms, in our prototype these agents are Java class packages (jar files), carrying SPKI certificates within themselves. The agents are named as A_S for the agent eventually running at the server S, and as A_i for the agents running at the intermediate nodes N_i.

It is crucial to note that when the execution begins, the user U typically does not know the identity of the server S, the intermediate nodes N_i, or the agents A_S, A_i. Instead, she has expressed her confidence towards a number of administrators (described below), who in turn certify the trustworthiness of S and N_i. Correspondingly, the server S has no idea about the user U or the nodes N_i. Again, it trusts a number of administrators to specify an explicit security policy on its behalf.

5.1 Trust requirements

Since we assume that the nodes in the network do not necessarily nor implicitly trust each other or the executable agents, a number of trust conditions must be met and explicitly expressed.

First, from the user's point of view, the following conditions must be met.

- The user U must trust the server S to provide the desired service S_R granting access to the resource R. This trust is expressed through a sequence of trust administrators TA_i, where the last administrator TA_k confirms that S indeed is a server that provides the service S_R.
- The user U must trust the agent A_S, and delegate the right of accessing the resource R to it. However, the actual runtime identity (i.e, the temporary public key) of the particular activation of A_S, running on S on the behalf of U on this occasion, is not initially known but created runtime. On the other hand, U must certify the code of A_S so that it may be loaded on her behalf.
- The user U must consider each of the intermediate nodes N_i to be trustworthy enough to execute code on and to participate in accessing the resource R on her behalf. For simplicity, in this case we have assumed that the trustworthiness of the nodes is certified by a single trust authority TA_N, directly trusted by the user U.
- The user U must trust the intermediate agents A_i, while running on the nodes N_i, to execute on her behalf and to participate in the process. Again, the temporary public keys of the actual incarnations of the agents are created only at runtime.

From the server's point of view, a number of similar conditions must be met.

- The user U must be authorised to access the resource R. Since the resource R is controlled by the server S, the source of this authority must be S itself. Typically, this authorisation is achieved through a chain of independent security policy administrators PA_i.

- The server S must trust the intermediate nodes N_i to faithfully represent the user U [1]. This means, among other things, that when an agent is running on any of these nodes, S trusts that the node has faithfully created and certified the temporary key pair that represents the agent. For simplicity, we have assumed that the server S assumes the user U to be competent enough to determine which nodes to trust. Thus, in practice, the certificate chain used to delegate the right to access the resource R may be combined with the chain certifying U's proficiency in determining node trustworthiness.

5.2 Expressing the Trust Requirements with SPKI Certificates

Using SPKI certificates, it is possible to explicitly express the static and dynamic trust and delegation relationships. In the following, the appearance of the symbols U, S, N_i, TA_i, TA_N and PA_i as the issuer or the subject of the certificates denotes the (static) public key of the respective principal. On the other hand, to explicitly communicate the dual nature of the agents as dynamically loaded code and dynamically created key pairs that represent them, $h(A)$ denotes a hash code calculated over the code of the agent A, and $K_{A,N}$ denotes a temporary key that the node N has created for the agent A. Furthermore, the symbol R is used to denote the permission to access the resource R.

Normal SPKI certificates are represented as 4-tuples (I, S, D, A), where the validity field is left out. Correspondingly, SPKI name certificates are represented as $((I's\ name), S)$, denoting that the issuer I has bound the *name* for the principal S.

User trust requirements. First, U's trust on S is represented through a certificate chain Cert. 1 ... Cert. 3.

$$(U, TA_1, true, S_R)$$
Cert. 1

...
Cert. 2

$$(TA_k, S, false, S_R)$$
Cert. 3

Second, U must further certify that the agents, when run, may use whatever rights U has granted to the agents as code. Since U does not know where the agents will be run, SPKI certificates containing indirect naming are used to denote this delegation.

$$(U, (U's\ N's\ h(A_i)), false, \text{act as } h(A_i))$$
Cert. 4

where $(N's\ h(A_i))$ is an SPKI name denoting the running agent A_i, running on an arbitrary node N, named by U.

Next, U must certify that the nodes are trustworthy to execute code. U has delegated this right to TA_N; thus, a chain of two certificates is needed for each node. In practice, the right of running code on the issuer's behalf is represented by a number of SPKI naming certificates that transfer the node name N, used above, from U's name

---

[1] More generally, the server S must trust the intermediate nodes to faithfully represent any user, or at least any user that has the authority and a need to access the resource R.

space to the name space of the trust authority TA_N. The trust authority TA_N, on it's behalf, names a specific node N_i as a node N, which, consecutively, has the authority to bind the agent hash $h(A_i)$ to a public key.

$$((U's\ N), (TA_N's\ N)) \hspace{4cm} \text{Cert. 5}$$

$$((TA_N's\ N), N_i) \hspace{4.5cm} \text{Cert. 6}$$

Furthermore, the user U must certify the actual code of the agents A_i. In a real situation, this would happen through another certificate chain. However, for simplicity, we assume that the user has written the agents herself, and therefore certifies their code directly.

$$(U, h(A_i), true, R) \hspace{4.5cm} \text{Cert. 7}$$

Server trust requirements. Similar to the user, the server S must authorise the user U to access the resource R, represented as the chain Cert. 8 ... Cert. 10.

$$(S, PA_1, true, R) \hspace{4.8cm} \text{Cert. 8}$$

$$\cdots \hspace{6.5cm} \text{Cert. 9}$$

$$(PA_k, U, true, R) \hspace{4.8cm} \text{Cert. 10}$$

Since the user is allowed to directly denote which nodes she trusts, no other certificates are needed on the server's behalf.

Initial reductions. Reducing Certificates 1–3, one gets the certificate

$$(U, S, false, S_R) \hspace{4.8cm} \text{Cert. 11}$$

This is sufficient for the user, and to anybody acting on the user's behalf, to verify that the server S really provides the desired service S_R, which allows one to access the resource R.

Respectively, reducing the Certificates 4–6, the result is

$$(U, (N_i's\ h(A_i)), false, \text{act as } h(A_i)) \hspace{2cm} \text{Cert. 12}$$

denoting that the user U has delegated to the agent A_i, as named by the node N_i, the right to use the rights assigned to the agent's code[1].

5.3 Runtime Behaviour

The run time permission delegation is advanced step by step, from the user through the intermediate nodes to the server. We next describe the initial step, a generic intermediate step, and the final step at the server.

Initiation of action. As the user U initiates her access, she contacts the first intermediate node N_1. The node loads the agent A_1, generates a temporary key K_{A_1, N_1} for the agent, and creates an SPKI name certificate (Cert. 13) to name the agent.

$$((N_1's\ h(A_1)), K_{A_1, N_1}) \hspace{4cm} \text{Cert. 13}$$

---

[1] The reader should notice that this, naturally, allows N_i to delegate this right to itself. However, this is acceptable and inevitable, as the node N_i is trusted for creating and signing the agent's public key.

Reducing this with Cert. 12 gives the newly created key the acting right.

$$(U, K_{A_1, N_1}, false, \text{act as } h(A_i)) \hspace{3cm} \text{Cert. 14}$$

Combining this, on the semantic level[1], with Certificates 7–10, results in the creation of Cert. 15 that finally denotes that the newly created key has the S delegated permission to access R, and to further delegate this permission.

$$(S, K_{A_1, N_1}, true, R) \hspace{3cm} \text{Cert. 15}$$

Intermediate delegation. Let us next consider the situation where the node N_i has gained the access right.

$$(S, K_{A_i, N_i}, true, R) \hspace{3cm} \text{Cert. 16}$$

The node initiates action on the next node, N_{i+1}, that launches and names the agent running on it.

$$((N_{i+1}'s\ h(A_{i+1})), K_{A_{i+1}, N_{i+1}}) \hspace{3cm} \text{Cert. 17}$$

Reducing this with the chain leading to Cert. 12 results in

$$(U, K_{A_{i+1}, N_{i+1}}, false, \text{act as } h(A_{i+1})) \hspace{3cm} \text{Cert. 18}$$

Having this, together with the Cert. 12 chain, A_i can be sure that it is fine to delegate the right expressed with Cert. 16 further to A_{i+1}.

$$(K_{A_i, N_i}, K_{A_{i+1}, N_{i+1}}, true, R) \hspace{3cm} \text{Cert. 19}$$

Combining Cert. 19 with Cert. 16 results in

$$(S, K_{A_{i+1}, N_{i+1}}, true, R) \hspace{3cm} \text{Cert. 20}$$

which effectively states that A_{i+1}, running on node N_{i+1}, is permitted to access the resource R and to further delegate this permission.

Final step. In the beginning of the final step, agent A_k, executing on node N_k, has gained the right to access R.

$$(S, K_{A_k, N_k}, true, R) \hspace{3cm} \text{Cert. 21}$$

Agent A_k now launches agent A_S to run on the server S. S creates a temporary key K_{A_S} for the agent, and publishes it as a certificate.

$$((S's\ h(A_S)), K_{A_S}) \hspace{3cm} \text{Cert. 22}$$

Again, combining this with the Cert. 12 chain gives

$$(U, K_{A_S}, false, \text{act as } h(A_S)) \hspace{3cm} \text{Cert. 23}$$

which allows the agent A_k to decide to delegate the right to access the resource R.

$$(K_{A_k, N_k}, K_{A_S}, false, R) \hspace{3cm} \text{Cert. 24}$$

Reducing Cert. 24 with Cert. 21 results in Cert. 25.

$$(S, K_{A_S}, true, R) \hspace{3cm} \text{Cert. 25}$$

---

[1] With semantic level we mean here that mere syntactic SPKI reduction is not enough, but that the interpreter of the certificates must interpret the expression "act as $h(A_i)$".

The final certificate, Cert. 25, can now be trivially closed into a certificate loop by S, since S itself has created the key K_{A_S}, and therefore can trivially authenticate it. In other words, this can be seen easily to reduce into a virtual self-certificate Cert. 26.

$$(S, S, false, R) \hspace{4cm} \text{Cert. 26}$$

Cert. 26, closed on the behalf of the agent A_S, finally assures the server S that the agent A_S does have the right to access the protected resource R.

5.4 Preserving privacy

Using SPKI Certificate Reduction Certificates (CRC) provides the user U a simple way to stay anonymous while still securely accessing the resource R. If any of the policy administrators PA_i on the trust path leading from S to U is available online and willing to create CRCs, the user can feed it the relevant items of Cert. 9, Cert. 10, and Certs 4–6 and Cert. 7. This allows the policy administrator PA_i to create CRCs Cert. 27 and Cert. 28, for Certs 4–6 and Cert. 7, respectively.

$$(PA_i, (N_i's \ h(A_i)), false, \text{act as } h(A_i)) \hspace{2cm} \text{Cert. 27}$$

$$(PA_i, h(A_i), true, R) \hspace{3.5cm} \text{Cert. 28}$$

Then, in the rest of the algorithm, Cert. 27 is used instead of Cert. 12, and Cert. 28 is used instead of Cert. 7. Using this technique, other nodes than N_1 do not see U's key at all. The only identity information they can infer is that the user who effectively owns the computation is some user whom PA_i has directly or indirectly delegated the permission to access the resource R.

To further strengthen privacy, PA_i may encrypt parts of the certificates that it issues. Since these certificates will be used by PA_i itself for creating CRCs only, nobody else but PA_i itself needs to be able to decrypt the encryption. This makes it virtually impossible to find out the identities of the users that PA_i has issued rights in the first place.

6 Implementing the architecture

We are building a JDK 1.2 based prototype, where distinct JVM protection domains could delegate Java Permission objects, in the form of SPKI certificates, between each other. At this writing (September 1998), we have completed the integration of SPKI certificates to the basic JVM security policy system [25], implemented the basic functionality of ECDSA in pure Java [15], and integrated these two together so that the SPKI certificates are signed with ECDSA signatures, yielding improved performance in key generation.

Our next steps include facilities for transferring SPKI certificates between the Java Virtual Machines, and extending the Java security policy objects to recognize and support dynamically created delegations. Initially, we plan to share certificates through the file system between a number of JVMs running as separate processes under the UNIX operating system.

In addition, we are building a prototype of the ISAKMP [18] security protocol framework. This will allow us to create secure connections between network separated JVMs. The ISAKMP also allows us to easily transfer SPKI certificates and certificate chains between the virtual machines.

In order to support dynamic search and resolving of distributedly created SPKI certificate chains [3], we are integrating the Internet Domain Name System (DNS) certificate resource record (RR) format into our framework. This will allow us to store and retrieve long living SPKI certificates in the DNS system [22].

7 Conclusions

In this paper we have shown how authorisation certificates combined with relatively fast, elliptic curve based public key cryptography can be used to dynamically delegate authority in a distributed system. We analyzed the trust requirements of such a system in a fairly generic setting (Sect. 5.1), illustrated the details of how these trust requirements can be represented and verified with SPKI certificates (Sect. 5.2), and explained how the agents delegate permissions at run time by creating new key pairs and certificates. Finally, we outlined how the system can be utilized in a way that the user's identity is kept anonymous while still keeping all authorisations and connections secure (Sect. 5.4).

We are in the process of implementing a prototype of the proposed system. At the moment, we have completed the basic integration of SPKI certificates into the JDK 1.2 access control system (Sect. 3) and our first pure Java implementation of the ECDSA algorithms (Sect. 4). The next step is to integrate these with a fully distributed certificate management and retrieval system. The resulting system will allow distributed management of distributed systems security policies in fairly generic settings. In our view, the system could be used, e.g., as an Internet wide, organization borders crossing security policy management system.

References

1. Amoroso, E., *Fundamentals of Computer Security Technology*, Prentice Hall, Englewood Cliffs, New Jersey, 1994.
2. Arnold, K. and Gosling, J., *The Java Programming Language*, Addison-Wesley, 1996.
3. Aura, T. , "Comparison of Graph-Search Algorithms for Authorisation Verification in Delegation", *Proceedings of the 2nd Nordic Workshop on Secure Computer Systems, Helsinki*, 1997.
4. Beth, T., Borcherding, M., Klein, B., *Valuation of Trust in Open Networks*, University of Karlsruhe, 1994.
5. Blaze, M., Feigmenbaum, J., and Lacy, J., "Decentralized trust management", *Proceedings of the 1996 IEEE Computer Society Symposium on Research in Security and Privacy*, Oakland, CA, May 1996.

152

6. Chadwick, D., Young, A., "Merging and Extending the PGP and PEM Trust Models - The ICE-TEL Trust Model", *IEEE Network Magazine*, May/June, 1997.
7. Ellison, C. M., Frantz, B., Lampson, B., Rivest, R., Thomas, B. M. and Ylönen, T., *Simple Public Key Certificate*, Internet-Draft `draft-ietf-spki-cert-structure-05.txt`, work in progress, Internet Engineering Task Force, March 1998.
8. Ellison, C. M., Frantz, B., Lampson, B., Rivest, R., Thomas, B. M. and Ylönen, T., *SPKI Certificate Theory*, Internet-Draft `draft-ietf-spki-cert-theory-02.txt`, work in progress, Internet Engineering Task Force, March 1998.
9. Ellison, C. M., Frantz, B., Lampson, B., Rivest, R., Thomas, B. M. and Ylönen, T., *SPKI Examples*, Internet-Draft `draft-ietf-spki-cert-examples-01.txt`, work in progress, Internet Engineering Task Force, March 1998.
10. Ellison, C., "Establishing Identity Without Certification Authorities", In Proceedings of the *USENIX Security Symposium*, 1996.
11. Gong, Li, *Java™ Security Architecture (JDK 1.2)*, DRAFT DOCUMENT (Revision 0.8), `http://java.sun.com/products/jdk/1.2/docs/guide/security/spec/security-spec.doc.html`, Sun Microsystems, March 1998.
12. Gong, Li and Schemers, R., "Implementing Protection Domains in the Java Development Kit 1.2", *Proceedings of the 1998 Network and Distributed System Security Symposium*, San Diego, CA, March 11–13 1998, Internet Society, Reston, VA, March 1998.
13. International Telegraph and Telephone Consultative Committee (CCITT): *Recommendation X.509, The Directory - Authentication Framework*, CCITT Blue Book, Vol. VIII.8, pp. 48-81, 1988.
14. Kohl, J. and Neuman, C., *The Kerberos Network Authentication Service (V5)*, RFC1510, Internet Engineering Task Force, 1993.
15. Kortesniemi, Y., "Implementing Elliptic Curve Cryptosystems in Java 1.2", in *Proceedings of NordSec'98*, 6-7 November 1998, Trondheim, Norway, November 1998.
16. Landau, C., Security in a Secure Capability-Based System, *Operating Systems Review*, pp. 2-4, October 1989.
17. Lehti, I. and Nikander, P., "Certifying trust", *Proceedings of the Practice and Theory in Public Key Cryptography (PKC) '98*, Yokohama, Japan, Springer-Verlag, February 1998.
18. Maughan, D., Schertler, M., Schneider, M. and Turner, J., *Internet Security Association and Key Management Protocol (ISAKMP)*, Internet-Draft `draft-ietf-ipsec-isakmp-10.txt`, work in progress, Internet Engineering Task Force, July 1998.
19. McMahon, P.V., "SESAME V2 Public Key and Authorisation Extensions to Kerberos", in *Proceedings of 1995 Network and Distributed Systems Security*, February 16-17, 1995, San Diego, California, Internet Society 1995.
20. Nikander, P. and Karila, A., "A Java Beans Component Architecture for Cryptographic Protocols", *Proceedings of the 7th USENIX Security Symposium*, San Antonio, Texas, Usenix Association, 26-29 January 1998.

21. Nikander, P. and Partanen, J., "Distributed Policy Management for JDK 1.2", In *Proceedings of the 1999 Network and Distributed Systems Security Symposium,* 3-5 February 1999, San Diego, California, Internet Society, February 1999.

22. Nikander, P. and Viljanen, L., "Storing and Retrieving Internet Certificates", in *Proceedings of NordSec'98*, 6-7 November 1998, Trondheim, Norway, November 1998.

23. OMG, *CORBAservices: Common Object Services Specification, Revised Edition,* Object Management Group, Farmingham, MA, March 1997.

24. Partanen, J. and Nikander, P., "Adding SPKI certificates to JDK 1.2", in *Proceedings of NordSec'98*, 6-7 November 1998, Trondheim, Norway, November 1998.

25. Partanen, J., *Using SPKI certificates for Access Control in Java 1.2*, Master's Thesis, Helsinki University of Technology, August 1998.

26. Rivest, R. L. and Lampson, B., "SDSI — a simple distributed security infrastructure", *Proceedings of the 1996 Usenix Security Symposium*, 1996.

27. Wilhelm, G. U., Staamann, S., Buttyán, L., "On the Problem of Trust in Mobile Agent Systems", In *Proceedings of the 1998 Network And Distributed System Security Symposium,* March 11-13, 1998, San Diego, California, Internet Society, 1998.

28. Yahalom, R., Klein, B., Beth, T., "Trust Relationships in Secure Systems - A Distributed Authentication Perspective", In *Proceedings of the IEEE Conference on Research in Security and Privacy*, 1993.

Unknown Key-Share Attacks on the Station-to-Station (STS) Protocol

Simon Blake-Wilson[1] and Alfred Menezes[2]

[1] Certicom Research, 200 Matheson Blvd. W., Suite 103
Mississauga, Ontario, Canada L5R 3L7
sblakewi@certicom.com
[2] Department of Combinatorics & Optimization
University of Waterloo, Waterloo, Ontario, Canada N2L 3G1
ajmeneze@cacr.math.uwaterloo.ca

Abstract. This paper presents some new unknown key-share attacks on STS-MAC, the version of the STS key agreement protocol which uses a MAC algorithm to provide key confirmation. Various methods are considered for preventing the attacks.

1 Introduction

Key establishment is the process by which two (or more) entities establish a shared secret key. The key may subsequently be used to achieve some cryptographic goal, such as confidentiality or data integrity. Ideally, the established key should have precisely the same attributes as a key established face-to-face — for example, it should be shared by the (two) specified entities, it should be distributed uniformly at random from the key space, and no unauthorized (and computationally bounded) entity should learn anything about the key.

Key establishment protocols come in various flavors. In *key transport* protocols, a key is created by one entity and securely transmitted to the second entity, while in *key agreement* protocols both parties contribute information which is used to derive the shared secret key. In *symmetric* protocols the two entities a priori possess common secret information, while in *asymmetric* protocols the two entities share only public information that has been authenticated. This paper is concerned with two-party key agreement protocols in the asymmetric setting.

Unfortunately, the requirement that key agreement protocols have the same properties as face-to-face key establishment is too vague to be much help to protocol designers, who instead focus on designing protocols to meet more explicit requirements. Implicit key authentication and key confirmation are two explicit requirements that are often considered essential.

Let A and B be two honest entities, i.e., legitimate entities who execute the steps of a protocol correctly. Informally speaking, a key agreement protocol is said to provide *implicit key authentication* (of B to A) if entity A is assured that no other entity aside from a specifically identified second entity B can possibly learn the value of a particular secret key. Note that the property of implicit key authentication does not necessarily mean that A is assured of B actually possessing the key. A key agreement protocol which provides implicit key authentication to both participating entities is called an *authenticated key agreement (AK)* protocol.

Informally speaking, a key agreement protocol is said to provide *explicit key confirmation* (of B to A) if entity A is assured that the second entity B *has actually* computed the agreed key. The protocol provides *implicit key confirmation* if A is assured that B *can* compute the agreed key. While explicit key confirmation appears to provide stronger assurances to A than implicit key confirmation (in particular, the former implies the latter), it appears that, for all practical purposes, the assurances are in fact the same. That is, the assurance that A requires in practice is merely that B can compute the key rather than that B has actually computed the key. Indeed in practice, even if a protocol does provide explicit key confirmation, it cannot guarantee to A that B will not lose the key between key establishment and key use. Thus it would indeed seem that implicit key confirmation and explicit key confirmation are in practice very similar.

If both implicit key authentication and (implicit or explicit) key confirmation (of B to A) are provided, then the key establishment protocol is said to provide *explicit key authentication* (of B to A). A key agreement protocol which provides explicit key authentication to both participating entities is called an *authenticated key agreement with key confirmation (AKC)* protocol.

In addition to implicit key authentication and key confirmation, a number of other desirable security attributes of key agreement protocols have been identified including known-key security, forward secrecy, key-compromise impersonation, and unknown key-share. These are typically properties possessed by face-to-face key establishment which may be more or less important when a key establishment protocol is used to provide security in real-life applications.

An *unknown key-share* (UKS) attack on an AK or AKC protocol is an attack whereby an entity A ends up believing she shares a key with B, and although this is in fact the case, B mistakenly believes the key is instead shared with an entity $E \neq A$. The significance of UKS attacks on AK and AKC protocols is further discussed in §3.

This paper presents some new on-line UKS attacks on STS-MAC, the variant of the station-to-station (STS) [11] AKC protocol which uses a MAC to provide key confirmation. For an extensive survey on key establishment, see Chapter 12 of [25]. For a recent survey on authenticated Diffie-Hellman key agreement protocols, see [10]. Formal definitions of authenticated key agreement can be found for the symmetric setting in [7] and for the asymmetric setting in [9].

The remainder of this paper is organized as follows. The STS protocol is described in §2. In §3 we present the new on-line UKS attacks on STS-MAC, and consider ways of preventing the attacks. In §4, we examine the plausibility of an assumption regarding signature schemes that is required in order for the attacks to succeed. §5 makes concluding remarks.

2 Description of STS

The station-to-station (STS) protocol [11] is a Diffie-Hellman-based AKC protocol that purports to provide both (mutual) implicit key authentication and (mutual) key confirmation, and additionally appears to possess desirable security attributes such as forward secrecy and key-compromise impersonation. The STS protocol, as described in [11], provides (explicit) key confirmation by using the agreed key K in a symmetric-key encryption scheme; we call this protocol STS-ENC. A variant of STS mentioned in [11], which we call STS-MAC, provides (explicit) key confirmation by using the agreed key K in a MAC algorithm.

STS-MAC may be preferred over STS-ENC in many practical scenarios because of existing export or usage restrictions on secure encryption. Moreover, the use of encryption to provide key confirmation in STS-ENC is questionable — traditionally the sole goal of encryption is to provide confidentiality and if an encryption scheme is used to demonstrate possession of a key then it is shown by decryption, not by encryption. One advantage of STS-ENC over STS-MAC is that the former can facilitate the provision of anonymity.

Many protocols related to STS have appeared in the literature (e.g., [5], [14], [18]). It should be noted, however, that these protocols cannot be considered to be minor variants of STS — as this paper shows, the former protocols have some security attributes that are lacking in STS.

The following notation is used throughout the paper.

Notation

A, B	Honest entities.
E	The adversary.
S_A	A's (private) signing key for a signature scheme S.
P_A	A's (public) verification key for S.
$S_A(M)$	A's signature on a message M.
Cert_A	A's certificate containing A's identifying information, A's public signature key P_A, and possibly some other information.
$E_K(M)$	Encryption of M using a symmetric-key encryption scheme with key K.
$\text{MAC}_K(M)$	Message authentication code of M under key K.
G, α, n	Diffie-Hellman parameters; α is an element of prime order n in the finite multiplicative group G.
r_A	A's ephemeral Diffie-Hellman private key; $1 \leq r_A \leq n - 1$.
K	Ephemeral Diffie-Hellman shared secret; $K = \alpha^{r_A r_B}$.

The two STS variants are presented below (see also [11, 25, 32]). In both descriptions, A is called the *initiator*, while B is called the *responder*.

STS-MAC protocol. The STS-MAC protocol is depicted below. Initiator A selects a random secret integer r_A, $1 \leq r_A \leq n - 1$, and sends to B the message (1). Upon receiving (1), B selects a random secret integer r_B, $1 \leq r_B \leq n - 1$, computes the shared secret $K = (\alpha^{r_A})^{r_B}$, and sends message (2) to A. Upon receiving (2), A uses Cert_B to verify the authenticity of B's signing key P_B, verifies B's signature on the message $(\alpha^{r_B}, \alpha^{r_A})$, computes the shared secret $K = (\alpha^{r_B})^{r_A}$, and verifies the MAC on $S_B(\alpha^{r_B}, \alpha^{r_A})$. A then sends message (3) to B. Upon receipt of (3), B uses Cert_A to verify the authenticity of A's signing key P_A, verifies A's signature on the message $(\alpha^{r_A}, \alpha^{r_B})$, and verifies the MAC on $S_A(\alpha^{r_A}, \alpha^{r_B})$. If at any stage a check or verification performed by A or B fails, then that entity terminates the protocol run, and rejects.

(1) $A \to B$ A, α^{r_A}

(2) $A \leftarrow B$ $\text{Cert}_B, \alpha^{r_B}, S_B(\alpha^{r_B}, \alpha^{r_A}), \text{MAC}_K(S_B(\alpha^{r_B}, \alpha^{r_A}))$

(3) $A \to B$ $\text{Cert}_A, S_A(\alpha^{r_A}, \alpha^{r_B}), \text{MAC}_K(S_A(\alpha^{r_A}, \alpha^{r_B}))$

STS-ENC protocol. The STS-ENC protocol is given below. For the sake of brevity, the checks that should be performed by A and B are henceforth omitted.

(1) $A \to B$ A, α^{r_A}

(2) $A \leftarrow B$ $\text{Cert}_B, \alpha^{r_B}, E_K(S_B(\alpha^{r_B}, \alpha^{r_A}))$

(3) $A \to B$ $\text{Cert}_A, E_K(S_A(\alpha^{r_A}, \alpha^{r_B}))$

3   Unknown key-share attacks

An *unknown key-share* (UKS) attack on a key agreement protocol is an attack whereby an entity A ends up believing she shares a key with B, and although this is in fact the case, B mistakenly believes the key is instead shared with an entity $E \neq A$. In this scenario, we say that B has been led to false beliefs. If B is the protocol's initiator, then the attack is called a UKS attack *against the initiator*. Otherwise, the attack is called a UKS attack *against the responder*.

It is important to note that if an AK or AKC protocol succumbs to a UKS attack in which E is a dishonest entity (this is the case with the attacks presented in this paper), then this does not contradict the implicit key authentication property of the protocol — by definition, the provision of implicit key authentication is only considered in the case where B engages in the protocol with an honest entity (which E isn't).

AN ATTACK SCENARIO. A hypothetical scenario where a UKS attack can have damaging consequences is the following; this scenario was first described in [11]. Suppose that B is a bank branch and A is an account holder. Certificates are issued by the bank headquarters and within each certificate is the account information of the holder. Suppose that the protocol for electronic deposit of funds is to exchange a key with a bank branch via an AKC protocol. At the conclusion of the protocol run, encrypted funds are deposited to the account number in the certificate. Suppose that no further authentication is done in the encrypted deposit message (which might be the case to save bandwidth). If the UKS attack mentioned above is successfully launched then the deposit will be made to E's account instead of A's account.

ANOTHER ATTACK SCENARIO. Another scenario where a UKS attack can be damaging is the following. Suppose that B controls access to a suite of sensitive applications (e.g. salary databases). Each application has a password associated with it. The password is chosen and securely distributed by a CA to B and to all entities entitled to access that application. The CA also certifies public keys of all potential users of one (or more) of the applications. A user A gains access to an application by supplying to B the password that is specific to that application. This can be done securely as follows. When A wants to gain access to the application, she and B engage in a single run of an AKC protocol to establish shared keys K_1 and K_2 (K_1 and K_2 are derived from the shared secret established). A then authenticates and encrypts the password using the keys and sends the result to B. B checks the encrypted authenticated password and supplies access to A. Once access has been granted, the application establishes new keys with A to secure the subsequent use of the application.

If the AKC protocol does not provide unknown key-share, an active adversary E can induce B into believing that he shares the keys K_1 and K_2 with E, while A correctly believes that she shares the keys with B. E may then use the encrypted authenticated password sent by A to gain access to the application.

SIGNIFICANCE OF UKS ATTACKS. The importance of preventing UKS attacks has been debated in the literature. It is interesting to note that prevention of UKS attacks was one of the original design principles of STS [11]. Here we make two observations about the relevance of UKS attacks. First, notice that traditional, face-to-face key establishment is not susceptible to UKS attacks. Therefore anyone implementing a key establishment protocol that does not prevent UKS attacks as a drop-in replacement for face-to-face key establishment must check whether UKS attacks represent a security concern in the application. Second, notice that a UKS attack on an AKC protocol is more serious than a UKS attack on an AK protocol (which does not provide key confirmation). As stated in [9], keys established using AK protocols should be confirmed prior to cryptographic use. Indeed, some standards such as [4] take the conservative approach of mandating key confirmation of keys agreed in an AK protocol. If appropriate key confirmation is subsequently provided, then the attempt at a UKS attack will be detected. For this reason, the above hypothetical banking scenario (in particular, the assumption that no further authentication is performed after termination of the key agreement protocol) is realistic if an AKC protocol is used (since key confirmation has already been provided), and unrealistic if an AK protocol is used (since key confirmation has not yet been provided).

The remainder of this section discusses UKS attacks on STS-MAC and STS-ENC. §3.1 describes well-known public key substitution UKS attacks (for example, see [24, 25]). These attacks can be prevented if a CA checks possession of private keys during the certification process. §3.2 presents new on-line UKS attacks on STS-MAC that are not prevented simply by checking knowledge of private keys during certification. It suggests other methods which may be used to prevent the new attacks. The attacks are similar in spirit to Kaliski's recent attack [20] on the AK protocol of [21] — however the attacks we present are more damaging because, unlike Kaliski's attack, they are not prevented by appropriate key confirmation. Finally, in §3.3 we consider possible UKS attacks on STS-ENC which may not be prevented by checking knowledge of private keys during certification. The attacks in §3.3 are considerably more far-fetched than the attacks in §3.2, but they demonstrate the value of public-key validation and formal protocol analysis.

3.1 Public key substitution UKS attacks

This section describes well-known public key substitution UKS attacks on STS-MAC and STS-ENC.

Attack against the responder. In this UKS attack against the responder, the adversary E registers A's public key P_A as its own; i.e., $P_E = P_A$. When A sends B message (1), E intercepts it and replaces the identity A with E. E then passes message (2) from B to A unchanged. Finally E intercepts message (3), and replaces Cert_A with Cert_E. Since $P_A = P_E$, we have $S_A(\alpha^{r_A}, \alpha^{r_B}) = S_E(\alpha^{r_A}, \alpha^{r_B})$. Hence B accepts the key K and believes that K is shared with E, while in fact it is shared with A. Note that E does not learn the value of K. The attack is depicted below. The notation $A \hookrightarrow B$ means that A transmitted a message intended for B, which was intercepted by the adversary and not delivered to B.

(1) $A \hookrightarrow B$ A, α^{r_A}
(1') $E \to B$ E, α^{r_A}
(2) $E \leftarrow B$ $\text{Cert}_B, \alpha^{r_B}, S_B(\alpha^{r_B}, \alpha^{r_A}), \text{MAC}_K(S_B(\alpha^{r_B}, \alpha^{r_A}))$
(2') $A \leftarrow E$ $\text{Cert}_B, \alpha^{r_B}, S_B(\alpha^{r_B}, \alpha^{r_A}), \text{MAC}_K(S_B(\alpha^{r_B}, \alpha^{r_A}))$
(3) $A \hookrightarrow B$ $\text{Cert}_A, S_A(\alpha^{r_A}, \alpha^{r_B}), \text{MAC}_K(S_A(\alpha^{r_A}, \alpha^{r_B}))$
(3') $E \to B$ $\text{Cert}_E, S_A(\alpha^{r_A}, \alpha^{r_B}), \text{MAC}_K(S_A(\alpha^{r_A}, \alpha^{r_B}))$

Attack against the initiator. E can similarly launch a UKS attack against the initiator A by registering B's public P_B as its own. The attack is depicted below.

(1) $A \to E$ A, α^{r_A}
(1') $E \to B$ A, α^{r_A}
(2) $A \leftarrow B$ $\text{Cert}_B, \alpha^{r_B}, S_B(\alpha^{r_B}, \alpha^{r_A}), \text{MAC}_K(S_B(\alpha^{r_B}, \alpha^{r_A}))$
(2') $A \leftarrow E$ $\text{Cert}_E, \alpha^{r_B}, S_B(\alpha^{r_B}, \alpha^{r_A}), \text{MAC}_K(S_B(\alpha^{r_B}, \alpha^{r_A}))$
(3) $A \to E$ $\text{Cert}_A, S_A(\alpha^{r_A}, \alpha^{r_B}), \text{MAC}_K(S_A(\alpha^{r_A}, \alpha^{r_B}))$
(3') $E \to B$ $\text{Cert}_A, S_A(\alpha^{r_A}, \alpha^{r_B}), \text{MAC}_K(S_A(\alpha^{r_A}, \alpha^{r_B}))$

Preventing the attacks. Both these public key substitution attacks are well-known and are usually prevented by requiring that entities prove to the certificate-issuing authority possession of the private keys corresponding to their public keys during the certification process. The attacks can also be launched against STS-ENC; it this case, an alternate way to prevent the attacks is to encrypt certificates using the shared key K.

3.2 On-line UKS attacks on STS-MAC

This section describes the new on-line UKS attacks on STS-MAC. The following assumptions are made in order for the attacks to be effective.

1. The signature scheme S used in STS has the following *duplicate-signature key selection* property. Suppose that P_A (A's public key) and A's signature s_A on a message M are known. Then the adversary is able to select a key pair (P_E, S_E) with respect to which s_A is also E's signature on the message M. The plausibility of this assumption is examined in §4, where it is shown that the RSA, Rabin, ElGamal, DSA and ECDSA signature schemes all possess the duplicate-signature key selection property in certain situations.

2. E is able to get its public key certified during a run of the STS protocol. This assumption is plausible, for instance, in situations where delays in the transmission of messages are normal, and where the CA is on-line.

Attack against the responder. This new UKS attack on STS-MAC is similar to the public key substitution attack against the responder in §3.1. After A sends message (3), E intercepts it and selects a key pair (P_E, S_E) for the employed signature scheme such that $S_E(\alpha^{r_A}, \alpha^{r_B}) = S_A(\alpha^{r_A}, \alpha^{r_B})$. E then obtains a certificate $Cert_E$ for P_E, and transmits message (3') to B.

Attack against the initiator. This new UKS attack on STS-MAC is similar to the public key substitution attack against the initiator in §3.1. After B sends message (2), E intercepts it and selects a key pair (P_E, S_E) for the employed signature scheme such that $S_E(\alpha^{r_B}, \alpha^{r_A}) = S_B(\alpha^{r_B}, \alpha^{r_A})$. E then obtains a certificate $Cert_E$ for P_E, and transmits message (2') to A.

Preventing the attacks. In the on-line UKS attacks, the adversary knows the private key S_E corresponding to its chosen public key P_E. Hence, unlike the case of the public key substitution attacks, the on-line attacks cannot be prevented by requiring that entities prove to the certificate-issuing authority possession of the private keys corresponding to their public keys during the certification process.

The following outlines some measures that can be taken to prevent the on-line UKS attacks on STS-MAC.

1. If A sends its certificate $Cert_A$ in flow (1) rather than in flow (3), then the on-line UKS attack against the responder cannot be launched; however the on-line UKS attack against the initiator still succeeds.

2. If certificates are exchanged a priori, i.e., prior to the protocol run, then the on-line UKS attacks fail. A priori exchanges of certificates may be undesirable in practice because it increases the number of protocol flows.

3. Including the identities of the sender and intended receiver as well as the flow number[1] in the messages being signed prevents the on-line UKS attacks. Inclusion of the flow number and the identity of the message sender may help guard against attacks yet to be discovered. (See [26] for an example

---

[1] In this paper, we assume that message fields such as flow numbers, identities, and group elements, are represented using fixed-length encodings and concatenated. Otherwise, some other unique prefix-free encoding such as ASN.1 DER [15, 16] should be used.

of how inclusion of flow numbers can help guard against certain attacks on entity authentication mechanisms.) These modifications add negligible computational overhead to the protocol and follow the generic philosophy expounded in [9] and [21]. The revised protocol is shown below.

(1) $A \to B$ A, α^{r_A}

(2) $A \leftarrow B$ $\text{Cert}_B, \alpha^{r_B}, S_B(2, B, A, \alpha^{r_B}, \alpha^{r_A})$,
                     $\text{MAC}_K(S_B(2, B, A, \alpha^{r_B}, \alpha^{r_A}))$

(3) $A \to B$ $\text{Cert}_A, S_A(3, A, B, \alpha^{r_A}, \alpha^{r_B}), \text{MAC}_K(S_A(3, A, B, \alpha^{r_A}, \alpha^{r_B}))$

4. In the original STS-MAC protocol and the modification presented in item 3 above, the agreed key K is used as the MAC key for the purpose of providing *explicit* key confirmation. A passive adversary now has some information about K — the MAC of a known message under K. The adversary can use this to distinguish K from a key selected uniformly at random from the key space[2]. The elegant general principle that in the face of a computationally bounded adversary a computationally indistinguishable key can later be used in place of a traditional face-to-face secret key anywhere without sacrificing security can therefore not be applied (and security must be analyzed on a case-by-case basis). Another drawback of providing explicit key confirmation in this way is that the agreed key K may be subsequently used with a different cryptographic mechanism than the MAC algorithm — this violates a fundamental cryptographic principle that a key should not be used for more than one purpose.

An improvement, therefore, is to provide *implicit*, rather than explicit, key confirmation. Two keys K and K' are derived from $\alpha^{r_A r_B}$ using a cryptographic hash function H. In practice, this can be achieved by setting $K \| K' = H(\alpha^{r_A r_B})$, or $K = H(01, \alpha^{r_A r_B})$ and $K' = H(10, \alpha^{r_A r_B})$. K' is used as the MAC key for the session, while K is used as the agreed session key. The revised protocol is depicted below.

(1) $A \to B$ A, α^{r_A}

(2) $A \leftarrow B$ $\text{Cert}_B, \alpha^{r_B}, S_B(2, B, A, \alpha^{r_B}, \alpha^{r_A})$,
                     $\text{MAC}_{K'}(S_B(2, B, A, \alpha^{r_B}, \alpha^{r_A}))$

(3) $A \to B$ $\text{Cert}_A, S_A(3, A, B, \alpha^{r_A}, \alpha^{r_B}), \text{MAC}_{K'}(S_A(3, A, B, \alpha^{r_A}, \alpha^{r_B}))$

We imagine that this protocol (and also the protocol in item 6 below) can be analyzed by modelling the hash function H as a random oracle [6].

5. Instead of including the identities of the entities in the signed message, one could include them in the *key derivation function*, whose purpose is to derive the shared key from the shared secret $\alpha^{r_A r_B}$. In the protocol of item 3, the shared secret key would be $K = H(\alpha^{r_A r_B}, A, B)$, while in the 2 protocols of item 4, the shared keys would be (i) $K \| K' = H(\alpha^{r_A r_B}, A, B)$ and (ii) $K' = H(01, \alpha^{r_A r_B}, A, B)$ and $K = H(10, \alpha^{r_A r_B}, A, B)$.

However, key derivation functions have not been well-studied by the cryptographic community. In particular, the desirable security properties of a key derivation function have not yet been specified. For this reason, the protocols presented in items 3 and 4 are preferred over the variants which include identities in the key derivation function.

---

[2] The key space here is $\mathcal{K} = \{\alpha^i : 1 \leq i \leq n - 1\}$.

6. The protocols in item 4 provide implicit key confirmation. While the assurance that the other entity has actually computed the shared key K is not provided, each entity does get the assurance that the other has computed the shared secret $\alpha^{r_A r_B}$. Implicit key confirmation is still provided (to a somewhat lesser degree) if the MACs are not included in the flows. The revised protocol is shown below:

   (1) $A \rightarrow B$ A, α^{r_A}

   (2) $A \leftarrow B$ $\text{Cert}_B, \alpha^{r_B}, S_B(2, B, A, \alpha^{r_B}, \alpha^{r_A})$

   (3) $A \rightarrow B$ $\text{Cert}_A, S_A(3, A, B, \alpha^{r_A}, \alpha^{r_B})$

7. ISO 11770-3 has one variant each of the STS-ENC and STS-MAC protocols — these are included as "Key agreement mechanism 7" in [18]. Both these variants resist the on-line UKS attacks. The ISO variant of STS-MAC, which we call ISO-STS-MAC, is the following:

   (1) $A \rightarrow B$ A, α^{r_A}

   (2) $A \leftarrow B$ $\text{Cert}_B, \alpha^{r_B}, S_B(\alpha^{r_B}, \alpha^{r_A}, A), \text{MAC}_K(\alpha^{r_B}, \alpha^{r_A}, A)$

   (3) $A \rightarrow B$ $\text{Cert}_A, S_A(\alpha^{r_A}, \alpha^{r_B}, B), \text{MAC}_K(\alpha^{r_A}, \alpha^{r_B}, B)$

   Notice that, unlike the original description of STS-MAC, identities of the intended recipients are included in the signatures in ISO-STS-MAC. This was apparently done in order to be conformant with the entity authentication mechanisms in ISO 9798-3 [17], rather than because of a security concern with STS without the inclusion of identities. Another difference between ISO-STS-MAC and STS-MAC is that in the former the MAC algorithm is applied to the message that is signed, rather than to the signature of the message.

   We note that Bellare, Canetti and Krawczyk [5] have recently provided a model and security definitions under which ISO-STS-MAC without the inclusion of the MACs is provably secure. How their model compares with the model of [9] is not entirely clear.

3.3 Other UKS attacks

The on-line UKS attacks of §3.2 cannot, in general, be launched on STS-ENC because the signatures $S_A(\alpha^{r_A}, \alpha^{r_B})$ and $S_B(\alpha^{r_B}, \alpha^{r_A})$ are not known by the adversary. Is it possible to extend the attacks to provide UKS attacks on STS-ENC that cannot be prevented by checking knowledge of private keys during certification? This section suggests a possible (although unlikely) scenario in which such (off-line) attacks on STS-ENC (and STS-MAC) may be successful. The attack illustrates two points:

1. A complete description of STS-ENC should include a complete specification of the underlying symmetric-key encryption and signature schemes, together with a statement of the security properties they are assumed to possess; and

2. Performing public-key validation [19] of signature keys is a sensible measure to take. (Rationale for performing key validation of public keys for use in Diffie-Hellman-based key agreement protocols is provided in [23].)

The attack is similar to the attack presented in §3.2, but relies on the following assumption on the signature scheme: E is able to certify a key pair (P_E, S_E) such that A's signature on any message M is also valid as E's signature on message M. Note that deterministic signature schemes cannot possess this property and be secure, since E knows S_E and can therefore compute A's signatures using S_E. However it is possible that some probabilistic signature schemes possess this property. This is illustrated by the following example.

Suppose that the underlying signature scheme is the ElGamal signature scheme (see §4.3). Suppose that entities select their own domain parameters p and g, as may be the case in high security applications. Suppose further that when certifying an entity E's public key $P_E = (p, g, y)$ (where $y = g^e \pmod p$ and e is E's private key), the CA does not perform public-key validation; that is, the CA does not verify that p, g and y possess the requisite arithmetic properties — that p is prime, g is a generator of $\mathbb{Z}_p^*$, and $1 \leq y \leq p - 1$. Finally, suppose that the CA verifies that E possesses the private key corresponding to its public key by asking E to sign a challenge message.

If a dishonest entity E selects $g = 0$ (which is *not* a generator of $\mathbb{Z}_p^*$), then $y = 0$. In this case, every pair of integers (r, s), where $1 \leq r \leq p - 1$ and $1 \leq s \leq p - 2$, is a valid signature for E on any message M since the ElGamal signature verification equation (see §4.3) $g^m \equiv y^r r^s \pmod p$ is satisfied. In particular, if the CA does not validate E's public key, then it will accept E's proof of possession of its private key.

Having obtained a certificate Cert_E of such an invalid public key $P_E = (p, 0, 0)$ (where the prime p is greater than the prime moduli of A and B), E can now launch UKS attacks against the responser or the initiator in both STS-ENC and STS-MAC in exactly the same way as described in §3.1. For example, in the attack against the initiator, E replaces A's identity with its own identity in flow (1), and then replaces Cert_A with Cert_E in flow (3). Note that these are not online attacks since E can get its public key certified in advance of the attack. Note also that these attacks are different from the public key substitution attacks of §3.1, because in the former E has indeed demonstrated possession of its private key to the CA during the certification process.

As precautionary measures, we recommend that public-key validation of signature keys be performed, and that STS-ENC be modified so that either the flow number and identities of the sender and intended recipient are included in the signed message[3] or that the identities be included in the key derivation function (as in item 5 in §3.2).

4   Duplicate-signature key selection

This section examines whether commonly used signature schemes possess the duplicate-signature key selection property that is required in §3.2: given A's

---

[3] The resulting revised protocols are the same as the ones presented in items 3 and 4 in §3.2 with the data $(S_A(m), \text{MAC}_K(S_A(m)))$ replaced by $E_K(S_A(m))$, and $(S_B(m), \text{MAC}_K(S_B(m)))$ replaced by $E_K(S_B(m))$.

public key P_A for a signature scheme S, and given A's signature s_A on a message M, can an adversary select a key pair (P_E, S_E) for S such that s_A is also E's signature on the message M? We demonstrate that, in certain circumstances, the RSA [31], Rabin [30], ElGamal [12], DSA [1, 27], and ECDSA [3] signature schemes all possess this property. In the RSA scheme, it is assumed that each entity is permitted to select its own encryption exponent e. In the ElGamal, DSA and ECDSA schemes, it is assumed that entities are permitted to select their own domain parameters; this is what might be done in high security applications.

It must be emphasized that possession of the duplicate-signature key selection property does not constitute a weakness of the signature scheme — the goal of a signature scheme is to be existentially unforgeable against an adaptive chosen-message attack [13].

In the following, H denotes a cryptographic hash function such as SHA-1 [28].

4.1 RSA

Key pair: A's public key is $P_A = (N, E)$, where N is a product of two distinct primes P and Q, and $1 < E < \Phi$, $\gcd(E, \Phi) = 1$, where $\Phi = (P-1)(Q-1)$. A's private key is D, where $1 < D < \Phi$ and $ED \equiv 1 \pmod{\Phi}$.

Signature generation: To sign a message M, A computes $m = H(M)$ and $s = m^D \bmod N$. A's signature on M is s. Here, H may also incorporate a message formatting procedure such as the ones specified in the ANSI X9.31 [2], FDH [8] and PSS [8] variants of RSA.

Signature verification: Given an authentic copy of A's public key, one can verify A's signature s on M by computing $m = H(M)$, and verifying that $s^E \equiv m \pmod{N}$.

Adversary's actions: Given A's public key P_A and A's signature s on M, E does the following.

1. Compute $m = H(M)$.
2. Select a prime p such that:
   (a) $p - 1$ is smooth; and
   (b) s and m are both generators of $\mathbb{Z}_p^*$.
3. Select a prime q such that:
   (a) $pq > N$;
   (b) $q - 1$ is smooth;
   (c) $\gcd(p - 1, q - 1) = 2$; and
   (d) s and m are both generators of $\mathbb{Z}_q^*$.
4. Since $p - 1$ is smooth, E can use the Pohlig-Hellman algorithm [29] to efficiently find an integer x_1 such that $s^{x_1} \equiv m \pmod{p}$.
5. Similarly, since $q - 1$ is smooth, E can efficiently find an integer x_2 such that $s^{x_2} \equiv m \pmod{q}$.
6. Compute $n = pq$, $\phi = (p - 1)(q - 1)$, and $\lambda = \phi/2$.

7. Find the unique integer e, $1 < e < \lambda$, such that $e \equiv x_1 \pmod{(p-1)}$ and $e \equiv x_2 \pmod{(q-1)}$. This can be done by first solving the congruence

$$t(p-1)/2 \equiv (x_2 - x_1)/2 \pmod{(q-1)/2}$$

for t (note that $x_2 - x_1$ is indeed even), and then setting $e = x_1 + t(p-1) \bmod \lambda$. Note also that since m is a generator of $\mathbb{Z}_p^*$, we have $\gcd(x_1, p-1) = 1$; similarly $\gcd(x_2, q-1) = 1$. If follows that $\gcd(e, \phi) = 1$.
8. Compute an integer d, $1 < d < \phi$, such that $ed \equiv 1 \pmod{\phi}$.
9. E forms $P_E = (n, e)$; E's private key is d.

Observe that s is also E's signature on M since

$$s^e \equiv s^{e \bmod (p-1)} \equiv s^{x_1} \equiv m \pmod{p}$$

and

$$s^e \equiv s^{e \bmod (q-1)} \equiv s^{x_2} \equiv m \pmod{q},$$

whence

$$s^e \equiv m \pmod{n}.$$

Remarks

1. The following is a heuristic analysis of the expected number of candidate p's and q's that are chosen before primes satisfying the conditions in steps 2 and 3 are found.

   Suppose that the desired bitlength of both p and q is k. Candidates p and q can be selected by first choosing $p-1$ and $q-1$ to be products of small prime powers (thus ensuring conditions 2(a) and 3(b)); the primes occurring in the two products should be pairwise distinct, except for a 2 which occurs exactly once in each product (this ensures that $\gcd(p-1, q-1) = 2$). The candidate p is then subjected to a primality test. By the prime number theorem [25, Fact 2.95], the expected number of trials before a prime p is obtained is $(\frac{1}{2} \ln 2)k$. Given that p is prime, the probability that both m and s are generators of $\mathbb{Z}_p^*$ is (see [25, Fact 2.102])

$$\left(\frac{\phi(p-1)}{(p-1)} \right)^2 < \left(\frac{1}{6 \ln \ln(p-1)} \right)^2.$$

   If either m or s does not generate $\mathbb{Z}_p^*$, then another candidate p is selected. Hence, the expected number of trials before an appropriate p is found is

$$\left(\frac{1}{2} \ln 2 \right) k(6 \ln \ln(p-1))^2 = O(k(\ln k)^2).$$

   It follows that the expected number of candidates p and q before appropriates primes are found is also $O(k(\ln k)^2)$.
2. Observe that (n, e) is a valid RSA public key, and that E knows the corresponding private key d.

3. To reduce the amount of on-line work required, the adversary could use A's public key to precompute several candidate pairs of primes p and q which satisfy conditions 2(a), 3(a), 3(b), and 3(c). Subsequently, when the adversary sees A's signature s on M, it can choose a precomputed pair of primes which also satisfy conditions 2(b) and 3(d).

4.2 Rabin

Key pair: A's public key is $P_A = N$, where N is a product of two distinct primes P and Q. A's private key is (P, Q).

Signature generation: To sign a message M, A computes $m = H(M)$, and finds a square root s of m modulo N: $s^2 \equiv m \bmod N$. A's signature on M is s. (If m is not a quadratic residue modulo N, then m should be adjusted in a predetermined way so that the result is one.)

Signature verification: Given an authentic copy of A's public key, one can verify A's signature s on M by computing $m = H(M)$, and verifying that $s^2 \equiv m \pmod{N}$.

Adversary's actions: Given A's public key P_A and A's signature s on M, E computes $n = (s^2 - m)/N$ and forms $P_E = n$. Observe that s is also E's signature on M since $s^2 \equiv m \pmod{n}$.

Remarks

1. The bitlength of n is expected to be the same as the bitlength of N.
2. n is most likely not the product of two distinct primes, and hence is not a valid Rabin public key. (Assuming that n is a random k-bit integer, the expected total number of prime factors of n is approximately $\ln k$; [25, Fact 3.7(iii)].) However, it is difficult, in general, to test whether a composite integer is a product is of two distinct primes; hence Rabin public-key validation is usually not performed in practice.
3. Assuming that n is a random k-bit integer, the probability that the bitlength of the second-largest prime factor of n is $\leq 0.22k$ is about $\frac{1}{2}$ [25, Fact 3.7(ii)]. Thus, for example, if 512-bit moduli are being used, then the probability that the bitlength of the second-largest prime factor of n is ≤ 113 is about $\frac{1}{2}$. Such n can be readily factored with the elliptic curve factoring algorithm [22]. Given the prime factorization of n, E can hope to convince the CA that it knows the corresponding private key (even though one may not exist — n may not be a product of 2 distinct primes), by signing (computing square roots modulo n, as with the Rabin scheme) a message of the CA's choice.

4.3 ElGamal

Domain parameters: A safe prime p (i.e., $q := (p - 1)/2$ is prime), and a generator g of $\mathbb{Z}_p^*$.

Key pair: A's private key is an integer a, $1 \leq a \leq p - 2$. A's public key is $P_A = (p, g, y)$, where $y = g^a \bmod p$.

Signature generation: To sign a message M, A selects a random integer k, $1 \le k \le p - 2$, such that $\gcd(k, p - 1) = 1$, and computes $m = H(M)$, $r = g^k \bmod p$, and $s = k^{-1}(m - ar) \bmod (p - 1)$. A's signature on M is (r, s).

Signature verification: Given an authentic copy of A's public key, one can verify A's signature (r, s) on M by computing $m = H(M)$, and verifying that $g^m \equiv y^r r^s \pmod{p}$.

Adversary's actions: Given A's public key P_A and A's signature (r, s) on M, E does the following. If $\gcd(s, p - 1) \ne 1$ or if $\gcd(m, r) = 2$ or q, then E terminates with failure. Otherwise, E selects an arbitrary integer c, $1 \le c \le p - 2$, such that $\gcd(t, p - 1) = 1$, where $t = m - cr$. E then computes $\overline{g} = (r^s)^{t^{-1} \bmod (p-1)} \bmod p$ and forms $P_E = (p, \overline{g}, \overline{y})$, where $\overline{y} = \overline{g}^c \bmod p$.

Observe that (r, s) is also E's signature on M since

$$\overline{g}^{(-m)} \overline{y}^r r^s \equiv \overline{g}^{-(m-cr)} r^s \equiv (r^s)^{-t^{-1} t \bmod (p-1)} r^s \equiv 1 \pmod{p}.$$

Remarks. The condition $\gcd(s, p - 1) = 1$ ensures that r^s, and hence also $\overline{g}$, is a generator of $\mathbb{Z}_p^*$. The condition $\gcd(m, r) \ne 2, q$ ensures that there exists a c for which $\gcd(t, p - 1) = 1$; it also implies that a non-negligible proportion of all c's satisfy $\gcd(t, p - 1) = 1$. If we make the heuristic assumption that r, s and m are distributed uniformly at random from $[1, p - 1]$, then we see that the success probability of the adversary is about $\frac{3}{8}$.

4.4 DSA

Domain parameters: Primes p and q such that q divides $p - 1$, and an element $g \in \mathbb{Z}_p^*$ of order q. Typically p has bitlength 1024 and q has bitlength 160.

Key pair: A's private key is an integer a, $1 \le a \le q - 1$. A's public key is $P_A = (p, q, g, y)$, where $y = g^a \bmod p$.

Signature generation: To sign a message M, A selects a random integer $k \in [1, q - 1]$, and computes $m = H(M)$, $r = (g^k \bmod p) \bmod q$, and $s = k^{-1}(m + ar) \bmod q$. A's signature on M is (r, s).

Signature verification: Given an authentic copy of A's public key, one can verify A's signature (r, s) on M by computing $m = H(M)$, $u_1 = s^{-1} m \bmod q$, $u_2 = s^{-1} r \bmod q$, and verifying that $r = (g^{u_1} y^{u_2} \bmod p) \bmod q$.

Adversary's actions: Given A's public key P_A and A's signature (r, s) on M, E selects a random integer $c \in [1, q - 1]$ such that $t := ((u_1 + cu_2) \bmod q) \ne 0$. E then computes $r_1 = g^{u_1} y^{u_2} \bmod p$ and $\overline{g} = r_1^{t^{-1} \bmod q} \bmod p$, and forms $P_E = (p, q, \overline{g}, \overline{y})$ where $\overline{y} = \overline{g}^c \bmod p$. Note that $\mathrm{ord}(\overline{g}) = q$, so P_E is a valid DSA public key.

Observe that (r, s) is also E's signature on M since

$$\overline{g}^{u_1} \overline{y}^{u_2} \equiv \overline{g}^{u_1 + cu_2} \equiv \overline{g}^t \equiv r_1 \pmod{p},$$

whence $r = (\overline{g}^{u_1} \overline{y}^{u_2} \bmod p) \bmod q$.

4.5 ECDSA

ECDSA is the elliptic curve analogue of the DSA and is specified in [3].

Domain parameters: An elliptic curve E defined over the finite field $\mathbb{F}_q$ with $\#E(\mathbb{F}_q) = nh$ and n prime, and a point $P \in E(\mathbb{F}_q)$ of order n.

Key pair: A's private key is an integer a, $1 \le a \le n-1$. A's public key is $P_A = (p, E, n, P, Q)$, where $Q = aP$.

Signature generation: To sign a message M, A selects a random integer k, $1 \le k \le n-1$, and computes $m = H(M)$, $R = kP$, $r = x(R) \bmod n$, and $s = k^{-1}(m + ar) \bmod n$. Here, $x(R)$ denotes the x-coordinate of the point R. A's signature on M is (r, s).

Signature verification: Given an authentic copy of A's public key, one can verify A's signature (r, s) on M by computing $m = H(M)$, $R = s^{-1}mP + s^{-1}rQ$, and verifying that $r = x(R) \bmod n$.

Adversary's actions: Given A's public key P_A and A's signature (r, s) on M, E selects an arbitrary integer c, $1 \le c \le n-1$, such that $t := ((s^{-1}m + s^{-1}rc) \bmod n) \ne 0$. E then computes $R = s^{-1}mP + s^{-1}rQ$ and $\overline{P} = (t^{-1} \bmod n)R$, and forms $P_E = (p, E, n, \overline{P}, \overline{Q})$, where $\overline{Q} = c\overline{P}$. Note that $\operatorname{ord}(\overline{P}) = n$, so P_E is a valid ECDSA public key.

Observe that (r, s) is also E's signature on M since

$$s^{-1}m\overline{P} + s^{-1}r\overline{Q} = (s^{-1}m + s^{-1}rc)\overline{P} = t\overline{P} = R, \tag{1}$$

whence $r = x(R) \bmod n$.

Remarks. E's domain parameters are the same as A's, with the exception of the base point $\overline{P}$. If the elliptic curve was chosen verifiably at random using a canonical seeded hash function (e.g., as specified in ANSI X9.62 [3]), then E can use the same (non-secret) seed as selected by A to demonstrate to the CA that the curve was indeed selected verifiably at random. There is no requirement in ANSI X9.62 for generating the base point verifiably at random. Hence, performing domain parameter validation as specified in ANSI X9.62 does not foil the adversary.

5 Conclusions

This paper presented some new unknown key-share attacks on the STS-MAC key agreement protocol. The attacks are a concern in practice since STS-MAC purports to provide both implicit key authentication and key confirmation. There are various ways in which the attacks can be circumvented. Our preferred way is to include flow numbers and identities in the messages being signed, and to separate keys used to provide key confirmation from derived shared secret keys.

Acknowledgements

The authors would like to thank Don Johnson and Minghua Qu for their valuable comments on earlier drafts of this paper.

References

1. ANSI X9.30 (Part 1), *Public Key Cryptography Using Irreversible Algorithms for the Financial Services Industry – Part 1: The Digital Signature Algorithm (DSA)*, 1995.
2. ANSI X9.31, *Digital Signatures Using Reversible Public Key Cryptography for the Financial Services Industry (rDSA)*, working draft, March 1998.
3. ANSI X9.62, *The Elliptic Curve Digital Signature Algorithm (ECDSA)*, working draft, August 1998.
4. ANSI X9.63, *Elliptic Curve Key Agreement and Key Transport Protocols*, working draft, October 1998.
5. M. Bellare, R. Canetti and H. Krawczyk, "A modular approach to the design and analysis of authentication and key exchange protocols", *Proceedings of the 30th Annual Symposium on the Theory of Computing*, 1998. A full version of this paper is available at http://www-cse.ucsd.edu/users/mihir
6. M. Bellare and P. Rogaway, "Random oracles are practical: a paradigm for designing efficient protocols", *1st ACM Conference on Computer and Communications Security*, 1993, 62–73. A full version of this paper is available at http://www-cse.ucsd.edu/users/mihir
7. M. Bellare and P. Rogaway, "Entity authentication and key distribution", *Advances in Cryptology – Crypto '93*, LNCS **773**, 1993, 232-249. A full version of this paper is available at http://www-cse.ucsd.edu/users/mihir
8. M. Bellare and P. Rogaway, "The exact security of digital signatures—how to sign with RSA and Rabin", *Advances in Cryptology – Eurocrypt '96*, LNCS **1070**, 1996, 399-416.
9. S. Blake-Wilson, D. Johnson and A. Menezes, "Key agreement protocols and their security analysis", *Proceedings of the sixth IMA International Conference on Cryptography and Coding*, LNCS **1355**, 1997, 30-45. A full version of this paper is available at http://www.cacr.math.uwaterloo.ca/
10. S. Blake-Wilson and A. Menezes, "Authenticated Diffie-Hellman key agreement protocols", *Proceedings of SAC '98*, LNCS, to appear.
11. W. Diffie, P. van Oorschot and M. Wiener, "Authentication and authenticated key exchanges", *Designs, Codes and Cryptography*, **2** (1992), 107-125.
12. T. ElGamal, "A public key cryptosystem and a signature scheme based on discrete logarithms", *IEEE Transactions on Information Theory*, **31** (1985), 469-472.
13. S. Goldwasser, S. Micali, and R. Rivest, "A digital signature scheme secure against adaptive chosen message attacks", *SIAM Journal on Computing*, **17** (1988), 281-308.
14. IPSEC Working Group, *The OAKLEY Key Determination Protocol*, Internet Draft, Internet Engineering Task Force, available from http://www.ietf.cnri.reston.va.us/
15. ISO/IEC 8824-1, *Information Technology – Open Systems Interconnection – Abstract Syntax Notation One (ANS.1) – Part 1: Specification of Basic Notation.*
16. ISO/IEC 8825-3, *Information Technology – Open Systems Interconnection – Specification of ASN.1 Encoding Rules – Part 3: Distinguished Canonical Encoding Rules.*
17. ISO/IEC 9798-3, *Information Technology – Security Techniques – Entity Authentication Mechanisms – Part 3: Entity Authentication Using a Public-Key Algorithm* 1993.

18. ISO/IEC 11770-3, *Information Technology – Security Techniques – Key Management – Part 3: Mechanisms Using Asymmetric Techniques*, draft, (DIS), 1996.

19. D. Johnson, Contribution to ANSI X9F1 working group, 1997.

20. B. Kaliski, Contribution to ANSI X9F1 and IEEE P1363 working groups, June 17 1998.

21. L. Law, A. Menezes, M. Qu, J. Solinas, S. Vanstone, "An efficient protocol for authenticated key agreement", Technical report CORR 98-05, Department of C&O, University of Waterloo, 1998. Also available at http://www.cacr.math.uwaterloo.ca/

22. H.W. Lenstra, "Factoring integers with elliptic curves", *Annals of Mathematics*, **126** (1987), 649-673.

23. C. Lim and P. Lee, "A key recovery attack on discrete log-based schemes using a prime order subgroup", *Advances in Cryptology – Crypto '97*, LNCS **1294**, 1997, 249-263.

24. A. Menezes, M. Qu and S. Vanstone, "Some new key agreement protocols providing mutual implicit authentication", *Workshop on Selected Areas in Cryptography (SAC '95)*, 22-32, 1995.

25. A. Menezes, P. van Oorschot and S. Vanstone, *Handbook of Applied Cryptography*, CRC Press, 1997.

26. C. Mitchell and A. Thomas, "Standardising authentication protocols based on public key techniques", *Journal of Computer Security*, **2** (1993), 23-36.

27. National Institute of Standards and Technology, *Digital Signature Standard*, FIPS Publication 186, 1994.

28. National Institute of Standards and Technology, *Secure Hash Standard (SHS)*, FIPS Publication 180-1, 1995.

29. S. Pohlig and M. Hellman, "An improved algorithm for computing logarithms over $GF(p)$ and its cryptographic significance", *IEEE Transactions on Information Theory*, **24** (1978), 106-110.

30. M.O. Rabin, "Digitalized signatures and public-key functions as intractable as factorization", MIT/LCS/TR-212, MIT Laboratory for Computer Science, 1979.

31. R.L. Rivest, A. Shamir and L.M. Adleman, "A method for obtaining digital signatures and public-key cryptosystems", *Communications of the ACM*, **21** (1978), 120-126.

32. P. van Oorschot, "Extending cryptographic logics of belief to key agreement protocols", *1st ACM Conference on Computer and Communications Security*, ACM Press, 1993, 232-243.

Toward Fair International Key Escrow *
– An Attempt by Distributed Trusted Third Agencies with Threshold Cryptography –

Shingo Miyazaki[1] and Ikuko Kuroda[2] and Kouichi Sakurai[1][**]

[1] Dept. of Computer Science and Communication Engineering, Kyushu Univ.
Hakozaki, Higashi-ku, Fukuoka, 812-8581, JAPAN.
{shingo,sakurai}@csce.kyushu-u.ac.jp
[2] Project TEAM - 4, NTT Human Interface Laboratories,
1-1 Hikarino-oka, Yokosuka-shi, Kanagawa, 239-0847, JAPAN
ikuko@mistral.hil.ntt.co.jp

Abstract. We consider key escrow system for international communication between multiple domains with different policies. In intercepting international communications between two domains serious problems on unfairness may arise when one government has not authorized the message interception in legal. We solve this problem by incorporating a mechanism that allows message interception by law enforcement parties subject to the consent of both governments involved in the communication. That mechanism involves the establishment of an independent International Trusted Third Party (ITTP) that has the ultimate authority to check of the security policies of each country and permit or deny the interception of international messages.

We present a scheme with multiple Diffie-Hellman type key distribution protocoland the ITTP copes with only the secret-key corresponding to its own public-key.

We can also make the ITTP "multiple", and we apply recent developed techniques on distributed (threshold) cryptography to our multiple ITTPs. Thus, the establishment and control of an international trusted third party can done with incorporating by each governments.

Key Words : *Key escrow/recovery system, Diffie-Hellman key distribution, Trusted Third Party, Distributed Cryptography, Security policy*

1 Introduction

1.1 International aspects of Key Escrow

Various key escrow systems (KES) and key recovery systems have been proposed recently [DB96]. These systems make it possible, under certain conditions, for authorized third party (referred to as law Enforcement Parties (LEP) in the following) to intercept encrypted messages sent between users.

A key escrow mechanism suitable for international use was recently proposed by Jefferies, Mitchell, and Walker [JMW95] (JMW-mechanism), and revised schemes are presented [GCHQ96, CGM96, BDHJ97] for use among multiple domains.

---

* This work is inspired by Prof. Tsujii's remark [Tsu96] on unfairness hidden in some existing escrow-scheme.

** Partially done while visiting in Columbia Univ. Computer Science Dept.

In the JWM-mechanism, a session key for users' end-to-end encryption is established based on Diffie-Hellman key exchange [DH76]. So, it is possible for the court to permit "edge surveillance", in which only communication between sender A and receiver B can be decrypted from one of keys from A or B unlike Clipper. The JWM-mechanism also introduces a licensed Trusted Third Party to escrow users' private keys.

As an international aspect of the JWM-mechanism, Chen et al. considers key escrow in mutually mistrusting domains: the countries involved do not trust one another. And to solve this problem, it proposes to share the information of escrowed key using the method of Pedersen [P91]. Bao et al [BDHJ97] proposes an improved one of above method that enables to efficiently share the information between several countries.

1.2 Our discussed problem

The previous methods [CGM96, BDHJ97] premise that both two countries have authorized the interception, and that keys are escrowed fairly between both countries with no other parties appearing.

For interception of international communication, particularly between a country that has authorized the interception and one that has not, however, such JMW-mechanism may become a demerit. The reason is that, when LEP has carried out a proper law enforcement process, LEP can arbitrarily intercept encrypted messages, regardless of the security policy of the other country. Considering that every country should respect the security policies of other countries to the utmost limit, it is not desirable that one country should be able to arbitrarily intercept the communications from and/or to another country. The law enforcement process should be such that it is not possible for LEP to intercept encrypted communications without the cooperation or at least the consent of the other country. Unfortunately, there have not been any discussions on these international features, however, in papers referred to above.

Compares to this, we consider a system for intercepting international communications that can adapt to various security policies freely designed by each country, including not authorizing the interception as its policy.

1.3 Our contributions

Requirements: Our proposed key escrow system enjoys the following.

1. When international communications are the target of communication surveillance, it must not be possible for the investigator to intercept encrypted messages without obtaining the consent of the other country.
2. The ITTP provides the investigator the crucial information for the law enforcement process on condition that the party obtains the consent of the other country.
3. No agency or organization preserves the knowledge of each user's international private key, by which users communicates with other users in the other domain. Chances of interception are limited depending on time.
4. The encrypted communication protocol uses only published or fixed data, and not data with randomness.
5. Our ITTP can be distributed, or can be eliminated: multiple domains jointly generate ITTP's public-key and collectively decrypt the message encrypted with ITTP's secret-key.

How to compromise with ITTP: We set up an international trusted third party (ITTP) hierarchically in advance. When intercepting an international communication, this is only made to be possible with the consent of both countries and cooperation of ITTP. This approach is an implementation of the idea as Frankel and Yung are insisting in [FY95] that "Trusted agents trusted by both countries are necessary between countries that can not be trusted one another."

The technique used first is to construct multiple Diffie-Hellman type keys as in [CGM96], and to make it escrowed a part of the secret information to ITTP which we are setting up in our proposal. Through the method above, the possibility of intercepting international communications is limited to only when ITTP cooperates under both countries' consent.

In our proposed scheme, unlike the previous ones [JMW95, GCHQ96], the common key between two communicating users cannot be obtained without the user's international private key or the national secret key. The user's international private key is not deposited anywhere and only ITTP manages the national secret key, so it is not possible for LEP to obtain those keys. Furthermore, in the law enforcement protocol, also, ITTP does not provide the users' communicating key itself to LEP. Therefore, there is no possibility of LEP obtaining the common key between two communicating users. The user's national private key that is deposited with the key escrow agencies is used by the key escrow agencies in the law enforcement protocol. The information supplied by the key escrow agencies, however, is always constructed of a combination of the user's national private key and system secret information. Because LEP does not possess the means to separate that secret information, there is no possibility of LEP obtaining the user's national private key from the information that is available when the law enforcement protocol is executed.

On the other hand, each key escrow agency manages only a part of the user's segmented national private key. The purpose of having multiple key escrow agencies, each of which manages only a part of the user's segmented national private key, is to reduce the risk of infringement on the privacy of users by a key escrow agency.

Accordingly, it is not desirable, for that purpose, for a key escrow agency to be able to obtain the user's national private key itself. In the law enforcement protocol proposed here, the information that is available to each key escrow agency always involves an unknown constant that is the segmental system secret information possessed only by the other key escrow agencies. This is to say that the deletion of the unknown constant is done when LEP obtains KS finally; within the processing by the key escrow agencies the unknown constants cannot be deleted. There is therefore no possibility that any of the key escrow agencies can obtain the user's national private key from the information that is available when the law enforcement protocol is executed unless there is collusion among all of the key escrow agencies.

Distributed ITTPs: A criticism from the practical view point is that the use of a single International TTP sitting over all other national jurisdictions is too idealistic, and naive or completely unworkable solution. So, we also consider a further improvement on multiple third parties, who are trusted collectively but not individually, for answering this criticism.

De Santis, Desmedt, Frankel and Yung [DDFY94] presented an idea to use threshold cryptography for key escrow. We make use of recent developed techniques in threshold cryptography [Des92, FY98]. Each government jointly makes an ITTP. Then, the ITTP and all governments shares the secret keys of an organization. We should remark that any public-key scheme (e.g., RSA and ElGamal) is applicable to our ITTP's encryption scheme.

In particular, our system gives a solution to the following open problem remarked in [CGM96]:

> *Can a practical key escrow scheme be designed for the case where more than two domains are involved, and where escrow agencies are not permitted to span more than one domain ?*

We utilize techniques in threshold cryptography for restricting the escrow agency's tapping power only within his domain.

Against subliminal channel via randomness: The reason that the data with randomness is not involved in the encrypted communication protocol is for protection against subliminal channel [KL95]. When users communicating, in the escrow system involved the data with randomness they might communicate by transmitting the data itself with randomness as the ciphertext to the other. In this case, since the ordinary message put in the formal position as dummy is deciphered in a law enforcement, this shadow-communication is hardly detectable. For avoiding this attack, in our system all data involved in the communication protocol including a session key is public or fixed data within a period (e.g. hour, day, week, etc.) without randomness.

Time-related session key establishing: Our basic scheme for domestic communication is a modification of the previous [JMW95, GCHQ96] for restricting investigator's tapping conversation.

In a GCHQ system [GCHQ96], a time stamp is added to the concept of the system described in [JMW95], whereas the system described in [JMW95] does not use a time stamp. As for the system described in [GCHQ96], it is not efficient in practice since users must access key escrow agencies each time on starting communication to generate a session key.

So, we make use of a time stamp: for embedding a tiem-stamp into the generator of discrete log. for Diffie-Hellman key exchange. Thus, this enables an efficient encrypted communications without accessing key escrow agencies when starting communication to generate a session key.

Comparison: Ours vs Previous: Some works have discussed international aspects of KES. The comparison to the related works is described in Table 1.

Chen, Gollmann, and Mitchell [CGM96] points out the problem that there is no guarantee to trust one another's key escrow agencies between the two countries that have authorized the interception. And to solve this problem, they proposes to share the information of escrowed key using the method of Pedersen [P91]. Chen et al. [BDHJ97] proposes an improved one of above method that enables to efficiently share the information between several countries. These methods above premise that both two countries have authorized the interception, and that keys are escrowed fairly between both countries with no other parties appearing.

In the scheme [GCHQ96] and ours, the investigator cannot peep into the communication between users over the period permitted by the court. in the scheme proposed in [VT97], the investigator must perform the law enforcement protocols so many the target communications.

In the schemes [GCHQ96, JMW95], TTP which generates the secret key of user and transmits it to the user preserves it without the need of the key deposit. The scheme introduced in [VT97], in which users need not to deposit their own secret key, is applicable to the communication under various states same as ours. However, in the system, the investigator cannot obtain in advance of the target communication to monitor in *real time*, because the sender generates randomly the session key when communicating.

In the previous scheme [CGM96, BDHJ97], key escrow agencies (TTPs) can obtain the secret key of the target user in the law enforcement process, However, in our proposed scheme, the knowledge of the key escrow agency, does not increase even after the law enforcement process is done: The key escrow agencies, in our scheme, cannot access the perfect secret key of users, since the key escrow agencies, in the law enforcement process, computes the crucial data with the partial secret key preserved and transfer the result to the investigator. Due to this, the user need not to do his key renewal even after a law enforcement.

Young and Yung [YY98] recently proposed a key-escrow systems with multiple trusted agencies. Though they have no discussion on international aspects on key-escrow, their scheme could be applicable to international communication. However, they presented the new *double decker* scheme and a hierarchical key-escrow system [YY99]. The system can be applicable to international communication. In the Young-Yung schemes [YY98, YY99], only a ciphertext is decrypted via a law enforcing process. Then, if multiple ciphertexts should be recovered, too many law enforcing tasks have to be performed. Whereas, in our scheme, the investigator can decrypt any messages encrypted within a limited period, which is allowed for a session key recovered via a law enforcing protocol. This gap is due to the difference of the recovered target, which is a content of encrypted message in Young-Yung scheme while a session key of being effective with a limited term in our system.

Gressel, Granot and Dror [GGD95] presented the first approach to the key escrow scheme (Fortress KISS) taking account of a crypto law over the international communication. Their scheme is different from ours in two points below. One is that the session key for encrypting the communication is independent of user's private key in Fortress KISS. In our scheme, in order to exclude the randomness concealing the shadow message, the session key is uniquely generated from valid public (secret) keys of users and the date. The other is that Fortress KISS discloses the private key itself of target user in the law enforcing protocol. On the other hand, in our system, the only selected message permitted by the court can be recovered without revealing the private key of target user. This idea is pointed out in [DDFY94].

2 Our proposed system

2.1 System configuration

Our proposed system consists of the following parties:

User $U_i (i = A, B, \cdots)$: This is a party engaged in encrypted communication. There are multiple users. Each user deposits his own national private key in the key escrow agencies of his own country by dividing into several parts. Without revealing the information on the international private key, each user must register the international public key with the certificate authority related to international communication.

	Consent of the other	Country's policy	Time-bounded tapping	Deposit of secret keys	Real-time Monitoring
[CGM96]	None	Both EGs	None (required key renewal a commu.)	Required	Possible
[GCHQ96]	None	Both EGs	One day	Required (TTP's generated keys)	Possible
[JMW95]	None	Both EGs	None (required key renewal a commu.)	Required (TTP's generated keys)	Possible
[BDHJ97]	None	Both EGs	None (required key renewal a commu.)	Required	Possible
[VT97]	None	—	A commu.	Not required	None
[YY99]	(Required)	Both EGs	A commu.	(Not) Required	(Possible)
Ours	Required	(N)EG vs. (N)EG	A period set up	(Required)	Possible

(N)EG : (None) Escrowing Government,   commu. : communication

Table 1. The comparison to related works

[CGM96], [BDHJ97]	DH key-exchange, Pedersen's VSS
[JMW95], [GCHQ96]	DH key-exchange, TTP (as Key producer)
[VT97]	ElGamal cryptosystem, Data binding
[YY99]	Double decker exponentiation (RSA, ElGamal)
Ours	DH key-exchange, Any (Distributed) PKP for ITTP,

Table 2. Basic technique used

Investigator : An organization that, after obtaining the court permission, has the authority to perform the interception of the encrypted messages of the user specified in the court order with the cooperation of key escrow agencies.

Key Escrow Agency $T_j (j = 1, 2, \cdots, k)$: It holds a segmental private key of each user as well as a part of the one-time secret system information distributed by the court. There are multiple key escrow agencies in a country, of which the government has the affirmative policy for the key escrow. In a law enforcement process, it checks the validity of the court order and presents to the investigator the information computed from the partial private key only when the consent is given.

Court of Justice : An organization that considers the appropriateness of requests by the investigator to perform the interception, and when deemed appropriate, issues an order permitting that interception. This is a trusted organization.

International Trusted Third Party (ITTP) : This is an internationally trusted organization for asking the final determination of permission to intercept the international communications. In a law enforcement process, it provides the investigator of the country that wants to perform the interception with the information, which makes deciphering of the target messages possible, only when the country has obtained the consent of the other country involved. In an emergency related to the international problem, ITTP presents the crucial information without the consent of the other country. (Section 4 discusses how to make ITTP "multiple" for distributed ITTPs: $ITTP_j$ $(j = 1, 2, \ldots, m)$.)

Certificate Authority (CA) : It authenticates the international public key of users. There are multiple certificate authorities. The CA manages the list of the public keys or issues the certification of the public key by using the technique such as the digital signature.

2.2 Setting up the system

A prime number p and a primitive element g mod p are published as public system information. Each user preserves two different types of the key pair for the international and the domestic, respectively.

In order to communicate with users in the same domain (country), U_A generates a domestic secret key S_A and computes the the corresponding domestic public key P_A. If the country has the affirmative policy for the key escrow, U_A deposits the segmental domestic secret key S_{Ai} to each key escrow agency T_i as follows.

$$S_A = S_{A1} + S_{A2} + \cdots + S_{Ak} \tag{1}$$

The country authenticates $P_A = g^{S_A} \pmod{p}$ as the domestic public key of U_A. On the other hand, the country, of which the government has a negative policy against escrow, only authenticates the domestic public key of the citizen.

U_A, who wants to communicate with the person in the other domain (country), generates the secret key x_A for the international communication. Then, the international public key $y_A = g^{x_A} \pmod{p}$ of U_A is computed and sent to the CA managing the list of the public keys for the international communication. After verifying the validity of y_A via the digital signature on the challenge, the CA register y_A to the list as the international public key of U_A. The certification of y_A is issued by CA and sent to U_A.

Every law enforcement process the court in the country promoting the policy of key escrow generates the secret system information (I_s, i_s) satisfying the following equations.

$$I_s = \prod_{j=1}^{k} I_{sj} = I_{s1} I_{s2} \cdots I_{sk} \pmod{p} \tag{2}$$

$$i_s = I_s^{-1} = \sum_{j=1}^{k} i_{sj} = i_{s1} + i_{s2} + \cdots + i_{sk} \pmod{q} \tag{3}$$

Then, the partial information (I_{si}, i_{si}) is transmitted to each key escrow agency T_i confidentially. Each key escrow agency T_i preserves (I_s, i_s) secretly and provides the investigator with the partial result computed from the partial information during a law enforcement process.

2.3 Basic scheme for domestic communication

We describe the protocol for U_A of a country conducting the encrypted communication with U_B in the same domain (country).

2.4 Encrypted communication protocol

Step 1: U_A calculates the master key $K_{AB} = P_B^{S_A} \pmod{p}$ from his own domestic private key S_A of U_A and the domestic public key P_B of U_B. Then, U_A computes the session key $KS = D^{K_{AB}} \pmod{p}$ by using K_{AB} and the time-data.

Step 2: U_A encrypts a message M with a symmetric cryptosystem f_2, using KS to obtain a ciphertext $C = f_1(M, KS)$. U_A sends C and $LEAF = (P_A\|P_B\|D)$ to U_B.

Step 3: U_B extracts D from $LEAF$ and computes the master key $K_{AB} = P_A^{S_B} \pmod{p}$ from his own domestic private key S_A and the domestic public key P_A.

Step 4: U_B computes KS from D and K_{AB}. Then, U_B decrypts C with KS to obtain the message $M = f_1^{-1}(C, KS)$.

Law enforcing protocol: We depict the protocol for the case in which the investigator performs the interception on U_B. Here, the investigator already gets encrypted communication between U_A and U_B and records the ciphertext C and $LEAF$.

Step 1: The investigator petitions the court of justice for an order permitting the law enforcement to the communication between U_A and U_B.

Step 2: The court decides whether or not to permit the surveillance. If permission is to be granted, the court issues an order that clearly specifies the verification date and the name of the user who will be subject to the surveillance (U_B).

Step 3: The investigator presents to each key escrow agency T_j the court order regarding U_B and D.

Step 4: Each key escrow agency T_j computes $K_j = I_{sj} P_A^{S_{Bj}} \pmod{p}$ and sends K_j to the investigator.

Step 5: The investigator computes $K^* = \prod_{j=1}^{k} K_j \pmod{p}$ and sends K^* to each key escrow agency T_j.

Step 6: Each key escrow agency T_j computes $K_j' = D^{i'_{sj} K^*}$ and sends K_j' to the investigator.

Step 7: The investigator computes the session key KS from K_j':

$$\prod_{j=1}^{k} K_j' = D^{I_s \cdot K_{AB} \cdot \sum_{j=1}^{k} i_{sj}} = D^{I_s \cdot i_s \cdot K_{AB}} = KS \pmod{p} \qquad (4)$$

and then can decrypt C to obtain the message $M = f_2^{-1}(C, KS)$.

2.5 Unfairness in law enforcement without agreement

We consider the arising unfairness in law enforcement of communication between two domains with different escrowing policies: one domain P is negative against escrow and the other Q is positive for escrow. Consider two users: User U_A is a citizen of one domain P, and User U_B is in the other domain Q.

Then, the domestic secret key of the user in the country P is not required to deposit to the key escrow agencies (The government P might have no such agencies.). On the other hand, the government of the domain Q might promote the policy of the key escrow and decrypt the encrypted communication between users under the law. Executing the encrypted communication protocol described in the section 2.3 for the international communication between U_A and U_B, causes the following problem.

In the protocol the communication between U_A and U_B is encrypted with the session key KS, which consists of both time-data D and the Diffie-Hellman key K_{AB} of a common key between U_A and U_B. After obtaining the court order's permission of intercepting U_B, the investigator can decrypt the encrypted communication between U_A and U_B with help of key escrow agencies' by submitting their segmental secret key of U_B. The country Q can execute the law enforcement protocol keeping the interception secret from the country P since the investigator in the country Q can access the communication between U_A and U_B without the help of the country P.

Step 1: The investigator of the country Q petitions the court of justice in the own country for an order permitting the law enforcement to the communication between U_A and U_B.

Step 2: The court decides whether or not to permit the surveillance. If permission is to be granted, the court issues an order that clearly specifies the verification date and the name of the user who will be subject to the surveillance (U_B).

Step 3-7: By executing the same process Step 3–7 in subsection 2.4, the investigator can independently decipher the encrypted communication between U_A and U_B without the help of any agencies in the country P.

We should remark that the previous international KES with multiples domains [CGM96, GCHQ96, VT97] suffer from the similar defect of this "unfairness". In the other system [JMW95, BDHJ97], the investigator in a country can perform the law enforcement process with the "unfairness" except when monitoring in real-time (In the real-time monitoring, the investigator in advance obtains the session key or related key from the law enforcement before the target communication is done).

2.6 Our scheme for international communication

Encrypted communication protocol We describe the protocol for U_A of the country P conducting encrypted communication with U_B of the country Q.

Step 1: U_A computes the international master key $IK_{AB} = y_B^{x_A} \pmod{p}$ from his own international private key x_A and the international public key y_B of U_B. Then, U_A enciphers D with the the symmetric cryptosystem f_1, using IK_{AB} to obtain $E_D = f_1(D, IK_{AB})$.

Step 2: U_A calculates $K_{AB} = P_B^{S_A} \pmod{p}$ from his own national secret key S_A and the national public key P_B of U_B. Then, U_A computes the session key $KS = D^{K_{AB} \cdot E_D} \pmod{p}$ from K_{AB} and D. Moreover, U_A enciphers a message M with the symmetric cryptosystem f_2 using KS obtained ($C = f_2(M, KS)$).

Step 3: U_A enciphers $(E_D, D, C, y_A, y_B, P_A, P_B)$ with the asymmetric cryptosystem $Enc(\cdot)$, using the ITTP's public key P_I to obtain $Inf = Enc((E_D\|D\|C\|y_A\|y_B\|P_A\|P_B), P_I)$. Then, U_A sends C and $LEAF = (y_A\|y_B\|P_A\|P_B\|D\|Inf)$ to U_B.

Step 4: U_B extracts D and Inf from $LEAF$ and computes $IK_{AB} = y_A^{x_B} \pmod{p}$ from his own international secret key x_B and the international public key y_A of

U_A. Then, U_B enciphers D with the symmetric cryptosystem f_2, using IK_{AB} to obtain $E_D = f_1(D, IK_{AB})$.

Step 5: U_B verifies the soundness of Inf in $LEAF$ using E_D computed. U_B computes Inf' by enciphering $(E_D\|D\|C\|y_A\|y_B\|P_A\|P_B)$ with $Enc(\cdot)$, using the ITTP's public key P_I, where E_D is computed in Step 4. If $Inf' = Enc((E_D\|D\|C\|y_A\|y_B\|P_A\|P_B), P_I)$ computed and Inf in $LEAF$ is not identical, the processing is halted.

Step 6: U_B calculates $K_{AB} = P_A^{S_B} \pmod{p}$ from the national public key P_A of U_A and his own national secret key S_B. Then, U_A computes the session key $KS = D^{K_{AB} \cdot E_D} \pmod{p}$ and finally deciphers C with KS to obtain the message $M = f_2^{-1}(C, KS)$.

Law enforcing protocol We depict the protocol for the case in which the investigator of the country Q performs the interception on U_B in the same country. Here, the investigator of country Q already gets encrypted communication between U_A and U_B and records the ciphertext C and $LEAF$.

Step 1: The investigator of the country Q petitions the court of justice in his own country for an order permitting the law enforcement to the communication between U_A and U_B.

Step 2: The court decides whether or not to permit the surveillance. If the permission is to be granted, the court issues an order that clearly specifies the verification date and the name of the user who will be subject to the surveillance (U_B).

Step 3: The investigator petitions the country P for the agreement on the tapping of the communication line.

Step 4: The country P decides whether or not to permit the surveillance. If the permission is to be granted, the country P issues the consent bond for the tapping.

Step 5: The investigator presents to the ITTP both the court order and the consent bond of the country P.

Step 6: After verifying the validity of both the court order and the consent bond, the ITTP deciphers Inf with his own secret key S_I to obtain $(E_D, D', C, y_A, y_B, P_A, P_B)$.

$$Dec(Inf, S_I) = E_D, D', C, y_A, y_B, P_A, P_B \tag{5}$$

If and only if D' and D in the $LEAF$ is identical, the ITTP sends E_D to the investigator of the country Q.

Step 7: The investigator presents to each key escrow agency T_j both the court order regarding to U_B and D and the consent bond of the country Q.

Step 8: Each key escrow agency T_j computes $K_j = I_{sj} y_A^{S_{Bj}} \pmod{p}$ and sends K_j to the investigator.

Step 9: The investigator computes $K^* = \prod_{j=1}^{k} K_j \pmod{p}$ and sends K^* to each key escrow agency T_j.

Step 10: Each key escrow agency T_j computes $K_j' = D^{i_{sj} K^* E_D}$ and sends K_j' to the investigator.

Step 11: The investigator computes the session key KS from K_j'.

$$\prod_{j=1}^{k} K_j' = D^{I_s \cdot K_{AB} \cdot E_D \cdot \sum_{j=1}^{k} i_{sj}} = KS \pmod{p} \tag{6}$$

Then, the investigator deciphers C to obtain the message $M = f_2^{-1}(C, KS)$.

3 Discussion

3.1 Why two types of keys are introduced

In our system, we have introduced two public-private key pairs for each user. One is a domestic key pair which is used for both domestic and international communication and the other is an international key pair which is only used for international communication.

The reason we have introduced two types of keys for each user is, to maintain an independency of key escrow policy of each country as long as the communication is within the country (domestic), but to prevent either country from executing a wiretap on one's own judgement (authority) for international communication.

In our original key escrow system, we have set up only one key for each user assuming that there are only domestic communication. The key has been shared among TTPs within the country. On extending the system involving international communication, the problem was if the key is shared among both domestic TTPs and international TTPs the key escrow policy within domestic communication will be affected by international TTPs' decision. Thus we have set up another key (distinct from the domestic one) for international communication. Both domestic and international policy must be taken into consideration for wiretapping international communication. This is why both keys are used for international communication, what is therefore leading to introduce in our system two types of keys for each user.

3.2 Setting the fixed data within a period as a generator

At the equation 2.6, the difference between setting the primitive element g of the system parameter p as a generator and putting the fixed data within a period D (in this paper, date/time as D) is discussed here. A session key is computed as $g^{K_{AB} \cdot E_D}$ in the former while $D^{K_{AB} \cdot E_D}$ in the latter. In the former case, once the investigator obtains the session key from key escrow agencies in a law enforcement process, he can calculate the fixed data $g^{K_{AB}}$ of U_A and U_B by computing KS^{E_D}. The data $g^{K_{AB}}$ computed allows the investigator to calculate the session key used in the communication between U_A and U_B without the cooperation of key escrow agencies, only with E_D provided by the ITTP.

While the investigator, in the latter case, only obtains the ad hoc data $D^{K_{AB}}$, even if he computes KS^{E_D} as well as the former. In this case, when the law enforcement process is performed, the investigator must collude with the key escrow agencies every time the fixed data D has changed.

According to the policy for the law enforcement or the efficiency of the process, two types of the key construction should be appropriately chosen.

3.3 One-timeness of the secret system information (I_s, i_s)

The court of justice issues the secret system information (I_s, i_s) for every law enforcement process. This information allows key escrow agencies to provide the investigator with the partial result that enables the access to the communication between users, with not revealing the knowledge itself of the segmental secret key. If the same (I_s, i_s) is used in the different law enforcement process, the problem described below arises.

The investigator of a country, say Q, might in prior communicate with U_B as a dummy user $U_{B'}$ (or in collusion with $U_{B'}$). Then, the investigator petitions the court of justice in his own country for an order to permit the law enforced recovery of the communication between U_A and $U_{B'}$. If the offer is accepted, the investigator obtains $K^* = I_s K_{AB'}$ in the law enforcement process. The investigator preserving the secret key of $U_{B'}$ can compute the master key $K_{AB'}$ and then calculate I_s from $K_{AB'}$ and K^* as follows:

$$K^*/K_{AB'} = I_s K_{AB'}/K_{AB'} = I_s. \tag{7}$$

After that, when the law enforcement process for the domestic communication between U_X and U_Y in the country Q is performed, the investigator with a part I_s of the secret system information can obtain K_{XY} by computing the following equation:

$$K^*/I_s = I_s K_{XY}/I_s = K_{XY}. \tag{8}$$

Finally, without help of key escrow agencies the investigator can decipher the encrypted communication between U_X and U_Y by himself anytime.

For avoiding this attack, the court generates the secret system information (I_s, i_s) every law enforcement protocol and distributes a part of it to each key escrow agency.

4 Distributed ITTPs (or Without an ITTP)

Our proposed International TTP publishes its international public key, and does nothing related with any user's secret key. Thus, even in international communication between two domains, the users need no communication with the ITTP. However, a criticism from the practical view point is that the use of such a single International TTP sitting over all other national jurisdictions is too idealistic, and naive or completely unworkable solution.

We have a solution against this criticism: we can distribute the role of such unique ITTP to multiple agencies by using recent developed techniques in threshold cryptography [Des92, FY98]. Our idea is the following. E ach government jointly makes an ITTP. Then, the ITTP and all governments shares the secret keys of an organization. In such a distributed (threshold) cryptosystem, without cooperation by all (or more than k) governments the ITTP cannot decrypt the ciphertext encrypted by the public key of the organization. This approach allows the investigator to make a law enforcement protocol with the approvals of all governments or more than k members.

We should remark that any public-key scheme (e.g., RSA and ElGamal) is applicable to our ITTP's encryption scheme.

Suppose that the ITTPs select the ElGamal cryptography as his own asymmetric cryptosystem. In this case, n ITTPs share the secret key of an organization by the Pedersen's scheme [Ped91b]. When processing the law enforcement, each ITTP computes the partial result from the partial secret key preserved, using the deciphering protocol described in [DF89]. The combination of the partial result enables the investigator to decipher the data encrypted with the public key of the organization, which consists of n ITTPs, to obtain E_D. This technique is applicable to the distribution of the national secret key. In other words, our system has no problem even if users deposits the segmental national secret key to each key escrow agency by the k-out-of-n sharing scheme instead of the n-out-of-n sharing. (Appendix A describes the concrete scheme of the discrete-log based distributed ITTP.)

As the public cryptosystem of ITTPs, also RSA can be also applicable. ITTPs share the secret key of an organization by applying the method of the shared RSA key generation [BF97, FMY98]. When the law enforcement protocol is executed, each

ITTP computes partial result same as the ElGamal. The investigator combines of the partial result to access E_D. Also our system gives a solution to the following open problem remarked in [CGM96]:

Can a practical key escrow scheme be designed for the case where more than two domains are involved, and where escrow agencies are not permitted to span more than one domain ?

A requirement for international key escrow stated in [CGM96] is that "the interception authorities in any domain can gain access to an escrowed key without communicating with any domain independently."

We utilize techniques in threshold cryptography for restricting the escrow agency's tapping power only within his domain. We should remark that a communication in our system is done between two domains (say domain P and domain Q), so our solution answers to a weaker requirement that "the key is capable of being escrowed by one domain P with cooperation of other domains except the other Q."

Furthermore, by applying distributed public-key techniques [FY98], our proposed system can be flexibly modified for being satisfied variants of requirements of security policies.

Acknowledgments: The authors would like to thank Shigeo Tsujii for having inspired the authors to the fair international key escrow problem. Thanks also to an anonymous referee for pointing out the reference [GGD95]. The first author wants to express his thanks to Atsushi Fujioka for discussing the design of fair key escrow system while his visiting NTT-lab. The third author wishes to thanks Zvi Galil and Moti Yung for their hospitality while his visiting Columbia Univ.

References

[Abe97]   H. Abelson et al., "*The risks of key recovery, key escrow, and trusted third-party encryption*," Final Report – 27 May 1997.
http://www.crypto.com/key_study/

[BDHJ97] F. Bao, R. Deng, Y. Han, A. Jeng, "*Design and Analyses of Two Basic Protocols for Use in TTP-Based Key Escrow*," Proceedings of ACISP'97, pp.261-270, 1997.

[BF97]   D. Boneh, M. Franklin, "*Efficient generation of shared RSA keys*," Advances in Cryptology – CRYPTO '97, LNCS 1294, pp. 425-439, 1997.

[BG97]   M. Bellare, S. Goldwasser, "*Verifiable Partial Key Escrow*," 4th ACM Conference on Computer and Communications Security, pp.78-91, 1997.

[CGM96]   L. Chen, D. Gollmann and C. J. Mitchell, "*Key Escrow in Mutually Mistrusting Domains*," Proceedings of Security Protocols, LNCS 1189, pp. 139-153, 1996.

[DB96]   E. D. Denning and D. K. Branstad, "*A taxonomy for key escrow encryption systems*," Comm. ACM, 39(3): pp.34-40, 1996.

[DB97]   E. D. Denning and D. K. Branstad, "*A taxonomy for key recovery encryption systems*," May 1997 paper on key recovery terminology and approaches, revised version of [DB96], 1997.

[DDFY94] A. De Santis, Y. Desmedt, Y. Frankel and M. Yung, "*How to share a function security*," Proc. of the 26th Annual ACM Symposium on the Theory of Computing, pp. 522-533, 1994.

[Des92]   Y. Desmedt, "*Threshold cryptosystems*," Advances in Cryptology – Auscrypt'92, LNCS 718, pp. 3-14, 1992.

[DF89]   Y. Desmedt and Y. Frankel, "*Threshold cryptosystems*," Advances in Cryptology – CRYPTO '89, LNCS 435, pp. 307-315, 1989.

[DH76] W. Diffie, M. E. Hellman, *"New Directions in Cryptography,"* IEEE Transactions in Information Theory IT-22, pp. 644-655, 1976.

[EES93] E. F. Brickell, D. E. Denning, S. T. Kent, D. P. Maher, W. Tuchman, *"SKIPJACK Review Interim Report,"* July 28, 1993.

[FMY98] Y. Frankel, P. D. MacKenzie and M. Yung, *"Robust efficient distributed RSA-key generation,"* Proc. ACM STOC, pp. 663-672, 1998.

[FY95] Y. Frankel, M. Yung, *"Escrow encryption systems visited:attacks, analysis and designs,"* Proceedings of Advances in Cryptology–CRYPTO'95, LNCS 963, pp. 222-235, 1995.

[FY98] Y. Frankel, M. Yung, *"Distributed Public Key Cryptosystems,"* (Invited) PreProc. of PKC'98, 1998.

[GCHQ96] CESG, *"Securing Electronic Mail within HMG – part 1:Infrastructure and Protocol,"* document T/3113TL/2776/11, 21 March, 1996.
http://www.rdg.opengroup.org/public/tech/security/pki/casm/casm.htm

[GGD95] C. Gressel, R. Granot, and Itai Dror, *"International Cryptographic Communication without Key Escrow; KISS: Keep the Invaders (of Privacy) Socially Sane,"* presented at the International Cryptography Institute 1995: Global Challenges, Sept. 21-22, 1995. Short paper is available at http://www.cosc.georgetown.edu/~denning/crypto/Appendix.html

[JMW95] N. Jefferies, C. Mitchell, M. Walker, *"A Proposed Architecture for Trusted Third Party Services,"* Proceedings of Cryptography: Policy and Algorithms, LNCS 1029, pp. 98-104, 1995.

[KL95] J. Kilian and T. Leighton, *"Fair cryptosystems, revised,"* Advances in Cryptology-CRYPTO '95, LNCS 963, pp. 208-221, 1995.

[LWY95] A. K. Lenstra, P. Winkler, Y. Yacobi, *"A Key Escrow System with Warrant Bounds,"* Advances in Cryptology-CRYPTO '95, LNCS 963, pp. 198-207, 1995.

[Mc88] K. S. McCurley, *"A Key Distribution System Equivalent to Factoring,"* Journal of Cryptology, pp. 95-105, 1988.

[Mic93] S. Micali, *"Fair Public-Key Cryptosystems,"* Technical Report 579, MIT Lab. For Computer Science, 1993.

[Mic95] S. Micali, *"Guaranteed partial key escrow,"* MIT Laboratory for Computer Science Technical Memo. 537, 1995.

[MN97] C. W. Man, R. Safavi-Naini, *"Democratic Key Escrow Scheme,"* Proceedings of ACISP'97, pp.249-260, 1997.

[Ped91a] T. P. Pedersen, *"Distributed provers with applications to undeniable signatures,"* Advances in Cryptology – Eurocrypt '91, LNCS 547, pp. 221-238, 1991.

[Ped91b] *"A threshold cryptosystem without a trusted party,"* Advances in Cryptology – Eurocrypt '91, LNCS 547, pp. 522-526, 1991.

[Sim83] G. J. Simmons, *"A 'weak' privacy protocol using the RSA cryptoalgorithm,"* Cryptologia, vol. 7, pp. 180-182, 1983.

[Sti95] D. R. Stinson, *"CRYPTOGRAPHY:Theory and Practice,"* CRC Press, Inc. Boca Raton, Florida, U.S.A., 1995.

[Tsu96] S. Tsujii, *"A remark on the problem in an international key escrow,"* Personal Communication with the third author, November 1996.

[VT97] E. R. Verheul, H. C. A. van Tilborg, *"Binding ElGamal: A Fraud-Detectable Alternative to Key-Escrow Proposals,"* Advances in Cryptology – EUROCRYPT '97, LNCS 1233, pp. 119-133, 1997.

[YY98] A. Young and M. Yung, *"Auto-recoverable auto-certifiable cryptosystems,"* Advances in Cryptology – EUROCRYPT '98, LNCS 1403, pp. 17-31, 1998.

[YY99] A. Young and M. Yung, *"Auto-recoverable cryptosystems with faster initialization and the escrow hierarchy,"* These Proceedings of PKC '99, 1999.

A A discrete-log based implementation of our Distributed-ITTPs

A.1 Basic techniques

VSS with Dealer [Ped91a] Pedersen proposed a VSS scheme [Ped91a], in which the dealer who knows the secret key itself distributes the share to each party P_j ($1 \leq j \leq n$) as follows. Any $k(< n)$ P_js can computes the secret key S of the dealer.

Step.1: The dealer generates $k - 1$ random integers $f_1, f_2, \ldots f_{k-1} \in Z_q^*$ and computes $s_j = f(j)(1 \leq j \leq m)$ with the polynomial $f_z = f_0 + f_1 z + \ldots + f_{k-1} z^{k-1}$. Here, f_z satisfies $f_0 = S$.

Step.2: The dealer sends each $P_j (1 \leq j \leq n)$ the share s_j and the verification vector $V = (g^{f_0}, g^{f_1}, \ldots, g^{f_{k-1}})$.

Step.3: Each $P_j (1 \leq j \leq n)$ verifies if $g^{s_j} h_i = \prod_{l=0}^{k-1} (g^{f_j})^{j^l}$

VSS without Dealer [Ped91b] Pedersen also presented another VSS scheme [Ped91b] without the dealer, in which multiple parties $P_j (1 \leq j \leq n)$ shares the secret key of the group, generating their key pair of public and secret key. We describes the protocol below, where let $k(< n)$ be a value of threshold.

Step.1: Each party P_i generates x_i and $k - 1$ random integers $f_{i1}, f_{i2}, \ldots f_{i,k-1} \in Z_q^*$ chooses a polynomial $f_i(z) = f_{i0} + f_{i1} z + \ldots + f_{i,k-1} z^{k-1}$. For $1 \leq i \leq n$, P_i calculates $S_{ij} = f_i(j)$, where $f_{i0} = x_i$.

Step.2: P_i sends each $P_j (1 \leq j \leq n)$ the share S_{ij} and the verification vector $V = (g^{f_{i0}}, g^{f_{i1}}, \ldots, g^{f_{i,k-1}})$.

Step.3: Each $P_i (1 \leq i \leq n)$ verifies the validity of each share S_{ji} from each P_j, by checking $g^{S_{ji}} \stackrel{?}{=} \prod_{l=0}^{k-1} (g^{f_{jl}})^{i^l}$. If and only if all verification is validly accepted, go to next step.

Step.4: Each P_i calculates $S_i = \sum_{j=1}^n S_{ji}$ and stores the partial secret S_i as the share of secret key $S = x_1 + x_2 + \cdots + x_n$

Distributed deciphering protocol Now, a set Λ of any t P_j can computes the secret key S as follows.

$$S = \sum_{j \in \Lambda} S_j \lambda_{j, \Lambda} \quad , \quad \lambda_{j, \Lambda} = \prod_{l \in \Lambda \setminus \{j\}} \frac{l}{l - j}$$

Based on the above technique, Desmedt and Frankel proposed the distributed deciphering algorithm in the ElGamal cryptosystem. Suppose that the entity $\mathcal{X}$ has a message M encrypted with the public key (y, q, p), where $C = (C_1, C_2) = (g^r \bmod p, M y^r \bmod p)$. The key y of the group composed by multiple P_j satisfies $y = g^S \pmod p$.

The entity X has distributed parties decrypt the ciphertext with each share as follows.

Step.1: X sends C_1 to each party P_j ($\in \Lambda$).

Step.2: Each P_j calculates a partial result $R_j = C_1^{\lambda_{j, \Lambda} S_j} \pmod p$ and sends R_j to X.

Step.3: X incorporates t partial results to obtain the message M.

$$C_2 / R = M y^r / \prod_{j \in \Lambda} R_j = M y^r / (g^r)^S = M \pmod p$$

The algorithm allows distributed party to decrypt the ciphertext encrypted by the public key of group without revealing their share and computing the secret key S. Remark that the algorithm is different from the above technique computing S itself from t shares revealed by each party P_j.

Distributed ITTPs The ITTP, which is only involved in the law enforcement protocol for the communication between the users who belong to different countries, can allows the tapping of communication to be performed with the consent of both countries. The arrangement is in consideration of the communication between different countries whose policy for the key escrow is affirmative and negative respectively. When the affirmative country wants to tap such a communication, the consent of the negative country should be needed so as not to incur the government's wrath.

The distributed ITTP generates and shares the group secret key u using the Pedersen's scheme [Ped91b] described in section A.1. Let $h = g^u$ be the corresponding public key of the ITTP. Any k out of m ITTPs can produce the output with the secret key u.

Setting up the parameters of users Each user generates the domestic key and the national key as follows.

Domestic Key: The user in the negative country generates the secret and public key and registers the public key as the domestic key via the certificate authority. On the other hand, the user in the affirmative country deposits and registers the own secret key as follows. Each user U_i generates the domestic secret key x_i and computes $y_i = g^{x_i} \pmod{p}$ as the domestic public key. Then, each user distributes the share of x_i to each T_j in own country, using the Pedersen's technique [Ped91a] with a dealer. The y_i is registered as the domestic key of the user U_i only when the shares are distributed in a regular manner.

International Key: Each user U_j who want to make international communications generates the international secret key S_j and computes the public key $P_i = g^{S_i} \pmod{p}$. Then, the user U_j makes the registration of the international public key P_i in the $\mathcal{CA}$ for international keys only. Rote that the secret key S_j has no requirement of depositing to any institution and the ITTP cannot be involved at the key registration stage.

A.2   International Communication

The protocol for U_A in the country P conducting the encrypted communication with U_B in the country Q is the same as the protocol for single ITTP described in 2.6. The difference is in the following Law enforcing protocol.

Law enforcing protocol The following protocol is performed when the investigator in the country Q starts on tapping the encrypted communication of U_B. Here, the investigator has already obtained the encrypted message C and $LEAF$ in the communication. For simplicity, the $T_1, T_2, \ldots, T_k$ amoung the m TTPs in the country Q are involved in this protocol.

Step 1:   The investigator of the country Q petitions the court of justice in his own country for an order permitting the law enforcement to the communication of U_B.

Step 2:   The court decides whether or not to permit the surveillance. If the permission is to be granted, the court issues an order that clearly specifies the verification date and the name of the user who will be subject to the surveillance (U_B).

Step 3:   The court of justice generates the parameters (I_s, i_s) satisfying the following formula.

$$I_s = I_{s1} I_{s2} \cdots I_{sk} \pmod{p}$$
$$i_s = I_s^{-1} = i_{s1} + i_{s2} + \cdots + i_{sk} \pmod{q}$$

The court of justice transmits both the warrant and (I_{sj}, i_{sj}) to each $T_j (1 \leq j \leq k)$ in the country Q.

Step 4:   The investigator petitions the country P for the agreement on the tapping of the communication line.

Step 5 : The country P decides whether or not to permit the surveillance. If the permission is to be granted, the country P issues the consent bond for the tapping.

Step 6 : The investigator submits the consent bond of the country P to t ITTPs attending (let Γ be a set of any t ITTPs).

Step 7 : After verifying the validity of both the court order and the consent bond, each ITTP$_j$ computes a partial result R_j with the share u_j and the appropriate Lagrange coefficient $\gamma_{j,\Gamma}$ and sends R_j to the investigator (See section A.1), where

$$u = \sum_{j \in \Gamma} u_j \gamma_{j,\Gamma} \quad , \quad \gamma_{j,\Gamma} = \prod_{l \in \Gamma \setminus \{j\}} \frac{l}{l-j}.$$

Step 8 : The investigator incorporates the partial result R_j from ITTP$_j$ to obtain Inf successfully $(Dec(Inf) = E_D, D', C, y_A, y_B, P_A, P_B)$. If and only if the extracted D' and the D in the $LEAF$ is identical, the investigator sends the court order to the related $T_j (1 \leq j \leq k)$. Here, let Λ be the set of k key escrow agencies.

Step 9 : Each T_j computes a partial result K_j with the preserved share S_{Bj} and sends $K_j = I_{sj} P_A^{\lambda_{j,\Lambda} S_{Bj}}$ (mod p) to the investigator.

Step 10 : The investigator incorporates k partial results K_j to obtain K^* and transmits $K^* = \prod_{j=1}^{t} K_j$ (mod p) to each T_j.

Step 11 : Each T_j computes $K_j' = D^{i_{sj} K^*}$ (mod p) and sends K_j' to the investigator.

Step 12 : The investigator computes the session key KS with partial results K_j'.

$$(\prod_{j=1}^{t} K_j')^{E_D} = (D^{I_s \cdot K_{AB} \cdot \sum_{j=1}^{k} i_{sj}})^{E_D} = (D^{I_s \cdot i_s \cdot K_{AB}})^{E_D} = KS \ (\text{mod } p)$$

The investigator decrypts the ciphertext C with the computes KS to obtain the message $M = f_2^{-1}(C, KS)$.

How to Copyright a Function ?

David Naccache

Gemplus Card International
34 rue Guynemer
Issy-les-Moulineaux, 92447, France
naccache@compuserve.com

Adi Shamir

Weizmann Institute of Science
Applied Mathematics Department
Rehovot, 76100, Israel
shamir@wisdom.weizmann.ac.il

Julien P. Stern

UCL Cryptography Group
Bâtiment Maxwell, place du Levant 3
Louvain-la-Neuve, 1348, Belgium
stern@dice.ucl.ac.be

Université de Paris-Sud
Laboratoire de Recherche en Informatique
Bâtiment 490, 91405, Orsay, France
stern@lri.fr

Abstract. This paper introduces a method for tracking different copies of functionally equivalent algorithms containing identification marks known to the attacker. Unlike all previous solutions, the new technique does not rely on any marking assumption and leads to a situation where each copy is either traceable or so severely damaged that it becomes impossible to store in polynomial space or run in polynomial time.

Although RSA-related, the construction is particularly applicable to confidential block-ciphers such as SkipJack, RC4, GOST 28147–89, GSM A5, COMP128, TIA CAVE or other proprietary executables distributed to potentially distrusted users.

1 Introduction

Although software piracy costs $11.2 billion per year [3], impedes job growth and robs governments millions of dollars in tax revenues, most existing protections still rely on legal considerations or platform-specific assumptions.

The most common solutions are based on electronic extensions (dongles) containing memory tables or cheap 4-bit microcontrollers; to rely on these, the protected program periodically challenges the dongle via to the computer's parallel port and makes sure that the retrieved answers are correct. Unfortunately, given enough time, skill and motivation, it is always possible to disassemble the program, find the dongle calls and remove them from the code. In some sense, this approach mixes tamper-resistance and steganography.

A somewhat more efficient solution (mostly used in the playstation industry) consists of executing strategic code fragments in the dongle. As an example, a chess program (exchanging with the player a couple of bytes per round) can be executed in the dongle while less important game parts such as graphics, sounds and keyboard-interfaces can be left unprotected on a CD, useless for playing without the dongle.

A third approach consists of dividing the protected media into two partitions: a first (conventionally formatted) area contains a program called *loader* while the second, formatted in a non-standard way, contains the protected software itself. When the loader is executed, it reads-out the second partition into the RAM and jumps into it. Since operating system commands are unable to read the second partition, its contents are somewhat protected, although patient attackers can still analyze the loader or copy the executable directly from the RAM.

By analogy to the *double-spending problem* met in e-cash schemes, it seems impossible to prevent duplication without relying on specific hardware assumptions, simply because digital signals are inherently copyable. This difficulty progressively shifted research from *prevention* to *detection*, assuming that the former is achieved by non-technical (legal) means. In such models, users generally get personalized yet very similar copies of a given data (referred to as *equivalent*) where the slight dissimilarities (*marks*) between copies are designed to resist collusion, be asymmetric or offer anonymity and other cryptographic features [5, 10, 11].

It is important to stress that all such systems rely on the hypothesis that the marks are scattered in a way that makes their location, alteration or destruction infeasible (*marking assumption*). In practice, marking heavily depends on the nature of the protected data and the designer's imagination [1]. Different strategies are used for source code, images and texts and vary from fractal coding [2], statistical analysis [14] or stereometric image recordings [4] to paraphrasing information exchanged between friendly intelligence agencies [9].

This paper shows that at least as far as functions, algorithms or programs are concerned, marking assumptions can be replaced by regular complexity ones; consequently, we will assume that all identification marks (and their positions) are known to the attacker and try to end-up in a situation where each copy is either traceable or so severely damaged that it becomes impossible to store in polynomial space or run in polynomial time.

The new construction appears particularly suitable to proprietary cryptosystems such as SkipJack, RC4, GOST 28147–89, GSM A5, COMP128 or CAVE TIA, distributed to potentially distrusted users. Although it seems unlikely that an important number (≥ 100) of copies will be marked in practice, we believe that the new method can be useful in the following contexts where a few copies are typically distributed :

• Proprietary standardization committees (such as the TIA-AHAG, the GSM consortium or the DVB group) could distribute different yet equivalent functions to each member-company. Although such a deployment does not incriminate individuals, it will point out the company which should be held collectively responsible.

- In an industrial development process, different descriptions of the same function could be given to each involved department (*e.g.* software, hardware, integration and test) and the final client.

Although acceptable, the performances of our solution degrade when the number of users increases; we therefore encourage researchers and implementers to look for new variants and improvements of our scheme.

2   The formal framework

The new protocol involves a distributor and several users; the distributor is willing to give each user a morphologically different, yet functionally equivalent, implementation of a function. Hereafter, the word *function* will refer to the mathematical object, while *implementations* will represent electronic circuits or programs that compute a function (more formally, implementations can be looked upon as polynomial circuits that compute the function).

Definition 1: *Let M and L be sets of integers. A distribution of the function $f : M \rightarrow L$ is a set of implementations F such that:*

$$\forall F \in \mathcal{F}, \ \forall x \in M \ \ f(x) = F[x]$$

Definition 2: *Let M and L be sets of integers. A keyed distribution of the function $f : M \rightarrow L$ is an implementation F and a set of integers K such that:*

$$\forall k \in K, \ \forall x \in M \ \ f(x) = F[x, k]$$

A keyed distribution can be regarded as a monolithic device that behaves like the function f when fed with a key belonging to K, whereas a distribution is simply a set of independent software or hardware devices that behave like the function f. Note that both definitions are equivalent: a keyed distribution is a specific distribution and a keyed distribution can be constructed from a distribution by collecting all the implementations and calling the one corresponding to the key; we will therefore use the simpler definition of keyed distribution.

These definitions do not capture the fact that several implementations might be trivially derived from each other. If, for instance, $F[x, k] = kx$ then it is easy to find an implementation F' such that $F'[x, 2k] = kx$. (F' can be $F[x, 2k]/2$). To capture this, we define an *analyzer*:

Definition 3: *Let $\{F, K\}$ be a keyed distribution of f. An analyzer Z of this distribution is an algorithm that takes as input $\{F, K\}$, an implementation F' of f and tries to find the key $k \in K$ used in F'. Z may either fail or output k.*

In other words, when an opponent receives a legitimate implementation of f keyed with k and modifies it, the analyzer's role consists of trying to recover k despite the modifications. The analyzer consequently behaves as a detective in our construction.

2.1 Adversarial model

As usual, the adversary's task consists of forging a new implementation which is unlinkable to those received legitimately. We distinguish two types of opponents: *passive* adversaries which restrict themselves to re-keying existing implementations and *active* adversaries who may re-implement the function in any arbitrary way. When distribution is done through hardware tokens (decoders, PC-cards, smart-cards) where keys are stored in EEPROM registers or battery-powered RAM cells, passive adversaries are only assumed to change the register's contents while active ones may re-design a whole new hardware from scratch.

Definition 4: *Let c be a security parameter. A keyed distribution $\{F, \mathcal{K}\}$ for the function f is c-copyrighted against a passive adversary if given $C \subset \mathcal{K}$, $|C| < c$, finding a $k \notin C$ such that $\{F, k\}$ implements f is computationally hard[1].*

Definition 5: *Let c be a security parameter. A keyed distribution $\{F, \mathcal{K}\}$ with analyzer $\mathcal{Z}$ for f is c-copyrighted against an active adversary if given $C \subset \mathcal{K}$, $|C| < c$, finding an implementation F' of f such that the analyzer $\mathcal{Z}$, given input F', outputs either a integer k in $\mathcal{K} \setminus C$ or fails is computationally hard.*

3 The new primitive

The basic observation behind our construction is that in many public-key cryptosystems, a given public-key corresponds to infinitely many integers which are homomorphic to the secret key, and can be used as such.

For instance, using standard notations, it is easy to see that a DSA key x can be equivalently replaced by any $x + kq$ and an RSA key e can be looked upon as the inverse of any $d_k = e^{-1} \mod \phi(n) + k\phi(n)$. We intend to use this flexibility to construct equivalent modular exponentiation copies.

At a first glance it appears impossible to mark an RSA function using the above observation since given n, e and d_k, a user can trivially find $\phi(n)$ (hereafter ϕ) and replace d_k by some other $d_{k'}$. Nevertheless, this difficulty can be circumvented if we assume that the exponentiation is only a building-block of some other primitive (for instance a hash-function) where e is not necessary.

We start by presenting a solution for two users and prove its correctness; the two-user case will then be used as a building-block to extend the construction to more users.

When only two users are concerned, a copyrighted hash function can be distributed and traced as follows:

Distribution: The designer publishes a conventional hash function h and an RSA modulus n, selects a random $d < \phi$ and a couple of random integers $\{k_0, k_1\}$, computes the quantities $d_i = d + k_i\phi$, keeps $\{\phi, d, k_0, k_1\}$ secret and discloses the implementation $H[x, i] = h(h(x)^{d_i} \mod n)$ to user $i \in \{0, 1\}$.

---

[1] with respect to the parameters of the scheme used to generate $\mathcal{K}$.

Tracing: Upon recovery of a copy, the designer analyzes its exponent. If d_0 or d_1 is found, the leaker is identified and if a third exponent d' appears, both users are identified as a collusion.

4 Analysis

One can easily show that the essential cryptographic properties of the hash function are preserved and that the distribution is 1-copyrighted against passive adversaries. It seems difficult to prove resistance against general active adversaries; however, we show that if such opponents are bound to use circuits performing arithmetic operations modulo n, then we can exhibit an analyzer that makes our distribution 1-copyrighted.

Theorem 1: *h and H are equally collision-resistant.*

PROOF: Assume that a collision $\{x, y\}$ is found in h; trivially, $\{x, y\}$ is also a collision in H; to prove the converse, assume that a collision $\{x', y'\}$ is found in H. Then either $h(x')^d = h(y')^d \bmod n$ and $\{x', y'\}$ is also a collision in h, or $h(x')^d \neq h(y')^d \bmod n$ and $\{h(x)^d \bmod n, h(y)^d \bmod n\}$ is a collision in h. $\square$

Lemma 1: *Finding a multiple of $\phi(n)$ is as hard as factoring n.*

PROOF: This lemma, due to Miller, is proved in [6]. $\square$

Theorem 2: *If factoring is hard, $\{H, \{d_0, d_1\}\}$ is 1-copyrighted against a passive adversary.*

PROOF: Assume, without loss of generality, that an adversary receives the implementation H and the key d_0. Suppose that he is able to find $d' \neq d_0$ such that $H[., d_0] = H[., d']$. Then, $d_0 - d'$ is a multiple of $\phi(n)$ and by virtue of Miller's lemma, n can be factored. $\square$

Theorem 3: *If factoring is hard, then $\{H, \{d_0, d_1\}\}$ is 1-copyrighted against an active adversary restricted to performing arithmetic operations modulo n.*

PROOF: (Sketch) We show that an active adversary is not more powerful than a passive one. We build $\mathcal{Z}$ as follows: $\mathcal{Z}$ first extracts the exponentiation part. He then formally evaluates the function computed by this part, with respect to its constants $\{c_1, \ldots, c_w\}$ and input x, replacing modular operations by regular ones. This yields a rational function P/Q with variable x and coefficients depending only on $\{c_1, \ldots, c_w\}$. He finally evaluates all these coefficients modulo n. A careful bookkeeping of the non zero monomials shows that either the adversary has obtained a multiple of $\phi(n)$ (and can therefore factor n) or that P divides Q. This means that the rational function is in fact reduced to a single monomial, from which we can compute the value of the corresponding exponent and the security of the construction follows from the security against the passive adversary. $\square$

Note that resistance against active adversaries is more subtle than our basic design: assuming that d is much longer than ϕ, adding random multiples of ϕ to d will not alter its most significant bits up to a certain point; consequently, there is a finite number of ℓ-bit exponents, congruent to $d \bmod \phi$ and having a given bit-pattern (say u) in their most significant part; the function: $h(h(x)^{d_i} \oplus u)$ will thus admit only a finite number of passive forgeries.

5 Tracing more users

Extending the previous construction to more users is somewhat more technical; obviously, one can not simply distribute more than two exponents as this would blind the collusion-detection mechanism.

System setup is almost as before: letting t be a security parameter, the designer publishes a hash function h and t RSA moduli $\{n_1, \ldots, n_t\}$, selects t random triples $\{d[j] < \phi_j, k[0, j], k[1, j]\}$ and computes the t pairs:

$$d[i, j] = d[j] + k[i, j]\phi_j \quad \text{for } i \in \{0, 1\}$$

Then, the designer selects, for each user, a t-bit string ω. We will call ω the ID or the codeword of this user. Each user receives, for each j, one out of the two keys $d[0, j], d[1, j]$ (he receives $d[0, j]$ if the j-th bit of ω is zero and $d[1, j]$ otherwise). The exact codeword generation process will be discussed later.

Let s be a security parameter ($0 < s \leq t$). The function is now defined as follows: the input x is hashed and the result $h(x)$ is used to select s keys among the t keys of a user. For simplicity, let us rename these s keys $\{a_1, \ldots, a_s\}$ for a given user.

We now define $H[x] = H[s, x]$ recursively by:

$$H[1, x] = h(x^{a_1} \bmod n_1) \qquad \text{and}$$
$$H[j, x] = h(H[j - 1, x]^{a_j} \bmod n_j) \quad \text{for } j > 1$$

A simple (and sometimes acceptable) approach would be to distribute copies with randomly chosen codewords. However, by doing so, logarithmic-size collusions could recover the exponents with constant probability and forge new implementations; therefore, specific sets of codewords must be used. Letting $\mathcal{C}$ be a coalition of c users provided with codewords $\omega[1], \ldots, \omega[c]$. $\mathcal{C}$ can not change $d[i, j]$, if and only if all codewords match on their j-th bit. Hence, the problem to solve boils down to the design of a set of codewords, amongst which any subset, possibly limited to a given size, has elements which match on enough positions to enable tracing. This problem was extensively studied in [4] which exhibits a set of codewords of polylogarithmic ($\mathcal{O}(\log^6 t)$) length, capable of tracing logarithmic size coalitions.

While [4]'s hidden constant is rather large, our marks are a totally independent entity and their size is not related to the size of the function (which is *not* the case when one adds marks to an image or a text); hence, *only complexity-theoretic considerations* (the hardness of factoring n) may increase the number of symbols in H.

Finally, the new construction allows to adjust the level of security by tuning s accordingly. Although pirates could try to distribute copies with missing exponents in order not to get traced, such copies become almost unusable even if only a few exponents are omitted. This approach (detecting only copies which are usable enough) is similar to the one suggested by Pinkas and Naor in [8]. Assuming that m of the exponents are missing and that each computation requires s exponents out of t, the correct output probability is:

$$\Pr[t, m, s] = \frac{(t - s)!(t - m)!}{t! \,(t - m - s)!}$$

Given $\Pr[t, m, s]$'s quick decay (typically $\Pr[100, 10, 10] \cong 3/10$) and the fact that repeated errors can be detected and traced, it is reasonable to assume that these untraceable implementations are not a serious business threat. No one would buy a pirate TV decoder displaying only three images out of ten (the perturbation can be further amplified by CBC, in which case each error will de-synchronize the image decryption until the next stream-cipher initialization).

6 Applications

Building upon a few well-known results, a variety of traceable primitives can be derived from H: Feistel ciphers can be copyrighted by using H as a round function, traceable digital signatures can use H in Rompel's construction [13] and traceable public-key encryption can be obtained by using [7] with a composite modulus (e-less RSA) or by post-encrypting systematically any public-key ciphertext with a watermarked block-cipher keyed with a public constant. Interactive primitives such as zero-knowledge protocols or blind signatures can be traced using this same technique.

The construction also gives birth to new fundamental protocols; a web site could, for example, sell marked copies of a MAC-function and record in a database the user IDs and their exponents. Since all functions are equivalent, when a user logs-in, he does not need to disclose his identity; but if an illegit imate copy is discovered, the web owners can look-up the faulty ID in the database[2].

Another application consists of restricting software to registered users. In any scenario involving communication (file exchange, data modulation, payment, etc), the protected software must simply encrypt the exchanged data with a copyrighted block-cipher. Assuming that a word processor systematically encrypts its files with a copyrighted block-cipher (keyed with some public constant), unregistered users face the choice of getting traced or removing the encryption layer from their copies (the word processor will then be unable to read files produced by legitimate users and will create files that are unreadable by registered programs); consequently, users of untraceable (modified) programs are forced to *voluntarily* exclude themselves from the legitimate user community.

---

[2] care should be taken not to restrict the MAC's input space too much as polynomially small I/O spaces could be published as look-up tables.

Finally, our scheme can also be used for TV tracing instead of the usual broadcast encryption/traitor tracing techniques. In broadcast schemes, the message is usually block-encrypted, each block being made of a *header* (which allows each user to recover a random key) and a *ciphertext* block (which is the encryption of the data under this random key). The main advantage of our scheme is its very low communication overhead: the header can be a simple encryption of the secret key, as all the users receive an equivalent decryption function. There are, however, several disadvantages: we totally lose control over the access structure allowed to decrypt. This means that new keys need to be sent to all registered users from time to time.

Surprisingly, in our setting smart-cards suddenly become a powerful... piracy tool; by programming one of the H_i into a smart-card, a pirate can manufacture and distribute executable hardware copies of his function and rely on the card's tamper-resistance features to prevent the designer from reading the exponents that identify him.

7 Conclusion and open questions

We presented a new (public-domain) marking technique which applies to a variety of functions and relies on regular complexity assumptions; while we need a large amount of data to personalize an implementation when many users are involved, the construction is fairly efficient and can be adjusted to variable security levels.

There remains, however, a number of fundamental and practical questions such as the existence of DLP-based copyright mechanisms or the design of a copyright mechanism that allows to serve more than two users in a single (non-iterated) function. From a practical standpoint, it seems easy to compress the set $\{n_1 \ldots n_t\}$ to only $N + t \log N$ bits (this is done by generating t moduli having identical MSBs). Reducing the size of the exponent set is an interesting challenge.

References

1. J.-M. Acken, *How watermarking adds value to digital content*, Communications of the ACM, vol. 41-7, pp. 75-77, 1998.

2. P. Bas, J.-M. Chassery and F. Davoine, *Self-similarity based image watermarking*, Proceedings of EUSIPCO'98, Ninth European signal processing conference, European association for signal processing, pp. 2277-2280.

3. *The huge costs of software piracy*, Computer Fraud and Security Bulletin, 09/1997, Elsevier Science, page 3.

4. D. Boneh and J. Shaw, *Collusion-secure fingerprinting for digital data*, Advances in cryptology CRYPTO'95, Springer-Verlag, Lectures notes in computer science 963, pp. 452–465, 1995.

5. B. Chor, A. Fiat and M. Naor, *Tracing traitors*, Advances in cryptology CRYPTO'94, Springer-Verlag, Lectures notes in computer science 839, pp. 257–270, 1994.

6. G. Miller, *Riemann's hypothesis and tests for primality*, Journal of computer and system sciences, vol. 13, pp. 300–317, 1976.

7. D. Naccache and J. Stern, *A new public-key cryptosystem*, Advances in cryptology EUROCRYPT'97, Springer-Verlag, Lectures notes in computer science 1233, pp. 27–36, 1997.

8. M. Naor and B. Pinkas, *Theshold Traitor Tracing*, Advances in cryptology CRYPTO'98, Springer-Verlag, Lectures notes in computer science 1462, pp. 502–517, 1998.

9. V. Ostrovsky, *The other side of deception*, Harper-Collins Publishers, New-York, page 38, 1995.

10. B. Pfitzmann and M. Schunter, *Asymmetric fingerprinting*, Advances in cryptology EUROCRYPT'96, Springer-Verlag, Lectures notes in computer science 1070, pp. 84–95, 1996.

11. B. Pfitzmann and M. Waidner, *Anonymous fingerprinting*, Advances in cryptology EUROCRYPT'97, Springer-Verlag, Lectures notes in computer science 1233, pp. 88–102, 1997.

12. R. Rivest, A. Shamir and L. Adleman, *A method for obtaining digital signatures and public-key cryptosystems*, Communications of the ACM, vol. 21-2, pp. 120-126, 1978.

13. J. Rompel, *One way functions are necessary and sufficient for secure digital signatures*, Proceedings of the 22-nd Annual ACM Symposium on the Theory of Computing, pp. 387–394, 1990.

14. K. Verco and M. Wise, *Plagiarism à la mode: a comparison of automated systems for detecting suspected plagiarism*, The Computer Journal, vol. 39-9, pp. 741–750, 1996.

On the Security of RSA Screening

Jean-Sébastien Coron[1+2]

1. École Normale Supérieure
45 rue d'Ulm
Paris, F-75230, France
coron@clipper.ens.fr

David Naccache[2]

2. Gemplus Card International
34 rue Guynemer
Issy-les-Moulineaux, F-92447, France
{coron,naccache}@gemplus.com

Abstract. Since many applications require the verification of large sets of signatures, it is sometimes advantageous to perform a simultaneous verification instead of checking each signature individually. The simultaneous processing, called *batching*, must be *provably* equivalent to the sequential verification of all signatures.

In EUROCRYPT'98, Bellare *et al.* [1] presented a fast RSA batch verification scheme, called *screening*. Here we successfully attack this algorithm by forcing it to accept a false signature and repair it by implementing an additional test.

1 Introduction

Many industrial applications require the verification of large sets of signatures. For example, real-time applications such as web-servers or toll-highway gates must verify many coins in a short time-frame. A well-known speed-up strategy is *batching*, a probabilistic test that verifies the correctness of n signatures much faster than n sequential verifications. Batching is probabilistic in the sense that if (at least) one signature is false, the algorithm rejects the whole set with high probability but always accepts sets of correct signatures.

A new batching strategy suggested in [1] (called *screening*) provides faster verification at the cost of weaker guarantees. Just as batching, screening fails with high probability if one of the signatures was never produced by the signer, but might succeed if the signer signed all the signatures in the past, although one of them has since been modified.

1.1 Batch verification

Let R be a boolean relation taking as input an instance I and outputting a bit (meaning true or false). For example, R can be RSA's verification algorithm [8] where $R(x,y) = 1 \iff x \equiv y^e \bmod N$.

A *batch instance* for R (a sequence $\{I_1, \ldots, I_n\}$ of instances of R) is said to be correct if $R(I_i) = 1$ for all $i = 1, \ldots, n$ and incorrect otherwise (*i.e.* there exists an $i \in \{1, \ldots, n\}$ such that $R(I_i) = 0$).

A *batch verifier* $\mathcal{V}$ for R is a probabilistic algorithm that takes as input a batch instance $X = \{I_1, \ldots, I_n\}$ and a security parameter ℓ and satisfies the two following properties :

1. If X is correct then $\mathcal{V}$ outputs 1.
2. If X is incorrect then the probability that $\mathcal{V}$ outputs 1 is at most $2^{-\ell}$.

If at least one I_i is incorrect, the verifier must reject X with probability greater than $1 - 2^{-\ell}$. In practice, ℓ should be greater than 64, reducing the error probability to 2^{-64}.

1.2 Signature screening

A *signature scheme* consists of three components :

1. A probabilistic key generation algorithm $\mathsf{generate}(1^k) \overset{R}{\to} \{P, S\}$, where P is the public key and S the secret key.
2. A private signature algorithm $\mathsf{sign}_S(M) \to x$ where M is the message and x the signature.
3. A public verification algorithm $\mathsf{verify}_P(M, x) \to \{0, 1\}$.

$$\mathsf{verify}_P(M, x) = 1 \iff x = \mathsf{sign}_S(M)$$

A weaker notion of batch verification, called *screening* is introduced in [1].

A batch instance for signature verification consists of a sequence :

$$B = \{\{M_1, x_1\}, \ldots, \{M_n, x_n\}\}$$

where x_i is a purported signature of M_i with respect to some public key P.

A screening test screen is a probabilistic algorithm that takes as input a batch instance and outputs a bit. It must satisfy the two following properties :

1. Validity : correct signatures are always accepted :

$$\mathsf{verify}_P(\{M_i, x_i\}) = 1 \text{ for all } i = 1, \ldots, n \text{ implies } \mathsf{screen}_P(B) = 1$$

2. Security : if a message $M_i \in B$ was never signed by sign_S, B will be rejected with high probability.

2 RSA signature screening

Bellare *et al.*'s screening algorithm for hash-then-decrypt RSA signatures proceeds as follows :

The public key is $\{N, e\}$ and the secret key is d, where N is an RSA modulus, $e \in \mathbb{Z}^*_{\varphi(N)}$ an encryption exponent and d the corresponding decryption exponent : $ed \equiv 1 \bmod \varphi(N)$. Let H be a public hash function.

The signature algorithm is :

$$\mathsf{sign}_{\{N, d\}}(M) = H(M)^d \bmod N$$

and the corresponding verification algorithm is :

$$\text{verify}_{\{N,e\}}(M, x) = 1 \iff x^e \equiv H(M) \bmod N$$

The security of this scheme was studied in [2], where it was shown that H should ideally hash strings uniformly into $\mathbb{Z}_N^*$. This was called the *full domain hash* scheme (FDH).

FDH-RSA screening [1] is very simple, given N, e, an oracle access to the hash function H and :

$$\{\{M_1, x_1\}, \ldots, \{M_n, x_n\}\} \text{ with } x_i \in \mathbb{Z}_N^*$$

the screener outputs 1 if $(\prod_{i=1}^n x_i)^e \equiv \prod_{i=1}^n H(M_i) \bmod N$ and 0 otherwise.

The test is efficient as it requires n hashings, $2n$ multiplications and a single exponentiation, instead of n hashings and n exponentiations for the sequential verification of all signatures.

3 The attack

The flaw in this screening protocol is based on Davida's homomorphic attack [4] and reminds the Fiat-Shamir implementation detail pointed-out in [6]. By repeating a data element a certain number of times, we compensate the forgery's effect and force the verifier to accept an instance containing a piece of data that was never signed. The attack is illustrated for $e = 3$ but could work with any reasonably small exponent (although less secure, small exponents are often used to speed-up RSA verifications).

Let $M_1 \neq M_2$ be two messages and $x_1 = \text{sign}_S(M_1)$ which implies :

$$x_1^3 \equiv H(M_1) \bmod N$$

Let B' be the batch instance :

$$B' = \{(M_1, x_1 H(M_2) \bmod N), \{M_2, 1\}, \{M_2, 1\}, \{M_2, 1\}\}$$

Then $\text{screen}_P(B') = 1$ although M_2 was never signed.

An attacker $\mathcal{A}$ may thus produce a batch instance which contains a forgery (a message that was never signed by the signer) that gets undetected by the verifier. In the next section we explain how to prevent this attack and correct the scheme's security proof.

4 Preventing the attack

To prevent the attack the verifier must check that no message appears more than once in the batch. This can be done in $\mathcal{O}(n \log n)$ and suffices to reject B' where $\{M_2, 1\}$ appeared three times. Note that making the comparison only on x_i will not be a satisfactory repair.

The following corrects the security proof given in [1] and shows that screening plus message comparisons is provably secure unless inverting RSA is easy. Since the security of screening is based on the hardness of RSA, we recall the formalization given in [2].

The security of RSA is quantified as a trapdoor permutation f. The RSA$_e$ function $f : \mathbb{Z}_N^* \to \mathbb{Z}_N^*$ is defined by :

$$f(x) = x^e \bmod N$$

which inverse f^{-1} is :

$$f^{-1}(y) = y^d \bmod N$$

where N is a k-bit modulus, product of two $(k/2)$-bit primes, e the public exponent and d the secret exponent.

RSA$_e$ is said to be (t, ϵ)-secure if an attacker, given a randomly chosen $y \in \mathbb{Z}_N^*$ and a limited running time $t(k)$, succeeds in finding $f^{-1}(y)$ with probability at most $\epsilon(k)$.

The following theorem states that if RSA$_e$ is secure, then an adversary can not produce an acceptable FDH-RSA screening instance that contains a message that was never signed by the signer. The proof assumes the random oracle model where the hash function is seen as an oracle giving a truly random value for each new query. If the same query is asked twice, the answers are of course identical.

Theorem 1 : *Assume that RSA$_e$ is (t', ϵ')-secure. Let $\mathcal{A}$ be an adversary who after a chosen message attack on the FDH-RSA signature scheme, outputs a batch instance with n distinct messages, in which at least one message was never signed. Assume that in the chosen message attack $\mathcal{A}$ makes q_s FDH signature queries and q_h hash queries and suppose that the total running time of $\mathcal{A}$ is at most $t(k) = t'(k) - \Omega(k^3) \times (n + q_s + q_h)$. Then the probability that the FDH-RSA signature screening test accepts the batch instance is at most $\epsilon(k) = \epsilon'(k) \times (n + q_s + q_h)$.*

PROOF : The proof is easily derived from [1]; the only correction consists in ensuring that the equation :

$$y_m \times \prod_{i=1, i \neq m}^{n} y_{M_i} \equiv \prod_{i=1}^{n} x_i^e \bmod N$$

can be solved for $y_m = y_{M_m}$. Namely that if all the messages M_i in the batch instance are distinct, the term y_{M_m} differs from the other terms y_{M_i} with overwhelming probability and we get :

$$y_m = \frac{\prod_{i=1}^{n} x_i^e}{\prod_{i=1,i\neq m}^{n} y_{M_i}} \mod N$$

□

5 Conclusion and further research

We have presented a succesful attack against Bellare *et al.*'s EUROCRYPT'98 screening algorithm and a repair that makes it provably secure against signature forgery.

Alternative repair strategies such as the splitting of the batch instance into buckets also seem possible although their implementation seems to require more delicate security adjustments.

Note that the repaired algorithm does not *formally* respect the validity principle stated in section 1.2 as the batch instance :

$$\{\{M, H(M)^d \mod N\}, \{M, H(M)^d \mod N\}\}$$

will be rejected (as M appears more than once) although M was correctly signed. This is easily fixed by deleting from the batch instance all identical signatures except one.

Finally, it is interesting to observe that the requirement that each element must appear only once is *probably* too restrictive (this point should, however, be carefully investigated !) as the attack does not *seem* to apply when the number of identical messages is not congruent to zero modulo e; extending the proof to this case does not seem trivial at a first glance.

Screening DSA-like signatures is a challenging problem : in EUROCRYPT'94, Naccache *et al.* [7] presented a candidate (*cf.* appendix A) which did not appear in the proceedings but seems to be a promising starting point [5].

References

1. M. Bellare, J. Garray and T. Rabin, *Fast batch verification for modular exponentiation and digital signatures*, Advances in Cryptology - EUROCRYPT'98 Proceedings, Lecture Notes in Computer Science vol. 1403, K. Nyberg ed., Springer-Verlag, 1998. Full on-line version via http://www-cse.ucsd.edu/users/mihir, 1998.

2. M. Bellare, P. Rogaway, *The exact security of digital signatures : How to sign with RSA and Rabin*, Advances in Cryptology - EUROCRYPT'96 Proceedings, Lecture Notes in Computer Science vol. 1070, U. Maurer ed., Springer-Verlag, 1996.

3. M. Bellare, P. Rogaway, *Random oracles are practical : A paradigm for designing efficient protocols*, First ACM Conference on computer and communications security, ACM, 1994.

4. G. Davida, *Chosen signature cryptanalysis of the RSA (MIT) public-key cryptosystem*, Technical report TR-CS-82-2, Department of EECS, University of Wisconsin, 1982.

5. C. Lim & P. Lee, *Security of interactive DSA batch verification*, Electronic Letters, vol. 30, no. 19, pp. 1592–1593, 1994.

6. D. Naccache, *Unless modified Fiat-Shamir is insecure*, Proceedings of the third symposium on state and progress of research in cryptography : SPRC'93, Fondazione Ugo Bordoni, W. Wolfowicz ed., Roma, Italia, pp. 172–180, 1993.

7. D. Naccache, D. M'raïhi, S. Vaudenay & D. Raphaeli, *Can DSA be improved ? Complexity trade-offs with the digital signature standard*, Advances in Cryptology - EUROCRYPT'94 Proceedings, Lecture Notes in Computer Science vol. 950, A. de Santis ed., Springer-Verlag, pp. 77–85, 1995.

8. R. Rivest, A. Shamir, L. Adleman, *A method for obtaining digital signatures and public-key cryptosystems*, Communications of the ACM, vol. 21, pp. 120–126, 1978.

APPENDIX A
(FROM EUROCRYPT'94'S PRE-PROCEEDINGS)

The signature collection protocol is :

for $i = 1$ to n

- The signer picks $k_i \in_R \mathbb{Z}_q$ and sends $\lambda_i = g^{k_i} \bmod p$,
- The verifier replies with an e-bit message randomizer b_i,
- and the signer sends :

$$s_i = \frac{\text{SHA}(m_i|b_i) + x\lambda_i}{k_i} \bmod q$$

The batch verification criterion (with cut-&-choose in case of failure) is :

$$\prod_{i=1}^{n} \lambda_i = g^{\sum_{i=1}^{n} w_i \text{SHA}(m_i|b_i)} y^{\sum_{i=1}^{n} w_i \lambda_i} \bmod p \quad \text{where} \quad w_i = \frac{1}{s_i} \bmod q$$

This scheme is essentially as fast as a single DSA verification $(3(n-1)|q| \cong 480n$ modular multiplications are saved). Its security was assumed to result from the following argumentation : assume that $j-1$ messages were signed and denote :

$$\alpha = \prod_{i=1}^{j-1} \lambda_i \bmod p$$

$$\beta = g^{\sum_{i=1}^{j-1} w_i \text{SHA}(m_i|b_i)} y^{\sum_{i=1}^{j-1} w_i \lambda_i} \bmod p$$

$$\gamma = \frac{\alpha\lambda_j}{\beta} \bmod p$$

If at this point a cheater can produce a λ_j such that he can later solve (by some algorithm $\mathcal{C}(\alpha, \beta, \lambda_j, m_j, b_j, p, q, g, y) = s_j$ the equation :

$$\gamma^{s_j} = g^{\text{SHA}(m_j|b_j)} y^{\lambda_j} \bmod p \tag{1}$$

then he can pick, by his own means, any random couple $\{b_1, b_2\}$, find

$$\mathcal{C}(\alpha, \beta, \lambda_j, m_j, b_i, p, q, g, y) = s_{j,i}$$

for $i = 1, 2$ and compute directly :

$$x' = \frac{\text{SHA}(m_j|b_1)s_{j,2} - \text{SHA}(m_j|b_2)s_{j,1}}{\lambda_j(s_{j,1} - s_{j_2})} \bmod q$$

which satisfies $g^{x'} = y \bmod p$ and breaks DSA.

This is proved by dividing formula 1 for $i = 1$ by formula 1 for $i = 2$, extracting γ from the resulting equality and replacing it back in formula 1 for $i = 1$ which becomes $g^{x'} = y \bmod p$.

This article was processed using the LaTeX macro package with LLNCS style

The Effectiveness of Lattice Attacks Against Low-Exponent RSA

Christophe Coupé[1], Phong Nguyen[2], and Jacques Stern[2]

[1] coupe@ens-lyon.fr, École Normale Supérieure de Lyon, Département de Mathématiques et d'Informatique, 46 allée d'Italie, 69364 Lyon Cedex 07, France
[2] {pnguyen,stern}@ens.fr, http://www.dmi.ens.fr/~{pnguyen,stern}/
École Normale Supérieure, Laboratoire d'Informatique,
45 rue d'Ulm, 75230 Paris Cedex 05, France

Abstract. At Eurocrypt '96, Coppersmith presented a novel application of lattice reduction to find small roots of a univariate modular polynomial equation. This led to rigorous polynomial attacks against RSA with low public exponent, in some particular settings such as encryption of stereotyped messages, random padding, or broadcast applications à la Håstad. Theoretically, these are the most powerful known attacks against low-exponent RSA. However, the practical behaviour of Coppersmith's method was unclear. On the one hand, the method requires reductions of high-dimensional lattices with huge entries, which could be out of reach. On the other hand, it is well-known that lattice reduction algorithms output better results than theoretically expected, which might allow better bounds than those given by Coppersmith's theorems. In this paper, we present extensive experiments with Coppersmith's method, and discuss various trade-offs together with practical improvements. Overall, practice meets theory. The warning is clear: one should be very cautious when using the low-exponent RSA encryption scheme, or one should use larger exponents.

1 Introduction

One longstanding open problem in cryptography is to find an efficient attack against the RSA public key cryptosystem [13]. In the general case, the best-known method is factoring, although the equivalence of factorization and breaking RSA is still open (note that recent results [3] suggest that breaking RSA might be easier than factoring). However, under certain conditions, more efficient attacks are known (for a survey, see [2]). One of these conditions is when the public exponent is small, *e.g.* 3. This is the so-called low-exponent RSA, which is quite popular in the real world.

The most powerful known attack against low-exponent RSA is due to Coppersmith [5, 6]. At Eurocrypt '96, Coppersmith presented two applications [5, 4] of a novel use of the celebrated LLL algorithm [12]. Both applications were searches for small roots of certain polynomial equations: one for univariate modular equations, the other for bivariate integer equations. Instead of using lattice reduction algorithms as shortest vector oracles, Coppersmith applied the LLL algorithm to determine a subspace containing all reasonably short lattice points. He then deduced rigorous polynomial attacks, as opposed to traditional heuristic lattice-based attacks.

Finding small integer roots of a modular polynomial equation has great practical significance, for instance with the low-exponent RSA encryption scheme, or the KMOV cryptosystem (see [1]). More precisely, in the case of low-exponent RSA, such roots are related to the problems of encryption of stereotyped messages, random padding and broadcast applications.

However, Coppersmith did not deal with practical issues: the practical behaviour of his attack was unclear. On the one hand, the method would *a priori* require reductions of high-dimensional lattices with huge entries, in order to achieve the theoretical bounds. For instance, with a small example such as 512-bit RSA and a public exponent of 3, Coppersmith's proofs suggest to reduce matrices of dimension over 300, and 17000-digit entries. Obviously, some adjustements need to be made. On the other hand, it is well-known that lattice reduction algorithms output better results than theoretically expected. Moreover, one could apply improved reduction algorithms such as [14], instead of LLL. Thus, if one uses smaller parameters than those suggested by Coppersmith's theorems, one might still obtain fairly good results.

In this paper, we present extensive experiments with Coppersmith's method applied to the low-exponent RSA case, and discuss various trade-offs together with practical improvements. To our knowledge, only limited experiments (see [1, 9]) had previously been carried out. Our experiments tend to validate Coppersmith's approach. Most of the time, we obtained experimental bounds close to the maximal theoretical bounds. For instance, sending e linearly related messages to participants with the same public exponent e is theoretically insecure. This bound seems unreachable in practice, but we were able to reach the bound $e + 1$ in a very short time. The warning is clear: one should be very cautious when using low-exponent RSA encryptions, or one should use larger exponents.

The remainder of the paper is organized as follows. In Section 2, we review Coppersmith's method. In Section 3, we recall applications of this method to the low-exponent RSA encryption scheme. We describe our implementation, and discuss practical issues in Section 4. Finally, Section 5 presents the experiments, which gives various trade-offs.

2 Coppersmith's Method

In this section, we recall Coppersmith's method, as presented in [6]. Let N be a large composite integer of unknown factorization, and $p(x) = x^{\delta} + p_{\delta-1}x^{\delta-1} + \cdots + p_2 x^2 + p_1 x + p_0$, be a monic integer polynomial. We wish to find an integer x_0 such that, for some $\varepsilon > 0$:

$$p(x_0) \equiv 0 \pmod{N} \tag{1}$$

$$|x_0| < X = \frac{N^{(1/\delta)-\varepsilon}}{2} \tag{2}$$

(2) means that we look for a reasonably short solution. We select an integer h such that:

$$h \geq \max \left(\frac{\delta - 1 + \varepsilon\delta}{\varepsilon\delta^2}, \frac{7}{\delta} \right) \tag{3}$$

Let $n = h\delta$. For $(i,j) \in [0..\delta-1] \times [1..h-1]$, let the polynomial $q_{i,j}(x) = x^i p(x)^j$, for which $q_{i,j}(x_0) \equiv 0 \pmod{N^j}$.

A rational triangular matrix M is built using the coefficients of the polynomials $q_{i,j}(x)$, in such a way that an integer linear combination of the rows of M corresponding to powers of x_0 and y_0 will give a vector with relatively small Euclidean norm. Multiplying by the least common denominator produces an integer matrix on which lattice basis reduction can be applied. This will disclose a certain linear relation satisfied by all sufficiently short vectors. Finally, this relation will translate to a polynomial relation on x_0 over $\mathbb{Z}$ (not mod N) of degree at most n, which we can solve over $\mathbb{Z}$ to discover x_0.

The matrix M of size $(2n - \delta) \times (2n - \delta)$ is broken into four blocks:

$$M = \begin{pmatrix} A & B \\ 0 & C \end{pmatrix}.$$

The $n \times (n - \delta)$ block B has rows indexed by $g \in [0..n - 1]$, and columns indexed by $\gamma(i,j) = n + i + (j - 1)\delta$ with $(i,j) \in [0..\delta] \times [1..h - 1]$, so that $n \leq \gamma(i,j) < 2n - \delta$. The entry at $(g, \gamma(i,j))$ is the coefficient of x^g in the polynomial $q_{i,j}(x)$. The $(n - \delta) \times (n - \delta)$ block C is a diagonal matrix, with the value N^j in each column $\gamma(i,j)$. The $n \times n$ block A is a diagonal matrix, whose value in row g is a rational approximation to $X^{-g}/\sqrt{n}$, where X is defined by (2).

The rows of M span a lattice. In that lattice, we are interested in a target vector $\mathbf{s}$, related to the unknown solution x_0. Namely, we define $\mathbf{s} = \mathbf{r}M$, where $\mathbf{r}$ is a row vector whose left-hand elements are $r_g = x_0^g$, and whose right-hand elements are $r_{\gamma(i,j)} = -x_0^i y_0^j$ with $y_0 = p(x_0)/N$. The vector $\mathbf{r}$ and the matrix M were constructed in order to make $\mathbf{s}$ a short lattice point, with norm strictly less than 1. Indeed, $\mathbf{s}$ has left-hand elements given by $s_g = (x_0/X)^g/\sqrt{n}$, and right-hand elements equal to zero, as $s_{\gamma(i,j)} = q_{i,j}(x_0) - x_0^i y_0^j N^j$. In other words, the blocks B and C translate the polynomial modular equations $q_{i,j}(x)$. The fact that x_0 satisfies these equations makes the right-hand elements of $\mathbf{s}$ equal to zero. And the upper bound of (2) on the root x_0 is expressed by the block A. The diagonal coefficients "balance" the left-hand elements of $\mathbf{s}$.

In traditional lattice-based attacks, one would reduce the matrix M, and hope that the first vector of the reduced basis is equal to the target vector $\pm\mathbf{s}$. But Coppersmith notices that computing this vector explicitly is not necessary. Indeed, it suffices to confine the target vector in a subspace, which we now detail.

As the right-hand elements $n - \delta$ of the desired vector $\mathbf{s}$ are 0, we restrict our attention to the sublattice $\widehat{M}$ of M consisting of points with right-hand elements 0, namely $M \cap (\mathbb{R}^n \times \{0\}^{n-\delta})$. It is possible to compute explicitly this sublattice, by taking advantage of the fact that $p(x)$ and hence $q_{i,j}(x)$ are monic polynomials: certain $n - \delta$ rows of the block B form an upper triangular matrix with 1 on the diagonal. Thus, we can do elementary row operations on M to produce a block matrix $\widetilde{M}$ of the form:

$$\widetilde{M} = \begin{pmatrix} ? & 0 \\ ? & I \end{pmatrix},$$

where I is the $(n - \delta) \times (n - \delta)$ identity matrix. The $n \times n$ upper-left block represents the desired sublattice: an n-dimensional lattice, of which $\mathbf{s}$ is one relatively short element. In particular, M and $\widetilde{M}$ have the same volume.

Next, we compute an LLL-reduced basis $(\mathbf{b}_1, \ldots, \mathbf{b}_n)$ of the matrix $\widetilde{M}$. From the theoretical bounds of the LLL algorithm and the value of the volume of $\widetilde{M}$ (which can be bounded thanks to (3) and (2)), Coppersmith proved that any lattice point of norm strictly less than 1 must lie in the hyperplane spanned by $\mathbf{b}_1, \mathbf{b}_2, \ldots, \mathbf{b}_{n-1}$. In particular, $\mathbf{s}$ is such a lattice point. In terms of the larger matrix M, there is an n-dimensional space of vectors $\mathbf{r}$ such that $\mathbf{r}M = \mathbf{s}$ has 0's in its right-hand $n - \delta$ entries. And those integer vectors $\mathbf{r}$ which additionally satisfy $\mathbf{s} < 1$ must lie in a space of dimension one smaller, namely dimension $n - 1$. This gives rise to a linear equation on the entries $r_g, 0 \le g < n$. That is, we compute coefficients c_g such that: for any integer vector $\mathbf{r} = (r_g, r_{\gamma(i,j)})$ such that $\mathbf{s} = \mathbf{r}M$ has right-hand entries 0 and $\|\mathbf{s}\| < 1$, we must have $\sum c_g r_g = 0$. In particular:

$$\sum_{g=0}^{n-1} c_g x_0^g = 0.$$

This is a polynomial equation holding in $\mathbb{Z}$, not just modulo N. We can solve this polynomial for x_0 easily, using known techniques for solving univariate polynomial equations over $\mathbb{Z}$ (for instance, the Sturm sequence [11] suffices). This shows:

Theorem 1 (Coppersmith). *Let $p(x)$ be a polynomial of degree δ in one variable modulo an integer N of unknown factorization. Let X be the bound on the desired solution x_0. If $X < \frac{1}{2} N^{1/\delta - \varepsilon}$, then in time polynomial in $(\log N, \delta, 1/\varepsilon)$, we can find all integers x_0 with $p(x_0) \equiv 0 \pmod{N}$ and $|x_0| < X$.*

Corollary 2 (Coppersmith). *With the same hypothesis, except that $X \le N^{1/\delta}$, then in time polynomial in $(\log N, 2^\delta)$, we can find all integers x_0 such that $p(x_0) \equiv 0 \pmod{N}$ and $|x_0| \le X$.*

Proof. See [6]. The result is obtained by applying the previous theorem four times, with $\varepsilon = 1/\log_2 N$. □

This is a major improvement over the bound $N^{2/[\delta(\delta+1)]}$ which was previously obtained in [17]. But, theoretically, one would *a priori* need the following parameters in order to achieve the theoretical bound $N^{1/\delta}$: $\varepsilon = 1/\log_2 N$ and $h \approx (\delta - 1) \log_2 N / \delta^2$. For example, if we take $\delta = 3$ and a 512-bit number N, this means reducing several 341×341 matrices with entries at least as large as N^{h-1}, that is 17000-digit numbers ! Unfortunately, that appears to be a drawback of Coppersmith's improvement. Indeed, instead of using only the polynomial $p(x)$ (such as in [17]), Coppersmith introduced shifts and powers of this polynomial. This enlarges the volume of the lattice M, which is what makes the target vector more and more short compared to other lattice points, but at the expense of the size of the entries. In other words, the larger the entries are, the better the bound is supposed to be, and the more expensive the reduction is. This leads to several questions: is Coppersmith's method of any use in real life ? How much can we achieve in practice ? How do the practical bounds compare with the theoretical bounds ? We will answer these questions in Sections 4 and 5.

3 Applications to Low-Exponent RSA

We briefly review some applications of Coppersmith's method. More can be found in [6].

3.1 Stereotyped messages

Suppose the plaintext m consists of two pieces: a known piece $B = 2^k b$, and an unknown piece x. If this is RSA-encrypted with an exponent of 3, the ciphertext c is given by $c = m^3 = (B + x)^3 \pmod{N}$. If we know B, c and N we can apply the previous results to the polynomial $p(x) = (B + x)^3 - c$, and recover x_0 satisfying

$$p(x_0) = (B + x_0)^3 - c \equiv 0 \pmod{N},$$

as long as such an x_0 exists with $|x_0| < N^{1/3}$. The attack works equally well if the unknown x_0 lies in the most significant bits of the message m rather than the least significant bits.

3.2 Random padding

Suppose two messages m and m' satisfy an affine relation, say $m' = m + r$. Suppose we know the RSA-encryptions of the two messages with an exponent of 3:

$$c \equiv m^3 \pmod{N}$$
$$c' \equiv (m')^3 \equiv m^3 + 3m^2 r + 3mr^2 + r^3 \pmod{N}$$

We can eliminate m from the two equations above by taking their resultant, which gives a univariate polynomial in r of degree 9, modulo N:

$$r^9 + (3c - 3c')r^6 + (3c^2 + 21cc' + 3(c')^2)r^3 + (c - c')^3.$$

Thus, if $|r| < N^{1/9}$, we can theoretically recover r, from which we can derive the message $m = r(c' + 2c - r^3)/(c' - c + 2r^3) \pmod{N}$ (see [7]).

3.3 Broadcast attacks

As was pointed out in [15, 1], Coppersmith's result improves known results of Håstad [8]. We consider the situation of a broadcast application, where a user sends linearly related messages m_i to several participants with public exponent e_i and public modulus N_i. That is, $m_i \equiv \alpha_i m + \beta_i \pmod{N_i}$, for some unknown m and known constants α_i and β_i. This precisely happens if one sends a similar message with different (known) headers or time-stamps which are part of the encryption block.

Let $e = \max e_i$. If k such messages m_i are sent, the attacker obtains k polynomial equations $p_i(m) \equiv 0 \pmod{N_i}$ of degree $e_i \leq e$. Then we use the Chinese Remainder Theorem to derive a polynomial equation of degree e:

$$p(m) \equiv 0 \pmod{N}, \text{where } N = \prod_{i=1}^{k} N_i.$$

And thus, by Coppersmith's method, we can theoretically recover m if $|m| < N^{1/e}$. In particular, this is satisfied if $k \geq e$. This improves the previous bound $k > e(e+1)/2$ obtained by Håstad.

4 Implementation

In Section 2, we saw that Coppersmith's method required reductions of high-dimensional lattices with huge entries. This is because the proof uses the parameter ε which induces a choice of h. Actually, ε is only of theoretical interest, as h is the natural parameter. In practice, one would rather choose h and ignore ε, so that the matrix and its entries are not too large. To compute the theoretical maximal rootsize (for a fixed h), one needs to look back at Coppersmith's proof. However, we will obtain this maximal rootsize from another method, due to Howgrave-Graham (see [9]). It can be shown that from a theoretical point of view, the two methods are strictly equivalent: they provide the same bounds, and they have the same complexity. But Howgrave-Graham's method is simpler to implement and to analyze, so that the practical behaviour of Coppersmith's method is easier to explain with this presentation.

4.1 Howgrave-Graham's method

We keep the notations of Section 2: a monic polynomial $p(x)$ of degree δ; a bound X for the desired solutions modulo N; and h a fixed integer. In both methods, one computes a polynomial $r(x)$ of degree at most $n = h\delta$ for which small modular roots of $p(x)$ are also integral roots of $r(x)$. In Coppersmith's method, such a polynomial is deduced from the hyperplane generated by the first vectors of a reduced basis of a certain n-dimensional lattice. In Howgrave-Graham's method, any sufficiently short vector of a certain n-dimensional lattice can be transformed into such a polynomial. Actually, these two lattices are related to each other by duality. Coppersmith uses lattice reduction to find a basis for which sufficiently short vectors are confined to the hyperplane generated by the first vectors of the basis. But this problem can also be viewed as a traditional short vector problem in the dual lattice, a fact that was noticed by both Howgrave-Graham [9] and Jutla [10].

Given a polynomial $r(x) = \sum a_i x^i \in \mathbb{Z}[x]$, define $\|r(x)\| = \sqrt{\sum a_i^2}$.

Lemma 3 (Howgrave-Graham). *Let $r(x) \in \mathbb{Z}[x]$ of degree n, and let X be a positive integer. Suppose $\|r(xX)\| < M/\sqrt{n}$. If $r(x_0) \equiv 0 \,(mod\,M)$ and $|x_0| < X$, then $r(x_0) = 0$ holds over the integers.*

Proof. Notice that $|r(x_0)| = |\sum a_i x_0^i| \le \sum |a_i X^i| \le \|r(xX)\|\sqrt{n} < M$. Since $r(x_0) \equiv 0 \,(mod\,M)$, it follows that $r(x_0) = 0$. □

The lemma shows that a convenient $r(x) \in \mathbb{Z}[x]$ is a polynomial with small norm having the same roots as $p(x)$ modulo N. We choose such a polynomial as an integer linear combination of the following polynomials (similar to the $q_{i,j}$'s of Coppersmith's method):

$$q_{u,v}(x) = N^{h-1-v} x^u f(x)^v.$$

Since x_0 is a root of $q_{u,v}(x)$ modulo N^{h-1}, $r(xX)$ must have norm less than $N^{h-1}/\sqrt{n}$ to use the lemma. But this can be seen as a short vector problem in the lattice corresponding to the $q_{u,v}(xX)$. So we define a lower triangular $n \times n$ matrix M whose i-th row consists of the coefficients of $q_{u,v}(xX)$, starting by the low-degree terms, where $v = \lfloor (i-1)/\delta \rfloor$ and $u = (i-1) - \delta v$. It can be shown that:

$$\det(M) = X^{n(n-1)/2} N^{n(h-1)/2}.$$

We apply an LLL-reduction to the lattice spanned by the rows of M. The first vector of the reduced basis corresponds to a polynomial of the form $r(xX)$. And its Euclidean norm is equal to $\|r(xX)\|$.

One the one hand, to apply the lemma, we need :

$$\|r(xX)\| \le N^{h-1}/\sqrt{n}.$$

On the other hand, the theoretical bounds of the LLL algorithm guarantee that the norm of the first vector satisfies:

$$\|r(xX)\| \le 2^{(n-1)/4} \det(M)^{1/n} \le 2^{(n-1)/4} X^{(n-1)/2} N^{(h-1)/2}.$$

Therefore, a sufficient condition for the method to work is:

$$2^{(n-1)/4} X^{(n-1)/2} N^{(h-1)/2} \le N^{h-1}/\sqrt{n}.$$

Hence, for a given h, the method is guaranteed to find modular roots up to X if:

$$X \le \frac{1}{\sqrt{2}} N^{(h-1)/(n-1)} n^{-1/(n-1)} \tag{4}$$

This is also the expression found by Coppersmith in [6] (p. 241). And the limit of this expression, when h grows to ∞, is $\frac{1}{\sqrt{2}} N^{1/\delta}$. But what is worth noticing is that the logarithm of that expression, as a function of h, is quite concave (see Figure 1). This means that small values of h should already give results close to the limits. And hopefully, with a small h, the lattice is low-dimensional and its entries are not excessively large. This indicates that Coppersmith's method should be useful in real life. Fortunately, we will see that experiments confirm this prediction.

Fig. 1. Bit-length of the bound X for $\delta = 3$ and RSA-512, as a function of h.

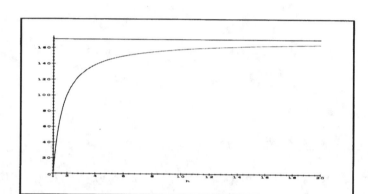

4.2 Limits of the method

It is well-known that lattice reduction algorithms perform better in practice than theoretically expected. And when the LLL algorithm does not provide sufficiently short vectors, one can turn to improved lattice reduction algorithms such as Schnorr's [14]. However, a simple argument shows that Coppersmith's method and its variants are inherently limited, no matter how good the reduction algorithm is.

Indeed, if we assume that the lattice M to be reduced is "random", there are probably no lattice points of M significantly shorter than $\det(M)^{1/n}$, that is $X^{(n-1)/2} N^{(h-1)/2}$. And therefore, since the conditions of lemma 3 are quite tight, any lattice reduction algorithm will not detect roots much larger than:

$$N^{(h-1)/(n-1)} n^{-1/(n-1)}.$$

Compared to (4), only the factor $1/\sqrt{2}$ is removed, which is a very small improvement. Thus, it is likely that when the LLL algorithm fails to provide the solution, other lattice reduction algorithms will not help. The bound provided by (4) is probably tight.

4.3 Complexity

In both Coppersmith's method and Howgrave-Graham's method, the most expensive step is the lattice reduction step. The matrices to be reduced have the same dimension $n = h\delta$, and the size of their entries are similar. Therefore, from a theoretical point of view, the methods have the same complexity. We assume that X is chosen less than $N^{1/\delta}$.

The worst-case complexity of the LLL algorithm is $O(n^5 d \log^3 R)$ where n is the lattice dimension, d is the space dimension and R an upper bound for the squared norms of the basis vectors. So the method has worst-case complexity $O(n^6 \log^3 R)$ where R is an upper bound for all the $\|q_{u,v}(xX)\|^2$. We have:

$$\|q_{u,v}(xX)\|^2 = N^{2(h-1-v)} X^{2u} \|p(xX)^v\|^2.$$

All the coefficients of $p(xX)$ are less than N^2. It follows that:

$$\|p(xX)^v\|^2 \le N^{4v} \|(1 + x + \cdots + x^\delta)^v\|^2 \le N^{4v}(\delta + 1)^{2v}.$$

Therefore:

$$\|q_{u,v}(xX)\|^2 \le N^{2(h-1+v)} X^{2u}(\delta + 1)^{2v} \le N^{2h-4} X^{2\delta-2}(\delta + 1)^{2h-2}.$$

Thus, the complexity is $O(n^6[(2h - 4 + (2\delta - 2)/\delta) \log N + (2h - 2)(\delta + 1)]^3)$, that is:

$$O(h^9 \delta^6 [\log^3 N + \delta \log^2 N + \delta^2 \log N + \delta^3]).$$

For large N compared to δ, this is $O(h^9 \delta^6 \log^3 N)$. And that means large values of h and δ are probably not realistic. It also means that the running time of the method should be more sensitive to an increase of h, than an increase of δ, or an increase of the size of the modulus N.

5 Experiments

Our implementation uses the NTL library [16] of Victor Shoup. Due to the size of the entries, we had to use the floating point versions of reduction algorithms with extended exponent. Timings are given for a 500 MHz DEC Alpha. We used two sorts of computers: 64-bit 500 MHz DEC Alpha using Linux and 64-bit 270 MHz Sparc Ultra-2i using Solaris. It is worth noticing that for large reductions, the Alpha was about 6 times faster than the Ultra. In part, this is because we were able to use a 64-bit compiler for the Alpha, but not for the Ultra; and the clock frequency of the Alpha is twice as high than the one of the Ultra.

We implemented both Coppersmith's method and its variant by Howgrave-Graham. The running times and the results are very similar, but Howgrave-Graham's method is simpler to implement. Therefore, the tables given here hold for both methods.

5.1 Running times

Tables 1, 2 and 3 show the running time of the reduction stage, as a function of the parameter h and the polynomial degree δ, for different sizes of moduli. The polynomial was randomly chosen. The other parts of the method, such as computing the integral roots of the polynomial found, are negligible compared to the reduction stage.

In Section 4, we saw that the worst-case complexity was $O(h^9 \delta^6 \log^3 N)$. The running times confirm that an increase in h is more expensive than an increase in δ. But the dominant factor is $n = h\delta$. If δ is not small, only small values of h are realistic. And if h is chosen large, only small values of δ are possible.

Doubling the size of the modulus from RSA-512 to RSA-1024 roughly multiplies by 5 the running times. And doubling the size of the modulus from RSA-1024 to RSA-2048 roughly multiplies by 5.5 the running times. From the complexity, one would expect a multiplication by 8. It turns out that the method is practical even for very large N. And therefore, one would expect broadcast attacks with small exponent to be practical, as they multiply the size of the modulus by the number of linearly related messages, but keep the (low) polynomial degree unchanged.

Table 1. Running time (in seconds), as a function of h and δ, for RSA-512.

Parameter h	Polynomial degree δ								
	2	3	4	5	6	7	8	9	10
2	0	0.04	0.12	0.29	0.57	0.98	1.71	2.8	4.4
3	0.07	0.34	1.02	2.66	5.71	11	21	36	56
4	0.27	1.48	5.09	14	33	64	120	191	318
5	0.84	4.99	19	53	123	242	455	773	1170
6	2.21	14	55	161	368	764	1395	2341	3773
7	5.34	37	150	415	919	1868	3417	6157	9873
8	11	82	331	912	2146	4366	7678	13725	21504
9	21	166	646	1838	4464	8777	17122	27314	42212
10	38	323	1234	3605	8343	15997	30992		
11	70	598	2239	6989	16050				
12	126	994	4225	11650					
13	194	1582	6598						
14	311	2498	10101						
15	496	3967	16347						

5.2 Experimental bounds

For a given choice of h and δ, one can theoretically find roots as large as $X = N^{(h-1)/(n-1)} n^{-1/(n-1)}/\sqrt{2}$, where $n = h\delta$. However, in practice, one has to use floating point versions of lattice reduction algorithms, because exact versions

Table 2. Running time (in seconds), as a function of h and δ, for RSA-1024.

Parameter h	Polynomial degree δ								
	2	3	4	5	6	7	8	9	10
2	0.03	0.13	0.37	0.83	1.68	3.02	5.17	8.53	13
3	0.24	1.19	3.76	9.19	21	42	76	128	209
4	1.16	5.89	21	57	134	270	492	813	1306
5	3.69	21	82	238	541	1111	2030	3426	5745
6	9.68	66	264	752	1736	3423	6272	11064	17040
7	25	175	699	2017	4521	9266	17746		
8	53	392	1623	4748	10858	21662			
9	103	815	3277	9800	22594	44712			
10	204	1605	6512	18608					
11	364	2813	11933						
12	627	5191	20947						
13	1028	8530							

Table 3. Running time (in seconds), as a function of h and δ, for RSA-2048.

Parameter h	Polynomial degree δ								
	2	3	4	5	6	7	8	9	10
2	0.09	0.46	1.29	3.01	5.93	11	19	31	48
3	1.04	5.11	16	42	93	187	343	598	928
4	5.21	29	97	277	635	1308	2386	4151	6687
5	19	107	405	1185	2780	5616	10584	17787	28458
6	52	337	1355	3922	9129	18776			
7	123	920	3729	10697	25087				
8	282	2122	8697	25089	58258				
9	555	4503	18854	53345					
10	1072	9313	36468						
11	2008	16042	68669						
12	3499	28187							
13	5796								

(using only integer arithmetic) are quite expensive, especially with this size of entries. This means that the basis obtained is not guaranteed to be LLL-reduced, and therefore, the upper bound X cannot be guaranteed either. But, in practice, in all our experiments, the basis obtained was always LLL-reduced, and thus, we have always been able to find roots as large as the bound. Approximation problems occur only when the lattice dimension is very high (larger than say, 150), which was not the case here. When the LLL algorithm failed to provide a sufficiently short vector, we applied improved lattice reduction algorithms. But as expected (see the previous section), it did not help: the method is inherently limited by the value of the lattice determinant.

We only made experiments with the case of an RSA encryption using 3 as a public exponent. Coppersmith-like attacks are useful only for a very small exponent such as 3, because the polynomial degree must be very small for efficiency, and the roots cannot be much larger than the size of the modulus divided by the polynomial degree. For instance, a public exponent of 65537 is not threatened by Coppersmith's method. One should also note that these attacks do not recover the secret factorization: they can only recover the plaintext under specific conditions.

Stereotyped messages. This case corresponds to $\delta = 3$. Table 4 give the bounds obtained in practice, and the corresponding running times. The bound of (4) is tight: we never obtained an experimental bound X more than twice as large as the theoretical bound. There is a value of h which gives the best compromise between the maximal rootsize and the running time. Of course, this value depends on the implementation. If one wants to compute roots larger than the corresponding rootsize, one should treat the remaining bits by exhaustive search, rather than by increasing h. Here, this value seems to be slightly larger than 13.

Table 4. Bounds and running time for stereotyped messages

Size of N	Data type	Parameter h												
		2	3	4	5	6	7	8	9	10	11	12	13	∞
512	Size of X	102	128	139	146	150	153	156	157	159	160	161	162	170
	Seconds	0.05	0.36	1.54	5	15	36	82	161	308	542	910	1501	
768	Size of X	153	192	209	219	226	230	234	236	238	240	241	242	256
	Seconds	0.09	0.76	3.39	12	35	90	211	418	853	1490	2563	4428	
1024	Size of X	204	256	279	292	301	307	311	315	318	320	322	323	341
	Seconds	0.14	1.28	6	23	66	179	393	823	1634	3044	5254	9224	

Random padding. This case corresponds to $\delta = 9$. Table 5 give the bounds obtained in practice, and the corresponding running times. Note that for this case, the experimental bound X had a few bits more than the theoretical bound for small values of h, which is why we added new data in the table. Again, there is a value of h which gives the best compromise between the maximal rootsize and the running time. This value seems to be $h = 6$ for RSA-512 and RSA-768, and $h = 7$ for RSA-1024. In all these cases, the running time is less than than a few minutes, and the corresponding rootsize is not far from the maximal theoretical rootsize (corresponding to $h = \infty$).

Note that the running time is significantly less than the one given in tables 1, 2 for $\delta = 9$. This is because the polynomial of degree 9 is of particular form here, as it is quite sparse.

Table 5. Bounds and running time for random padding

Size of N	Data type	Parameter h										
		2	3	4	5	6	7	8	9	10	∞
512	Experimental size of X	34	42	46	48	50	51	51	52	52	
	Theoretical size of X	30	39	44	46	48	49	50	51	52	57
	Seconds	0.28	2.07	8	29	76	190	396	769	1307	
768	Experimental size of X	51	63	69	73	75	76	77	78	79	
	Theoretical size of X	45	59	66	70	72	75	76	77	77	85
	Seconds	0.46	3.76	17	55	163	396	835	1713	3095	
1024	Experimental size of X	68	85	93	97	100	102	103	104	105	
	Theoretical size of X	60	79	88	93	96	99	101	102	103	114
	Seconds	0.74	6	28	97	298	733	1629	3468	6674	

Broadcast applications. We consider the situation of a broadcast application, where a user sends k linearly related messages m_i (built from an unknown message m) to several participants with public exponent $e_i \leq e$ and public modulus N_i. Theoretically, Coppersmith's method should recover the message m, as soon as $k \geq e$. The problem is that the case $k = e$ corrresponds to a large value of h, which is unrealistic in practice, as shown in Table 3. Table 6 give the bounds obtained in practice, and the corresponding running times for a public exponent of 3 (which corresponds to $\delta = 3$), depending on the number of linearly related messages and the size of the modulus N. When one allows $e + 1$ messages, the attack becomes practical. We have always been able to recover the message when $e = 3$ and 4 messages are sent, with a choice of $h = 4$ (the value is $h = 3$ is a bit tight). The corresponding running time is only a few minutes, even with RSA-1024. For larger exponents (and thus, a larger number of necessary messages), the method does not seem to be practical, as the running time is very sensitive to the polynomial degree δ and the parameter h.

Table 6. Bounds and running time for broadcast attacks with public exponent 3

Size of N	Messages	Data type	Parameter h					
			2	3	4	5	6	∞
512	2	Size of X	204	256	279	292	301	341
		Seconds	0.12	1.27	6	22	67	
	3	Size of X	307	384	419	439	452	511
		Seconds	0.28	2.85	15	55	164	
	4	Size of X	409	512	558	585	602	682
		Seconds	0.45	5	28	104	329	
768	2	Size of X	307	384	419	439	452	511
		Seconds	0.27	2.72	15	55	169	
	3	Size of X	460	576	628	658	677	767
		Seconds	0.57	7	36	135	435	
	4	Size of X	614	768	837	877	903	1022
		Seconds	0.93	12	67	272	873	
1024	2	Size of X	409	512	558	585	602	682
		Seconds	0.48	5	29	107	340	
	3	Size of X	614	768	837	877	903	1024
		Seconds	1.41	13	71	283	896	
	4	Size of X	819	1024	1117	1170	1204	1364
		Seconds	1.89	25	144	567	1793	

6   Conclusion

We presented extensive experiments with lattice-based attacks against RSA with low public exponent, which validate Coppersmith's novel approach to find small roots of a univariate modular polynomial equation. In practice, one can, in a reasonable time, achieve bounds fairly close to the theoretical bounds. We also showed that these theoretical bounds are essentially tight, in the sense that one cannot expect to obtain significantly better results in practice, regardless of the lattice reduction algorithm used.

The experiments confirm that sending stereotyped messages with a small public exponent e is dangerous when the modulus size is larger than e times the size of the hidden part (consecutive bits). Random padding with public exponent 3 is also dangerous, as while as the modulus size is larger than 9 times the padding size. Interestingly, Håstad-like attacks are practical: if a user sends 4 linearly related messages encrypted with public exponent 3, then one can recover the unknown message in a few minutes, even for 1024-bit modulus. Note that this improves the former theoretical bound of 7 messages obtained by Håstad. For 3 messages, one can recover the message if the unknown part has significantly less bits than the modulus.

This stresses the problems of the low-exponent RSA encryption scheme. However, it only applies to the case of very small public exponents such as 3. It does not seem to threaten exponents such as 65537. And these attacks do not seem to apply to the RSA signature scheme with a small validating exponent.

Acknowledgements. We would like to thank the anonymous referees for their helpful comments.

References

1. D. Bleichenbacher. On the security of the KMOV public key cryptosystem. In *Proc. of Crypto '97*, volume 1294 of *LNCS*, pages 235–248. Springer-Verlag, 1997.
2. D. Boneh. Twenty years of attacks on the RSA cryptosystem. *Notices of the AMS*, 1998. To appear. Available at http://theory.stanford.edu/~dabo/.
3. D. Boneh and R. Venkatesan. Breaking RSA may not be equivalent to factoring. In *Proc. of Eurocrypt '98*, volume 1233 of *LNCS*, pages 59–71. Springer-Verlag, 1998.
4. D. Coppersmith. Finding a small root of a bivariate integer equation; factoring with high bits known. In *Proc. of Eurocrypt '96*, volume 1070 of *LNCS*, pages 178–189. Springer-Verlag, 1996.
5. D. Coppersmith. Finding a small root of a univariate modular equation. In *Proc. of Eurocrypt '96*, volume 1070 of *LNCS*, pages 155–165. Springer-Verlag, 1996.
6. D. Coppersmith. Small solutions to polynomial equations, and low exponent RSA vulnerabilities. *J. of Cryptology*, 10(4):233–260, 1997.
7. D. Coppersmith, M. Franklin, J. Patarin, and M. Reiter. Low-exponent RSA with related messages. In *Proc. of Eurocrypt '96*, volume 1070 of *LNCS*, pages 1–9. Springer-Verlag, 1996.
8. J. Hastad. Solving simultaneous modular equations of low degree. *SIAM J. Comput.*, 17(2):336–341, April 1988.
9. N. Howgrave-Graham. Finding small roots of univariate modular equations revisited. In *Cryptography and Coding*, volume 1355 of *LNCS*, pages 131–142. Springer-Verlag, 1997.
10. C. S. Jutla. On finding small solutions of modular multivariate polynomial equations. In *Proc. of Eurocrypt '98*, volume 1233 of *LNCS*, pages 158–170. Springer-Verlag, 1998.
11. D. Knuth. *The Art of Computer Programming vol. 2: Seminumerical Algorithms.* Addison-Wesley, 1981. Section 4.6.1.
12. A. K. Lenstra, H. W. Lenstra, and L. Lovász. Factoring polynomials with rational coefficients. *Math. Ann.*, 261:515–534, 1982.
13. R.L. Rivest, A. Shamir, and L. Adleman. A method for obtaining digital signatures and public-key cryptosystems. *Communications of the ACM*, 21(2):120–126, 1978.
14. C.-P. Schnorr. A hierarchy of polynomial lattice basis reduction algorithms. *Theoretical Computer Science*, 53:201–224, 1987.
15. H. Shimizu. On the improvement of the Håstad bound. In *1996 IEICE Fall Conference*, volume A-162, 1996. In Japanese.
16. V. Shoup. Number Theory C++ Library (NTL) version 3.1. Can be obtained at http://www.cs.wisc.edu/~shoup/ntl/.
17. B. Vallée, M. Girault, and P. Toffin. How to guess ℓ-th roots modulo n by reducing lattice bases. In *Proc. of AAECC-6*, volume 357 of *LNCS*, pages 427–442. Springer-Verlag, 1988.

A Trapdoor Permutation Equivalent to Factoring

Pascal Paillier

GEMPLUS

Cryptography Department

34 Rue Guynemer

Issy-Les-Moulineaux

paillier@gemplus.com

ENST

Computer Science Department

46, rue Barrault

75634 Paris Cedex 13

paillier@inf.enst.fr

Abstract. In Eurocrypt'98 [1], Okamoto *et al.* exhibited a new trapdoor function based on the use of a special moduli (p^2q) allowing easy discrete logarithm computations. The authors proved that the scheme's resistance to chosen-plaintext attacks is equivalent to factoring n. Unfortunately, the proposed scheme suffers from not being a permutation (the expansion rate is $\cong 3$), and hence cannot be used for public-key signatures.

In this paper, we show how to refine the function into a trapdoor permutation that can be used for signatures. Interestingly, our variant still remains equivalent to factoring and seems to be the second known trapdoor permutation (Rabin-Williams' scheme [3] being the first) provably as secure as a primitive problem.

1 The Okamoto-Uchiyama Cryptosystem

In Eurocrypt'98, Okamoto and Uchiyama proposed a new public-key cryptosystem based on the ability of computing discrete logarithms in a particular subgroup. Namely, if p is a large prime and $\Gamma_p \subset \mathbf{Z}_{p^2}^*$ is

$$\Gamma_p = \{x < p^2 \mid x = 1 \bmod p\} \, ,$$

then Γ_p has a group structure with respect to the multiplication modulo p^2 and $\sharp \Gamma_p = p$. The function $\log(.) \; : \; \Gamma_p \longrightarrow \mathbf{Z}_p$ which associates $(x-1)/p$ to x is clearly well-defined on Γ_p and presents interesting homomorphic properties. In particular,

$$\forall x, y \in \Gamma_p \quad \log(xy \bmod p^2) = \log(x) + \log(y) \bmod p$$

whereby, as a straightforward generalization,

$$\forall g \in \Gamma_p, m \in \mathbf{Z}_p \quad \log(g^m \bmod p^2) = m \log(g) \bmod p \, .$$

Key Setup. Generate two k-bit primes p and q (typically $3k = 1023$) and set $n = p^2q$. Randomly select and publish a number $g < n$ such that

$$g_p = g^{p-1} \bmod p^2$$

is of order p in $\mathbf{Z}_{p^2}^*$ and keep g_p secret (note that $g_p \in \Gamma_p$). Similarly, choose $g' < n$ at random and publish

$$h = g'^n \bmod n .$$

The triple (n, g, h) forms the public key. The secret key is (p, q).

Encryption. Pick $r < n$ uniformly at random and encrypt the k-bit message m by :

$$c = g^m h^r \bmod n .$$

Decryption. Proceed as follows :

1. $c' = c^{p-1} \bmod p^2 = g^{m(p-1)} g'^{nr(p-1)} = g_p^m \bmod p^2$,
2. $m = \log(c') \log(g_p)^{-1} \bmod p$.

We refer the reader to [1] for a thorough description of the scheme. Although provably equivalent to factoring [5] as far as chosen-plaintext attacks are concerned, the scheme suffers from the fact that ciphertexts are about three times longer than plaintexts. As a result, it is impossible to use [1]'s trapdoor as a signature scheme.

The next section shows how to extend the scheme to a trapdoor permutation [4] over $\mathbf{Z}_n^*$. Interestingly, the security analysis presented in section 3 shows that the new encryption function is still as secure as factoring.

2 The New Trapdoor Function

Using the same notations as before, let the message be $3k - 2$-bit long and define $m = m_1 \| m_2$ where $m_1 < 2^{k-1}$, $m_2 < 2^{2k-1}$ and $\|$ stands for concatenation. The encryption procedure is as follows.

Encryption. Split m into m_1 and m_2 and encrypt by :

$$c = g^{m_1} m_2^n \bmod n .$$

This presents an expension rate of :

$$\rho = \frac{\log_2 n}{3k - 2} \cong 1 + \frac{2}{3k} ,$$

which is very close to 1 for common values of k.

Decryption. Compute

$$c' = c^{p-1} \bmod p^2 = g_p^{m_1} \bmod p^2 ,$$

and

$$m_1 = \log(c') \log(g_p)^{-1} \bmod p ,$$

as in [1] and

1. deduce $m_2^n \bmod pq = g^{-m_1} c \bmod pq$
2. obtain $m_2 \bmod pq = (m_2^n \bmod pq)^{n^{-1} \bmod (p-1)(q-1)} \bmod pq$
3. conclude by $m = m_1 \| m_2$.

3   Equivalence to Factoring

In this section, we prove the one-wayness of our encryption function under the factoring assumption :

Theorem 1. *Inverting the new encryption function is equivalent to factoring n.*

Proof (sketch). Assuming that there exists a probabilistic polynomial time Turing machine $\mathcal{M}$ which decrypts ciphertexts for a given (n, g) with a non-negligible probability, we transform $\mathcal{M}$ into a PPT machine $\mathcal{M}'$ that factors n with non-negligible probability. We directly re-use the proof arguments from Theorem 6 of [1] for showing the statistical closeness of distributions of ciphertexts. Feeding $\mathcal{M}$ with $g^z \bmod n$ for random $(k + 1)$-bit numbers z, we need a single correct answer $m = m_1 \| m_2$ to recover a nontrivial factor of n by $\gcd(z - m_1, n)$.   □

Alternatively, the encryption and decryption functions can be used for digital signatures as well. To achieve this, a signer computes the signature $s = s_1 \| s_2$ of the message m such that

$$g^{s_1} s_2^n = h(m) \bmod n \, ,$$

where h is a collision-free one-way hash function. Note however that since $s_1 \in \mathbf{Z}_p$ and $s_2 \in \mathbf{Z}_{pq}^*$, some information about p and q will leak out at each signature. Namely, collecting N signatures (of arbitrary messages) will allow an attacker to recover $\mathcal{O}(\log(N))$ bits of p. We therefore recommand to regularly re-generate the scheme's parameters, possibly according to an internal counter.

It is worthwhile noticing that our scheme presents underlying homomorphic properties which could be useful for designing distributed cryptographic protocols (multi-signatures, secret sharing, threshold cryptography and so forth).

4   Further Research

Okamoto-Uchiyama's trapdoor technique is inherently new in the sense that it profoundly differs from RSA and Diffie-Hellman. It makes no doubt that this technique could be declined in various ways for designing new public-key cryptosystems in near future.

References

1. T. Okamoto and S. Uchiyama, *A New Public-Key Cryptosystem as secure as Factoring*, LNCS 1403, Advances in Cryptology, Proceedings of Eurocrypt'98, Springer-Verlag, pp. 308–318, 1998.
2. W. Diffie and M. Hellman, *New Directions in Cryptography*, IEEE Transaction on Information Theory, IT-22,6, pp. 644–654, 1995.

3. M. Rabin, *Digitalized Signatures and Public-Key Functions as Intractable as Factorization*, Technical Report No. 212, MIT Laboratory of Computer Science, Cambridge, pp. 1–16, 1979.

4. L. Goubin and J. Patarin, *Trapdoor One-Way Permutations and Multivariate Polynomials*, Proceedings of ICICS'97, LNCS 1334, Springer-Verlag, pp 356–368, 1997.

5. E. Okamoto and R. Peralta, *Faster Factoring of Integers of a Special Form*, IEICE Trans. Fundamentals, Vol. E79-A, No 4, pp 489–493, 1996.

Low-Cost Double-Size Modular Exponentiation or How to Stretch Your Cryptoprocessor

Pascal Paillier

GEMPLUS

Cryptography Department

34 Rue Guynemer

92447 Issy-Les Moulineaux

paillier@gemplus.com

ENST

Computer Science Department

46, rue Barrault

75634 Paris Cedex 13

paillier@inf.enst.fr

Abstract. Public-key implementers often face strong hardware-related constraints. In particular, modular operations required in most cryptosystems generally constitute a computational bottleneck in smart-card applications. This paper adresses the size limitation of arithmetic coprocessors and introduces new techniques that virtually increase their computational capacities. We suspect our algorithm to be nearly optimal and challenge the cryptographic community for better results.

1 Introduction

Since most public-key cryptosystems involve modular arithmetic over large integers, fast modular multiplication techniques have received considerable attention in the last two decades. Although most efforts focused on conventional 8, 16, 32 or 64-bit architectures (we refer the reader to [7, 1, 2]), we will specifically consider hardwired devices such as cryptoprocessors (see [5]).

Interestingly, most chip manufacturers provide cryptographic cores capable of performing fast regular/modular operations (addition, subtraction, modular reduction, modular multiplication) on 512 or 1024-bit integers. Although such hardware is fully adapted to the processing context required in cryptography, it inherits inescapable operand size limitations (conversely, conventional CPUs can handle data of quasi-arbitrary length, which is only bounded by the available RAM resource). As an illustrative example, one can hardly use a 512-bit cryptoprocessor for adding two 768-bit integers (no carry management is provided in general) as they exceed the 512-bit arithmetic registers. Subsequently, it seems very hard to perform a 768-bit modular exponentiation based on such an architecture. More formally, one could define the task as a more general computational problem :

Problem 1. How to optimally implement nk-bit modular operations using k-bit modular operations ?

This problem raises interesting both practical and theoretical questions[1].

---

[1] this is somehow related to the formal decomposition of an algebraic operation with respect to a set of others.

From a cryptographic standpoint, we will essentially focus on designing an nk-bit modular multiplication *in virtue* of its immediate utility in modular exponentiation. Since most complexity-consuming parts will come from k-bit multiplications, our interest will be to tightly investigate :

Problem 2. How to implement an nk-bit modular multiplication using k-bit modular operations with a minimal number of k-bit multiplications ?

In this paper, we develop new algorithmic techniques that solve Problem 2 for an arbitrary n, if we authorize a Montgomery-like constant to appear in the result. Moreover, we propose specifically optimized variants for $n = 2$ that require 9 k-bit modular multiplications in the general case, and only 6 if one of the two operands is previously known like in modular exponentiation. The author is strongly confident in the optimality of these bounds and offers a 9˙999 yens cash reward (as a souvenir from PKC'99) for any better results.

In next section, we briefly recall the main principles of Residue Number Systems (RNS). In section 3, we introduce the notions of modular and radix-compliant RNS bases, show their relevance to Problem 2 and give a concrete example of their implementation in the context of RSA signatures. Note that we will sometimes adopt the notation $[a_i]$ instead of mod a_i for visual comfort.

2 Radix versus Modular Representations

We begin by briefly introducing radix and RNS integer representations. A representation is a function that bijectively transforms a number into a sequence of smaller ones. Although there exist various ways of representing numbers, the most commonly used is the 2^k-radix form: if x denotes a nk-bit nonnegative integer smaller than $N_{\max} < 2^{nk}$, its radix representation is given by the vector

$$(x) = (x_0, \cdots, x_{n-1}) ,$$

where $x_i < 2^k$ for $i = 0, \ldots, n-1$ and

$$x = x_0 + x_1 2^k + \ldots + x_{n-1} 2^{(n-1)k} .$$

Let $a = \{a_1, \ldots, a_r\}$ be a set of r arbitrary integers (called set of moduli or RNS base) such that

$$A = \gcd(a_1, \cdots, a_r) \geq N_{\max} . \tag{1}$$

The modular (also called chinese in digital signal processing) representation of x with respect to this base is the function that associates to x the vector

$$<x>_a = (x[a_1], \ldots, x[a_r]) .$$

The bijection between an integer and its modular representation is guaranteed by the Chinese Remainder Theorem correspondance [3]. More precisely, for all $x < A$ and *a fortiori* for all $x < N_{\max}$, by noting

$$\rho_i = \text{lcm}(a_1, \cdots, a_r)/a_i \quad \text{for } i = 1, \cdots, t ,$$

and defining

$$\theta_i = \rho_i(\rho_i^{-1}[a_i]) \quad \text{for } i = 1, \cdots, t ,$$

it is known that

$$x = (x[a_1]\theta_1 + \cdots + x[a_r]\theta_r)[A] .$$

When modular representations are employed in divide-and-conquer computation techniques, the RNS base is chosen in such a way that $\gcd(a_i, a_j) = 1$ for increased performance. We will therefore assume the pairwise relative primality of the moduli throughout the paper and, as a consequence, Eq. (1) yields

$$A = \prod_{i=1}^{r} a_i \geq N_{\max} . \tag{2}$$

Clearly, regular addition and multiplication (relevant only when the result happens to be smaller than A) can be efficiently computed componentwise in modular representation, that is

$$<x + y>_a = ((x + y)[a_1], \ldots, (x + y)[a_r])$$
$$<xy>_a = (xy[a_1], \ldots, xy[a_r]) .$$

In this setting, evaluating $x + y$ leads to carry-free parallelizable computations. Furthermore, multiplying x by y usually requires less computational resources than direct multiplication since

$$(\log_2 A)^2 > \sum_{i=1}^{r} (\log_2 a_i)^2 . \tag{3}$$

This clearly shows one advantage or modular approaches. Interestingly, modular representation appears well-suited for computations on large integers, but remains rather incompatible with common representation in base 2^k. This strongly motivates deeper investigations of Radix/Modular and Modular/Radix representation conversions. The next section sheds light on these specific RNS bases for which conversions from one type into an other may be achieved at very low cost.

3 Fast Representation Conversions

Definition 3. A set of moduli $a = \{a_1, \cdots, a_r\}$ is said to be $(N_{\max})$-*modular-compliant* (respectively $(N_{\max})$-*radix-compliant*) when $A \geq N_{\max}$ and for all $x < N_{\max}$, the conversion

$$(x) \longrightarrow <x>_a \quad (\text{resp.} <x>_a \longrightarrow (x))$$

requires only $\mathcal{O}(1)$ operations of low (at most linear) complexity.

It is not obvious that a given set of moduli fulfills compliance regarding conversion $(x) \rightarrow <x>_a$, because modular reductions are then to be achieved in linear time. Moreover, switching back into radix representation in linear complexity is even far more intricate. In a general context, getting out a number x from its modular representation is done by Chinese remaindering. For achieving this with a minimum amount of storage, one cascades Garner's method that computes $x < a_1 a_2$ given $x[a_1]$ and $x[a_2]$ in the following way. There exists $x_1 < a_2$ and $x_2 < a_1$ such that

$$x = x_1 a_1 + x[a_1]$$
$$= x_2 a_2 + x[a_2] \ ,$$

wherefrom

$$x_1 = x_1[a_2] = \frac{x[a_2] - x[a_1]}{a_1} [a_2] \ ,$$

which yields

$$x[a_1 a_2] = \left(\frac{x[a_2] - x[a_1]}{a_1} [a_2] \right) a_1 + x[a_1] \ .$$

This combination has then to be iterated $r-1$ times on other RNS components to retrieve $x = x[a_1 \cdots a_r]$. This requires to precompute and store $r-1$ constants, for instance

$$a_1^{-1}[a_2]$$
$$(a_1 a_2)^{-1}[a_3]$$
$$\vdots$$
$$(a_1 \cdots a_{r-1})^{-1}[a_r] \ ,$$

or other (computationnally equivalent) precomputable constants, depending on the chosen recombination sequence. The total recombination thus requires no less than $r-1$ modular multiplications all along the computation, that is, implies a complexity of $\mathcal{O}\left(\sum (\log_2 a_i)^2\right)$.

Radix-compliant RNS bases, by definition, are expected to allow CRT reconstruction without any multiplication. By comparison, using them to switch from modular to radix representation will only cost $\mathcal{O}(\sum \log_2 a_i)$, which assuredly reaches a minimum of complexity.

3.1   Application to RSA Signature Generation

We show here a concrete example of utilizing radix-compliant bases in the context of RSA with Chinese remaindering. Suppose that the cryptoprocessor is limited to k-bit modular computations (typically $k = 512$ or 1024). After computing the k-bit integers

$$m^d \bmod p \quad \text{and} \quad m^d \bmod q \ ,$$

one generally uses Garner's algorithm to recombine the two parts of the signature :

$$s = m^d [pq] = \left(\frac{m^d [p] - m^d [q]}{q} [p] \right) q + m^d [q] . \tag{4}$$

The main problem here resides in computing the regular multiplication of the two k-bit numbers q and $(m^d [p] - m^d [q])/q [p]$ since this operation is a *priori* not supported by the cryptographic processor. Although common implementations take advantage of the 8 or 32-bit host CPU to externally execute the work[2], we will preferably rely on a simple radix-compliant RNS base. Setting

$$a_1 = 2^k \quad \text{and} \quad a_2 = 2^k - 1 ,$$

one notices that $\gcd(a_1, a_2) = 1$ and $s < pq < (2^k - 1)^2 < a_1 a_2$. Additionally, for all $x = x_1 2^k + x_0$ such that $x < pq$, $<x>_a$ can be efficiently computed in linear complexity since

$$x [a_1] = x_0$$
$$x [a_2] = (x_1 + x_0) [a_2] ,$$

and conversely,

$$x_0 = x [a_1] \tag{5}$$
$$x_1 = (x [a_2] - x [a_1]) [a_2] , \tag{6}$$

which makes (a_1, a_2) a (pq)-radix *and* modular-compliant RNS base for all p and q. As a direct consequence, one can compute $<s>_a$ from equation (4) by multiplying separately mod a_1 and mod a_2. Finally, the representation of s in 2^k-radix form is obtained by performing steps (5) and (6).

4 Working in Modular Representation

Let $N \leq N_{\max}$, $x < N$ and $x < N$ be three nk-bit numbers given under their respective modular representations $<x>$, $<y>$ and $<N>$ for some RNS base to be defined. Although one would preferably compute the direct modular product $<xy [N]>$, we will authorize a Montgomery-type constant factor to appear in the result : it is known that the constant can be left unchanged through an arbitrary number of multiplications and eventually vanishes when some additional low-cost pre(and post)-computations are done. Montgomery's well-known modular multiplication [1] is based on a transformation of the form

$$xy \longrightarrow \frac{xy + (-xyN^{-1} [B]) N}{B} , \tag{7}$$

where B is generally chosen such that operations mod B and div B are particularly efficient (or easier to implement) compared to operations mod N and

---

[2] this makes the multiplication feasible but is particularly time-consuming.

div N. Although B is usually a power of the base in radix representation, we will use here for B a product of (N_{max})-modular-compliant moduli. Namely (wlog),

$$B = b_1 \times \cdots \times b_t .$$

We will then choose to compute Eq. (7) while working in modular representation with respect to the base $a \cup b$ where $a = \{a_1, \cdots, a_r\}$ is a (N_{max})-radix-compliant base. Observe first that due to representation constraints, all expected intermediate results have to remain smaller than the total product of the moduli, *i.e.* we must have

$$N^2 + BN \le AB ,$$

which can be satisfied if A and B are chosen in such a way that

$$N_{max}^2 + BN_{max} \le AB . \tag{8}$$

We now describe how to implement Equation (7) in RNS representation with base $a \cup b$. The algorithm is given on Fig. 1.

Algorithm 1.

Input: $<x>_{a \cup b}$, $<y>_{a \cup b}$ and $<N>_{a \cup b}$ where $x, y < N$ and $N \le N_{max}$.

Output: $<z>_{a \cup b}$ with $z = xyB^{-1}[N]$ or $z = xyB^{-1}[N] + N$.

Precomputations: $\alpha_i = -(N \prod_{l<i} b_l)^{-1}[b_i]$ for $i = 1, t$ and $B^{-1}[a_j]$ for $j = 1, r$.

Step 1. $u_1 = x[b_1] y[b_1] \alpha_1 \bmod b_1$,

Step 2. $u_2 = (x[b_2] y[b_2] + u_1 N[b_2]) \alpha_2 \bmod b_2$,

Step 3. $u_3 = (x[b_3] y[b_3] + (u_1 + b_1 u_2) N[b_3]) \alpha_3 \bmod b_3$,

$\vdots$

Step t. $u_t = (x[b_t] y[b_t] + (u_1 + b_1 u_2 + \cdots + \prod_{i=1}^{t-2} b_i u_{t-1}) N[b_t]) \alpha_t \bmod b_t$,

Step t + 1. For $j = 1$ to r, compute

$$z[a_j] = \frac{x[a_j] y[a_j] + (u_1 + b_1 u_2 + \cdots + \prod_{i=1}^{t-1} b_i u_t) N[a_j]}{\prod_{i=1}^{t} b_i} \bmod a_j ,$$

Step t + 2 convert $<z>_a \to (z)$ (low-cost due to radix-compliance of a),

Step t + 3 convert $(z) \to <z>_b$ (low-cost due to modular-compliance of b).

Fig. 1. Montgomery-type Multiplication in Modular Representation.

The correctness of the algorithm is guaranteed by the following statement :

Theorem 4 (Correctness). *Assuming that condition (8) holds, Algorithm 1 outputs either*

$$<xyB^{-1}[N]>_{a \cup b} \quad or \quad <xyB^{-1}[N] + N>_{a \cup b} .$$

Proof. We have to prove (i) that $z = xyB^{-1}[N]$ and (ii) that $z < 2N$. Let

$$v = u_1 + b_1 u_2 + \cdots + \prod_{i=1}^{t-1} b_i u_t \ .$$

One can easily check that the number $xy + vN$ is a multiple of B : it is straitforward that $(xy+vN)[b_1] = 0$ and by definition of the α_is, we get $(xy+vN)[b_i] = 0$ by induction on $i = 1, t$. Therefore the division $(xy + vN)/B$ is implicitly realized in $\mathbf{Z}$, and z is a well-defined integer which fulfills the equality (i). (ii) is due to $B \geq N_{\max} \geq N$ (coming from the $(N_{\max})$-modular-compliance of b) which implies $xy + vN < N^2 + BN \leq 2BN$. $\qquad\square$

Theorem 5 (Complexity Analysis). *Algorithm 1 runs in $\rho(n)$ k-bit multiplications where*

$$\rho(n) = \begin{cases} \frac{n}{2}(3n + 7) & \text{if } N_{\max} \leq \left\lfloor \frac{B_n}{2}\left(\sqrt{1 + 4\frac{A_n}{B_n}} - 1\right)\right\rfloor, \\ \frac{n}{2}(7n + 15) & \text{otherwise}, \end{cases} \tag{9}$$

where A_n and B_n are defined as

$$A_n = \max\left\{\prod_{i=1}^{n} a_i \mid \{a_1, \cdots, a_n\} \text{ is radix-compliant and } a_i \leq 2^k \text{ for } i = 1, n\right\}$$

$$B_n = \max\left\{\prod_{i=1}^{n} b_i \mid \{b_1, \cdots, b_n\} \text{ is modular-compliant and } b_i \leq 2^k \text{ for } i = 1, n\right\} \ .$$

Proof (Sketch). By construction, a_i and b_i must be (at most) k-bit integers. For $i = 1, \ldots, t$, the i-th step of the algorithm requires $i + 1$ k-bit modular multiplications. Then the r following iterations require $t + 2$ modular multiplications each. Therefore, the total amount of k-bit multiplication can be expressed as

$$\frac{t(t+1)}{2} + t + r(t+2) = \frac{1}{2}(t^2 + 2rt + 3t + 4r) \ ,$$

which shows that r and t should be tuned to be as small as possible. The minimum values of r and t are reached when $r = t = n$ and this forces the inequality given by (9) because of condition (8). If $N_{\max}$ is greater than the given bound, we optimally choose $r = n + 1$ and $t = n$. $\qquad\square$

It is worthwhile noticing that previous works such as [4] are based on quite a similar approach, but often interleave heavy representation conversions during the computation or impose hybrid (MRS) representation of operands.

Algorithm 2.

Input: $<x>_{a \cup b}$, $<y>_{a \cup b}$ and $<N>_{a \cup b}$ where $x, y < N$ and $N \le N_{max}$.
Output: $<z>_{a \cup b}$ with $z = xyB^{-1}[N]$ or $z = xyB^{-1}[N] + N$.
Precomp. : $\alpha_1 = -N^{-1}[b_1]$, $\alpha_2 = -(b_1 N)^{-1}[b_2]$, $(b_1 b_2)^{-1}[a_1]$ and $(b_1 b_2)^{-1}[a_2]$.

Step 1. $u_1 = x[b_1] \, y[b_1] \, \alpha_1 \bmod b_1$
Step 2. $u_2 = (x[b_2] \, y[b_2] + u_1 N[b_2]) \alpha_2 \bmod b_2$

Step 3. $z[a_1] = \dfrac{x[a_1] \, y[a_1] + (u_1 + b_1 u_2) N[a_1]}{b_1 b_2} \bmod a_1$

Step 4. $z[a_2] = \dfrac{x[a_2] \, y[a_2] + (u_1 + b_1 u_2) N[a_2]}{b_1 b_2} \bmod a_2$

Step 5. compute $(z) = (z_1, z_0)$ from $(z[a_1], z[a_2])$ and
Step 6. deduce missing coordinates $(z[b_1], z[b_2])$ from (z).

Fig. 2. Double-Size Montgomery Multiplication in RNS base $\{b_1, b_2, a_1, a_2\}$.

5 Size-Doubling Techniques

Double-size computations are obtained by in the particular case when $r = t = n = 2$. Then, Algorithm 1 turns into the algorithm depicted on Fig. 2. The correctness of the algorithm is ensured by Theorem 4. The (quadratic part of the) complexity appears to be of exactly $\rho(2) = 13$ k-bit modular multiplications. In the setting of size-doubling, however, this number can be substantially decreased by utilizing particular RNS bases $\{a_1, a_2\}$ and $\{b_1, b_2\}$ which, under the conditions of compliance and (8), also verify useful properties that simplify computations of Algorithm 2. Namely, the numbers

$$b_1[a_1]$$
$$b_1[a_2]$$
$$b_1^{-1} b_2^{-1}[a_1]$$
$$b_1^{-1} b_2^{-1}[a_2]$$
$$a_1^{-1}[a_2] \text{ or } a_2^{-1}[a_1] \ ,$$

have to be as "simple" as possible. This is achieved by taking the following moduli :

$$\begin{aligned} b_1 &= 2^k + 1 & b_2 &= 2^{k-1} - 1 \\ a_1 &= 2^k & a_2 &= 2^k - 1 \, , \end{aligned}$$

which happen to be pairwise relatively prime for common even values of k (512 or 1024 in practice). This choice allows a particularly fast implementation in 9 k-bit multiplications as shown on Fig. 3. We state :

Theorem 6. *Algorithm 3 computes a $2k$-bit modular multiplication for any $N \le N_{max}$ such that $N_{max} \le (2^k + 1)(2^{k-1} - 1)$ in 9 k-bit modular multiplications.*

Algorithm 3.

Input: $<x>_{a\cup b}$, $<y>_{a\cup b}$ and $<N>_{a\cup b}$ where $x, y < N$ and $N \leq N_{max}$.
Output: $<z>_{a\cup b}$ with $z = xyB^{-1}[N]$ or $z = xyB^{-1}[N] + N$.
Precomputations: $\alpha_1 = -N^{-1}[b_1]$, $\alpha_2 = -(b_1 N)^{-1}[b_2]$.

Step 1. $u_1 = x[b_1] \times y[b_1] \times \alpha_1 \bmod b_1$
Step 2. $u_2 = (x[b_2] \times y[b_2] + u_1 \times N[b_2]) \times \alpha_2 \bmod b_2$
Step 3. $z[a_1] = -(x[a_1] \times y[a_1] + (u_1 + u_2) \times N[a_1]) \bmod a_1$
Step 4. If $z[a_1]$ is odd then $z[a_1] = z[a_1] + 2^{k-1}$
Step 5. $z[a_2] = -(x[a_2] \times y[a_2] + (u_1 + 2u_2) \times N[a_2]) \bmod a_2$
Step 6. $z_1 = (z[a_2] - z[a_1]) \bmod a_2$
Step 7. deduce $z[b_1] = (-z_1 + z[a_1]) \bmod b_1$ and
Step 8. $z[b_2] = (2z_1 + z[a_1]) \bmod b_2$.

Fig. 3. Double-Size Multiplication in RNS base $\{2^k + 1, 2^{k-1} - 1, 2^k, 2^k - 1\}$.

Proof. Let us first prove the correctness of steps 3 through 8 :

steps 3 and 4: b_1 disappears from the general expression (see step 3 of Algorithm 2) because $b_1 = 1 \bmod a_1$; also $(b_1 b_2)^{-1} = b_2 \bmod a_1$ and multiplying some number g by $b_2 \bmod a_1$ leads to $-g \bmod a_1$ if g is even or $-g \bmod a_1 + 2^{k-1}$ otherwise,

step 5 : we have $b_1 = 2 \bmod a_2$; also $(b_1 b_2)^{-1} = -1 \bmod a_2$,

steps 6, 7, 8 : are easy to check.

From the inequality

$$N_{max} \leq \left\lfloor \frac{B}{2} \left(\sqrt{1 + 4\frac{A}{B}} - 1 \right) \right\rfloor,$$

due to condition (8) and $A/B = 2 + 2/(2^k + 1)(2^{k-1} - 1)$, we get

$$\frac{\left(\sqrt{1 + 4\frac{A}{B}} - 1 \right)}{2} \cong 1 + 2/3(2^k + 1)(2^{k-1} - 1),$$

wherefrom

$$N_{max} \leq B(1 + \frac{2}{3B}) \cong B.$$

Finally, looking at Algorithm 3 shows that only 9 k-bit modular multiplications are required throughout the whole computation. $\square$

As input and output numbers are given in modular representation, Algorithm 3 can be re-iterated at will, thus providing an algorithmic base for double-size exponentiation, if modular squaring is chosen to be computed by the same way. Conversions from radix to modular representation in base $a \cup b$ for the message and the modulus will then have to be executed once during the initialization phase, and so will the conversion of the result from modular to radix representation after the Square-and-Multiply exponent-scanning finishes.

Remark. At this level, note also that modular exponentiating leads to constantly multiply the current accumulator by the same number (the base), say $<g>_{a \cup b}$. As a consequence, the modular multiplier shown above can be simplified again in this context, by replacing the precomputed constants α_1 and α_2 by

$$\alpha_1' = g\alpha_1 = -gN^{-1} \bmod b_1 \;,$$

and

$$\alpha_2' = g\alpha_2 = -g(b_1 N)^{-1} \bmod b_1$$
$$\alpha_2'' = N\alpha_2 = -b_1^{-1} = -\frac{1}{3} \bmod b_2 \;,$$

and replacing Algorithm 3 by the more specific multiplication algorithm shown on Fig. 4 which uses only 7 k-bit multiplications. Note that this improvement cannot be applied *ad hoc* for modular squaring.

Algorithm 4.

Input: $<x>_{a \cup b}$, $<g>_{a \cup b}$ and $<N>_{a \cup b}$ where $x, g < N$ and $N \leq N_{\max}$.
Output: $<z>_{a \cup b}$ with $z = xgB^{-1}[N]$ or $z = xgB^{-1}[N] + N$.
Precomputations: $\alpha_1' = -gN^{-1}[b_1], \alpha_2' = -g(b_1 N)^{-1}[b_1]$.

Step 1. $u_1 = x[b_1] \times \alpha_1' \bmod b_1$
Step 2. $u_2 = x[b_2] \times \alpha_2' + u_1 \times \alpha_2'' \bmod b_2$

Step 3. $z[a_1] = -(x[a_1] \times y[a_1] + (u_1 + u_2) \times N[a_1]) \bmod a_1$

Step 4. If $z[a_1]$ is odd then $z[a_1] = z[a_1] + 2^{k-1}$

Step 5. $z[a_2] = -(x[a_2] \times y[a_2] + (u_1 + 2u_2) \times N[a_2]) \bmod a_2$

Step 6. $z_1 = (z[a_2] - z[a_1]) \bmod a_2$
Step 7. deduce $z[b_1] = (-z_1 + z[a_1]) \bmod b_1$ and
Step 8. $z[b_2] = (2z_1 + z[a_1]) \bmod b_2$.

Fig. 4. Double-Size Multiplier in RNS base $\{2^k + 1, 2^{k-1} - 1, 2^k, 2^k - 1\}$ specific to Modular Exponentiation.

Remark. Note also that the multiplication $u_1 \times \alpha_2''[b_2] = u_1/3[b_2]$ can be advantageously replaced by the (linear in k) following operation :

1. determine which number among $\{u_1, u_1 + 1, u_1 + 2\}$ is divisible by 3 (using repeated summations on u_1's bytes for instance),
2. divide $u_1 + i$ by 3 in $\mathbf{Z}$ by some linear technique as Arazi-Naccache fast algorithm (see [6]) to get an integer u,
3. correct the result by adding i times α_2'' to u modulo b_2.

This decreases the complexity again down to 6 k-bit multiplications.

From a practical point of view, the technique is (to the best of our knowledge) the only one that makes it possible to perform $2k$-bit modular exponentiations on k-bit cryptographic processors at reasonable cost.

6 Hardware Developments

Size-doubling techniques are an original design strategy for cryptoprocessor hardware designers. In particular,

- total independance of computations at steps 3 and 5 of Algorithm 3 (or the r iterations at step $t + 1$ of Algorithm 1) could lead to a high parallelization of computational resources (typically the arithmetic core),
- the specific choice of the RNS base allows specific treatments of modular multiplications, for instance $xy \bmod 2^k$ and $xy \bmod 2^k - 1$,
- the cascades of steps 1 and 2 of Algorithm 3 (or the t first steps of Algorithm 1) appear to be pipeline-suitable for so-equiped hardware designs.
- division by 3 using Arazi-Naccache's fast algorithm can be implemented in hardware very easily.

7 Conclusions

In this paper, we have introduced new efficient techniques for multiplying and exponentiating double-size integers using arithmetic operations over k-bit integers. These techniques are particularly adapted to enhance the computational capabilities of size-limited cryptographic devices. From a theoretic viewpoint, we state that :

- multiplying two arbitrary $2k$-bit integers (up to a given bound $N_{\max}$) modulo a third $2k$-bit given number $N < N_{\max}$ leads to a complexity of 9 k-bit modular multiplications essentially,
- multiplying an arbitrary $2k$-bit integer by a $2k$-bit given number modulo a third $2k$-bit given number $N < N_{\max}$ leads to 6 k-bit modular multiplications.

Although we believe that no other algorithm could offer better results regarding Problem 2, the bounds we provide are not *proven* optimal so far, and the question of showing that minimality is reached or not remains open.

8 Acknowledgements

I would like to thank David Naccache, Helena Handschuh and Jean-Sébastien Coron for helpful discussions and significative improvements on certain algorithms presented in this paper.

References

1. P. Montgomery, *Modular Multiplication without Trial Division*, Mathematics of Computation 44(170), pp 519–521, July 1997.

2. E. Brickell, *A Survey of Hardware Implementations for RSA*, Advances in Cryptology, Proceedings of Crypto'89, 1990.

3. C. Ding, D. Pei and A. Salomaa, *Chinese Remainder Theorem - Applications in Computing, Coding, Cryptography*, World Scientific Publishing, 1996.

4. J. C. Bajard, L. S. Didier and P. Kornerup, *An RNS Montgomery Modular Multiplication Algorithm*, Proceedings of ARITH13, IEEE Computer Society, pp 234–239, July 1997.

5. H. Handschuh and P. Paillier, *Smart-Card CryptoCoProcessors for Public-Key Cryptography*, CryptoBytes Vol. 4, Num. 1, Sum. 1998

6. B. Arazi and D. Naccache, *Binary to Decimal Conversion Based on the Divisibility of 255 by 5*, Electronic Letters, Vol. 28, Num. 23, 1992.

7. J. F. Dhem, *Design of an Efficient Public-Key Cryptographic Library for RISC-based Smart Cards*, PhD Thesis, UCL, 1998

Evaluating Differential Fault Analysis of Unknown Cryptosystems

Pascal Paillier

GEMPLUS	ENST
Cryptography Department	Computer Science Department
34 Rue Guynemer	46, rue Barrault
92447 Issy-Les Moulineaux	75634 Paris Cedex 13
paillier@gemplus.com	paillier@inf.enst.fr

Abstract. Recently [1], Biham and Shamir announced an attack (Differential Fault Analysis, DFA for short) that recovers keys of arbitrary cryptosystems in polynomial (quadratic) complexity. In this paper, we show that under slightly modified assumptions, DFA is not polynomial and would simply result in the loss of *some* key-bits. Additionally, we prove the existence of cryptosystems on which DFA cannot reach the announced workfactor.

1 Introduction

Boneh, DeMillo and Lipton's 1997 paper [11], suggesting a cryptanalytic approach based on the generation of hardware faults, motivated investigations on either improving the attacks (see [6, 2, 5]), or evaluating its practicality [9, 10].

Extending fault-based attacks to block-ciphers [4], Biham and Shamir described a cryptanalysis of DES with 200 ciphertexts where one-bit errors were assumed to be induced by environmental stress. In [3], the same authors explored another fault model based on memory asymetry and introduced Differential Fault Analysis as a tool for breaking unknown cryptosytems.

In this paper, we further investigate DFA in the context of unknown cryptosystems. We show that under slightly modified assumptions, DFA would simply amount to the loss of some key-bits. Additionally, we prove the existence of cryptosystems on which the original attack cannot reach the workfactor announced in [1].

2 The Differential Fault Model

The main assumption behind DFA's fault model consists in approximating the physical properties of memory devices by a perfect asymetric behaviour. In other words, when submitted to physical stress, EEPROM cells containing key bits would only be expected to switch off from ones to zeroes[1]. In this setting, Biham

---

[1] or alternatively from zeroes to ones depending on the technology-dependant coding convention.

and Shamir's approach consists in applying successive stress pulses to an n-bit key register between repeated encryption requests of the same message m. As a result, the sequence of ciphertexts $\{c_0, \cdots, c_r\}$ returned by the device will correspond to a sequence $\{k_0, \cdots, k_r\}$ of keys obtained from the original key k_0 by resetting the 1 bits one by one up to the empty key $k_r = 0^n$ where $r \simeq n/2$. We will hereafter denote by $k_t \rightarrow_i k_{t+1}$ the binary relation "k_{t+1} is obtained by flipping the i-th bit of k_t".

During the second phase, the attacker retrieves the 1-bit positions in k_0 by backtracking. Supposedly able to replace the key register by any data of his choice, he simply explores the sequence $\{k_r, \cdots, k_0\}$ by searching at each step $k_{t+1} \rightarrow k_t$ the missing position of the 1-bits. This is done in at most $\mathcal{O}(n^2)$ encryptions.

Let us assume that the register bits induce independent random sequences and denote by p_1 the probability (uniform over all bits) of flipping a one bit to a zero during a stress pulse. Naturally, p_1's value would entirely depend on the employed technology, the amplitude, nature and specific physical parameters of the attack's environment. We will denote by $p_{1,i}$ the value of p_1 during the i-th stress period.

Since $p_{1,i}$ is intentionally small, it appears that particular events for which $h(k_{i-1}) - h(k_i) \geq 2$, where h denotes the Hamming weight, happen with negligible probability : as a consequence, we always have $h(k_i) = h(k_{i-1}) - 1$ for all $i = 1, \ldots, r$. Let n_i be the number of identical ciphertexts generated consecutively by the same key k_{i-1} ; n_i may also be looked upon as the number of attempts necessary to erase a bit from the current key while applying the i-th stress pulse. Basically, we have :

$$\overline{n_i} = \frac{1}{1 - (1 - p_{1,i})^{h(k_{i-1})}} , \tag{1}$$

and therefore,

$$N = \sum_{i=1}^{r} \overline{n_i} = \sum_{i=1}^{r} \frac{1}{1 - (1 - p_{1,i})^{h(k_{i-1})}}$$

$$\cong \sum_{i=1}^{r} \frac{1}{p_{1,i} h(k_{i-1})} = \sum_{i=1}^{h(k_0)} \frac{1}{p_{1,i}(h(k_0) + 1 - i)} .$$

If $p_{1,i} = p_1$ is kept constant throughout the attack, the total average number of encryptions is :

$$N = \frac{1}{p_1} \sum_{i=1}^{h(k_0)} \frac{1}{(h(k_0) + 1 - i)}$$

$$= \frac{1}{p_1}(1 + \frac{1}{2} + \cdots + \frac{1}{h(k_0)}) = \mathcal{O}\left(\frac{1}{p_1} \ln \left(\frac{n}{2}\right)\right) . \tag{2}$$

Since N grows logarithmically with n for small p_1, there is no need to impose a particular $p_{1,i}$ sequence to minimize N. The attacker can thus apply successive constant-strength pulses throughout the attack. In this respect, the next section refines [1]'s model and analyses its characteristics.

3 A More Elaborate Model

Biham and Shamir's DFA relies on a strong asymmetric assumption. In this section, we show that under slightly modified hypothesis, the attack inherits an inescapable exponential workfactor.

3.1 The Zero-Probability Assumption

Although some specific types of memories do present an asymetric behavior when submitted to certain physical *stimuli*, tamper-protected EEPROM cells are usually efficiently protected from specific external influences[2].

However, one may still try physical/chemical/electronical attacks (or a simultaneous combination of these) on a protected chip, even though this implies more intricate operations and totally unpredictible results. This being said, we will focus our investigation on registers that are characterized by a weaker differential influence, *i.e.* for which stressing the targetted zone flips some one bits to zeroes, while a much smaller fraction of zero bits is supposed to be transformed into ones.

3.2 Flipping Key-Bits : A Statistical Equilibrium

Assuming that some zero bits of the key register may additionnally flip to one bits with a small probability during physical stress pulses, the attacker (whose aim still remains to shift one bits into zero bits) cannot avoid to simultaneously cause a back-to-one-flipping phenomenon.

Let p_0 be the probability of flipping a zero bit to a one. As in section 2, this probability is assumed to be uniform over all the register bits. Now consider the sequence $h(k_i)$ formed by the Hamming weights of successive keys stored in the device. The average number of one bits that disappeared during the i-th stress pulse is $u_i = n_i p_1 h(k_{i-1})$. At the same time about $z_i = n_i p_0(n - h(k_{i-1}))$ zeroes have been replaced by ones. Since $p_0 \leq p_1$ and noting that $n - h(k_0) \simeq h(k_0)$, we have necessarily $z_1 \leq u_1$. As the number of zero bits in the key $n - h(k_{i-1})$ increases in time, more and more zero-to-one transformations become likely to occur and z_i increases as u_i constantly decreases. The equilibrium is reached when $u_i = z_i$ and the sequence $h(k_i)$ thus converges to an h_∞ such that :

$$p_1 h_\infty = p_0(n - h_\infty) \, ,$$

---

[2] many smart card components contain security detectors that flush all the memory contents or reset the microprocessor if an abnormal event occurs (UV rays, clock glitches, depassivation, Vcc fluctuations, etc.).

that is

$$h_\infty = \frac{np_0}{p_0 + p_1} = \alpha n .$$

This equation expresses a statistical equilibrium, in which one-to-zero and zero-to-one inversions expectedly compensate each other. As a consequence, the family of faulty keys k_i will never stabilize on any particular key, but will oscillate inside the whole range of keys of Hamming weight h_∞ (there are $\binom{h_\infty}{n}$ such keys).

As an example, in the (favorable) case when α is Gilbert-Warshamov's constant $\alpha = 0.11$ ($p_0 = 0.1235 \times p_1$), we get :

$$\binom{\alpha n}{n} \cong 2^{\frac{n}{2}} .$$

Hence, although this type of DFA would allow the extraction of a part of the key, it will still remain exponential in n.

4 DFA-Immune Cryptosystems

In this section, we explore the original model's boundaries. Indeed, although Biham and Shamir will retrieve in theory the secret key from most cryptosystems, there exist DFA-immune cryptosystems.

In particular, specific implementations may present key-verifying mechanisms, providing a brief detection of a *priori* dangerous characteristics of the key, whenever encryption is sollicited. In this respect, key-checking operations may guarantee the use of random bit-patterns and are therefore expected to protect the cryptographic function against transmission errors or incorrectly chosen keys. The following illustrative example spots keys for which the difference between the number of zero-bits and one-bits is too large :

- $H(k) = k$ if $|h(k) - \frac{n}{2}| \leq m$,
- $H(k) = 0^n$ otherwise .

In this case, the key is replaced by 0 if its Hamming weight is too far from $n/2$. Under other implementations, the second event may just cause an internal function status flag to flip and an error is returned. Applying a DFA on such a design makes the first attack stage stop after $\simeq m$ encryptions. This, when completed by brute-force research, would result an $\mathcal{O}(2^{\frac{n}{2}-m}mn)$ complexity, which is exponential in n again.

4.1 Differential Fault Analysis on Parity-Protected Keys

Some error-detecting mechanisms use a part of the key material to authenticate the bits involved in the encryption process. A typical example is the DES key format defined by the NIST where a 7-byte key is parity-protected by an additionnal byte spread over the key string[3]. According to the standard, the 8-th bit of each key byte is computed by complementing the xor of the 7 other bits. To motivate further analysis, we will denote a parity-checking predicate V on a bitstring k as :

1. a partition $k = (k^1, k^2, \cdots, k^d)$ over k's bits into d key-blocks,
2. a set of d boolean functions $f_1, f_2, \cdots, f_d$ where each f_i is a linear function of k_i.
3. a d-bit vector v

Obviously, k fulfills a given V when $f_j(k^j) = v_j$ for all j. We will then denote by $\mathcal{V}$ the set of keys satisfying V. From the generic description of V given above, let us define on all n-bit strings the function $\phi : \{0,1\}^n \longrightarrow \{0,1\}^d$ such that :

$$\phi(k) = (f_1(k^1), \cdots, f_d(k^d)) \oplus v . \tag{3}$$

It is clear that $\phi(k) = 0^d$ if and only if $k \in \mathcal{V}$, that is $\mathcal{V} = \mathrm{Ker}(\phi)$; ϕ can thus be seen as a *canonic indicator* of V since its non-zero components indicate those blocks of k for which $f_j(k^j) \neq v_j$. From the linearity of the f_js, we can also infer that :

$$k \rightarrow_i k' \quad \Rightarrow \quad (\phi(k) \oplus \phi(k'))^j = \begin{cases} 1 & \text{if bit } i \text{ is in } k^j, \\ 0 & \text{otherwise} \end{cases} \tag{4}$$

expressing the fact that flipping a 1-bit of k to 0 will only make $\phi(k)$ and $\phi(k')$ differ at one coordinate. As a direct property, one can show that we necessarily have :

$$(k_1, k_2) \in \mathcal{V}^2 \quad \Rightarrow \quad |h(k_1) - h(k_2)| \text{ is even.} \tag{5}$$

Let us now assume that the device, sollicited to encrypt some constant message using the stored key k, spontaneously checks if $k \in \mathcal{V}$ and returns an error if not.

The Descent Stage. Since $k_0 \in \mathcal{V}$, the descent stage starts by making the device behave normally, that is, encrypt all given messages. After the first pulse, the memory contains k_1 which, due to Eq. (5), does not belong to $\mathcal{V}$ anymore. The attacker is then forced to apply successive stresses until the device re-accepts to encrypt (in which case the current key k_i belongs again to $\mathcal{V}$) and collect a sequence of valid keys which eventually may allow him to extract useful information about the initial key k_0 during the reconstruction stage. The end of the descent, caracterized by the sequence of keys $\{k_0, k_1, \cdots, k_r\}$ where $r = h(k_0)$ and stabilized on the all-zero key, is detectable only if $0^n \in \mathcal{V}$.

---

[3] the ANSI X3.92 standard recommends the systematic use of parity-checking before encrypting.

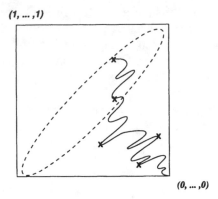

Fig. 1. Statistical search sequence in $\{0,1\}^n$ of valid keys (crosses).

The obtained information about k_0 thus depends on the average total number $\overline{N}$ of different plain/ciphertexts pairs for which keys comply with the integrity checking predicate. In this section, we will search a tight estimation of $\overline{N}$.

For a given k_0, let W_T represent the set of all possible sequences $\{k_0, k_1, \cdots, k_r\}$ likely to appear throughout the descent stage and W those sequences that contain a $k_i \in V$ for $i > 0$. For $w \in W$, we will note $|w|$ the smallest strictly positive index i such that k_i appears in w and $k_i \in V$. The probability that the descent fails is then :

$$P[\text{failure}] = \sum_{w \in W_T - W} P[w], \qquad (6)$$

and in this case, naturally, the attack will not give any particular advantage over a direct exhaustive search on k_0. Conversely, in case of success, we have for all $w \in W$

$$P[w \mid \text{success}] = \frac{P[w]}{P[\text{success}]} P[\text{success} \mid w]$$

$$= \frac{P[w]}{\sum_{w \in W} P[w]} .$$

For commodity, the normalized probability $P[w \mid \text{success}]$ will be refered to as $P(w)$. The average number of pulses to be applied on k_0 before obtaining a valid key during a succesfull descent stage is then :

$$\bar{t} = \sum_{w \in W} |w| \, P(w) . \qquad (7)$$

To each $w = \{k_0, \cdots, k_r\} \in W_T$, one may then associate $\phi(w)$ as the collection $\{\phi(k_0), \cdots, \phi(k_r)\}$. Because of Eq. (4) and the fact that $k_0 \in V$, $\phi(w)$ can be seen as a path in the natural graph induced by $\{0,1\}^d$ which, starting from the origin, follows the natural edges, that is, in one dimension at a time.

(1, ... ,1)

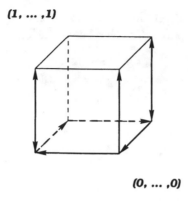

(0, ... ,0)

Fig. 2. Evolution of $\phi(k_t)$ in $\{0,1\}^d$ as t increases. The created circuit may appear for more than one key sequence w, *i.e.* ϕ is not injective.

From its definition given above, one can deduce that W is exactly the set of sequences w for which $\phi(w)$ is prefixed by a cycle starting and ending in 0^d. Denoting by C the set of such cycles and by $|c|$ the length of $c \in C$, we have for all c :

$$\sum_{\{w \in W \,|\, w \text{ realizes } c\}} |w|\ P(w) = |c| \sum_{\{w \in W \,|\, w \text{ realizes } c\}} P(w) = |c|\ P(c) .$$

Gathering terms in Eq. (7) therefore yields :

$$\bar{t} = \sum_{c \in C} |c|\ P(c) , \tag{8}$$

which relates to a classical graph calculation, as soon as the flipping probability remains uniform over all the key bits; the result is known to be :

$$\bar{t} = 2^d , \tag{9}$$

if cycles are accepted to be of arbitrary length. In our case $|c| \leq r$, and we will consider that Eq. (9) holds while imposing $r \geq 2^d$. As a result, the total number $\overline{N}$ of successful encryptions should be close to :

$$\overline{N} \simeq \frac{r}{\bar{t}} \simeq \frac{n}{2^{d+1}} . \tag{10}$$

The Key-Recovering Stage. To retrieve k_0, the attacker explores the sequence $\{k_0, \cdots, k_r\}$ backwards by positionning the r missing 1-bits as in section 2. The descent stage having brought the knowledge of valid keys in the sequence, he will face an additional workfactor coming from the gaps between those keys. Basically, the total complexity of the whole attack may be written as :

$$\overline{N} \times n^{\overline{i}} = \frac{n^{2^d+1}}{2^d} \,. \tag{11}$$

Although this expression remains polynomial in n, the exponent 2^d appears to be strongly dissuasive. Additionally, one notices that the average complexity grows (essentially) exponentially with d, which can then be tightly tuned ($d < n$) to reach an optimal protection against DFA.

4.2 Authenticating the Key

Similarly, various practical implementations of key-safety mechanisms use hash functions in order to authenticate the key : the CRC is then included in the key material. In a scenario where the critical data are stored in EEPROM as $P(k_0||H(k_0) \bmod 2^m)$ where H is a one-way hash function, P a secret permutation over the bit indexes of the key register and m a basic security parameter, flipping random key bits to zero results in a non-informative result, with a $1-2^{-m}$ probability. If $h(k_0)$ is the Hamming weight of the original key, the average total number of plain/ciphertext pairs successfully extracted from the device is :

$$N = \frac{2^{-m} \times h(k_0)}{1 - 2^{-m}} \,,$$

i.e. roughly

$$N = \frac{n}{2^{m+1} - 2} \,,$$

which reaches 0 as soon as $\lceil \log(n) \rceil \leq m$. This means that adding a $\lceil \log(n) \rceil$-bit CRC to the key guarantees a statistical inefficiency of DFA.

4.3 Key Equivalence

In this section, we notice that, if the data stored in the EEPROM are used to compute an effective key, the proposed attack may only recover *partial* information about the original data. More specifically, it may disclose a key which is *computationally equivalent* to the genuine one. As a typical illustration, consider the simple (cryptographically inefficient) design in which a plaintext m is encrypted by :

$$c = \text{DES} \left[\overline{k} \oplus \underline{k} \right] (m) \,,$$

where the 112-bit key is $k = \overline{k}||\underline{k}$. Applying DFA on this particular design allows the attacker to retrieve an equivalent k' such that

$$\overline{k'} \oplus \underline{k'} = \overline{k} \oplus \underline{k} \,, \tag{12}$$

but recovering the original key k information-theoretically imply a 2^{56}-step brute force research. In a more general context, DFA-immunity appears on cryptosystems which key input is fed by a non-injective function.

4.4 Intrinsic DFA-Immunity

Clearly, other cryptographic schemes present DFA-resistant features. In particular, any probabilistic algorithm such as El Gamal encryption or DSA signature scheme basically involves randomized computations which could not allow the attacker to perform the descent stage nor the key retrieval phase with a nonnegligible probability. In this case indeed, the attacker could not link ciphertexts (or signatures) to the message m when the function has processed a faulty secret key, and the attack simply cannot be successful.

5 Concluding remarks

We investigated the relevance of Differential Fault Analysis in particular contexts and showed that although the attack may sometimes offer substantial theoretical benefits, simple algorithmic countermeasures exist. This points out that DFA issues should essentially be looked upon as a research subject related to prudent engineering [7] and implementation-dependent security recommandations.

References

1. E. Biham and A. Shamir, *Differential Fault Analysis*, LNCS 1294, Advances in Cryptology, Proceedings of Crypto'97, Springer-Verlag, pp. 513–525, 1997.

2. F. Bao, R. Deng, Y. Han, A. Jeng, A. Narasimhalu and T. Ngair, *Breaking Public-Key Cryptosystems on Tamper-Resistant Devices in the Presence of Transient Faults*, LNCS 1361, Proceedings of Secure Protocal Workshop' 97, Springer-Verlag, pp. 115–124, 1997.

3. E. Biham and A. Shamir, *The next stage of differential fault analysis : How to break completely unknown cryptosystems*, Preprint, 1996.

4. E. Biham and A. Shamir, *A New Cryptanalytic Attack on DES : Differential Fault Analysis*, October 18, 1996. http//jya.com/dfa.htm.

5. A. Lenstra, *Memo on RSA Signature Generation in the Presence of Faults*, Sept. 28, 1996.

6. M. Joye, J-J. Quisquater, *Attacks on Systems using Chinese Remaindering*, Technical Report CG-1996/9 of UCL, 1996.

7. R. Anderson and R. Needham, *Robustness Principles for Public-Key Protocols*, LNCS 963, Advances in Cryptology, Proceedings of Crypto'95, Springer-Verlag, pp. 236–247, 1995.

8. R. Anderson and S. Vaudenay, *Minding your p's and q's*, LNCS 1163, Advances in Cryptology, Proceedings of Asiacrypt'96, Springer-Verlag, pp. 26–35, 1996.

9. R. Anderson and M. Kuhn, *Tamper Resistance - A Cautionary Note*, Usenix Workshop on Electronic Commerce, pp. 1–11, Nov. 1996.

10. R. Anderson and M. Kuhn, *Low-Cost Attacks on Tamper-Resistant Devices*, LNCS 1361, Security Protocol Workshop' 97, pp. 125–136, April 1997.

11. D. Boneh, R. DeMillo and R. Lipton, *On the Importance of Checking Cryptographic Protocols for Faults*, LNCS 1233, Advances in Cryptology, Proceedings of Eurocrypt'97, Springer-Verlag, pp. 37–51, 1997.

12. P. Kocher, *Timing Attacks on Implementations of Diffie-Hellman, RSA, DSS, and Other Systems*, LNCS 1109, Advances in Cryptology, Proceedings of Crypto'96, Springer-Verlag, pp. 104–113, 1996.

13. Federal Information Processing Standards. *Security Requirements for Cryptographic Modules*, FIPS Publication 140-1.

Removing Interoperability Barriers Between the X.509 and EDIFACT Public Key Infrastructures: The DEDICA Project

Montse Rubia, Juan Carlos Cruellas, and Manel Medina

Computer Architecture Department, Polytechnical University of Catalonia,
{montser,cruellas,medina}@ac.upc.es,
WWW home page: http://www.ac.upc.es/DEDICA

Abstract. This paper concerns the barriers to interoperability that exist between the X.509 and EDIFACT Public Key Infrastructures (PKI), and proposes a method to overcome them. The solution lies in the DEDICA[1] (Directory based EDI Certificate Access and management) TELEMATIC Project, funded by the European Union. The main objective of this project is to define and provide means to make these two infrastructures inter-operable without increasing the amount of information that they have to manage. The proposed solution is a gateway tool interconnecting both PKIs. The main purpose of this gateway is to act as a TTP that "translates" certificates issued in one PKI to the other's format, and then signs the translation to make it a new certificate. The gateway will in fact act as a proxy CA for the CAs of the other PKI.

1 Introduction

The growth and expansion of electronic means of communication has led to a need for certain mechanisms to secure these communications. These services are mostly based on asymmetric cryptography, which requires an infrastructure (PKI) to make the public keys available. Several initiatives around the world have led to the emergence of PKIs based on X.509 certificates, such as SET (Secure Electronic Transaction) or PKIX (Internet Public Key Infrastructure). X.509 is the authentication framework designed to support X.500 directory services. Both X.509 and X.500 are part of the X series of international standards proposed by the ISO and ITU.

Another type of PKI is the one based on EDIFACT certificates. Electronic Data Interchange (EDI) is the electronic transfer from one computer to another of commercial or administrative documents using an agreed standard to structure the transaction or message data. In the EDI world the internationally accepted standard is EDIFACT (EDI For Administration Commerce and Trade). Expert groups from different areas work on the development of EDIFACT compliant

---

[1] This project has been funded by the EC (TE-2005) and the Spanish government: CICYT (TEL-96/1644-CE), and has been selected by the G8 as one of the pilot projects to promote the use of telematic applications in SMEs.

messages, producing UN/EDIFACT (a set of internationally agreed standards, directories and guidelines for the electronic interchange of structured data) [8]. EDIFACT syntax defines a way of structuring information from a basic level involving sequences of characters (representing numbers, names, codes, etc.) to the highest level (the interchange) including sequences of messages (the electronic version of paper documents), which in turn are made up of sequences of qualitatively relevant pieces of information, the segments (to represent date and time, for instance), just as in paper documents one can link pieces of related information. The EDIFACT certificates are encoded in EDIFACT syntax, and are formed by segment groups related to general certificate information, algorithm and key information and the CAs (Certification Authority) digital signature (USC-USA(3)-USR). Since EDIFACT certificates are structured and encoded using EDIFACT syntax, they can be included within EDIFACT messages.

These infrastructures are not interoperable, mainly due to the fact that the certificates and messages are coded differently.

1.1 DEDICA Project : a solution to the problem of interoperability between the X.509-based PKI and the EDIFACT PKI

DEDICA (Directory based EDI Certificate Access and management) is a research and development project established by the European Commission under the Telematics Applications programme. Its main objective is to define and provide means to make the two above-mentioned infrastructures inter-operable without increasing the amount of information the must manage. The proposed solution involves the design and implementation of a gateway tool interconnecting both PKIs: the certification infrastructure, currently available, based on standards produced in the open systems world, and the existing EDI applications that follow the UN/EDIFACT standards for certification and electronic signatures mechanisms.

The main purpose of the gateway proposed by DEDICA is to act as a TTP (Trusted Third Party) that translates certificates issued in one PKI to the others format, and then signs the translation to make it a new certificate. For instance, any user certified within an X.509 PKI could get an EDIFACT certificate from this gateway without having to register in an EDIFACT Authority. The gateway will act in fact, as a proxy CA for the CAs of the other PKI.

The tools developed for the gateway can also be used in systems with a mixture of components, as they can allow CAs in one of the PKIs to behave as CAs in the other one. This gives a broader scope to the work and means it, could now be the starting point for further specifications and developments leading to inter-operability among other currently emerging PKIs (SPKI for instance).

In the figure below the DEDICA gateway context is shown. Each user is registered in his PKI and accesses the certification objects repository of this PKI. The DEDICA gateway must be able to interact with the users of both PKIs in order to respond to their requests. It must also be able to access the security objects stores of both PKIs, and to be certified in EDIFACT and X.509 CAs.

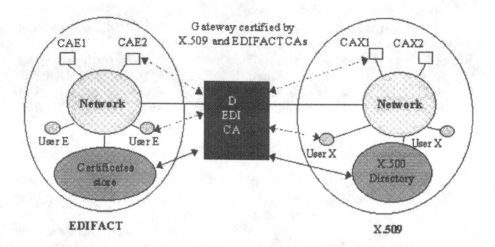

Fig. 1. DEDICA gateway context.

2 Functionality of the Gateway

The problem of interoperability between the X.509 and EDIFACT PKIs was approached on two levels by the DEDICA project: the different formats of the certificates and the different messages interchanged by the PKI entities.

To deal with the former, the DEDICA consortium, after in-depth study of the contents of both types of certificates, specified a set of mapping rules which permit two-way translation of both types of certificates.

In the case of the differences in messages and certification services: whereas in the EDIFACT world the UN/EDIFACT KEYMAN message is used to provide certification services, in the X.509 world a set of messages specified for each PKI (such as PKIX in Internet for instance) is used.

The DEDICA gateway is able to offer four services:

1. A request for an EDIFACT certificate from an X.509 certificate generated by an X.509 CA.
2. Verification of an EDIFACT certificate generated by the DEDICA gateway (from the mapping of an X.509 certificate).
3. A request for an X.509 certificate from an EDIFACT certificate generated by an EDIFACT CA.
4. Verification of an X.509 certificate generated by the DEDICA gateway (from the mapping of an EDIFACT certificate).

Figure 1 shows the DEDICA gateway context. This context is the following: An X.509 PKI with CAs, users and X.500 Directory access (the Directory operating as a repository of security objects), an EDIFACT PKI with CAs and users, and the DEDICA gateway, certified by CAs in both PKI and access to X.500 Directory.

The DEDICA gateway defines the terms *Initial certificates* and *Derived certificates* as follows :

Initial Certificate: any certificate supplied by the Certification Authority of any Public Key Infrastructure (EDIFACT or X.509).

Derived Certificate: certificate deriving from an initial certificate, generated by the DEDICA gateway through the mapping rules defined by DEDICA. The derived certificate depends on the initial one; if the initial certificate is revoked, then the derived certificate is also considered to be revoked.

2.1 Request for a derived certificate

In the scenario shown in figure 1, an X.509 user (user X) may wish to send EDIFACT messages to an EDIFACT user (user E) using digital signatures or any security mechanism that implies the management of certificates. This user needs a certificate from the other Public Key Infrastructure (in this case, the EDIFACT PKI). He then sends an interchange to the gateway requesting the production of an "equivalent" EDIFACT certificate. This interchange will contain a KEYMAN message (indicating a request for an EDIFACT certificate) and the X.509 certificate of this user in an EDIFACT package (EDIFACT structure able to carry binary information).

The gateway will validate the X.509 certificate. If the certificate is valid (the signature is correct, it has not been revoked, and it has not expired), it will perform the mapping process, and will generate the new derived EDIFACT certificate. After that, the gateway will send it to user X within a KEYMAN message.

Now user X can establish communication with user E using security mechanisms that imply the use of electronic certificates through the derived EDIFACT certificate, by sending an EDIFACT interchange with this derived certificate.

2.2 Validation of a derived certificate

The DEDICA gateway also validates derived certificates at users request.

Continuing with the process described in the previous section, user E, after receiving the interchange sent by user X, requests validation of the derived certificate by sending the corresponding KEYMAN message to the gateway.

The gateway determines whether the EDIFACT certificate has been generated by itself, and proceeds with the validation of the original X.509 certificate and the derived EDIFACT certificate. It will have to access the X.500 Distributed Directory to get both the original X.509, and the necessary Certificate Revocation Lists (CRL) for this process of certificate validation. The general process for the validation of derived certificates is the following:

1. First the validity of the derived certificate is verified. This implies checking:
   (a) That the signature matches the public key of the gateway.
   (b) That the certificate is within the validity period.
2. The X.500 Distributed Directory is accessed in order to obtain the original X.509 certificate and the necessary Certificate Revocation Lists.

3. The signature of the original certificate is verified and the validity period is checked.

4. The gateway verifies the certification path of the original X.509 certificate, and checks that the certificates have not been revoked.

If these steps are successfully accomplished, then the derived EDIFACT certificate can be considered as a valid certificate, and the gateway will send the validation response to the EDIFACT user within a KEYMAN message.

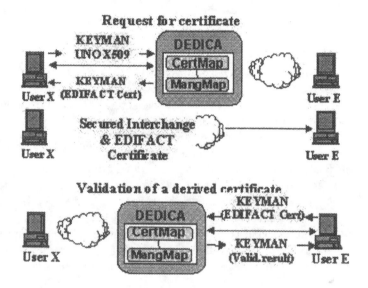

Fig. 2. Functionality of the DEDICA gateway.

3 Architecture of the gateway

The DEDICA gateway is made up of two main architectural blocks: The **CertMap** and the **MangMap** module. The former is responsible for mapping the certificates, and the latter converts the functionality of the KEYMAN message into equivalent X.509 PKI operations (including X.500 access).

3.1 CertMap module

The CertMap module is the module in charge of mapping certificates following the mapping rules that have been defined by the DEDICA project. Its operation will be launched by the MangMap module, which will give to it the needed input.

There will be two possible different inputs to the CertMap module:

- A X.509 certificate DER coded.

– An EDIFACT certificate coded following the rules of UN/EDIFACT syntax. There will be three possible different outputs from the CertMap module:

– A derived EDIFACT certificate coded according to the UN/EDIFACT syntax rules, if the input to the CertMap was a X.509 certificate DER coded and the derivation process has been successfully completed.

– A derived X.509 certificate DER coded; if the input to the CertMap was an EDIFACT certificate and the derivation process has been successfully completed.

– An error indication if it has not been possible for the CertMap to complete the generation of the derived certificate.

Comparison between X.509 and EDIFACT certificates. The CertMap module accomplishes the two- way translation of the certificates. It receives as input an EDIFACT certificate (printable characters) or X.509 (codified by the DER rules) and it respectively returns a new certificate X.509 or EDIFACT. But the X.509 and EDIFACT certificates have a lot of meaningful differences.

– The X.509 certificate is syntactically different from the EDIFACT certificate. The first incompatibility between both certificates is related to the syntax used for its definition. In the X.509 environment the ASN.1 Abstract Syntax is used, whereas in EDIFACT the certificates are specified following the EDIFACT syntax. Concerning the transfer syntax for the transmission, also it exists interoperability problems. In the X.509 environment is used the DER rules, on the other hand in EDIFACT the information is transmitted codified in printable characters.

– Other aspect to take into account is the different Name Systems used. In the X.509 world, the basic mechanism of identification is the Distinguished Name (DN), which is associated with an entry in the DIT (Directory Information Tree) of the X.500 Distributed Directory. Furthermore the X.509 certificate supports a variety of types of names apart from the DNS, as the RFC822 name, the URLs and even the EDI party names. On the other hand the EDIFACT certificate supports both codes (i.e. identifiers assigned by authorities) and EDI party names. However the new version of the EDIFACT certificate incorporates mechanisms that allow to carry Distinguished Names in certain fields of this certificate. The DEDICA gateway accomplishes a names mapping between the Distinguished Names and the EDI Names, according to some guidelines defined in EDIRA (EDIRA Memorandum of Understanding) [9]. EDIRA proposes an identification mechanism compatible with the DN strategy in X.500. In this way the EDI users will can make use of the X.500 Distributed Directory, using the entity registration for EDI entities proposed by EDIRA.

– The time information of the X.509 and EDIFACT certificates are also different. Whereas the EDIFACT certificate contains elements to specify the generation time and the revocation date of the certificate, the X.509 certificate does not maintain these data.

— Whereas the X.509 certificate version 3 uses the extension mechanism in order to include additional contents to the ones defined in version 1, the EDIFACT certificate does not apply any mechanism to expand its semantic. Below are listed some examples of these extensions.

- Certificate Policies and Policy Mappings. The X.509 certificate has the ability of identify the policies that define the use of the certificate and the keys related to the certificate, and it allows to specify a list of relations of equivalence between certificate policies.
- Certificate Path Constraints. X.509 allows the specification of constraints on certification paths. By means of a X.509 extension it is possible to identify whether the subject of the certificate is a CA and how deep a certification path may exist through that CA.
- Name Constraints. It is possible to indicate a name space within which all subject names in subsequent certificates in a certification path must be located.
- Alternative Names. It allows to specify alternative name formats for the subject and issuer of the certificate, as a X.500 Directory Name, a TCP/IP DNS name and IP address, RFC822 name, URLs and even EDI party names.

Specifications of CertMap Mapping Rules This section is mainly devoted to show the mapping rules that the DEDICA gateway will follow to convert certificates of one type (X.509 or EDIFACT) in certificates of other type (EDIFACT or X.509). Mapping rules must respect the semantics of data elements, fields and extensions, and must try to include as many information contained in the original certificate in the new certificate generated by the gateway. However, the high amount of extensions already defined in the X.509 version 3 implies that there will be situations when this will be impossible. There will be X.509 extensions that will not be mapped into data elements of standard EDIFACT certificates. However these EDIFACT certificate related to these X.509 certificates, can still be used in the EDIFACT world, because they will contain almost all the needed information that makes an initial EDIFACT certificate operative in these domains. As it has been said before, the UN/EDIFACT segments are made up by composite elements and simple data elements, and the composite elements by simple data elements. The notation that will be used in the following sections in order to specify an EDIFACT element is corresponded with a dotted notation, in which the element is named from the element more general to the element that is required to specify. In this way, if it is required to specify a simple data element that is included into a composite element of a segment, the notation will be the following :

```
<Segment>.<CompositeElement>.<SimpleDataElement>
```

This clause presents the global rules that the DEDICA gateway will apply to map the fields and extensions of X.509 certificate to data elements of EDIFACT certificate. Each field of the X.509 certificate that will be mapped in an element of the new EDIFACT certificate will be listed and its mapping specified. The fields that will no be mapped in any element, will not be listed below.

Serial Number

This element uniquely identifies one certificate issued by the CA. The DEDICA gateway numbers the certificates that it generates, and puts this generated serial number into the USC.0536 element.

Signature (algorithm)

This field specifies the hash algorithm used by the CA, and the algorithm to encipher this hash value.

EDIFACT owns two data element to contain both the hash applied by the CA and the algorithm used to encrypt this hash value, whereas the X.509 certificate only has one field that contain both the hash and encipher algorithm used by the CA. The hash value will be indicated in the USA[CAHashing].S502.0527, and the cipher algorithm in the USA[CASigning].S502.0527.

In DEDICA only two kinds of signatures are considered : `sha1withRsasignature` and `md5WithRsa`.

Validity

There are four USC.S501 time elements inside the EDIFACT certificate each one of them related to both the **validity before** and the **validity after** fields, in which these X.509 fields will be mapped. In the EDIFACT certificate there are two additional USC.S501 time elements. One of them specifies the certificate generation time, and its values will be generated by the DEDICA gateway, and the fourth one specifies the revocation time; and it will not appear in an EDIFACT derived certificate.

Subject

This field identifies the certificate owner, and it is mapped following the names mapping rules defined by DEDICA [5] in the USC.S500.0586 element related to the owner.

SubjectPublicKeyInfo

This field is used to carry the owner public key and identify the algorithm with which the key is used.

The EDIFACT certificate carries the public key in the USA[owner].S503 element. In the case of a RSA public key, this key is structured in three occurrences of this element: one of them is related to the key modulus, another one to the exponent, and the third one to the length in bits of the modulus. The owner public key carried in the *SubjectPublicKeyInfo* is mapped in these three occurrences of the USA[owner].S503 element.

The identification of the algorithm with which the key is used will be mapped in the USA[owner].S502.0527 element. Because in a first phase, only the rsa algorithm will be supported, the USA[owner].S502.0527 element of the EDIFACT certificate will specify the use of the RSA algorithm.

KeyUsage Extension

This field indicates the purpose for which the certified public key is used, and it is mapped in the USA[owner].S502.0523 element. If it specifies a digital signature use, then this EDIFACT element will contain a value indicating the certified public key is used by the issuer to sign. If it specify a key encipherment use, then the USA[owner].S502.0523 element will indicate that the public key is used by the owner to encipher. But if this extension specifies any other use, then this extension will not be mapped.

SubjectAltName Extension

This field contains one or more alternative names, using any of a variety of name forms, for the certificate subject.

If the name format that is used is *EDIPartyName*, then it can be mapped in the USC.S500.0586 element related to the owner.

AuthorityKeyIdentifier Extension

This extension identifies the CAs key used to sign the certificate, and it is mapped in the USC.S500.0538 element, corresponding to the USC.S500 related to the issuer.

SubjectKeyIdentifier Extension

This extension identifies the public key being certified, and it is mapped in the USC.S500.0538 element, corresponding to the USC.S500 related to the certificate owner.

The following tables show the mapping between X.509 fields/extensions and EDIFACT data elements. The first column is the initial X.509 field/extension of the X.509 certificate; the mapping result is filled in the EDIFACT data element of the second column.

Only the extensions that DEDICA can map are shown.

Table 1. Mapping between X.509 fields and extension, and EDIFACT data elements.

Field(X.509)	Data Element(EDIFACT)
version	USC.0545 CERTIFICATE SYNTAX VERSION,CODED
serialNumber	USC.0536 CERTIFICATE REFERENCE
tbsCertificate.signature	USA(CA-E).S502.0527 Algorithm, coded
	USA(CA-H).S502.0527 Algorithm, coded
	USA(CA-E).S502.0525 Crypt. mode of operation, coded
	USA(CA-H).S502.0525 Crypt. mode of operation, coded
issuer	Not mapped
validity	USC.S501 SECURITY DATE AND TIME
subject	(see Names Mapping Strategy, Deliverable DST2 [5])
subjectPublicKeyInfo	USA(OW).S502.0527 Algorithm , coded
issuerUniqueIdentifier	(field not mapped)
subjectUniqueIdentifier	(field not mapped)

Extension X.509	Data Element(EDIFACT)
KeyUsage	USA(OW).S502.0523 (Use of algorithm coded)
subjectAltName.ediPartyName	USC.S500.0586 (Security Party Name)
authorityKeyIdentifier	USC.S500.0538 (Key Name)
subjectKeyIdentifier	USC.S500.0538 (Key Name)

Internal Structure of the CertMap Module. In the internal design of the CertMap module, different kinds of modules have been identified :

- The **CM_Kernel** module (**CM_KE**). This module coordinates the operations performed by the rest of the modules in CertMap. It receives as input an original EDIFACT certificate (USC-USA(3)-USR) or a X.509 certificate DER encoded. If the derived certificate is successfully generated, CM_KE returns it to MangMap; in other case an error code is returned.
  Mapping Functions related to modules. A set of modules related to different functions needed during the mapping between the initial and the derived certificates has been identified. Below a short description of each one is given:
  - The **CM_Names** module (**CM_NM**) performs the mapping between the Edi Names and the X.509 Names (Distinguished Names).
  - The **CM_Algorithm** module (**CM_AL**) maps the identifiers of algorithms and cryptographic modes of operation.
  - The **CM_Time** module (**CM_TM**) maps the information related with dates and times of both certificates.
  - The **CM_Filter** module (**CM_FF**) applies the filter function specified, to the digital signature of a derived EDIFACT certificate, or to a public key.
  - The **CM_Keys** module (**CM_PK**) manage the mapping between keys and key names implied in the certificates.
- The **EDIFACT certificate coding/encoding** module (**CM_CE**). This module will be able to extract all the information contained in an EDIFACT certificate. The EDIFACT certificate information is stored in form of internal variables of an agreed structured data type to manipulate it during the mapping process. This module is also able to generate the characters stream corresponding to a derived EDIFACT certificate from an initial X.509 certificate.
- A set of **APIs** needed to allow the CM_KE to interact with external software tools. Two of these tools have been identified as necessary : an ASN.1 tool and a cryptographic tool. The APIs needed are the following :
  - The **CM_KE:ASN1 API**. This API will provide with means for the CM_KE to extract the information from the DER coded X.509 initial certificate. This information is stored in form of variables of an agreed type to allow the modules of the CertMap to manipulate it. It will also provide means for the CM_KE to order to the ASN.1 tool to get the DER stream corresponding to a derived X.509 certificate from an initial EDIFACT certificate.
  - The **CM_KE:CRYPTOGRAPHIC API**. This API will provide with means of the CM_KE to interact with cryptographic tools that will allow to sign the derived certificates.

In DEDICA, a table that contains mapping information was defined : **The Names Mapping Table**. This table will establish links between initial and derived certificates. These links are generated by CertMap module. In consequence, an explicit connection between CertMap and the Names Mapping Table must appear.

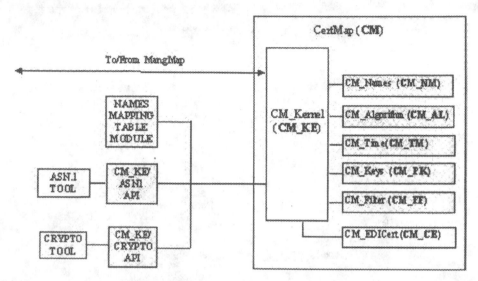

Fig. 3. CertMap module structure.

Sequence of operations In this clause, a more detailed view of the sequence of operations that will take place inside the CertMap to generate a derived certificate from the initial one, is shown.

Mapping from X.509 to EDIFACT. The figure below is a graphical representation of these operations. It shows how the CM_KE module co-ordinates the actuation of internal modules and external tools to generate a derived EDIFACT certificate from an initial X.509 one.

It can be seen how the different parts of the system take part in the generation of the derived certificate. It has to be pointed out that the effective mapping process is performed, as it has been said before by modules CM_NM, CM_AL, CM_TM, CM_PK and CM_FF. It has to be remarked that the filtering of the public key is part of the mapping of the public key in the certificate .

The following table shows a high level description of the tasks that allow to generate an EDIFACT derived certificate from an initial X.509 certificate.

Mapping from EDIFACT to X.509. The opposite sense is very similar to the previous case. In this case the CM_CE module extracts information of the original X.509 certificate, and puts it into a variable of agreed data type. The mapping modules make their tasks and the names, time, algorithm and public key information is mapped into the new X.509. Then the DER code for the *tobeSigned*

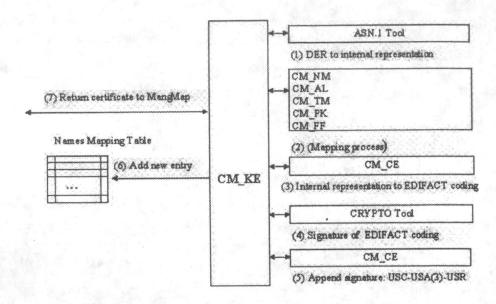

Fig. 4. Mapping process from X.509 to EDIFACT.

part of the X.509 certificate is generated by the ASN.1 tool, and the Cryptographic tool is used to sign the DER code of the *tobeSigned* part of the derived X.509 certificate. Since a new interrelationship between a X.509 and EDIFACT certificate is built, a new entry to the Names Mapping Table must be added. Now the ASN.1 tool is again used in order to generate the DER code for the whole X.509 derived certificate. Finally the new derived X.509 certificate is returned to the MangMap.

Table 2. Mapping between X.509 fields and extension, and EDIFACT data elements.

```
1. Extract information of the initial X.509 certificate using the ASN.1
   tool through the CM_KE:ASN1 API and put such information into a
   variable of agreed data type.
2. Map names, time, algorithm, and public key information.
3. Code the USC-USA (3) according to EDIFACT syntax.
4. Sign this character stream using the Cryptographic tool through the
   CM_KE:Cryptographic API.
5. Code the USR segment and add it to the USC-USA (3) stream.
6. Add new entry to the Names Mapping Table.
7. Return derived EDIFACT certificate.
```

3.2   MangMap module

The DEDICA gateway has to convert certain of the KEYMAN message operations into equivalent operations in the X.509 PKI (including X.500 access).

This is accomplished by the MangMap module of the DEDICA gateway. The MangMap module is also the general management module of DEDICA. It receives all the requests sent to the gateway and decides which information has to be recovered from external repositories, which type of translation is needed, and which results must be generated and sent to the requesting entity.

Internal structure of the MangMap module. The most important blocks in the MangMap are the following:

– **MangMap Kernel (MK) module**

The MangMap Kernel module handles different types of requests from both KM and XH and co-ordinates the execution of all the steps needed to perform the request.

– **KEYMAN Handling (KH) module**

This module can receive requests from an end user and from the kernel block. On reception of KEYMAN messages from an end user, it checks the protection applied to the KEYMAN, analyses it, interprets and converts the message into an internal request to the MangMap Kernel block. On reception of requests from the MangMap Kernel block, it builds KEYMAN messages, applies the required protection and makes the KEYMAN available to the communication services.

– **X.509 Public Key Infrastructure Messages Handling (XH) module**

On reception of relevant X.509 public key infrastructure messages from an end user, the XH module checks the protection applied to the message, analyses it and converts the message into an internal request to the MK.

It can also access the X.500 Directory in order to obtain X.509 certificates, revocation lists and certification paths. XH will be able to send requests to X.500 and to obtain and interpret answers from it.

On reception of requests from MK, it builds relevant X.509 public key infrastructure messages, applies the required protection and makes the message available to the communication service.

Figure 5 shows the building blocks of MangMap module and its relationships with the CertMap module.

Information flow example: Derived EDIFACT certificate request. This section shows the information flow inside the building blocks of MangMap module, when an X.509 certificated user requests a derived EDIFACT certificate. A slightly different flow occurs when validation of this certificate is required. The following list shows a high level description of the task performed by the building blocks in the gateway.

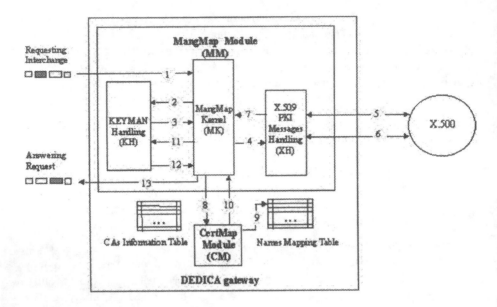

Fig. 5. Derived EDIFACT certificate request.

1. The requesting interchange arrives at the MangMap Kernel (MK) block in MangMap. This interchange will carry a KEYMAN message with a package containing the DER- coded X.509 certificate, or even the users DER-coded Distinguished Name.
2. MK identifies the request and passes the interchange to the KEYMAN Handling (KH) block.
3. KH analyses the KEYMAN message and sends the request information back to the MK in order to provide the derived certificate.
4. MK instructs the X.509 PKI Messages Handling block (XH) to access the X.500 DIT entries to retrieve all the necessary information to verify the validity of the initial X.509 certificate (the original X.509 certificate and CRLs).
5. XH retrieves the relevant Certificate Revocation List from the X.500 Directory and checks whether the initial certificate has been revoked.
6. XH retrieves the Certification Path from the X.500 Directory and verifies the signatures of the involved CAs.
7. If the initial certificate has not been revoked and the Certification Path has been successfully verified, XH notifies MK that the corresponding derived EDIFACT certificate can be generated.
8. MK then instructs the CertMap module to generate the EDIFACT certificate.
9. The CertMap generates the derived certificate and also creates a new entry in the Names Mapping Table associating both initial and derived certificates.
10. The CertMap module passes the derived certificate to the MK module.
11. MK passes the derived certificate to the KH module.

12. KH then builds the response and passes it to MK. This response will contain the KEYMAN message with the derived EDIFACT certificate. It can also contain a package with the initial X.509.

13. MK passes the answer interchange to the communication system.

X.500 Distributed Directory Access. As mentioned before, the DEDICA gateway needs to access the X.500 Distributed Directory in order to retrieve X.509 certificates and CRLs. This is accomplished mainly by the X.509 Public Key Infrastructure Messages Handler (XH module).

The management of the directory objects and the search methods that are used, are based on the standard defined in the X.500 recommendation of the ITU-T.

X.500 defines the Directory Access Protocol (DAP) for clients to use when contacting Directory servers. DAP is a heavyweight protocol that runs on a full OSI stack and requires a significant volume of computing resources to run.

Given the complexity of DAP, the X.509 Public Key Infrastructure Messages Handler uses a LDAP (Lightweight Directory Access Protocol) [12] interface to access the X.500 Directory. LDAP runs directly on TCP and provides most of the functionality of DAP at a much lower cost.

LDAP offers all the needed functionality to interact with the X.500 Directory. The conversion of requests from LDAP to DAP is achieved by an LDAP server, which operates as a DUA (Directory User Agent) of the Directory.

4 Systems where DEDICA is being integrated

The DEDICA consortium has developed both the gateway and client software that is being integrated within the existing EDI applications. Within the project several pilots schemes have been launched in the following fields: Customs, EDI software providers, electronic payment in banking and public administration application forms for Electronic Commerce.

DEDICA is also being integrated as part of the TEDIC system. The TEDIC system has been developed by ALCATEL/URACOM, and it offers a legal solution for the establishment of a specific "interchange agreement" between the involved parties for EDI Trade transactions, without any prior contact. The TEDIC system offers a set of security services for the different kinds of messages based on a range of security levels. It sets up a hierarchy based on a system of security policies, and allows dynamic and automatic negotiation of the transaction policy level. The integration of the DEDICA gateway in the TEDIC system implies that the TEDIC users can not only use the EDIFACT certification, but they can also use X.509 certificates. In this way all the users registered in an X.509 PKI can become TEDIC users, and they do not also need to register in an EDIFACT CA. DEDICA will generate X.509 certificates for the TEDIC users that wish to communicate with X.509 users.

A project is being developed by AECOC (the EAN Spanish representative)[2] and UPC (Technical University of Catalonia), whose main objective is to specify and develop tools that permit to secure EANCOM interchanges[3] and exchange them using Internet. The security services applied follow the standards developed by the UN/EDIFACT "Security Joint Working Group" (SJWG). In this scenario, DEDICA is being integrated into an X.509 Certification Authority developed by esCERT-UPC[4]. The esCERT-UPC organization provides help and advice on computer security and incident handling, and it is sponsored by UPC (Technical University of Catalonia), CICYT (Interministerial Science and Technology Commission), the Generalitat of Catalonia and the European Union. The integration of the DEDICA gateway and the esCERT-UPC X.509 Certification Authority, makes it possible for X.509 CA to manage security objects of the EDI infrastructure.

The DEDICA gateway extends the range of users and the infrastructures with which the AECOC-UPC system can interact. The system is more heterogeneous, not only capable of acting in a closed EDI world, but also able to manage the security objects of other infrastructures, suche as the X.509 certificates of an X.509 PKI.

5 Future Work

Part of the DEDICA project consortium is still working in order to extend the gateways functionality, especially in the domain of validation and revocation management.

In EDIFACT, a Certificate Revocation List is a KEYMAN message, digitally signed by the CA, containing the identifiers of certificates that have been revoked by the issuing CA. A receiver of a signed EDIFACT message with a certificate can retrieve the CRL from a publicly accessible repository to determine whether that certificate is on the list of revoked certificates. Alternatively, a security domain could delegate the facility for validating individual certificates to a trusted authoritative entity. In this context, users wanting to validate a received certificate would request validation by sending a KEYMAN message to this trusted entity.

At present, revocation management is solved indirectly: the user can request the validation of a derived EDIFACT certificate from the gateway; the gateway then recovers the original X.509 certificate related to the derived certificate, and it searches for this certificate in appropriate CRLs published in the X.500 Directory.

---

[2] AECOC: Since 1977 AECOC has been the representative of EAN International in Spain. AECOC is responsible for the management and promotion of the bar-codes of products and services, and Electronic Data Interchange (EDI), http://www.aecoc.es

[3] EANCOM is responsible for the management of profiles of EDIFACT messages standardized by EAN.

[4] esCERT-UPC: Spanish Computer Emergency Response Team, http://escert.upc.es

The DEDICA gateways revocation management could then go through the EDIFACT Revocation Lists of derived certificates generated by the gateway. The DEDICA gateway could periodically check the status of the initial X.509 certificates. When an X.509 original certificate was revoked, the derived certificate related to it would also have to be considered as revoked. The gateway would generate the KEYMAN message with the corresponding revocation list of EDIFACT derived certificates, and it would publish it in the X.500 Distributed Directory.

When the DEDICA gateway received a validation request for an EDIFACT derived certificate, it would look at this EDIFACT CRL in the X.500. If this certificate was not on this list, it would follow the normal process previously outlined.

6 Conclusions

Interoperability between the X.509 and EDIFACT PKIs can be greatly enhanced by facilities such as the DEDICA gateway, which acts as a TTP capable of offering a basic set of certificates management services to user of both infrastructures.

The DEDICA project has developed a gateway to translate security objects between X.509 and EDIFACT. This solution also provides interoperability between EDIFACT and all the other tools used in electronic commerce, since all of them authenticate the entities using X.509 certificates.

The DEDICA gateway is presently being integrated into several pilots schemes and projects in the field of electronic certification, such as the TEDIC system, the AECOC-UPC EDI on Internet project, or in the esCERT X.509 Certification Authority

The DEDICA gateway should be of interest to both large-scale enterprise and SMEs, however it is especially useful for SMEs. This is because it allows for security in the interchange of messages, without the need to pay registration fees for several different infrastructures. This is the reason why the DEDICA project was selected as one of the G8 pilot projects to promote the use of Information Technology in SMEs. The sharing of the certification infrastructure between the e-mail or distributed applications users and the EDI users will quickly satisfy the EDI users requirements for global service provision. The integration of public key certificates from X.509 and EDI will provide means to share common information and infrastructure over the most widely used telematics application: email, and the most economical: EDI. The main advantage for the user will be the possibility of sharing the authentication mechanism (digital signature, tools, etc.) between the various applications, thus avoiding the burden of having to register for different services to satisfy one single user requirement.

Moreover, the service has been quickly deployed and made available, thanks to the fact that no additional registration infrastructure is needed, due to its compatibility with the EDIFACT and X.509 infrastructures. This service will promote the use of Internet by EDI applications (since it will allow them to secure the interchanges which have been identified) in contrast to the major barriers to the deployment of EDI over Internet which existed in the past.

Another functional advantage of the DEDICA gateway is the independence of the communication protocols used by the applications, and their transparency for both the PKI users. In this way, an EDI/X.509 user should not know that the certificate that he is managing is a certificate automatically generated by the DEDICA gateway, and deriving from an X.509/EDIFACT certificate.

As part of the the several pilots schemes have been launched to demonstrate the system in the following fields: customs, electronic chambers of commerce, tourism, electronic products manufacturers, EDI software providers and electronic payment in banking and public administration.

References

1. Security Joint Working Group, Proposed Draft of a MIG Handbook UN/EDIFACT Message KEYMAN, 30 June 1995.
2. Security Joint Working Group: Committee Draft UN/EDIFACT CD 9735-5, Electronic Data Interchange for Administration, Commerce and Transport (EDIFACT) - Application Level Syntax Rules, Part 5: Security Rules for Batch EDI (Authenticity: Integrity and Non-Repudiation of Origin, Release 1, 14. December 1995.
3. United Nations, Economic and Social Council, Economic Commission for Europe, Committee on the Development of Trade: TRADE/WP.4/R.1026/Add.2, EDIFACT Security Implementation Guidelines, 22 February 1994.
4. DEDICA Consortium, CEC Deliverable WP03.DST1: Technical description of X.509 and UN/EDIFACT certificates, July 1996.
5. DEDICA Consortium, CEC Deliverable WP03.DST2: Naming Conversion Rules Specifications Requirements, July 1996.
6. DEDICA Consortium, CEC Deliverable WP03.DST3: Final Specifications of CertMap Conversion Rules, July 1996.
7. Network Working Group, RFC 1779: A String Representation of Distinguished Names, ISODE Consortium, 1995.
8. UN/EDIFACT: Draft Directory. Part 1, http://www.unicc.org/unece/trade/untdid/.
9. EDIRA - Memorandum of Understanding for the Operation of EDI Registration Authorities, Final Draft. November, 1993.
10. Network Working Group, RFC 1617: Naming and Structuring Guidelines for X.500 Directory Pilots, 1994.
11. Network Working Group, INTERNET- DRAFT: A Summary of the X.500(96) User Schema for use with LDAPv3, 1997.
12. Tim Howes, M. Smith, RFC 1823: The LDAP Application Program Interface, Network Working Group, University of Michigan, 1995.
13. PKIX Working Group: Internet Public Key Infrastructure - Part III: Certificate Management Protocols, Internet Draft, June 1996.
14. Fritz Bauspie, Juan Carlos Cruellas, Montse Rubia, DEDICA Directory based EDI Certificate Access and Management, Digital Signature Conference, July, 1996.
15. Juan Carlos Cruellas, Hoyt L. Kesterson II, Manel Medina, Montse Rubia, EDI and Digital Signatures for Business to Business Electronic Commerce, Jurimetrics Journal, Spring 1998.

Hash Functions and the MAC Using All-or-Nothing Property

Sang Uk Shin[1], Kyung Hyune Rhee[1], and Jae Woo Yoon[2]

[1] Department of Computer Science, PuKyong National University,
599-1, Daeyeon-dong, Nam-gu, Pusan, 608-737, Korea
shinsu@woongbi.pknu.ac.kr , khrhee@dolphin.pknu.ac.kr,
WWW home page: http://unicorn.pknu.ac.kr/~soshin and ~khrhee
[2] Coding Technology Section,
Electronics and Telecommunications Research Institute,
161, Kajong-dong, Yusong-gu,Taejon, 305-350, Korea
jyoon@etri.re.kr

Abstract. All-or-nothing property is a new encryption mode proposed by Rivest and has the property that one must decrypt the entire ciphertext to determine any plaintext block. In this paper, we propose a hash function with all-or-nothing property. The proposed scheme can use the existing hash functions without changing their structures, and it is secure against all of known attacks. Moreover, the proposed method can be easily extended to the MAC(Message Authentication Code) and provide message confidentiality as well as authentication.

1 Introduction

Hash functions are functions that map bitstrings of arbitrary finite length into strings of fixed length. They play an important role in modern cryptography as a tool for providing integrity and authentication. The basic idea of hash functions is that a hash value serves as a compressed representative image of an input string and can be used for uniquely identifying that string. Hash functions are classified into two classes[6] : unkeyed hash function with single parameter - a message, and keyed hash function with two distinct inputs - a message and secret key. Keyed hash functions are used to construct the MAC(Message Authentication Code). The MAC is widely used to provide data integrity and data origin authentication.

Rivest proposed the new encryption mode, referred to the "all-or-nothing encryption mode"[11]. This mode has the property that one must decrypt the entire ciphertext before one can determine even one message block. One of the design principles of a hash function is to make hash value dependent on the entire input message and to make finding collision hard. For existing hash functions, it may find a collision by modifying any blocks of the input message. In this paper, we propose a secure hash function with all-or-nothing property which is a new encryption mode proposed by Rivest. The proposed scheme uses the existing hash functions without changing the hash algorithm, and makes them secure against known attacks. Also the proposed scheme can be easily extended to the MAC, which can provide a message confidentiality as well as authentication.

The remainder of this paper is organized as follows. In section 2, we summarize the hash function and in section 3, all-or-nothing property is described. In section 4, we propose and analyze a new construction scheme of the hash function using all-or-nothing property. Finally, we have conclusions in section 5.

2   Hash functions

Hash functions(more exactly cryptographic hash functions) are functions that map bitstrings of arbitrary finite length into strings of fixed length. This output is commonly called a hash value, a message digest, or a fingerprint. Given h and an input x, computing $h(x)$ must be easy. A one-way hash function must satisfy the following properties[6];

- *preimage resistance* : it is computationally infeasible to find any input which hashes to any pre-specified output. That is, given a y in the image of h, it is computationally infeasible to find an input x such that $h(x) = y$.
- *second preimage resistance* : it is computationally infeasible to find any second input which has the same output as any specified input. That is, given a x in the image of $h(x)$, it is computationally infeasible to find an input $x' \neq x$ such that $h(x') = y$.

A cryptographically useful hash function must satisfy the following additional property[6] :

- *collision resistance* : it is computationally infeasible to find a collision. That is, it is computationally infeasible to find a pair of two distinct inputs x and x' such that $h(x) = h(x')$.

Almost all hash functions are iterative processes which hash inputs of arbitrary length by processing successive fixed-size blocks of input. The input X is padded to a multiple of block length and subsequently divided into t blocks X_1 through X_t. The hash function h can then be described as follows:

$$H_0 = IV, \quad H_i = f(H_{i-1}, X_i), \quad 1 \leq i \leq t, \quad h(X) = H_t$$

Where f is the *compression function* of h, H_i is the *chaining variable* between stage $i - 1$ and stage i, and IV is the initial value.
The block diagram of the iterative hash function using the compression function is shown in the Fig. 1.

The computation of the hash value is dependent on the chaining variable. At the start of hashing, this chaining variable has a fixed initial value which is specified as part of the algorithm. The compression function is then used to update the value of this chaining variable in a suitably complex way under the action and influence of part of the message being hashed. This process continues

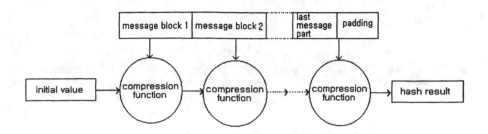

Fig. 1. The use of a compression function in an iterative hash function

recursively, with the chaining variable being updated under the action of different part of the message, until all the message has been used. The final value of the chaining variable is then output as the hash value corresponding to that message.

Based on the construction of the internal compression function, hash functions can be classified as followings[6];

- hash functions based on block ciphers
- hash functions based on modular arithmetic
- dedicated hash functions

Dedicated hash functions have fast processing speed and are independent of other system subcomponents such as block cipher and modular multiplication subcomponent. Most of existing dedicated hash functions have the structure similar to that of MD4[9] which is designed by R. Rivest in 1990. The typical examples of the dedicated hash functions are the MD family hash functions such as MD5[10], RIPEMD-160[3], SHA-1[4], HAVAL[14], and SMD[13].

According to the theory of Merkle[7] and Damgård[2], *MD-strengthening* denotes appending an additional block at the end of the input string containing its length. It is possible to relate the security of hash function h to the security of compression function f and output function g according to the following theorem.

Theorem 1. [5] Let h be an iterative hash function with MD-strengthening. Then finding preimage and second preimage on h have the same complexity as the corresponding attacks on the compression function f and the output function g.

An n-bit hash function has *ideal security* satisfies the following;

(a) Given a hash value, finding a preimage and second preimage require about 2^n operations.
(b) Finding collision pairs require about $2^{n/2}$ operations.

Given a specific hash function, it is desirable to be able to prove a lower bound on the complexity of attacking it. But such results are rarely known. Typically, the security of a hash function is the complexity of the applicable known attack.

3 All-or-nothing property

In 1997, Rivest proposed an all-or-nothing encryption, a new encryption mode for block ciphers[11]. This mode has the property that one must decrypt the entire ciphertext before one can determine even one message block. This means that brute-force searches against all-or-nothing encryption are slowed down by a factor equal to the number of blocks in the ciphertext.

The problem with most popular encryption modes is that the adversary can obtain one block of plaintext by decrypting just one block of ciphertext. This makes the adversary's key-search problem relatively easy, since decrypting a single ciphertext block is enough to test a candidate key.

Let us say that an encryption mode for a block cipher is *separable* if it has the property that an adversary can determine one block of plaintext by decrypting just one block of ciphertext. Rivest defined *strongly non-separable* mode as follows[11]:

Definition 1. Suppose that a block cipher encryption mode transforms a sequence $m_1, m_2, \ldots, m_s$ of s message blocks into a sequence $c_1, c_2, \ldots, c_t$ of t ciphertext blocks for some $t, t \geq s$. We say that the encryption mode is *strongly non-separable* if it is infeasible to determine even one message block m_i (or any property of a particular message block m_i) without decrypting all t ciphertext blocks.

Rivest proposed the strongly non-separable modes as follows[11]:

- Transform the message sequence $m_1, m_2, \ldots, m_s$ into a "pseudo-message" sequence $m'_1, m'_2, \ldots, m'_{s'}$ (for some $s' \geq s$) with an "all-or-nothing transform".
- Encrypt the pseudo-message with an ordinary encryption mode with the given cryptographic key K to obtain the ciphertext sequence $c_1, c_2, \ldots, c_t$.

We call encryption mode of this type "all-or-nothing encryption modes." To make this work, the all-or-nothing transform has to have certain properties as the following[11]:

Definition 2. A transform T mapping a message sequence $m_1, m_2, \ldots, m_s$ into a pseudo-message sequence $m'_1, m'_2, \ldots, m'_{s'}$ is said to be an *all-or-nothing transform* if

(1) The transform T is reversible: given the pseudo-message sequence, one can obtain the original message sequence.
(2) Both the transform T and its inverse are efficiently computable.
(3) It is computationally infeasible to compute any function of any message block if any one of the pseudo-message block is unknown.

An all-or-nothing encryption mode is strongly non-separable. The all-or-nothing transform is not itself encryption, since it makes no use of any secret key information. The actual encryption is the operation that encrypts the pseudo-message.

An all-or-nothing transform is a fixed public transform that anyone can perform on the message to obtain the pseudo-message, or invert given the pseudo-message to obtain the original message.

Rivest proposed the all-or-nothing transform which is referred to "package transform", as follows[11]:

(1) Let the input message be $m_1, m_2, \ldots, m_s$.
(2) Choose at random a key K for the package transform block cipher.
(3) Compute the output sequence $m'_1, m'_2, \ldots, m'_{s'}$ for $s' = s + 1$ as follows:
   - $m'_i = m_i \oplus E(K, i)$ for $i = 1, 2, 3, \ldots, s$.
   - Let

$$m'_{s'} = K \oplus h_1 \oplus \ldots \oplus h_s,$$

where

$$h_i = E(K_0, m'_i \oplus i) \ for \ i = 1, 2, \ldots, s,$$

where K_0 is a fixed, publically-known encryption key.

The block cipher for the package transform does not use a secret key, and needs not be the same as the block cipher for encrypting the pseudo-message. We assume that the key space for the package transform block cipher is sufficiently large that brute-force searching for a key is infeasible. It is easy to see that the package transform is invertible:

$$K = m'_{s'} \oplus h_1 \oplus \ldots \oplus h_s,$$

$$m_i = m'_i \oplus E(K, i) \ for \ i = 1, 2, \ldots, s.$$

If any block of pseudo-message sequence is unknown, the K can not be computed, and so it is infeasible to compute any message block.

An all-or-nothing transform is merely a pre-processing step, and so it can be used with already-existing encryption software and device, without changing the encryption algorithm. The legitimate communicants pay a penalty of approximately a factor of three in the time it takes them to encrypt or decrypt in all-or-nothing mode, compared to an ordinary separable encryption mode. However, an adversary attempting a brute-force attack pays a penalty of a factor of t, where t is the number of blocks in the ciphertext.

In the following section, we propose a construction scheme of hash function with all-or-nothing property. Our aim of a new design of the hash function is to obtain a fixed hash value dependent on the entire message, and to identify uniquely the message. Thus all-or-nothing property dependent on the entire message is suitable for constructing a hash function. In next section, we propose the construction scheme of the hash function with all-or-nothing property.

4 A hash function with all-or-nothing property

In this section, we propose the construction scheme of the hash function with all-or-nothing property. First, we propose three construction methods of all-or-nothing hash function and then analyze their security. Also, we apply them to the MAC, which can provide the message confidentiality as well as message authentication. We use the following notations on all of the paper:

- n : a length of an output and a chaining variable of a hash function
- k : a block size of a hash function
- X : an input message
- X' : a pseudo-message resulting from the all-or-nothing transform
- K : a randomly chosen k-bit key
- K_p : a fixed and publically-known k-bit key
- $h()$: an arbitrary hash function
- $h_x(y)$: hash an input y with an initial value x
- IV : initial value of a hash function
- $\oplus$: bitwise XOR
- $\|$: concatenation
- $\bar{Z}$: make n-bit Z to k-bit by iterating it

4.1 All-or-nothing hash function 1(AON hashing-1)

The simple all-or-nothing hash function works as follows:

A. Sender

(1) Partitioning the input message X into t k-bit block, $X_1, X_2, \ldots, X_t$
(2) Generating a random key k-bit K
(3) Compute the pseudo-message and the message digest as follows:
$H_0=IV$, $X'_{t+1} = K$
for $i = 1$ to t {
$\quad X'_i = X_i \oplus f(K, H_{i-1}, i)$
$\quad X'_{t+1} = X'_{t+1} \oplus g(K_p, X'_i, i)$
$\quad H_i = h_{H_{i-1}}(X'_i)$
}
$H_{t+1} = h_{H_t}(X'_i)$
(4) send $(X'\|H_{t+1})$.

B. Receiver

(1) Receive $(X'\|MD)$.
(2) Partitioning the pseudo-message X' into $t+1$ k-bit block, $X'_1, X'_2, \ldots, X'_{t+1}$
(3) Recover the random key K

$$K = X'_{t+1} \oplus g(K_p, X'_1, 1) \oplus \ldots \oplus g(K_p, X'_t, t)$$

(4) Recover the original message and check the message digest $H_0 = IV$
for $i = 1$ to t {
$\quad H_i = h_{H_{i-1}}(X'_i)$
$\quad X_i = X'_i \oplus f(K, H_{i-1}, i)$
}
$H_{t+1} = h_{H_t}(X'_{t+1})$

(5) If H_{t+1} is not equal to MD, reject the received message.

Here $f()$, $g()$ must be selected to satisfy the properties of the all-or-nothing transform described in section 3. Rivest proposed the construction scheme based on block cipher. This pays a penalty of approximately a factor of three in the time it takes them to encrypt or decrypt in all-or-nothing mode for legitimate communicants, compared to an ordinary separable encryption mode. For the efficient computation, We apply the round function of the block cipher. As a concrete example, we use SHA-1 hash function and the modified round function of RC6[12] which is submitted to AES. The simulation result shows that the performance of AON hashing-1 using the modified round function of RC6 is 12.17Mbytes/sec, while that of applying the entire block cipher is 3.66 Mbytes/sec.

As an another all-or-nothing transform, it is possible to apply the bijective function. First, choose the bijective function f mapping the entire input message to pseudo-message, and compute the pseudo-message $M' = f(M)$. Then encrypt the pseudo-message M' using the block cipher. The receiver can obtain the original message M by applying to $M = f^{-1}(M')$ after decrypting the ciphertext. Here, $f^{-1}()$ is the inverse of $f()$. The selected bijective function must satisfy that computing inverse of the bijective function is infeasible if any block of the pseudo-message is unknown. Even though there are some bijective functions satisfying above property, the careful considerations will be needed for practical purposes.

4.2 All-or-nothing hash function 2(AON hashing-2)

This scheme uses the hash function as an all-or-nothing transform instead of the block cipher.

A. Sender

(1) Partitioning the input message X into t n-bit block, $X_1, X_2, \ldots, X_t$.
(2) Generating a random key k-bit K.
(3) Compute the pseudo-message X' by an all-or-nothing transform.
   $X'_0 = IV$, $X'_i = X_i \oplus h_{X'_{i-1}}(K \oplus i)$, $i = 1, 2, \ldots, t$
(4) Compute the last pseudo-message block, X'_{t+1} (k-bit length).

$$X'_{t+1} = K \oplus \{\overline{h_{X'_1}(K_p \oplus 1) \oplus \ldots \oplus h_{X'_t}(K_p \oplus t)}\}$$

(5) Send $(X'||h_{IV}(X'))$.

B. Receiver

(1) Receive $(X'||MD)$ and check if $MD = h_{IV}(X')$.
(2) Partitioning the pseudo-message X' into t n-bit block, $X'_1, X'_2, \ldots, X'_{t+1}$ and k-bit X'_{t+1}.
(3) Recover the random key K.

$$K = X'_{t+1} \oplus \{\overline{h_{X'_1}(K_p \oplus 1) \oplus \ldots \oplus h_{X'_t}(K_p \oplus t)}\}$$

(4) Recover the original message.
$$X_0' = IV, \; X_i = X_i' \oplus h_{X_{i-1}'}(K \oplus i), \; i = 1, 2, \ldots, t$$

AON hashing-2 uses the hash function as the all-or-nothing transform. This scheme has also all properties of AON hashing-1. An adversary may try to attack after recovering the original message. The manipulation of the pseudo-message is not useful attack. If an attacker do not know any block of the pseudo-message, he can not recover the random key K correctly. So he can not obtain the original message. For an effective attack, he has to find a collision of the pseudo-message with the same hash value in advance, and then searches the message and random key mapped to this pseudo-message. Moreover, the fact that the $i - 1$th pseudo-message block is used to compute the ith pseudo-message block do increase the security. AON hashing-2 pays a penalty of approximately a factor of three compared to the original hash function. The simulation result shows that the performance of AON hashing-2 is 10.05 Mbytes/sec, which corresponds to about $1/3$ of the performance of SHA-1.

4.3 All-or-nothing hash function 3(AON hashing-3)

AON hashing-3 is an improved version of AON hashing-2. Here we assume K_p is a publically-known n-bit constant.

A. Sender

(1) Partitioning the input message X into t n-bit block, $X_1, X_2, \ldots, X_t$.
(2) Generating a random key k-bit K.
(3) Compute the pseudo-message X' by an all-or-nothing transform.

$$X_0' = IV, \; X_0 = 0, \; X_i' = X_i \oplus h_{X_{i-1}'}(K \oplus (\overline{X_{i-1}||i})), \; i = 1, 2, \ldots, t$$

(4) Compute the last pseudo-message block, X_{t+1}' (k-bit length).

$$MD = h_{K_p}(X_1'|| \ldots ||X_t'||h_{IV}(K_p)), \; X_{t+1}' = K \oplus \{\overline{MD}\}$$

(5) Send $(X'||h_{MD}(X_{t+1}'))$.

B. Receiver

(1) Receive $(X'||MD)$.
(2) Partitioning the pseudo-message X' into t n-bit block, $X_1', X_2', \ldots, X_{t+1}'$ and k-bit X_{t+1}'.
(3) Recover the random key K.

$$MD' = h_{K_p}(X_1'|| \ldots ||X_t'||h_{IV}(K_p)), \; K = X_{t+1}' \oplus \{\overline{MD'}\}$$

(4) Check if $MD = h_{MD'}(X_{t+1}')$.
(5) Recover the original message.

$$X_0' = IV, \; X_0 = 0, \; X_i = X_i' \oplus h_{X_{i-1}'}(K \oplus (\overline{X_{i-1}||i})), \; i = 1, 2, \ldots, t$$

This scheme is an improved version of AON hashing-2. All-or-nothing transform depends on the underlying hash function, and has all properties of AON hashing-2. It is more difficult to find the collision of pseudo-messages since all intermediate chaining variables are used in computing of the last pseudo-message blcok, X'_{t+1}. Also, we increase the security by using the hash value of the original message for computing of the pseudo-message. While AON hashing-2 pays a penalty of a factor of three, AON hashing-3 improves the efficiency by applying the hash function twice. The simulation result shows that the performance of 15.07 Mbytes/sec. Compared to AON hashing-2, the performance is improved about 50%.

4.4 Analysis of the security

To find collisions, the existing known attacks like those of MD4, MD5 and RIPEMD, can not be directly applicable to AON hashing. For the proposed scheme, we may guess that the best known attack for finding a collision is the birthday attack and it requires $2^{\frac{n}{2}}$ operations to find a collision pair for an n-bit hash function. It also requires same operations in AON hashing. If n is 160 bits, it can provide a sufficient security against the birthday attack.

Most of existing known attack for hash functions depends on manipulating of the message blocks. Since AON hashing transfers the pseudo-message instead of the original message, an adversary must intercept the pseudo-message and recover the original message. The manipulation of pseudo-message is not effective for the correct recovery of original message by the receiver because the random key K cannot be recovered exactly. Under this condition, if an attacker recover the original message and modify it(so the resulting of pseudo-message is altered), then the message digest would be different from the original one. Thus an adversary has to find the different pseudo-message with the same hash value in advance, and then compute the input message corresponding to the discovered pseudo-message. That is, an attacker has to search a collision of pseudo-message and find the random key K mapped the input message to the pseudo-message. This requires the search of random key K, as well as finding a collision pair. For finding preimage or second preimage, one must find a collision of pseudo-message with the same hash value in advance, which requires $2^{\frac{n}{2}}$ operations for AON hashing-1, and then find an original message mapped to this collision of pseudo-message. If a function f behaves randomly, it requires $2^{k \cdot t}$ operations. For AON hashing-2, finding a collision of pseudo-message requires $2^{\frac{n}{2}}$ operations, and finding a original message mapped to this collision of pseudo-message requires $2^{k \cdot t}$ operations. Similarly, for AON hashing-3, it requires total $2^{\frac{n}{2}+n \cdot t}$ operations.

For finding a collision message of a hash function, one may try to find a message having the same message digest independent on intermediate chaining variables. AON hashing-1 is secure against this attacks, because all intermediate chaining variables are used to generate the pseudo-message. AON hashing-2 uses the $i-1$th pseudo-message block to generate the ith pseudo-message block, and AON hashing-3 also uses the $i-1$th pseudo-message block and $i-1$th original message block to compute the ith pseudo-message block. Thus, AON hashing is secure against attacks by the manipulation of the message block.

By the above analysis, the proposed AON hashing maybe supposed to have the ideal security, which is secure against the existing known attacks.

4.5   An application of AON hashing

AON hashing can be easily applied to the MAC(Message Authentication Code). By using AON hashing, it is possible to provide both the authentication and confidentiality for message. In this case, both communication parties have to securely keep publically-known random constant K_p. This MAC construction may be considered as the variant of HMAC proposed by Bellare, et al[1].

$$HMAC_k(x) = h(\overline{k} \oplus opad, h(\overline{k} \oplus ipad, x))$$

The proposed MAC generates the pseudo-message by hashing(h) the message x, and then applies the pseudo-message to h once again. That is, the generation of pseudo-message from original message is considered as the inner hashing process of HMAC. Thus AON-MAC has the same security as that of HMAC.

Moreover, the proposed MAC can provide the message confidentiality as well as authentication. An attacker who does not know K_p may try to find the random key K for recovering the entire original message. For finding the random key K, AON hashing-1 requires the cryptanalysis of $g()$ and AON hashing-2 requires the finding K_p' having the same values as $h_{X_i'}(K_p \oplus i)$. For AON hashing-3, one must find the K_p' which generates the same values as $MD' = h_{K_p}(X_1'||\ldots||X_t'||h_{IV}(K_p))$. It corresponds to the envelope method which is one of the MAC construction using the hash function. The known best attack for this scheme is the divide-and- conquer attack proposed by Preneel and van Oorschot[8]. If we use SHA-1 or RIPEMD-160 which is considered as a secure hash function, this attack is computationally infeasible. An adversary who tries to decrypt the only one block must cryptanalyze the $f()$ for AON hashing-1. If the used random key K is 512-bit length, it is infeasible. For AON hashing-2 and AON hashing-3, it requires 2^n operations for decrypting the only one block. If n is more than or equal to 160-bit length, it is infeasible.

We can improve the security by adding some overheads to above schemes. We can encrypt the last pseudo-message block and message digest pair (X_{t+1}', MD) using the block cipher with the secret key K_s, and send it to the recipient. If X_{t+1}' is 512-bit length and MD is 160-bit length, the length of the encrypting block is total 672 bits. It rarely affects the performance. However an attacker must find the K_s and K_p for decrypting the entire message.

The confidentiality of the proposed MAC does not have the property that one must decrypt the entire ciphertext before one can determine even one message block. But it can provide both the authentication and confidentiality by only the hash functions. AON hashing-2 and AON hash-3 are constructed by only using the hash functions. They are more efficient than the all-or-nothing transform using the block cipher, and they can avoid the patent and the export restriction.

The proposed schemes pay a penalty of approximately a factor of two compared to an ordinary hash function, but they can be performed efficiently in parallel.

5 Conclusions

In this paper, we proposed hash functions using the all-or-nothing transform. The all-or-nothing transform which was proposed by Rivest has the property that one must decrypt the entire ciphertext before one can determine even one message block. Since hash functions must provide the hash value dependent on the entire input message, all-or-nothing property is suitable for the hash function. The proposed schemes use the existing hash functions without changing their structures, and make existing hash functions secure against known attacks. Moreover, the proposed schemes can be easily applied to construct the MAC, which can provide both the authentication and the confidentiality.

As further researches, we will study about the more efficient all-or-nothing transforms. As discussed in section 4, the carefule considerations are needed to devise efficient bijective functions and more efficient $f()$, $g()$ functions.

References

1. M. Bellare, R. Canetti, H. Krawczyk,: Keying Hash Functions for Message Authentication, Advances in Cryptology-Crypto'96, LNCS, vol. 1109. Springer-Verlag (1996) 1-15
2. I.B. Damgård,: A design principle for hash functions, Advances in Cryptology-CRYPTO 89, LNCS, vol. 435. Springer-Verlag (1990) 416-427
3. H. Dobbertin, A. Bosselaers, B. Preneel,: RIPEMD-160: A strengthened version of RIPEMD, Fast Software Encryption-Cambridge Workshop, LNCS, vol. 1039. Springer-Verlag (1996) 71-82
4. FIPS 180-1,: Secure hash standard, Federal Information Processing Standards Publication 180-1, U.S. Department of Commerce / Nist (1995)
5. L. Knudsen, B. Preneel,: Fast and secure hashing based on codes, Advances in Cryptology-CRYPTO 97, LNCS, vol. 1294. (1997) 485-498
6. A.J. Menezes, P.C. van Oorschot, S.A. Vanstone,: Handbook of Applied Cryptography, CRC Press (1997)
7. R. Merkle,: One way hash functions and DES, Advances in Cryptology-CRYPTO 89, LNCS, vol. 435. (1990) 428-446
8. B. Preneel, P. van Oorschot,: MDx-MAC and Building Fast MACs from Hash Functions, Advances in Cryptology-Crypto'95, LNCS, vol. 963. Springer-Verlag (1995) 1-14
9. R.L. Rivest,: The MD4 message-digest algorithm, Advances in Cryptology-CRYPTO 90, LNCS, vol. 537. Springer-Verlag (1991) 303-311
10. RFC 1321,: The MD5 message-digest algorithm, Internet request for comments 1321, R.L. Rivest, (1992)
11. R. L. Rivest,: All-Or-Nothing Encryption and The Package Transform, The Proceedings of the 1997 Fast Software Encryption Conference, LNCS, vol. 1267. Springer-Verlag (1997) 210-218

12. Ronald L. Rivest, M.J.B. Robshaw, R. Sidney, and Y.L. Yin,: The RC6 Block Cipher, a block cipher submitted for consideration as the new AES
13. Sang Uk Shin, Kyung Hyune Rhee, Dae Hyun Ryu, Sang Jin Lee,: A new hash function based on MDx-family and its application to MAC, PKC'98(International Workshop on Practice and Theory in Public Key Cryptography), LNCS, vol. 1431. Springer-Verlag (1998) 234-246
14. Y. Zheng, J. Pieprzyk, J. Sebery,: HAVAL - a one-way hashing algorithm with variable length of output, Advances in Cryptology-AUSCRYPT 92, LNCS, vol. 718. Springer-Verlag (1993) 83-104

Appendix: A simple example of f, g function used in AON hashing-1

Here we shows simple example of f, g function used in AON hashing-1. We use the round function of RC6 which is a block cipher submitted to AES candidates. The used function $f()$, $g()$ is as follows:

(1) $f()$ function : $f(K, H_i, i)$
Let K, K_p, X_i and X_i' be 512-bit length which is the length of the input block of the hash function. i denotes the number of the message block, and is the 64-bit length.
Step 1. Expand 8-byte i into 64-byte W as the Fig. 2:

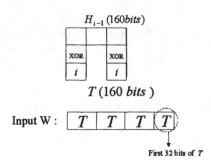

Fig. 2.

Step 2. Process W by 256 bits as the Fig. 3($W[i]$ and $K[i]$ is 32-bit length):

Here f function is $f(x) = x \times (2x + 1)$, and PHT(Pseudo-Hadamard Transform) is $PHT(a, b) = (2a + b, a + b)$ which is used in SAFER K-64 block cipher.

(2) $g()$ function : $g(K_p, X_i', i)$
Step 1. XOR i to begin and end of X_i'.
Step 2. This step is equal to Step 2 of $f()$ function.

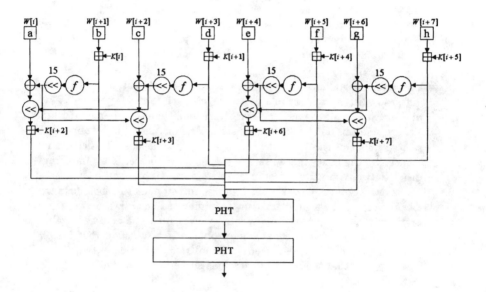

Fig. 3.

Decision Oracles are Equivalent to Matching Oracles

Helena Handschuh[*]   Yiannis Tsiounis[**]   Moti Yung[***]

Abstract. One of the key directions in complexity theory which has also filtered through to cryptographic research, is the effort to classify related but seemingly distinct notions. Separation or reduction arguments are the basic means for this classification.

Continuing this direction we identify a class of problems, called "matching problems," which are related to the class of "decision problems." In many cases, these classes are neither trivially equivalent nor distinct. Briefly, a "decision" problem consists of one instance and a supposedly related image of this instance; the problem is to decide whether the instance and the image indeed satisfy the given predicate. In a "matching" problem two such pairs of instances-images are given, and the problem is to "match" or "distinguish" which image corresponds to which instance. Clearly the decision problem is more difficult, since given a "decision" oracle one can simply test each of the two images to be matched against an instance and solve the matching problem. Here we show that the opposite direction also holds, presuming that randomization of the input is possible, and that the matching oracle is successful in all but a negligible part of its input set.

We first apply our techniques to show equivalence between the matching Diffie-Hellman and the decision Diffie-Hellman problems which were both applied recently quite extensively. This is a constructive step towards examining the strength of the Diffie-Hellman related problems. Then we show that in cryptosystems which can be uniformly randomized, non-semantic security implies that there is an oracle that decides whether a given plaintext corresponds to a given ciphertext. In the process we provide a new characteristic of encryption functions, which we call "universal malleability."

Keywords. Diffie-Hellman variants, randomized reductions, uniform reductions, public-key encryption, homomorphic encryption functions (ElGamal, Goldwasser-Micali, Okamoto-Uchiyama, Naccache-Stern), random self-reducibility, decision problems, matching problems, universal malleability.

---

[*] Gemplus Group/ENST, Paris. handschuh@gemplus.com
[**] GTE Laboratories, Inc., Waltham, MA. ytsiounis@gte.com
[***] CertCo Inc., New York, NY. moti@cs.columbia.edu

1 Introduction

Recently we have seen a number of constructions that are based on the difficulty of the decision Diffie-Hellman problem, ranging from ElGamal-based encryption [ElG85, Dam91, TY98, CS98], to electronic cash [FTY98], and to hash functions [Can97]. A few variations of this problem, called "matching Diffie-Hellman" have also appeared [FTY96, Oka95, CFT98], mainly in electronic cash systems. Our first goal in this paper is to investigate the relationships between these variations and the original problem. To this extent we conclude that the problems are equivalent; this can be seen either as a strengthening of the matching Diffie-Hellman assumptions, or as a weakening of the decision Diffie-Hellman assumption.

Since our reduction techniques for deriving this equivalence are general, they can be applied to other settings in order to transform matching oracles to decision oracles. One such setting is the setting of secure encryption, i.e., the concept of indistinguishability of encryptions. In this context we show, under a specific assumption about the encryption scheme, that distinguishability of encryptions allows us to decide whether a given plaintext corresponds to a given ciphertext. Loosely speaking, this direction enhances the relationship between indistinguishability and semantic security in the sense that it provides, even if only for a limited set of cryptosystems, a specific kind of information that can be retrieved about a ciphertext, if the encryption is not secure in the sense of indistinguishability.

In the course of defining the properties that we require from a cryptosystem that allows this "attack," we propose a new definition, that of *universally malleable* cryptosystems. Intuitively, these are encryption schemes in which, without knowledge of the secret key, one can randomize, independently, both the message and the ciphertext. Typically this property is derived from the random self-reducibility of some underlying problem. Examples of such systems are the ElGamal cryptosystem [ElG85], the Okamoto-Uchiyama factoring-based cryptosystem [OU98], the Naccache-Stern higher-order residue cryptosystem [NS98], and the Goldwasser-Micali quadratic-residue cryptosystem [GM84].

Finally, one can use our methodology to show equivalences between general decision and matching problems. However, the equivalence can be shown only when the "matching oracle" can operate on all but a negligible part of the problem set and when inputs to the oracle can be randomized; this is why the universal malleability is required for the case of encryption systems.

Organization: In section 2 we define the matching and decision Diffie-Hellman problems. We proceed to collapse the decision problem to the matching, i.e., prove equivalence, in section 3. In section 4 we apply our result to cryptosystems, and in section 5 we discuss additional variants of the matching Diffie-Hellman problem.

2 Matching Diffie-Hellman and Decision Diffie-Hellman

In this section we formally define the Matching Diffie-Hellman and the Decision Diffie-Hellman problems. We begin by defining the common setting.

Common setting. For security parameter n, primes P and Q are chosen such that $|P - 1| = \delta + n$ for a specified constant δ, and $P = \gamma Q + 1$, for a specified integer γ. Then a unique subgroup G_Q of prime order Q of the multiplicative group Z_P^* and a generator g of G_Q are defined. All the subsequent calculations are performed mod P, except operations involving exponents, which are performed mod Q.

Definition 1. (Decision Diffie-Hellman Problem) For security parameter n, P a prime with $|P-1| = \delta+n$ for a specified constant δ, for $g \in Z_P^*$ a generator of prime order $Q = (P - 1)/\gamma$ for a specified integer γ and for uniformly chosen $a, b \in_R G_Q$, given $[g^a, g^b, y]$ output 0 if $y = g^{ab} \pmod{P}$ and 1 otherwise, with probability better than $\frac{1}{2} + \frac{1}{n^c}$ for some constant c for large enough n.

The *decision Diffie-Hellman assumption* (DDH) states that it is infeasible for a p.p.t. adversary to solve the Decision Diffie-Hellman problem.

Definition 2. (Matching Diffie-Hellman Problem) For security parameter n, for uniformly chosen $a_i, b_i \in_R G_Q$ ($i \in \{0, 1\}$), P a prime with $|P - 1| = \delta + n$ for a specified constant δ, and for $g \in Z_P^*$ a generator of prime order $Q = (P - 1)/\gamma$ for a specified small integer γ, given $[g^{a_0}, g^{b_0}]$, $[g^{a_1}, g^{b_1}]$ and $g^{a_r b_r}, g^{a_{\bar{r}} b_{\bar{r}}}, r, \bar{r} \in_R \{1, 0\}, r \oplus \bar{r} = 1$, find r with probability better than $\frac{1}{2} + \frac{1}{n^c}$ for some constant c for large enough n.

The *matching Diffie-Hellman assumption* (MDH) states that it is infeasible for a p.p.t. adversary to solve the Matching Diffie-Hellman problem.

Clearly, the DDH problem is at least as hard as the MDH since via two calls to a decision oracle we can solve the matching problem. The goal of the next section is to show the equivalence of these two problems. Intuitively, the problem of mapping the right Diffie-Hellman triplets *together* seems related to deciding whether a given triplet is a *correct* Diffie-Hellman triplet or not. But it is not clear whether, and how, one can use the seemingly weaker *matching* oracle to solve the *decision* problem. Here we prove the reduction by giving an exact construction to achieve it. We only show one direction (matching oracle to decision oracle) since the converse is straightforward.

These results can be extended to the case where an adversary has to select which of two ciphertexts maps to which of two plaintexts (indistinguishability of encryptions), versus where she has to decide whether a given ciphertext is the encryption of a given plaintext. In other words, we show that indistinguishability of encryptions (and therefore semantic security) is equivalent to deciding whether a given ciphertext corresponds to a given plaintext. This however only holds under a specific assumption on the encryption scheme. Under this assumption, this is an extension of the notion of "matching" (distinguishability) of two ciphertext/plaintext pairs, as traditionally defined in [Gol93].

3 Matching Diffie-Hellman is at least as hard as Decision Diffie-Hellman

In this section we show how an attacker, given an oracle that solves the MDH problem with probability non negligibly better than $\frac{1}{2}$ (random guessing), can decide whether a given triplet is a correct Diffie-Hellman triplet or not with probability non negligibly better than random guessing. We are dealing with the uniform case.

Theorem 3. *Assume that there exists a probabilistic polynomial time Turing Machine which given an instance of the Matching Diffie-Hellman Problem gives the correct answer with probability better than $\frac{1}{2} + \frac{1}{n^c}$ for some constant c for large enough n. Then, there exists a p.p.t. TM which, given an instance of the Decision Diffie-Hellman Problem, gives the correct answer with probability better than $\frac{1}{2} + \frac{1}{n'^{c'}}$ for some constant c' for large enough n'.*

Proof. The proof is constructive. We show the steps that an adversary needs to take so that given a decision Diffie-Hellman problem she can solve it using the matching Diffie-Hellman oracle. This involves two phases.

1. **Testing Phase.**

   In this phase the oracle's behavior on incorrect inputs is tested. We will show that the oracle distinguishes either between two correct triplets and a correct and an incorrect one, *or* between a correct and an incorrect triplet and two incorrect ones. This fact will be used in the next phase to help us decide on whether the candidate Diffie-Hellman triplet is correct or not.

   First observe that if the oracle is given two random (i.e., non Diffie-Hellman) triplets, it cannot guess the attacker's random coin tosses for r, simply because no information (in the Shannon sense) about r is encoded in the input to the oracle. Formally, assume that the attacker uniformly and independently selects $r \in_R \{0,1\}, a_i, b_i \ (i \in \{0,1\}), v, w \in_R G_Q$, and then uses the oracle to estimate the quantity:[4]

$$\left| Pr[A([g^{a_0}, g^{b_0}], [g^{a_1}, g^{b_1}], g^v, g^w) = r] - \frac{1}{2} \right|,$$

   where $v, w \not\equiv a_i b_i \pmod{Q}$, for $i \in \{0,1\}$. It is clear that the probability of the oracle in finding r better than random guessing is negligible, since r is chosen randomly and independently of v, w and no information about r is included in the oracle's input. For clarity, we assume that the attacker

---

[4] Note that the notation $A[x] = r$ is a shortcut of saying that the adversary produces the correct "match". Thus we implicitly assume that an answer of 0 means that the first pair, in this case g^{a_0}, g^{b_0}, matches with the first number (g^v); and vice-versa, an answer of 1 means that the first pair matches with the second number.

has a success rate less than $\frac{1}{2n^c}$, i.e., that the oracle is run sufficiently many (polynomial) times so that the accuracy is $\frac{1}{2n^c}$. So we have that

$$\left| Pr[A([g^{a_0}, g^{b_0}], [g^{a_1}, g^{b_1}], g^v, g^w) = r] - \frac{1}{2} \right| \leq \frac{1}{2n^c} \tag{1}$$

On the other hand, from the assumption on the power of the oracle, we know that

$$Pr[A([g^{a_0}, g^{b_0}], [g^{a_1}, g^{b_1}], g^{a_r b_r}, g^{a_{\bar{r}} b_{\bar{r}}}) = r] - \frac{1}{2} > \frac{1}{n^c} . \tag{2}$$

In other words, the difference of behavior between two random triplets and two correct triplets is non-negligible. In particular, we have the following:

Lemma 4. *For every $a_i, b_i, c_i, d_i, i \in \{0, 1\}$, for uniformly and independently chosen $r \in_R \{0, 1\}$, $v, w \in_R G_Q$, and for large enough n, it holds that:*[5]

$$\Delta([a, b, 1, 1], [c, d, 0, 0]) = | \, Pr \, [A([g^{a_0}, g^{b_0}], [g^{a_1}, g^{b_1}], g^{a_r b_r}, g^{a_{\bar{r}} b_{\bar{r}}}) = r] -$$
$$Pr \, [A([g^{c_0}, g^{d_0}], [g^{c_1}, g^{d_1}], g^v, g^w) = r] \, | > \frac{1}{2n^c}$$

Proof. First, from equation (1) we have

$$- \left| Pr[A([g^{a_0}, g^{b_0}], [g^{a_1}, g^{b_1}], g^v, g^w) = r] - \frac{1}{2} \right| \geq - \frac{1}{2n^c}$$

Proceeding to prove the claim, we use the above together with equation (2) to get:

$$\Delta([a, b, 1, 1], [c, d, 0, 0]) = |Pr[A([g^{a_0}, g^{b_0}], [g^{a_1}, g^{b_1}], g^{a_r b_r}, g^{a_{\bar{r}} b_{\bar{r}}}) = r] -$$
$$Pr[A([g^{c_0}, g^{d_0}], [g^{c_1}, g^{d_1}], g^v, g^w) = r] \, | =$$
$$|(Pr[A([g^{a_0}, g^{b_0}], [g^{a_1}, g^{b_1}], g^{a_r b_r}, g^{a_{\bar{r}} b_{\bar{r}}}) = r] - \frac{1}{2}) -$$
$$(Pr[A([g^{c_0}, g^{d_0}], [g^{c_1}, g^{d_1}], g^v, g^w) = r] - \frac{1}{2}) \, | \geq$$
$$|Pr[A([g^{a_0}, g^{b_0}], [g^{a_1}, g^{b_1}], g^{a_r b_r}, g^{a_{\bar{r}} b_{\bar{r}}}) = r] - \frac{1}{2}| -$$
$$|Pr[A([g^{c_0}, g^{d_0}], [g^{c_1}, g^{d_1}], g^v, g^w) = r] - \frac{1}{2}| >$$
$$\frac{1}{n^c} - |Pr[A([g^{c_0}, g^{d_0}], [g^{c_1}, g^{d_1}], g^v, g^w) = r] - \frac{1}{2}| \geq$$
$$\frac{1}{n^c} - \frac{1}{2n^c} \geq \frac{1}{2n^c}$$

---

[5] The notation here is as follows: $[a, b, i, j]$ signifies that a pair of triplets is given, such that when i (resp. j) is 0 the first (resp. the second) triplet is incorrect, and when it is 1 the triplet is a correct D-H triplet.

Now we show how the actual testing phase proceeds. First the attacker uniformly selects $r \in_R \{0,1\}$, $v \in_R G_Q$ and estimates the difference

$$\Delta([a,b,1,1],[e,f,1,0]) = \mid Pr\left[A([g^{a_0},g^{b_0}],[g^{a_1},g^{b_1}],g^{a_r b_r},g^{a_{\bar{r}} b_{\bar{r}}}) = r\right] -$$
$$Pr\left[A([g^{e_0},g^{f_0}],[g^{e_1},g^{f_1}],g^x,g^y) = r\right] \mid,$$

where $x,y \in_R \{e_r f_r, v\}$. The estimate is given with accuracy $\frac{1}{16n^c}$. Now if the estimate is greater or equal to $\frac{3}{16n^c}$ then the actual difference is at least $\frac{3}{16n^c} - \frac{1}{16n^c} = \frac{1}{8n^c}$. In this case we will say that the attacker can distinguish between two correct triplets and one correct/one incorrect triplet. If the estimate on the other hand is less than $\frac{3}{16n^c}$ then the actual difference is less than $\frac{3}{16n^c} + \frac{1}{16n^c} = \frac{1}{4n^c}$. In this case we say that the attacker cannot distinguish.

Now we will show that if the attacker cannot distinguish as above, then it must be able to distinguish between one correct/one incorrect triplet and two incorrect triplets. Starting from lemma 4, we have (definitions of variables are similar as above; we omit details):

$$\frac{1}{2n^c} < \Delta([a,b,1,1],[c,d,0,0])$$
$$= \mid Pr[A([g^{a_0},g^{b_0}],[g^{a_1},g^{b_1}],g^{a_r b_r},g^{a_{\bar{r}} b_{\bar{r}}}) = r] -$$
$$Pr[A([g^{c_0},g^{d_0}],[g^{c_1},g^{d_1}],g^v,g^w) = r] \mid$$
$$= \mid Pr[A([g^{a_0},g^{b_0}],[g^{a_1},g^{b_1}],g^{a_r b_r},g^{a_{\bar{r}} b_{\bar{r}}}) = r] -$$
$$Pr[A([g^{e_0},g^{f_0}],[g^{e_1},g^{f_1}],g^x,g^y) = r] +$$
$$Pr[A([g^{e_0},g^{f_0}],[g^{e_1},g^{f_1}],g^x,g^y) = r] -$$
$$Pr[A([g^{c_0},g^{d_0}],[g^{c_1},g^{d_1}],g^v,g^w) = r] \mid$$
$$\leq \mid Pr[A([g^{a_0},g^{b_0}],[g^{a_1},g^{b_1}],g^{a_r b_r},g^{a_{\bar{r}} b_{\bar{r}}}) = r] -$$
$$Pr[A([g^{e_0},g^{f_0}],[g^{e_1},g^{f_1}],g^x,g^y) = r] \mid +$$
$$\mid Pr[A([g^{e_0},g^{f_0}],[g^{e_1},g^{f_1}],g^x,g^y) = r] -$$
$$Pr[A([g^{c_0},g^{d_0}],[g^{c_1},g^{d_1}],g^v,g^w) = r] \mid$$
$$= \Delta([a,b,1,1],[e,f,1,0]) + \Delta([e,f,1,0],[c,d,0,0])$$

Thus, for uniformly chosen $e_i, f_i, i \in \{0,1\}$, i.e., $Pr[(e_i,f_i)] = \frac{1}{|G_Q{}^2|}$, and for j enumerating all possible pairs, we have:

$$\Sigma_j \left[\Delta([a,b,1,1],[e,f,1,0]) + \Delta([e,f,1,0],[c,d,0,0])\right] > \Sigma_j \frac{1}{2n^c} \iff$$
$$\Sigma_j \Delta([a,b,1,1],[e,f,1,0]) + \Sigma_j \Delta([e,f,1,0],[c,d,0,0])] > |G_Q{}^2| \frac{1}{2n^c} \iff$$
$$\Sigma_j \frac{Pr[(e_i,f_i)]}{Pr[(e_i,f_i)]} \Delta([a,b,1,1],[e,f,1,0]) +$$
$$\Sigma_j \frac{Pr[(e_i,f_i)]}{Pr[(e_i,f_i)]} \Delta([e,f,1,0],[c,d,0,0])] > |G_Q{}^2| \frac{1}{2n^c} \iff$$
$$|G_Q{}^2| \Sigma_j Pr[(e_i,f_i)] \Delta([a,b,1,1],[e,f,1,0]) +$$

$$|G_Q{}^2|\Sigma_j\, Pr[(e_i, f_i)]\Delta([e, f, 1, 0], [c, d, 0, 0])] > |G_Q{}^2|\frac{1}{2n^c} \iff$$

$$\Sigma_j\, Pr[(e_i, f_i)]\Delta([a, b, 1, 1], [e, f, 1, 0]) +$$

$$\Sigma_j\, Pr[(e_i, f_i)]\Delta([e, f, 1, 0], [c, d, 0, 0])] > \frac{1}{2n^c} \iff$$

$$E[\Delta([a, b, 1, 1], [e, f, 1, 0])] + E[\Delta([e, f, 1, 0], [c, d, 0, 0])] > \frac{1}{2n^c} ,$$

where the expectancy is taken over the choice of the triplets (e_i, f_i). Therefore, if $E[\Delta([a, b, 1, 1], [e, f, 1, 0])] < \frac{1}{4n^c}$ then we have $E[\Delta([e, f, 1, 0], [c, d, 0, 0])] > \frac{1}{4n^c}$.

In summary, the oracle can be used to distinguish either between two correct triplets and one correct/one incorrect triplet, *or* between one correct/one incorrect triplet and two incorrect ones.

2. **Decision Phase.** Now we can use the result of the testing phase to decide whether the given triplet is a D-H triplet or not.

(a) Suppose the attacker can distinguish between two correct DH triplets and one correct/one random triplet. Then she can input a randomized sequence $[g^{a_0 s}, g^{a_1 t}]$, $[g^{x_0 u}, g^{x_1 v}]$ and $(g^{a_0 a_1 st}, Z^{uv})$ where $[g^{x_0}, g^{x_1}, Z]$ is the target Decision Diffie-Hellman triplet, to the MDH oracle. If the behavior on these inputs is different from the behavior when fed with a sequence of two randomized correct triplets, conclude that the target DDH triplet is *an incorrect Diffie-Hellman triplet*. Else, conclude that it is a correct Diffie-Hellman triplet.

In other words, the attacker uses the oracle to estimate the following difference:

$$\Delta([a, b, 1, 1], [(a, b), (x, y), 1, i]) =$$
$$|\, Pr[A([g^{a_0}, g^{b_0}], [g^{a_1}, g^{b_1}], g^{a_r b_r}, g^{a_{\bar{r}} b_{\bar{r}}}) = r] -$$
$$Pr[A([g^{a_0}, g^{b_0}], [g^x, g^y], X, Y) = r]\, | ,$$

where $X, Y \in_R \{g^{a_0 b_0}, Z\}$ and i is 1 or 0 depending on whether the candidate triplet is a correct or incorrect D-H triplet respectively. We implicitly assume here that the inputs to the oracle are randomized as described above. The estimate of the difference is given with accuracy $\frac{1}{32n^c}$. Now if $Z \neq g^{xy}$ then, as we know from the testing phase, the actual difference is at least $\frac{1}{8n^c}$ and the estimate must be larger than $\frac{1}{8n^c} - \frac{1}{32n^c} = \frac{3}{32n^c}$. Otherwise the actual difference would be 0 and the estimate would be smaller than $\frac{1}{32n^c}$. So depending on the estimate (greater than $\frac{3}{32n^c}$ or smaller than $\frac{1}{32n^c}$) the attacker decides whether the input is an incorrect, or respectively a correct Diffie-Hellman triplet.

(b) Otherwise, the oracle is able to distinguish between two random triplets and a correct and a random triplet. Then we can feed the MDH oracle with a randomized sequence $[g^{a_0 s}, g^{b_0 t}]$, $[g^{xu}, g^{yv}]$ and g^{wst}, Z^{uv} where

$[g^x, g^y, Z]$ is the target Decision Diffie-Hellman triplet and where w does not satisfy the equation $w \equiv a_0 b_0 \pmod{Q}$. If the behavior on these inputs is different from the behavior when fed with a sequence of two random triplets, conclude that the target DDH triplet is *a correct Diffie-Hellman triplet*. Else conclude that it is an incorrect Diffie-Hellman triplet.

In particular, the attacker uses the oracle to estimate the following difference:

$$\Delta([(x,y), (a,b), i, 0], [a, b, 0, 0]) = \mid Pr[A([g^x, g^y], [g^{a_0}, g^{b_0}], X, Y) = r] - $$
$$Pr[A([g^{a_0}, g^{b_0}], [g^{a_1}, g^{b_1}], g^{z_0}, g^{z_1}) = r] \mid ,$$

where $X, Y \in_R \{Z, g^{z_2}\}$, $z_0, z_1, z_2 \in_R G_Q$, and i is 1 or 0 depending on whether the candidate triplet is a correct or incorrect D-H triplet respectively. The estimate is given with accuracy $\frac{1}{16n^c}$. Now if $Z = g^{xy}$ then, as we know from the testing phase, the actual difference is at least $\frac{1}{4n^c}$ and the estimate must be larger than $\frac{1}{4n^c} - \frac{1}{16n^c} = \frac{3}{16n^c}$. Otherwise the actual difference would be 0 and the estimate would be smaller than $\frac{1}{16n^c}$, as analyzed in the testing phase above. So depending on the estimate (greater than $\frac{3}{16n^c}$ or smaller than $\frac{1}{16n^c}$) the attacker decides whether the input is a correct, or respectively an incorrect Diffie-Hellman triplet.

4 Universal malleability implies matching = decision

In this section we will show that for some special classes of cryptosystems indistinguishability of encryptions is equivalent to being able to decide whether a given ciphertext corresponds to a given plaintext. More precisely, we know [Gol93] that indistinguishability of encryptions is equivalent to semantic security. That is, if some information is leaked from the ciphertext then two ciphertext/plaintext pairs can be "matched" (distinguished); and vice-versa. What we do not know, however, is, given that indistinguishability does not hold, *what kind* of information can be extracted about the ciphertext.[6] Here we show that, under certain assumptions about the encryption, if indistinguishability/semantic security does not hold, then given a pair of plaintext and ciphertext it is possible to decide whether the ciphertext comes from this plaintext. Of course this implication only makes sense in either symmetric encryption or probabilistic asymmetric encryption, since in deterministic asymmetric encryption it is straightforward to make this decision: simply encrypt the plaintext and compare to the candidate ciphertext.

We begin by reiterating the definition of indistinguishability of encryptions.

---

[6] Of course the existing proofs of equivalence between semantic security and indistinguishability [Gol93] constructively extract some information, but this is limited to a specially fabricated function of some specified plaintext/ciphertext pairs.

Definition 5. (encryption secure in the sense of indistinguishability)
An encryption scheme (G, E, D) is said to be *secure in the sense of indistinguishability* if, for every probabilistic polynomial time algorithm F (for "Find"), for every probabilistic polynomial time algorithm A, for every constant $c > 0$ and for every sufficiently large n,

$$\Pr\left[F(1^n) = (\alpha, \beta, \gamma) \text{ s.t. } \Omega(\alpha, \beta, \gamma) > \frac{1}{n^c}\right] < \frac{1}{n^c} \, ,$$

with

$$\Omega(\alpha, \beta, \gamma) = \left|\Pr\left\{A((\gamma), E_{G(1^n)}(\alpha)) = 1\right\} - \Pr\left\{A(\gamma, E_{G(1^n)}(\beta)) = 1\right\}\right| \, ,$$

where the probability is taken over the coin tosses of F, A, E and G.

For our purposes, we need an additional assumption about the encryption scheme. Intuitively, we need to be able to "randomize" any plaintext/ciphertext pair, such that the resulting pair can obtain all possible values. We name the encryption schemes that satisfy this property "universally malleable," to be contrasted to non-malleable schemes [DDN91] that prohibit altering of the ciphertext. The formal definition follows.

Definition 6. (Universal malleability) An encryption scheme (G, E, D) is called *universally malleable* if for all but a negligible part of plaintext-ciphertext pairs $(a, E_{G(1^n)}(a)) \in (X_n, Y_n)$, there is a random variable Z_n and a p.p.t. TM T such that

- for every $z \in Z_n$, it holds that $T(a, E_{G(1^n)}(a), z) = (b, E_{G(1^n)}(b))$, and
- for all but a negligible part of pairs $(c, d) \in (X_n, Y_n)$ there is a $z' \in Z_n$ such that $T(a, E_{G(1^n)}(a), z') = (c, d)$.

Remark: this definition may seem too restrictive, but in fact there are several encryption schemes, at times provably semantically secure under some assumptions, which satisfy it. Examples include the ElGamal cryptosystem [ElG85], the Okamoto-Uchiyama cryptosystem [OU98], the Naccache-Stern higher-order residue cryptosystem [NS98], and the Goldwasser-Micali quadratic-residue cryptosystem [GM84]. Typically this property is derived from the random self reducibility of some underlying problem in which the encryption is based on—be it quadratic or higher order residuosity, the Diffie-Hellman problem, or factoring.

We now proceed to formally define and prove our statement. Again we work in the uniform model of computation.

Theorem 7. *Assume that a* universally malleable *encryption scheme* (G, E, D) *is not secure in the sense of indistinguishability. Then there exists a p.p.t. TM which, given a pair* $(a, E_{G(1^n)}(b))$, *can decide non-negligibly better than random guessing whether* $a = b$.

Proof. If an encryption is not secure in the sense of indistinguishability then there exists a p.p.t. adversarial algorithm A (which can be seen as the "oracle" that "breaks" the encryption scheme), a (polynomial) random variable Z_n and two independent (polynomial) random variables (X_n, Y_n) that have the same distribution, such that:

$$\exists\, c > 0, \exists\, N, \text{s.t. for infinitely many } n > N, \Pr[(X_n Y_n Z_n) \in B_n^c] > \frac{1}{n^c}, \text{where}$$

$$B_n^c = \left\{ (\alpha, \beta, \gamma) : \left| \Pr\left[A(\gamma, E_{G(1^n)}(\alpha)) = 1 \right] - \Pr\left[A(\gamma, E_{G(1^n)}(\beta)) = 1 \right] \right| > \frac{1}{n^c} \right\},$$

where the probabilities are taken over the coin tosses of the key generating algorithm G, the encryption algorithm $E_{G(1^n)}$, the adversarial algorithm A, and the selection of (α, β, γ).

We will show how this adversarial algorithm can be used by an attacker to decide whether $a = b$, in the given pair $(a, E_{G(1^n)}(b))$. For simplicity, we will write $(a, E(b))$.

The process requires three phases (including the preparation phase).

1. **Preparation phase.** In this phase the attacker finds two plaintexts whose ciphertexts she can distinguish. This is possible given the assumptions on the power of the adversarial algorithm A above.

Specifically, the attacker chooses a random message pair (m_0, m_1) from the distribution X_n and tries to estimate the following probability:

$$Pr[A([m_0, m_1], [E(m_r), E(m_{\bar{r}})]) = r] - \frac{1}{2}$$

where $r \in_R \{0, 1\}, r \oplus \bar{r} = 1$

with accuracy better than $\frac{1}{2n^c}$. Now if the estimate is greater than $\frac{3}{2n^c}$, the actual probability is greater than $\frac{3}{2n^c} - \frac{1}{2n^c} = \frac{1}{n^c}$ and the message pair is selected for the next step. Otherwise it is rejected and a new pair is selected. The number of experiments needed to estimate this probability with accuracy $\frac{1}{2n^c}$ is polynomially bounded since the encryption scheme is not secure in the sense of indistinguishability, and it can be computed using the Hoefding inequality.

Note that the estimation is performed by randomizing the input to algorithm A. This is where the property of *universal malleability* is crucial, in guaranteeing that the randomization will always succeed and that the randomized input can take all possible values: recall from the definition that for every $(m, E(m)) \in (X_n, Y_n)$ and $z' \in_R Z_n$ it holds that $T(m, E(m), z') = (b, E(b))$ for some $b \in X_n$, for all but a negligible part of plaintexts m. Therefore we can randomize the input sequence to the oracle. Now, from the second part of universal malleability we have that for all but a negligible part of pairs $(c, d) \in (X_n, Y_n)$ there is a $z' \in Z_n$ such that $T(m, E(m), z') = (c, d)$. Thus a randomization of $(m, E(m))$ achieved by T choosing a random $z' \in_R Z_n$ as above, results in a uniformly chosen pair from the distribution (X_n, Y_n), and all but a negligible fraction of those pairs can be generated by T in this manner.

Let m_0 and m_1 be the two messages that the algorithm can distinguish. We denote this as follows:

$$Pr[A([m_0, m_1], [E(m_r), E(m_{\bar{r}})]) = r] - \frac{1}{2} > \frac{1}{n^c} , \tag{3}$$

where $r \in_R \{0, 1\}, r \oplus \bar{r} = 1$.

2. **Testing phase.** As in section 3, assume that the attacker uniformly and independently selects $r \in_R \{0, 1\}, m_2, m_3 \in_R X_n, v, w \in_R Y_n$, and then uses the oracle to estimate:

$$\left| Pr[A([m_2, m_3], [v, w]) = r] - \frac{1}{2} \right| ,$$

where v, w do not encrypt m_2 nor m_3. Then again it is clear that the probability of the oracle in finding the attacker's random coin tosses for r is negligible (we formalize it as less than $\frac{1}{2n^c}$), since no information (in the Shannon sense) about r is included in the input of A. Thus, combining equation (3), we have the equivalent of lemma 4:

Lemma 8. *For every $m_2, m_3 \in_R X_n, r \in_R \{0, 1\}, r \oplus \bar{r} = 1, v; w \in_R Y_n$, and for large enough n it holds that*

$$\Delta([m_0, m_1, 1, 1], [m_2, m_3, 0, 0]) = |\, Pr\,[A([m_0, m_1], [E(m_r), E(m_{\bar{r}})]) = r] -$$
$$Pr\,[A([m_2, m_3], [v, w]) = r]| > \frac{1}{2n^c}$$

Now the attacker runs algorithm A in order to estimate the difference:

$$\Delta([m_0, m_1, 1, 1], [m_4, m_5, 1, 0]) = |\, Pr\,[A([m_0, m_1], [E(m_r), E(m_{\bar{r}})]) = r] -$$
$$Pr\,[A([m_4, m_5], [X, Y]) = r]| ,$$

where $X, Y \in_R \{E(m_4), t\}, t \in_R Y_n, r \in_R \{0, 1\}, \bar{r} \oplus r = 1$.

The estimate is given with accuracy $\frac{1}{16n^c}$; as in the preparation phase, we use the property of universal malleability to allow A to randomize the input and run the oracle as many times as dictated by the Hoefding inequality. As in section 3 we can test if the difference here is significant, i.e., greater than or equal to $\frac{3}{16n^c}$. In this case, the actual difference is at least $\frac{3}{16n^c} - \frac{1}{16n^c} = \frac{1}{8n^c}$, i.e. the attacker is able to distinguish between two correct plaintext/ciphertext pairs, and one correct and one incorrect one. If on the other hand the estimate is smaller than $\frac{3}{16n^c}$, the actual difference will be smaller than $\frac{3}{16n^c} + \frac{1}{16n^c} = \frac{1}{4n^c}$, and as in section 3 we can show that $\Delta([m_4, m_5, 1, 0], [m_2, m_3, 0, 0])$ will be greater than $\frac{1}{4n^c}$. In other words, the difference between two incorrect plaintext/ciphertext pairs, and one incorrect and one correct pair has to be significant. This is shown as follows:

$$\frac{1}{2n^c} < \Delta([m_0, m_1, 1, 1], [m_2, m_3, 0, 0])$$

$$= |Pr[A([m_0, m_1], [E(m_r), E(m_{\bar{r}})]) = r] - Pr[A([m_2, m_3], [v, w]) = r]|$$

$$= |Pr[A([m_0, m_1], [E(m_r), E(m_{\bar{r}})]) = r] - Pr[A([m_4, m_5], [X, Y]) = r]$$
$$\quad + Pr[A([m_4, m_5], [X, Y]) = r] - Pr[A([m_2, m_3], [v, w]) = r]|$$

$$\leq |Pr[A([m_0, m_1], [E(m_r), E(m_{\bar{r}})]) = r] - Pr[A([m_4, m_5], [X, Y]) = r]|$$
$$\quad + |Pr[A([m_4, m_5], [X, Y]) = r] - Pr[A([m_2, m_3], [v, w]) = r]|$$

$$= \Delta([m_0, m_1, 1, 1], [m_4, m_5, 1, 0]) + \Delta([m_4, m_5, 1, 0], [m_2, m_3, 0, 0])$$

Thus, for uniformly chosen $m_4, m_5 \in_R X_n$, i.e., $Pr[(m_4, m_5)] = \frac{1}{|X_n|^2}$, and for j enumerating all possible pairs, we have:

$$\Sigma_j \, [\Delta([m_0, m_1, 1, 1], [m_4, m_5, 1, 0]) + $$
$$\Delta([m_4, m_5, 1, 0], [m_2, m_3, 0, 0])] > \Sigma_j \frac{1}{2n^c} \iff$$
$$\Sigma_j \, \Delta([m_0, m_1, 1, 1], [m_4, m_5, 1, 0]) + $$
$$\Sigma_j \, \Delta([m_4, m_5, 1, 0], [m_2, m_3, 0, 0]) > |X_n|^2 \frac{1}{2n^c} \iff$$
$$\Sigma_j \, \frac{Pr[(m_4, m_5)]}{Pr[(m_4, m_5)]} \Delta([m_0, m_1, 1, 1], [m_4, m_5, 1, 0]) + $$
$$\Sigma_j \, \frac{Pr[(m_4, m_5)]}{Pr[(m_4, m_5)]} \Delta([m_4, m_5, 1, 0], [m_2, m_3, 0, 0]) > |X_n|^2 \frac{1}{2n^c} \iff$$
$$|X_n|^2 \Sigma_j \, Pr[(m_4, m_5)]\Delta([m_0, m_1, 1, 1], [m_4, m_5, 1, 0]) + $$
$$|X_n|^2 \Sigma_j \, Pr[(m_4, m_5)]\Delta([m_4, m_5, 1, 0], [m_2, m_3, 0, 0]) > |X_n|^2 \frac{1}{2n^c} \iff$$
$$\Sigma_j \, Pr[(m_4, m_5)]\Delta([m_0, m_1, 1, 1], [m_4, m_5, 1, 0]) + $$
$$\Sigma_j \, Pr[(m_4, m_5)]\Delta([m_4, m_5, 1, 0], [m_2, m_3, 0, 0]) > \frac{1}{2n^c} \iff$$
$$E[\Delta([m_0, m_1, 1, 1], [m_4, m_5, 1, 0])] + $$
$$E[\Delta([m_4, m_5, 1, 0], [m_2, m_3, 0, 0])] > \frac{1}{2n^c} \, ,$$

where the expected values are taken over the choice of the pair (m_4, m_5). Therefore, if $E[\Delta([m_0, m_1, 1, 1], [m_4, m_5, 1, 0])] < \frac{1}{4n^c}$ then it must be that $E[\Delta([m_4, m_5, 1, 0], [m_2, m_3, 0, 0])] > \frac{1}{4n^c}$.
This concludes the proof that the oracle may either distinguish between two correct plaintext/ciphertext pairs and one correct/one incorrect pair, *or* between one correct/one incorrect pair and two incorrect plaintext/ciphertext pairs.
We now proceed to the last phase.

3. **Decision phase.** In this phase we use the result of the testing phase accordingly. If the first difference is significant, then the attacker estimates the

difference

$$\Delta([m_0, m_1, 1, 1], [m_4, a, 1, i]) = \mid Pr \, [A([m_0, m_1], [E(m_r), E(m_{\bar{r}})]) = r] - $$
$$Pr \, [A([m_4, a], [X, Y]) = r] \mid ,$$

where $X, Y \in_R \{E(m_4), E(b)\}$. The estimate is given with accuracy $\frac{1}{32n^c}$, after polynomially many trials. In each trial each plaintext/ciphertext pair is randomized over all (but a negligible part) of possible combinations $(c, d) \in (X_n, Y_n)$; again we utilize the universal malleability property to do this, as in the preparation phase. Now as we know from the testing phase if $a \neq b$ the actual difference is at least $\frac{1}{8n^c}$, so the estimate in this case must be greater or equal to $\frac{1}{8n^c} - \frac{1}{32n^c} = \frac{3}{32n^c}$. Otherwise, if $a = b$ the actual difference is 0 and the estimate must be less or equal to $\frac{1}{32n^c}$. Therefore depending on the estimate (greater than $\frac{3}{32n^c}$ or smaller than $\frac{1}{32n^c}$) the attacker decides whether the input is a correct $(i = 1)$ or an incorrect $(i = 0)$ plaintext/ciphertext pair.

Accordingly, if the testing phase showed that the second difference is significant, then the attacker estimates

$$\Delta([a, m_5, i, 0], [m_2, m_3, 0, 0]) = \mid Pr \, [A([a, m_5], [X, Y]) = r] - $$
$$Pr \, [A([m_2, m_3], [v, w]) = r] \mid ,$$

where $X, Y \in_R \{E(b), t\}, t, v, w \in_R Y_n$. Here the required accuracy is $\frac{1}{16n^c}$. If $a = b$ then from the testing phase we know that the actual difference is at least $\frac{1}{4n^c}$, and therefore the estimate will be larger than $\frac{1}{4n^c} - \frac{1}{16n^c} = \frac{3}{16n^c}$. Otherwise, when $a \neq b$, the difference would be 0 and the estimate would be smaller than $\frac{1}{16n^c}$. Here again, the attacker can decide whether the input to algorithm A is a correct $(i = 1)$ or an incorrect $(i = 0)$ plaintext/ciphertext pair depending on the value of the estimated difference (above $\frac{3}{16n^c}$ or below $\frac{1}{16n^c}$). Again note that *universal malleability* is fundamental to this proof in order to be able to feed the oracle with a randomized input sequence.

5 Extensions

The original version of the matching Diffie-Hellman problem, defined in [FTY96], was slightly different from the one used in the analysis above. For convenience we name it "matching D-H II".

Definition 9. (Matching Diffie-Hellman Problem II) For security parameter n, for uniformly chosen $a_i, b_i \in_R G_Q$ $(i \in \{0, 1\})$, P a prime with $|P - 1| = \delta + n$ for a specified constant δ, and for $g \in Z_P^*$ a generator of prime order $Q = (P - 1)/\gamma$ for a specified small integer γ, given $[g^{a_0}, g^{a_0 b_0}], [g^{a_1}, g^{a_1 b_1}]$ and $g^{b_r}, g^{b_{\bar{r}}}, r, \bar{r} \in_R \{1, 0\}, r \oplus \bar{r} = 1$, find r with probability better than $\frac{1}{2} + \frac{1}{n^c}$ for some constant c for large enough n.

Using the same techniques of section 3 it can be shown that this version of the problem is also equivalent to the decision Diffie-Hellman problem, and therefore the two versions of the "matching" problem are equivalent.

References

[Can97] R. Canetti. Towards realizing random oracles: Hash functions that hide all partial information. In B. Kaliski, editor, *Advances in Cryptology — CRYPTO '97 Proceedings, LLNCS 1294*, pages 455–469, Santa Barbara, CA, August 17–21 1997. Springer-Verlag.

[CFT98] A. Chan, Y. Frankel, and Y. Tsiounis. Easy come–easy go divisible cash. In *Advances in Cryptology — Proceedings of Eurocrypt '98 (Lecture Notes in Computer Science 1403)*, pages 561–575, Helsinki, Finland, May 31–June 4 1998. Springer-Verlag. International patent pending. Available at http://www.ccs.neu.edu/home/yiannis/pubs.html.

[CS98] R. Cramer and V. Shoup. A practical public key cryptosystem provably secure against adaptive chosen ciphertext attack. In *Advances in Cryptology: Crypto '98, Proceedings (Lecture Notes in Computer Science 1462)*, pages 13–25, 1998. Available at http://www.cs.wisc.edu/ shoup/papers/.

[Dam91] I. B. Damgård. Towards practical public key systems against chosen ciphertext attacks. In J. Feigenbaum, editor, *Advances in Cryptology, Proc. of Crypto '91 (Lecture Notes in Computer Science 576)*, pages 445–456. Springer-Verlag, 1991.

[DDN91] O. Dolev, C. Dwork, and M. Naor. Non-malleable cryptography. In *Proceedings of the 23rd Annual Symposium on Theory of Computing*, 1991.

[ElG85] T. ElGamal. A public key cryptosystem and a signature scheme based on discrete logarithms. *IEEE Trans. Inform. Theory*, 31:469–472, 1985.

[FTY96] Y. Frankel, Y. Tsiounis, and M. Yung. Indirect discourse proofs: achieving fair off-line e-cash. In *Advances in Cryptology, Proc. of Asiacrypt '96 (Lecture Notes in Computer Science 1163)*, pages 286–300, Kyongju, South Korea, November 3–7 1996. Springer-Verlag. International patent pending. Available at http://www.ccs.neu.edu/home/yiannis/pubs.html.

[FTY98] Y. Frankel, Y. Tsiounis, and M. Yung. Fair off-line cash made easy. In *Advances in Cryptology, Proc. of Asiacrypt '98 (Lecture Notes in Computer Science)*. Springer-Verlag, October 18–22 1998. To appear. Available at http://www.ccs.neu.edu/home/yiannis/pubs.html.

[GM84] S. Goldwasser and S. Micali. Probabilistic encryption. *Journal of Computer and System Sciences*, 28(2):270–299, April 1984.

[Gol93] O. Goldreich. A uniform-complexity treatment of encryption and zero-knowledge. *Journal of Cryptology*, 6(1):21–53, 1993.

[NS98] D. Naccache and J. Stern. A new cryptosystem based on higher residues. In *ACM CCS '98—Communications and Computer Security*, 1998. To appear.

[Oka95] T. Okamoto. An efficient divisible electronic cash scheme. In Don Coppersmith, editor, *Advances in Cryptology, Proc. of Crypto '95 (Lecture Notes in Computer Science 963)*, pages 438–451. Springer-Verlag, 1995.

[OU98] T. Okamoto and S. Uchiyama. An efficient public-key cryptosystem. In *Advances in Cryptology – Eurocrypt 98 proceedings (Lecture Notes in Computer Science 1403)*, pages 308–318, Espoo, Finland, 1998. Springer-Verlag.

[TY98] Y. Tsiounis and M. Yung. On the security of El Gamal-based encryption. In *International workshop on Public Key Cryptography (PKC '98) (Lecture Notes in Computer Science 1431)*, pages 117–134, Yokohama, Japan, February 5–6 1998. Springer-Verlag. Available at http://yiannis.home.ml.org.

Shared Generation of Random Number with Timestamp: How to Cope with the Leakage of the CA's Secret[1]

Yuji Watanabe   Hideki Imai

Institute of Industrial Science
University of Tokyo
7-22-1 Roppongi, Minatoku, Tokyo 106-8558, Japan
Email: mue@imailab.iis.u-tokyo.ac.jp

Abstract. Public-key certificates play an important role in a public-key cryptosystem. In a public-key infrastructure, it is a presupposition that only the issuer of a signature knows the signing key. Since the security of all clients of the CA depends on the secrecy of the CA's signing-key, CA's will pose an attractive target for break-ins[1][2].

Once there is a leakage of information on the signing key, the whole system has to be reconstructed as quickly as possible in order to prevent the spread of damage. However, it requires a long time to reconstruct all certificates, because it involves large computation and communication.

In this paper, we present a practical solution to cope with the leakage of the CA's signing-key. In our protocol, two random number generators (RNG) generate distinct random numbers, and combine them to a random number utilized in the signature algorithm and the timestamp which cannot be forged without revealing the secret of both RNG. A verifier can check the timestamp and verify validity and time when the random number has been generated. That is, it is impossible for adversaries to forge arbitrary certificates without revealing the secret of both RNGs.

We show a concrete protocol suitable for a digital signature scheme based on the discrete logarithm.

1 Introduction

1.1 Motivation

With the spreading use of networks, digital signatures and public-key cryptosystems are often used to assure identity, as well as integrity. In these systems, a public-key certificate plays an important role in order to thwart attempts to substitute one public-key for another. A public-key certificate is someone's public key, signed by a trusted person (usually known as a certification authority, or CA). In the public-key infrastructure, it is a presupposition that only the issuer of signature knows the signing key. Since the security of all clients of the CA

---
[1] This work was performed in part of Research for the Future Program (RFTF) supported by Japan Society for the Promotion of Science (JSPS) under contact no. JSPS-RFTF 96P00604.

depends on the secrecy of the CA's signing-key, the CA's will pose an attractive target for break-ins[1][2].

Many solutions to keep the attractive information for adversaries secure have been already proposed[3][4][5][6]. Especially, the threshold cryptosystem (introduced by Desmedt and Frankel[7]) enhances the security of the key by sharing it among a group of servers. An attack to this threshold cryptosystem cannot be successful without revealing more than threshold of shares (within a given period of time). Using a sufficiently high threshold can practically assure the security of the CA's signing key.

However, if an adversary should reveal more than a threshold of shares and compute the original CA's signing key, the threshold cryptosystem provides no measure to cope with this critical situation. Accordingly, once this attack has been achieved, there is no practical way to repair the system except the total reconstruction of the system. Then, the CA has to produce a new signing key, renew all certificates that has been issued, and send them back to each client of the CA. However, it is a serious problem to renew the CA's signing key, because it takes a long time to renew a large number of certificates. On the other hand, the adversary who knows the CA's signing key can produce arbitrary forged certificates that pass the verification. Therefore, the renewal of all certificates has to be performed as quickly as possible before spreading a lot of forged certificates and increasing the damage over the network.

1.2 Checking Random Number and Timestamping

The purpose of this study is to show a practical solution to cope with the leakage of the CA's signing-key. What is significant in our protocol is that a verifier can verify the validity of the random number utilized in the CA's signature algorithm by checking the timestamp[8]. Since it is distinguishable whether the certificate is produced in accordance with regular procedures of the CA, the adversary cannot forge the certificate even after the leakage of the CA's signing-key. Moreover, we divide the procedure to generate the random number and to produce the timestamp into two parts. Two random number generators (RNG) generate distinct random numbers and the CA combines them to a single random number utilized in the signature generation algorithm and to produce a timestamp which cannot be forged without revealing the secret of both RNG.

We assume that the entire secret of the CA is revealed to an adversary at some point of time, while the secret of both RNGs is not revealed. On this assumption, we present a practical and secure protocol to generate the random number with a timestamp that allows the verifier to check the validity of certificate.

In our scheme, a verifier can check the validity of the random even after the leakage of the CA's signing-key. That is, our protocol plays a part as insurance for the existential faults. If the random number is correct, the client of the certificate gets the CA to issue a new one, otherwise, this certificate is rejected and disapproved in future. Since it is not necessary to renew the whole system immediately, the transaction for the CA to issue the certificates can be shared from the viewpoint of computation and communication. We present an efficient procedure to reconstruct the system and renew all of the certificates.

We show the concrete protocol suitable for a digital signature scheme based on the discrete logarithm problem (DLP)[9][10][11]. Our scheme is applicable to most of the digital signature scheme based on DLP and has many applications in the practical network.

1.3 Related Research

Before we discuss our protocol in detail, we discuss the background of our research and the difference between previous works and our result.

As a way to cope with attack to public-key certification scheme, various techniques to enhance the security have been always proposed.

If one of the certificates should be spoiled for any reason, the CA has to revoke it as soon as possible. This problem generally called "certification revocation", is still a difficult one to solve. The use of a CRL (certification revocation list) [12] is the most common way of revoking certificates. The CRL is a list of invalid certificates and it is published over a network. On checking the validity of the certificates, the verifiers can employ the CRL in order to check that a certain certificate is not listed as revoked. However, the CRL is effective only if the number of revoked certificates is considerably smaller than the number of total distributed ones. For the considered threat, namely, an exposure of the CA's signing key, a CRL is not enough, because the CA has to revoke all of the certificates that have been distributed before. Our proposed scheme is effective in this case, because the validity of certificates, i.e. whether the CA correctly generate the signature, is publicly verifiable by checking the random number used within the signature. As far as we know, little is known about the concrete method to cope with the exposure of CA's signing key efficiently.

To use the CRL together with our scheme can make it flexible to renew the CA's signing-key and all of certificates. When there is the leakage of the CA's signing key, it is necessary to renew all certificates, however, they cannot be renew all at once. A practical solution is to distribute the renewing transaction from the time's view. CRL is applied to the verification of certificates which has been issued before the leakage, and our renewal procedure gives certificates which has been issued after the leakage priority. Consequently, the combination of the CRL and our scheme reduces the load of the CA from the implementation's view.

Turning now to the way to make the CA's signing-key secure, the elegant solutions are well known, that are, threshold signature schemes[3][4]. Using a (t, n) threshold signature scheme, the secret key is shared by a group of n players and any coalition of $t(t < n)$ players can produce a new valid signature on a given message m. Our scheme and $(2, 2)$ threshold signature schemes seem to share certain similarities in that the coalition of two players (RNG, in our case) can produce a new valid signature on a given message m[13][14].

However, the threshold signature scheme is different from ours, from computation's and communication's view. The threshold signature scheme distributes the trust among parties symmetrically and achieves the high-level security even in the presence of a minority of a malicious party[15]. However, its protocol contains a number of computations and communications on a secure channel. Our scheme reduces the number of computations and communications substantially, such that our protocol is applicable to low-power devices that generate random sequences. Therefore, we consider no malicious devices, that is, we regard these devices as tamper-resistant and low-power devices. Indeed, the number of computation is only two and the number of modular exponentiation in each RNG is only one. In addition, our scheme is not an idea directly opposed to the threshold signature scheme. Since our scheme does not manipulate the signature scheme itself, it is easy to modify our scheme to work together with existing threshold signature schemes.

Our generation of random number is different from the previous generation that has been done in [16][17]. The previous one does not show any way for an outsider to check the random number. The random number generated by our scheme is publicly verifiable whether or not the random number is generated by the authenticated RNGs. Moreover, in our scheme, the authenticated random number cannot be generated without breaking both RNGs.

Digital signature schemes based on DLP are often used in various scenarios[9] [10] [11]. In such schemes, the random number r is required for generating a signature, and g^r appears at the verification of the signature. Since random numbers generated in our scheme satisfy the conditions required in general DLP-based signature schemes, our scheme is applicable to various systems without specifying the signature generation algorithm.

1.4 Outline

The rest of this paper is organized as follows: In Sect.2 we describe the protocols we use as building blocks and give the basic assumptions. In Sect.3 we describe our protocol. In Sect.4 we analyze the requirement and the efficiency of our protocol. Finally, Sect.5 contains conclusions.

2 Preliminaries

2.1 Definition

The following notations are used in the sequel:

CA (Certification Authority) An issuer of all certificates. We assume that there is the leakage of the entire secret of the CA (not including RNGs) to an adversary at some point in time.

RNG(Random Number Generator) The RNG is the random number generator. The RNG is tamper-resistant but computationally limited. In our scheme, two RNGs (denoted as RNG_1, RNG_2) generate the random numbers. Then, the CA combines their values to a value that is utilized as the random number in a signature generation. Therefore, Both RNG_1 and RNG_2 have the following property in communication.

- RNG_1 has secret communication channels to RNG_2 and the the CA.
- RNG_2 has secret communication channels from RNG_1 and to the CA.

User A member who has his own certificate and uses it in the verification. A user's certificate has to ber issued by the CA.

Verifier A member who verifies a certificate. Since the storage capacity of the verifier is limited, he cannot hold the information of all users.

Adversary A person who attempts and succeeds in break-ins to the CA at some point in time.

After this, we assume that a certificate means a signature *sig* appended to a message m, where m includes the user's identity, a value of the user's public-key, the time of issue, etc .

Finally, we will use the following definition of the parameters.

Definition 1. Let p and q be large primes such that $q|p-1$ and let g be an element of order q in Z_p^*. Let $H(.)$ denote a secure one-way hash function which maps from the integer space to Z_q^* and symbol $\|$ be the bit string concatenation. (p, q, g, H) is public.

2.2 Basic Protocol

Schnorr Signature Scheme We apply the Schnorr signature generation algorithm [11] (extended by Okamoto[18]) to timestamp the random numbers. In Schnorr's scheme, to generate a particular private/public key pair, Alice chooses a random number s from $0 < s < q$. This is her private key. Then she calculates

$$v := g^{-s} \bmod p$$

The result v is Alice's public key. Schnorr's scheme uses a secure one-way hash function. To sign a message m, Alice picks a random number $r \in Z_q^*$ and does the following computations:

$$e := H(g^r \bmod p\|m)$$

$$y := r + se \bmod q$$

The signature on the message m is the pair (e, y). To verify the signature, Bob computes:

$$z := g^y v^e \bmod p$$

and tests if e is equal to $H(m\|Z)$. If this test is true, Bob accepts the signature as valid.

In Schnorr's algorithm, most of the computation for signature generation can be completed in a processing stage, independent of the message being signed. Hence, it can be done during idle time and does not affect the signature speed[19]. These features are suitable for our purpose.

Combination of Random Number and Secret (*Comb*) In order to combine the random numbers generated by the RNGs to a random number utilized in the CA's signature generation, we adapt and optimize the technique of the 3-party distributed computation protocol in [20].

Alice and Bob possess $a_1 \in Z_q$ and $a_2, e_2 \in Z_q$ respectively. They generate random $r_1 \in Z_q$ and $r_2 \in Z_q$, respectively. They wish to let Carol know the information about $r = (a_1 + a_2)r_2 + e_2 r_1 \pmod q$ such that at the end of the computation Carol has no information about a_1, a_2, e_2, r_1, r_2. Simultaneously, Alice has no information about a_2, e_2, r_2, r and Bob has no information about a_1, r_1, r.

Definition 2. Two participants, Alice and Bob, secretly possess $a_1 \in Z_q$ and $a_2, e_2 \in Z_q$ respectively and choose at random $r_1 \in Z_q$ and $r_2 \in Z_q$ respectively. The distributed computation protocol *Comb* performs to let Carol know the information about $c = (a_1 + a_2)r_2 + e_2 r_1 \pmod q$ without revealing any additional information to each other. The protocol consists of three steps.

Step.1 Alice computes $\mathcal{MES}_{A \to C}(a_1, r_1)$ and $\mathcal{MES}_{A \to B}(a_1, r_1)$ using the algorithm Γ_1 and sends the former to Carol and the latter to Bob.

$$a_1, r_1 \xrightarrow{\Gamma_1} \underset{A \to B}{\mathcal{MES}}(a_1, r_1), \ \underset{A \to C}{\mathcal{MES}}(a_1, r_1)$$

Step.2 Bob computes $\mathcal{MES}_{B \to C}(a_2, e_2, r_2)$ using the algorithm Γ_2 and sends it to Carol.

$$\underset{A \to B}{\mathcal{MES}}(a_1, r_1), a_2, e_2, r_2 \xrightarrow{\Gamma_2} \underset{B \to C}{\mathcal{MES}}(a_2, e_2, r_2)$$

Step.3 Carol computes r using the algorithm Γ_3.

$$\underset{A \to C}{\mathcal{MES}}(a_1, r_1) + \underset{A \to C}{\mathcal{MES}}(a_2, e_2, r_2) \xrightarrow{\Gamma_3} r$$

We show the detail of the algorithm Γ_1, Γ_1 and Γ_3. We assume that x_A, x_B, x_C are public parameters corresponding Alice, Bob and Carol respectively and all arithmetic operation are done modulo q. The protocol works as follows:

Alice Alice picks two random lines $f_{a_1}(x)$ and $f_{r_1}(x)$ such that they intersect with the y-axis at a_1, r_1, respectively. She evaluates each line at three points x_A, x_B, x_C. Next, Alice picks three random numbers t_1, t_2, t_3 and a random quadratic polynomial $f_{rnd}(x)$ such that $f_{rnd}(0) = 0$. She computes:

$$r_A = (f_{a_1}(x_A) + t_1)t_2 + t_3 f_{r_1}(x_A) + f_{rnd}(x_A).$$

She computes and sends $\mathcal{MES}_{A \to B}(a_1, r_1)$ to Bob and $\mathcal{MES}_{A \to C}(a_1, r_1)$ to Carol (After this, we denote these Alice's computation Γ_1).

$$Alice \longrightarrow Bob : \underset{A \to B}{\mathcal{MES}}(a_1, r_1) = (f_{a_1}(x_B), f_{r_1}(x_B), f_{rnd}(x_B), t_1, t_2, t_3)$$
$$Alice \longrightarrow Carol : \underset{A \to C}{\mathcal{MES}}(a_1, r_1) = (f_{a_1}(x_C), f_{r_1}(x_C), f_{rnd}(x_C), r_A)$$

Bob Bob computes $t'_1 = (t_1 - a_2)/x_A$, $t'_2 = (t_2 - r_2)/x_A$ and $t'_3 = (t_3 - e_2)/x_A$. Note that the three lines $f_{a_2}(x) = t'_1 x + a_2$, $f_{r_2} = t'_2 x + r_2$ and $f_{e_2} = t'_3 x + e_2$ intersect with the y-axis at a_2, r_2, e_2 respectively and evaluate to t_1, t_2, t_3 at x_A. Next, Bob computes:

$$r_B = (f_{a_1}(x_B) + f_{a_2}(x_B))f_{r_2}(x_B) + f_{e_2}(x_B)f_{r_1}(x_B) + f_{rnd}(x_B)$$

and sends $\mathcal{MES}_{B \to C}(a_2, r_2, e_2)$ to Carol (After this, we denote these Bob's computation Γ_2).

$$Bob \longrightarrow Carol : \underset{B \to C}{\mathcal{MES}}(a_2, r_2, e_2) = (f_{a_2}(x_C), f_{r_2}(x_C), f_{e_2}(x_C), r_B)$$

Carol From $\mathcal{MES}_{A \to C}(a_1, r_1)$ and $\mathcal{MES}_{B \to C}(a_2, r_2, e_2)$, Carol computes:

$$r_C = (f_{a_1}(x_C) + f_{a_2}(x_C))f_{r_2}(x_C) + f_{e_2}(x_C)f_{r_1}(x_C) + f_{rnd}(x_C)$$

She then interpolates the quadratic polynomial $\alpha(x)$ that passes through the points $(x_A, r_A), (x_B, r_B), (x_C, r_C)$. Carol has $\alpha(0) = r$ (After this, we denote these Carol's computation Γ_3).

To see that $\alpha(0)$ indeed equals r observe that the polynomial $\alpha(x)$ satisfies

$$\alpha(x) = (f_{a_1}(x) + f_{a_2}(x))f_{r_2}(x) + f_{e_2}(x)f_{r_1}(x) + f_{rnd}(x)$$

Indeed, $\alpha(x_i) = r_i$ for $i = A, B, C$. It is clear that Alice and Bob cannot learn the secret information of each other, in addition to the value of r.

Lemma 3. *Given r, Carol can simulate each transcript of the protocol. Consequently, she learns nothing more than the value of r.*

Sketch of the Proof To simulate Carol's view, the simulator picks at random $(a_{1,c}, r_{1,c}, a_{2,c}, e_{2,c}, r_{2,c}, rnd_c)$ and computes $r_C = (a_{1,c} + a_{2,c})r_{2,c} + e_{2,c}r_{1,c} + rnd_c$ and then picks a random quadratic polynomial $\alpha(x)$ satisfying $\alpha(0) = r$ and $\alpha(x_C) = r_C$. It computes $r_A = \alpha(x_A)$ and $r_B = \alpha(x_B)$. These values are a perfect simulation of Carol's view $\square$.

The number of the messages during this protocol is only three: Alice sends $\mathcal{MES}_{A \to B}$ to Bob and $\mathcal{MES}_{A \to C}$ to Carol. Then Bob sends $\mathcal{MES}_{B \to C}$ to Carol. Moreover, this protocol is efficient in computation since no modular exponentiation is performed.

2.3 Basic Assumption

As a presupposition of our scenario, we assume the following conditions for considering the adversary.

Assumption 2.1 *The entire secret information of the CA is leaked to an adversary at some point in time, including the secret keys and the algorithm.*

Assumption 2.2 *The secret information of at least one of the RNGs is secure against break-ins by the adversary.*

The rest of the paper depends on the following assumption.

Assumption 2.3 *(Discrete Logarithm Assumption[15]) Let q be a large prime (e.g. $q \geq 2^{512}$) and α a generator of the multiplicative group Z_q^*; under the discrete logarithm assumption, when $q - 1$ has at least one large factor, the modular exponentiation function $f : x \rightarrow \alpha^x \mod q$ is hard to invert.*

Based on the above assumptions, we will give the description of our protocol to maintain the unforgeability of certificates and to facilitate a system reconstruction even after there is the leakage of the CA's secret.

3 Protocol

Our protocol consists of four parts, namely, the *preliminaries* by CA, the *shared generation of random numbers* by RNG_1 and RNG_2, *timestamp and signature generation* and *verification*.

3.1 Preliminary

The CA randomly chooses three elements s_1, s_2, a of order $q - 1$ in Z_q^* and chooses two integers a_1, a_2 such that $a = a_1 + a_2 \pmod{p}$, where (s_1, a_1) and (s_2, a_2) are the secret keys of RNG_1 and RNG_2, respectively. $h = g^a \pmod{p}$ and $v = g^{s_1} h^{s_2}$ are the public verification keys. The CA erases the value a.

3.2 Shared Generation of Random Number

At first, the CA inputs the value of $H(m)$ to RNG_1 and RNG_2.

RNG_1 RNG_1 picks a random number $r_1 \in Z_q^*$ and does the following computations:

$$RNG_1 \ : \ e_1 := H(g^{r_1} \mod p \| H(m) \| t)$$

$$RNG_1 \ : \ y_1 := r_1 + s_1 e_1 \mod q,$$

where H(m) is the message and t is the time and (e_1, y_1) is the Schnorr signature [11] on the value of $H(m) \| t$. Simultaneously, RNG_1 computes the two messages $\mathcal{MES}_{1 \rightarrow 2}(a_1, r_1)$, $\mathcal{MES}_{1 \rightarrow C}(a_1, r_1)$ using the algorithm Γ_1 in Definition 2.

$$RNG_1 \ : \ a_1, r_1 \xrightarrow{\Gamma_1} \underset{1 \rightarrow 2}{\mathcal{MES}}(a_1, r_1), \underset{1 \rightarrow C}{\mathcal{MES}}(a_1, r_1)$$

RNG_1 sends $(t, e_1, y_1, \mathcal{MES}_{1 \rightarrow 2})$ to RNG_2 and $(t, e_1, y_1, \mathcal{MES}_{1 \rightarrow C})$ to the CA.

$$RNG_1 \longrightarrow RNG_2 \ : \ t, e_1, y_1, \underset{1 \rightarrow 2}{\mathcal{MES}}(a_1, r_1)$$

$$RNG_1 \longrightarrow CA \ : \ t, e_1, y_1, \underset{1 \rightarrow C}{\mathcal{MES}}(a_1, r_1)$$

RNG_2 RNG_2 picks a random number $r_2 \in Z_q^*$ and does the following computations:

$$RNG_2 \ : \ e_2 := H(h^{y_1} \bmod p \| H(m) \| t)$$

$$RNG_2 \ : \ y_2 := r_2 + s_2 e_1 e_2 \bmod q$$

Simultaneously, RNG_2 computes the message $\mathcal{MES}_{2 \to C}(a_2, r_2, e_2)$ using the algorithm Γ_2 in Definition 2.

$$RNG_2 \ : \ \mathcal{MES}_{1 \to 2}(a_1, r_1), a_2, e_2, r_2 \xrightarrow{\Gamma_2} \mathcal{MES}_{2 \to C}(a_2, e_2, r_2)$$

RNG_2 sends $(t, e_2, y_2, \mathcal{MES}_{2 \to C}(a_2, e_2, r_2))$ to the CA.

$$RNG_2 \longrightarrow CA \ : \ t, e_2, y_2, \mathcal{MES}_{2 \to C}(a_2, e_2, r_2)$$

3.3 Timestamp & Signature Generation

The CA issues the certificate of user U, that is, the signature sig on the message m (including the identity of U, value of the user's public-key, the time of issue, etc .), and transmits it to U.

The CA computes $r = (a_1 + a_2)r_2 + e_2 r_1$ from $\mathcal{MES}_{1 \to C}$ and $\mathcal{MES}_{2 \to C}$ using the algorithm Γ_3 in Definition 2. The CA uses r as the random number for signature generation.

$$CA \ : \ \mathcal{MES}_{1 \to C}(a_1, r_1) + \mathcal{MES}_{2 \to C}(a_2, e_2, r_2) \xrightarrow{\Gamma_3} r$$

A set of values (t, e_1, e_2, y_2) is the timestamp on the random number r.

$$CA \ : \ timestamp(r) := (t, e_1, e_2, y_2)$$

The CA generates the certificates, that is, the signature sig on a given message m using the DLP based signature generation algorithm $\mathcal{SIG}$.

$$CA \ : \ m, r \xrightarrow{\mathcal{SIG}} sig$$

Finally, the CA sends $m, sig, timestamp(r)$ to U and erases r, y_1.

$$CA \longrightarrow U \ : \ m, sig, timestamp(r)$$

3.4 Verification

The verification procedure is different between before and after the adversary obtains the secret of the CA. There is hardly any increase in the number of operations in verification before the leakage of the CA's secret, even though we apply our protocol to the normal signature scheme. Since the attack under consideration here is the extremely rare case that the CA's signing key is completely leaked to an adversary, the increase in operations with respect to the ordinary process should be minimized if possible.

In case that the CA's secret has not been leaked yet, the timestamp generated by our scheme is not used. Therefore, we will consider the case that there is the leakage of the CA's secret for some reason, e.g. a corrupted administrator or break-ins.

The signature scheme SIG itself is not secure after this failure. Therefore, the verifier checks the random number utilized in the signature scheme. In this check, the additional information, namely, $timestamp(r)$, is used. Through the check of the correctness of the timestamp, the verifier can discriminate whether the random number used in the signature has been generated by authorized RNGs in a correct time.

The verification procedure works as follows. In the beginning, the verifier V computes $z = g^r \bmod p$ by SIG.

$$V \; : \; m, sig \xrightarrow{SIG} g^r (\equiv z) \bmod p$$

V computes:

$$V \; : \; \gamma := v^{e_1}(zh^{-y_2})^{1/e_2} \bmod p$$

and tests whether e_2 is equal to $H(\gamma \| H(m) \| t)$. If this test is true, V accepts the random number used in the signature as valid. If false, V sends that result to the CA.

4 Analysis

4.1 Verifiability

At first, we will show the verifiability of the correct timestamp.

Theorem 4. *If the timestamp (t, e_1, e_2, y_2) on random number r is correct, it passes the verification procedure.*

Theorem 5. *Our verification procedure can verify the correctness of the timestamp without revealing r itself.*

Sketch of the Proof

$$\begin{cases} y_1 = r_1 + s_1 e_1 \bmod q \implies g^{y_1} = g^{r_1} g^{s_1 e_1} \bmod p \\ \qquad\qquad\qquad\qquad \Longleftrightarrow g^{y_1 e_2} = g^{r_1 e_2} g^{s_1 e_1 e_2} \bmod p \\ y_2 = r_2 + s_2 e_1 e_2 \bmod q \implies h^{y_2} = h^{r_2} h^{s_2 e_1 e_2} \bmod p \end{cases}$$

$$\Longleftrightarrow g^{y_1 e_2} h^{y_2} \bmod p = g^{r_1 e_2} h^{r_2} (g^{s_1} h^{s_2})^{e_1 e_2} \bmod p$$
$$= g^r v^{e_1 e_2} \bmod p \quad (\text{because } r = a r_2 + r_1 e_2)$$

$$\Longleftrightarrow g^{y_1} = (g^r h^{-y_2})^{1/e_2} v^{e_1} \bmod p$$

$$\implies e_2 = H(g^{y_1} \bmod p \| H(m) \| t)$$
$$= H((g^r h^{-y_2})^{1/e_2} v^{e_1} \bmod p \| H(m) \| t) \bmod p \quad \square$$

4.2 Security

Now we examine the security of our scheme. According to the extent of the leakage, we have to consider four cases.

Case. 1 An adversary has no information about the secret of the CA, RNG_1 or RNG_2. That is, he knows several sets of $< m, sig, timestamp(r) >$.

Case. 2 The CA's secret has become known to an adversary, who has no information about the secret of RNG_1, RNG_2. That is, the adversary knows the algorithm SIG and several sets of $< m, sig, r, timestamp(r) >$.

Case. 3 The CA's secret and RNG_1's secret are known to an adversary, who has no information about the secret of RNG_2. That is, the adversary knows the algorithm SIG, the values of $< a_1, s_1 >$ and several sets of $< m, sig, r, timestamp(r), r_1, y_1 >$.

Case. 4 The CA's secret and RNG_2's secret are known to an adversary, who has no information about the secret of RNG_1. That is, the adversary knows the algorithm SIG, the values of $< a_2, s_2 >$ and several sets of $< m, sig, r, timestamp(r), r_2 >$.

Note that the random number r can be derived from a pair of $< m, sig >$ if there is the knowledge of the signing key, namely, SIG, like in most of the digital signature scheme based on the discrete logarithms.

We informally clarify the security that our protocol has to satisfy.

Secrecy of Remaining Secrets In our scenario, we assume that there is the leak of the secret. However, the remaining secret should be secure against various attacks after that. We will show the remaining secret that has not leaked yet is secure in the above cases.

Lemma 6. *For the cases 1, 2 and 4, the repetition of the distributed computation protocol $Comb$ reveals no information about the values of a_1 and r_1 in an information theoretic sense.*

Sketch of the Proof We consider the worst case, that is, the case.4. In this case, the adversary may know the values of r, e_2, y_2 and derive r_2 from y_2, s_2, e_1, e_2 every time he performs the protocol. As a consequence of repeating **Comb** n times, the adversary may know n equations and the $3n + 1$ values $< a_2, r, r^{(2)},$ $\ldots, r^{(n)}, r_2, r_2^{(2)}, \ldots, r_2^{(n)}, e_2, e_2^{(2)}, \ldots, e_2^{(n)} >$.

$$r = (a_1 + a_2)r_2 + e_2 r_1, \quad r^{(2)} = (a_1 + a_2)r_2^{(2)} + e_2^{(2)} r_1^{(2)}$$
$$, \cdots, r^{(n)} = (a_1 + a_2)r_2^{(n)} + e_2^{(n)} r_1^{(n)} \pmod q$$

However, $n + 1$ values of $< r_1, r_1^{(2)}, \ldots, r_1^{(n)}, a_1 >$ are unknown. Therefore, these simultaneous equations do not have a unique solution and the adversary cannot know the values of a_1 and r_1. $\square$

Lemma 7. *For the cases $1, 2$ and 3, the repeated execution of the distributed computation protocol* **Comb** *reveals no information about the values of a_2 and r_2 in an information theoretic sense.*

Sketch of the Proof We consider the worst case, that is, the case.3. In this case, the adversary may know the values of $< r, e_1, e_2, y_2 >$ every time he performs the protocol. As a consequence of repeating **Comb** n times, the adversary may know $2n$ equations and the $4n + 1$ values, including a_1.

$$r = (a_1 + a_2)r_2 + e_2 r_1, \quad r^{(2)} = (a_1 + a_2)r_2^{(2)} + e_2^{(2)} r_1^{(2)}$$
$$, \cdots, r^{(n)} = (a_1 + a_2)r_2^{(n)} + e_2^{(n)} r_1^{(n)}$$
$$y_2 = r_2 + s_2 e_1 e_2, \quad y_2^{(2)} = r_2^{(2)} + s_2 e_1^{(2)} e_2^{(2)}, \quad \cdots, \quad y_2^{(n)} = r_2^{(n)} + s_2 e_1^{(n)} e_2^{(n)} \pmod q$$

However, $2n + 2$ values of $< r_1, r_1^{(2)}, \ldots, r_1^{(n)}, r_2, r_2^{(2)}, \ldots, r_2^{(n)}, a_2, s_2 >$ are unknown. Therefore, these simultaneous equations do not have a unique solution and the adversary cannot know the value of a_2, s_2 and r_2. $\square$

Lemma 8. *The security of the value of s_1 is equivalent to that of the signing-key of the Schnorr signature scheme.*

Sketch of the Proof (e_1, y_1) is the Schnorr signature on the value of ($H(m)$ $\|t$). RNG_1 does not output any other useful information for revealing the value of s_1. $\square$

Using Lemmas 6 and 8, the following theorem has been shown.

Theorem 9. *The secret of RNG_1 is as secure as the Schnorr signature scheme against the leakage of the secret of RNG_2 and CA, even after the progress of the protocol.*

Similarly, the following theorem has been shown.

Theorem 10. *The secret of RNG_2 is as secure as the Schnorr signature scheme against the leakage of the secret of RNG_1 and CA, even after the progress of the protocol.*

The proofs are omitted due to space limitation.

Unforgeability We have to consider the unforgeability of the timestamp. An adversary wishes to generate a new signature for arbitrarily selected messages. The signature algorithm $\mathcal{SIG}$ itself is meaningless except for case 1, since the adversary can forge the arbitrary signature which passes the normal verification, using $\mathcal{SIG}$ and the random number which is selected by him at random. However, in our verification procedure, it is practically impossible to forge the signature without constructing the valid random number corresponding to the message m and the time t. Therefore, we will show that there is no efficient way to derive the valid random number from the published timestamps, the public parameters and the leaked information.

Theorem 11. *The timestamp of one message does not reveal any useful information about any other timestamps.*

Sketch of the Proof Let m be the message which has the timestamp (t, e_1, e_2, y_2) and let the random number be r. Let m' be a message on which the adversary wants to forge the random number r' and the timestamp (t', e_1', e_2', y_2'). At first, if the hash function $H(\cdot)$ is collision-free, it is difficult to find (m', t') such that $(r, t, e_1, e_2, y_2) = (r', t', e_1', e_2', y_2')$ and $(H(m)\|t) = (H(m')\|t')$. Next, if $(H(m)\|t) \neq (H(m')\|t')$ and H is secure, there is no correlation between e_2 and e_2'. Therefore, the knowledge about (r, t, e_1, e_2, y_2) is not useful for constructing the forged random number and the corresponding timestamp.

Theorem 12. *Any correlation between g and h cannot be found without knowing both the secrets a_1 and a_2.*

Sketch of the Proof Let somebody one know the value of a_1 such that $h = g^a = g^{a_1} g^{a_2}$. If $a_2 \neq a_2'$, $h = g^{a_1} g^{a_2}$ is not equal to $h' = g^{a_1} g^{a_2'}$, because $h/h' = g^{a_2/a_2'} \neq 1$. Therefore, the probabilistic distribution of h is uniform and equal to the distribution of a_2. The same is true to a_1. $\square$

Theorem 13. *Let α, β be elements of order q in Z_p^*. The non-trivial values of k_1, k_2 such that $\alpha^{k_1} = \beta^{k_2} \bmod p$ cannot be derived without the knowledge about the value $a = \log_\alpha \beta$.*

Sketch of the Proof If one can derive k_1 and k_2 without a, one can also compute $\log_\alpha \beta = k_1/k_2$. This fact contradicts to the assumption 2.3 $\square$

Theorem 14. *There is no efficient algorithm to derive a valid random number and the corresponding timestamp from the published timestamps, the public parameters and the leaked information.*

Sketch of the Proof From Theorem 11 and Theorem 12, the adversary has to decide the value $l_1, l_2 \in Z_q^*$ at first and compute:

$$e_2 = (g^{l_1} h^{l_2} \bmod p \| H(m) \| t).$$

After this, we consider the worst cases 3 and 4.

Case.3 An adversary knows the values of a_1, s_1, r. Let $\lambda_2 = h^{s_2} \bmod p$. Here,

$$
\begin{aligned}
g^{l_1} h^{l_2} &= v^{e_1}(zh^{-y_2})^{1/e_2} \\
&= g^{s_1 e_1} \lambda_2^{e_1} g^{r/e_2} h^{-y_2/e_2} \\
&= g^{s_1 e_1 + r/e_2} \lambda_2^{e_1} h^{-y_2/e_2} \pmod p
\end{aligned}
$$

From Theorem 12, the following equations have to be satisfied.

$$
g^{l_1} = g^{s_1 e_1 + r/e_2} \pmod p \Longrightarrow l_1 = s_1 e_1 + r/e_2 \pmod q \Longleftrightarrow e_1 = \frac{l_1 - r/e_2}{s_1}
$$

$$
h^{l_2} = \lambda_2^{e_1} h^{-y_2/e_2} \Longleftrightarrow h^{l_2 + y_2/e_2} = \lambda_2^{e_1} \pmod p
$$

From Theorem 13, a non-trivial pair of $l_2 + y_2/e_2$ and e_1 cannot be derived from the second equation. Therefore, the unforgeability of the timestamp holds in this case.

Case.4 An adversary knows the value of a_2, s_2, r. Let $\lambda_1 = h^{s_1} \bmod p$. Here,

$$
\begin{aligned}
g^{l_1} h^{l_2} &= v^{e_1}(zh^{-y_2})^{1/e_2} \\
&= \lambda_1^{e_1} h^{s_2 e_1} g^{r/e_2} h^{-y_2/e_2} \\
&= g^{r/e_2} \lambda_1^{e_1} h^{s_2 e_1 - y_2/e_2} \pmod p
\end{aligned}
$$

From Theorem 12, the following equations have to be satisfied.

$$
g^{l_1} = g^{r/e_2} \lambda_1^{e_1} \Longleftrightarrow g^{l_1 - r/e_2} = \lambda_1^{e_1} \pmod p
$$

$$
h^{l_2} = h^{s_2 e_1 - y_2/e_2} \pmod p \Longrightarrow l_2 = s_2 e_1 - y_2/e_2 \pmod q \Longleftrightarrow y_2 = e_2(s_2 e_1 - l_2)
$$

From Theorem 13, a non-trivial pair of $l_1 - r/e_2$ and e_1 cannot be derived from the first equation. Therefore, the unforgeability of the timestamp holds in this case as well. □

Randomness Since the random numbers generated by the RNGs are utilized in the signature generation, they should have the sufficient randomness.

Theorem 15. *The probabilistic distribution of r is equivalent to that of r_1 and r_2. Consequently, if r_1 and r_2 are random, r is also random.*

Sketch of the Proof r is the linear combination of r_1, r_2 such that $r = ar_2 + e_2 r_1 \pmod q$. Therefore, the distribution of r is obviously equal to that of r_1, r_2.

4.3 Efficiency

Modular Exponentiaion and Precomputation In our protocol, most of the computation for the timestamp generation, especially the modular exponentiation, can be completed in a processing stage, independent of the corresponding message and time. Hence, it can be done during idle time and does not affect the timestamping speed. Moreover, our protocol does not require any modular exponentiation at any timestamping stage. This is significant for the implementation, e.g. of the random number generator.

The Number of Communication Our protocol is also efficient in communication since the number of messages in our protocol is only three. This feature is suitable for a practical use.

The Length of Timestamp According to [10], e_1, e_2 y_1 are 160 bit and t is almost 64 bit long. Consequently, the total length of the timestamp is only 550 bit. This result is also practical.

5 Conclusion

In this paper, we presented a practical solution to cope with the leakage of a CA's signing-key. In our protocol, two random number generators (RNG) generate the distinct random numbers for they are combined to a single random number which is utilized in the signature algorithm and the timestamp which cannot be forged without revealing the secret of both RNGs. The verifier checks the timestamp and verifies the validity and the time when the random number has been generated. That is, it is impossible for adversaries to forge arbitrary certificates without revealing the secret of both RNGs.

The novel idea of our protocol is to combine the computational efficiency of the Schnorr signature scheme[11] (extended by Okamoto[18]) with the communicative efficiency of the idea of Boneh-Francklin's distributed computation protocol[20]. Accordingly, we could achieve a reduction of the computations and communications. Our protocol is efficient enough for practical use.

Our construction of the protocol is based on the discrete logarithm assumption. Digital signature schemes based on DLP are often used in various scenarios[9][10][11]. In such schemes, the random number r is required for generating a signature, and g^r appears at the verification of the signature. Since random numbers generated in our scheme satisfy the conditions required general DLP-based signature schemes, our scheme is applicable to various systems without specifying the signature generation algorithm.

In this paper, we examined the case of two RNGs. Our future work is to deal with more RNGs.

References

1. Y. Desmedt. Threshold cryptosystem. *European Transactions on Telecommunications*, 5(4):449–457, 1994.

2. Y. Frankel and M. Yung. Distributed public key cryptography. In *Proc. of PKC'98*, pages 1–13, 1998.
3. R. Gennaro, S. Jarecki, H. Krawczyk, and T. Rabin. Robust threshold DSS signatures. In *Proc. of EUROCRYPT'96*, pages 354–371, 1996.
4. R. Gennaro, S. Jarecki, H. Krawczyk, and T. Rabin. Robust and efficient sharing of RSA functions. In *Proc. of CRYPTO'96*, pages 157–172, 1996.
5. A. Herzberg, S. Jarecki, H. Krawczyk, and M. Yung. Proactive secret sharing, or: How to cope with perpetual leakage. In *Proc. of CRYPTO'95*, pages 339–352, 1995.
6. A. Herzberg, M. Jakobsson, S. Jarecki, and H. Krawczyk. Proactive public key and signature systems. In *Proc. of The 4-th ACM Symposium on Computer and Communication Security'97*, April 1997.
7. Y. Desmedt and Y. Frankel. Threshold cryptosystem. In *Proc. of CRYPTO'89*, pages 307–315, 1990.
8. S. Haber and W .S. Stornetta. How to time-stamp a digital document. In *Proc. of CRYPTO90*, pages 99–112, 1990.
9. T. ElGamal. A public key cryptosystem and signature scheme based on discrete logarithms. *IEEE Transaction on Information Theory*, 31:469–472, 1985.
10. National Institute for Standard and Technology. Digital signature standard(DSS). *Federal Register*, 56(169):20, Aug 1991.
11. C. P. Schnorr. Efficient signature generation for smart cards. In *Proc. of CRYPTO'89*, pages 239–252, 1990.
12. ITU-T. Information technology - open systems interconnection - the directory: Authentication framework. *ITU-T Recommendation X.509*, 1993.
13. I. Ingemarsson and G. J. Simmons. A protocol to set up shared secret schemes without the assistance of a mutually trusted party. In *Proc. of EUROCRYPT'90*, pages 266–282, 1991.
14. T. P. Pedersen. A threshold cryptosystem without a trusted party. In *Proc. of EUROCRYPT'91*, pages 129–140, 1991.
15. M. Cerecedo, T.Matsumoto, and H. Imai. Efficient and secure multiparty generation of digital signatures based on discrete logarithms. *IEICE Trans. Fundamentals*, E76-A(4):532–545, 1993.
16. D. Beaver and N. So. Global, unpredictable bit generation without broadcast. In *Proc. of EUROCRYPT'93*, pages 424–434, 1994.
17. A. De Santis, Y. Desmedt, Y. Frankel, and M. Yung. How to share a function securely. In *Proc. of STOC'94*, pages 522–533, 1994.
18. T. Okamoto. Provably secure and practical identification schemes and corresponding signature schemes. In *In Proc. of CRYPTO92*, pages 31–53, 1993.
19. B. Schneier. *Applied Cryptography*. John Wiley & Sons, 1996.
20. D. Boneh and M. Franklin. Efficient generation of shared RSA keys. In *Proc. of CRYPTO'97*, pages 425–439, 1997.

Auto-Recoverable Cryptosystems with Faster Initialization and the Escrow Hierarchy

Adam Young* and Moti Yung**

Abstract. In this paper we present a new Auto-Recoverable Auto-Certifiable Cryptosystem that is based on an algebraic problem different from the original system (of Eurocrypt'98). Specifically, our new cryptosystem uses generalized ElGamal and RSA. It has the following new advantages: (1) the escrow authority's key can be set-up much faster than in the original scheme; and (2) It can be used to implement the notion we introduce here of what we call "escrow hierarchy."

Key words: Key Escrow, Public Key, Auto-Recoverable Auto-Certifiable Cryptosystems, ElGamal, RSA, NIZK, software key escrow, escrow hierarchy.

1 Introduction

The problem of conducting software key escrow efficiently in the context of public key infrastructure (PKI) was recently solved in [YY98a]. In their paper, Young and Yung present a solution that is based on generalized ElGamal. In summary, their algorithm allows a user to generate an ElGamal key pair [ElG85], and a certificate of recoverability. The certificate can be used to prove that the user's private key is recoverable by the escrow authorities. Anyone in possession of the public key of the escrow authorities, the user's public key, and the certificate is capable of verifying that the user's private key is recoverable. The certificate itself is used by the escrow authorities to recover the private key.

It is important to have a variaty of options when implementing a cryptosystem, employing different algebraic problems. It is also interesting, due to the fact that the system is new, to improve the efficiency of the original scheme and to construct more functionality into the notion of auto recoverable systems. Indeed, we proposed a scheme which outputs an ElGamal public key for the user; the escrow authority's key is based on RSA.

Recall that in Young and Yung's algorithm, the system parameters r, q, and p must be generated such that $p = 2q + 1 = 4r + 3$ where r, q, and p are prime. Such values needed for generating the escrow authorities keys are difficult to find for $r > 1024$ bits. In [YY98b] the feasibility of that construction was carried out and shown to take considerable time (heuristically the time required becomes

---

* current address: Dept. of Computer Science, Columbia University Email: ayoung@cs.columbia.edu.

** current address: CertCo New York, NY, USA. Email: moti@certco.com, moti@cs.columbia.edu

proportional to the cube of the reciprocal of the probability of a number being prime).

Our results: (1) In our proposed system, it is much easier to generate the system parameters, since we only require a relationship between two rather than three large integers; this fact is true for a centralized escrow authority. Our system is still implementable in a distributed fashion due to a recent development regarding distributed RSA key generation. (2) We define the notion of escrow hierarchy and implement a two level hierarchy based on a combined system.

2 Background and Definitions

Informally, an Auto-Recoverable and Auto-Certifiable cryptosystem is a system that allows a user to generate auto-certifiable keys efficiently. The following is the formal definition from [YY98a].

Definition 1. An Auto-Recoverable and Auto-Certifiable Cryptosystem is an (m+2)-tuple (GEN,VER,REC_1,REC_2,...,REC_m) such that:

1. GEN is a publicly known poly-time probabilistic Turing Machine that takes no input and generates the triple (K_1,K_2,P) which is left on the tape as output. Here K_2 is a randomly generated private key and K_1 is the corresponding public key. P is a poly-sized certificate that proves that K_2 is recoverable by the escrow authorities using P.
2. VER is a publicly known poly-time deterministic Turing Machine that takes (K_1,P) on its input tape and returns a boolean value. With very high probability, VER returns true iff P can be used to recover the private key K_2.
3. REC_i, where $1 \leq i \leq m$ is a private poly-time deterministic Turing Machine that takes P as input and returns share i of K_2 on its tape as output, assuming that K_2 was properly escrowed. The Turing machines REC_i for $1 \leq i \leq m$ can be used collaboratively to recover K_2.
4. It is intractable to recover K_2 given K_1 and P without REC_1,..., REC_m.

It is assumed that the Certification Authority (CA) will not publish a public key unless it is verified that the corresponding private key is escrowed properly. Let EA_i denote Escrow Authority i. It is also assumed that EA_i knows only REC_i, in addition to what is publicly known. Our system is used as follows. To publish a public key, user U runs GEN and receives (K_1,K_2,P). U keeps K_2 private and encrypts the pair (K_1,P) with the public key of the CA. U then sends the resulting ciphertext to the CA. The CA decrypts this value, and recovers (K_1,P). The CA then computes VER(K_1,P), and publishes K_1 in the database of public keys iff the result is true. Otherwise, U's submission is ignored. The certificate P is not published in either case. We will explain the reason for this later. Suppose that U's public key is accepted and K_1 appears in the database of the CA. Given P, the escrow authorities can recover K_2 as follows. EA_i computes share i of K_2 by running $REC_i(P)$. The authorities then pool their shares and recover K_2.

The notion of a shadow public key system is due to [KL95]. In a shadow public key system, a conspiring user publishes his or her unescrowed public key within the information corresponding to his or her legitimate public key which is displayed in the public key database. Thus, the escrowed public key database is used as an unescrowed public key database by the conspirators. An escrow system is said to be shadow public key resistant if it is not possible for conspirators to do this. Young and Yung's system was argued to be shadow public key resistant so long as the certificates of recoverability are not published. The same also holds for the system that we propose herein. The system in fact has the numerous specifications of software key escrow given in [YY98a].

2.1 Mathematical Preliminaries

Our system requires the following cryptographic assumption.

Problem 1: Without knowing the factorization of n, find x where $x \in Z_{2tn}^*$, given x^e mod $2tn$ and g^x mod p. Here, $p = 2tn + 1$, $n = qr$, p, q, r, and large primes,t is a small prime, g generates a large subgroup of Z_p, and $\gcd(e, \phi(tn)) = 1$. In this work $e = 3$.

We were unable to prove that the above problem is a cryptographically hard problem. Thus, the difficulty of Problem 1 is a cryptographic assumption in regards to our system. We also assume that a modified version of the RSA problem is hard. Namely, that it is hard to compute the entire plaintext if we reduce modulo $2tn$, as opposed to reducing modulo n as in RSA. Recall that t is a small prime number[3].

Intuitively, it seems that problem 1 should be hard, since x^e mod $2tn$ is a presumed one-way trapdoor function of x, and g^x mod p is a presumed one-way function of x. Clearly, Problem 1 is not hard if cracking RSA is not hard, or if computing discrete logs is not hard.

Related Work

There is a wealth of proposed solutions to the problem of key escrow. Various hardware solutions have been proposed. Yet, it has been shown that these hardware solutions should not be automatically trusted due to their black-box nature [YY96, YY97a, YY97b]. Several protocol based solutions that can be implemented in software have been proposed [Mi92, KL95]. These solutions, namely, Fair Public Key Cryptosystems and Fail-safe Key Escrow systems, respectively, impose a significant amount of overhead for the user in excess of what is present in a typical unescrowed public key system. Recently, a "Fraud-Detectable Alternative to Key-Escrow Proposals" based on ElGamal was described in [VT97]. This system was shown not to be fraud-detectable in the case of colluding criminals [YY98a]. Furthermore, this solution operates at the session level, and the

---

[3] In our implementation we can actually give the CA the value mod n and always choose values which are fixed and known mod $2t$.

proofs involved introduce a significant amount of space overhead per communication session. Various other solutions (like the TTP and some industry proposals) require changes of the session level outside the PKI protocols which may not give a global solution due to the extensive required changes in applications and communications. The solution in [YY98a] is attractive for use as a key escrow system because, from the users perspective, the system is as easy to use as a typical public key system, and it does not require any changes outside the PKI protocols (along with many other properties, see [YY98a]).

A feature that an escrow system should have is the ability of the escrow authorities to recover selected messages of users, without being able to recover all of the messages [DDFY]. This capability is useful because it allows court orders to specify exactly which messages of a suspected criminal are to be decrypted, and hence does not completely compromise the privacy of the suspected user, who may be innocent. Our proposed system supports this capability. The system's set-up of the authority key can be done distributedly [BF97, FMY98].

3 The Scheme

The following is a description of our Auto-Recoverable and Auto-Certifiable cryptosystem.

3.1 System Setup

The escrow authority (authorities) generate a shared Blum integer $n = qr$, where q and r are prime. The escrow authorities then make sure that $\gcd(3, \phi(n)) = 1$. If this condition does not hold, then the escrow authorities generate a new n. The escrow authorities then compute $p = 2tn + 1$, where t is drawn from the first, say 256 strong primes starting from 11, inclusive. If p is found to be prime using one of these values for t, then the values for n and p have been found. If none of the values for t causes p to be prime, this entire process is repeated as many times as necessary. Note that $t = 2t' + 1$ where t' is prime. Since we insist that $t > 7$, we are guaranteed that $\gcd(3, \phi(tn)) = 1$. Once n and p are found, the escrow authorities generate the private shares $d_1, d_2, ..., d_m$ corresponding to $e = 3$. A value $g \in_R Z_{2tn}^*$ is chosen such that g has an order that is at least as large as the smallest of q and r, in the field Z_p (recall that the factorization of n is not known). The values t, n, and g are made public.

This system can be setup much faster than [YY98a] since the escrow authority can generate a composite modulus very quickly, and in order to find a prime p, t can be varied as needed. The expected time to find such a p is inversely proportional to the density of primes. In contrast, in [YY98a] the system setup relied on finding three primes with a rigid relationship between them. Heuristicly this means that sampling such primes may take an expected time which is inversely proportional to the density of the primes cubed.

3.2 Key Generation

GEN operates as follows. It chooses a value $x \in_R Z_{2tn}^*$ and computes $C = x^3 \bmod 2tn$. x is the user's ElGamal private key. GEN then computes $y = g^x \bmod p$. The user's ElGamal public key is (y, g, p). Note that g may not necessarily generate Z_p, but, we can make sure that it generates a large subgroup of Z_p. GEN also computes a non-interactive zero-knowledge proof based on C and y. The following is how this proof is constructed.

1. choose $r_1, r_2, ..., r_N \in_R Z_{2tn}^*$.
2. compute $C_i = r_i^3 \bmod 2tn$ for $1 \le i \le N$
3. compute $v_i = y^{r_i} \bmod p$ for $1 \le i \le N$
4. $b = H((C_1, v_1), (C_2, v_2), ..., (C_N, v_N)) \bmod 2^N$
5. $b_i = (2^i \ AND \ b) > 0$ for $1 \le i \le N$
6. $z_i = r_i x^{'b_i} \bmod 2tn$ for $1 \le i \le N$

Here N is the number of iterations in the NIZK proof (e.g., $N = 40$). Concerning step 1, technically the prover has a chance that one of the r_i will have q or r in its factorization, this is highly unlikely. Note that b_i in step 5 results from a boolean test. b_i is 1 if when we take the logical AND of 2^i and b we get a value greater than zero. It is 0 otherwise. The proof P is $(C, (C_1, v_1), (C_2, v_2), ..., (C_N, v_N), z_1, z_2, ..., z_N)$. GEN leaves $((y,g,p),x,P)$ on the output tape. Criterion 1 of definition 1 is therefore met. The use of H is akin to the Fiat-Shamir method to make the proofs non-interactive [FS86].

3.3 Public Escrow Verification

VER takes $((y,g,p),P)$ on its input tape and outputs a boolean value. VER verifies the following things:

1. $C^{b_i} C_i = z_i^3 \bmod 2tn$ for $1 \le i \le N$
2. $v_i = (y^{1-b_i} g^{b_i})^{z_i} \bmod p$ for $1 \le i \le N$

VER returns true both criterion are satisfied. Note that skeptical verifiers may also wish to check the parameters supplied by the escrow authorities (e.g., that n is composite, p is prime, etc.).

It is clear that this proof system is complete. The proof of soundness and an informal proof that this consititutes a proof of knowledge is given in the next section.

3.4 Key Recovery

REC_i recovers share i of the user's private key x as follows. REC_i takes C from P. It then recovers share s_i using the private share d_i. It outputs s_i on its tape. The authorities then pool their shares and x is computed. Criterion 3 of definition 1 is therefore met.

3.5   Recovering Plaintext Data

The escrow authorities can recover the plaintext of users suspected of criminal activity without recovering the user's private key itself. In this section, we assume that the method being used is [BF97]. In our case the private decryption exponent is $d = \sum_{i=1}^{m} d_i \bmod \phi(tn)$, and d is the inverse of 3 mod $\phi(tn)$. To decrypt the ElGamal ciphertext (a, b) of a user U the escrow authorities proceed as follows:

1. Each of the m escrow authorities receives C corresponding to U.
2. Escrow authority 1 computes $s_1 = a^{C^{d_1}} \bmod p$.
3. Escrow authority $i + 1$ computes $s_{i+1} = s_i^{C^{d_{i+1}}} \bmod p$.
4. Escrow authority m decrypts (a, b) by computing $b/(s_{m-1}^{C^{d_m}}) \bmod p$.

Since the escrow authorities do not reveal the values C^{d_i}, no one can recover x.

4   Security of the Trapdoor Values

Assuming the difficulty of computing discrete logs, it is intractable to find x given y as constructed by GEN. We would like to prove that it is intractable to find x given C and y. However, doing so would amount to proving that Problem 1 is hard. We have therefore shown that the trapdoor values in n, y, and C are secure, under the RSA mod $2tn$ assumption (where some $1 + \log t$ information theoretic bits may be leaked), the discrete log assumption, and assuming that Problem 1 is hard. Thus, under these assumptions, the three values n, y, and C can be published together without fear that the corresponding hidden values will be found. It follows that criteria 4 of definition 1 is met.

5   Security of the New Cryptosystem

We have to show that the additional information constitutes a proof system that assures that the user knows its public key and the recoverability (proof of knowledge), while not revealing additional information (i.e., being zero-knowledge).

The proof of completeness is immediate. Consider the proof of soundness. A prover can forge an invalid proof if he can find a C and a y such that $C^{1/3}$ is not congruent to x in $y = g^x \bmod p$, and have these two values pass the N verifications.

Claim 1 *If $C^{1/3}$ is not congruent to x in $y = g^x \bmod p$, then the prover will fail the proof with overwhelming probability.*

Proof. Assume that the prover knows t where $C^{1/3} = t \bmod 2tn$. Also, assume that the prover knows u where $y = g^u \bmod p$, and t is not congruent to $u \bmod 2tn$. Consider the case where the prover guesses that $b_i = 0$. The prover then follows the protocol and reveals $z_i = r_i$. The prover clearly passes the verifications in this case. Now suppose the prover guessed wrong, and $b_i = 1$. To pass the first verification in round i, the prover must reveal $z_i = tr_i \bmod 2tn$, because $(tr_i)^3 = CC_i \bmod 2tn$. But then the prover will fail the second verification. To see this note that $g^{z_i} = g^{tr_i} = (g^t)^{r_i} \bmod p$, but $g^t \neq y = g^u \bmod p$. Suppose that the prover guesses that b_i will be 1. The prover then chooses $w_i \in_R Z_{2tn}^*$ and computes $C_i = w_i{}^3/C \bmod 2tn$, and $v_i = g^{w_i} \bmod p$. The prover sends C_i, v_i, and $z_i = w_i$ to the verifier, and clearly passes if his guess is correct. Suppose the prover guesses wrong. To pass the second check, the prover must instead send $z_i = u^{-1}w_i \bmod 2tn$. This will pass since $y^{z_i} = (g^u)^{u^{-1}w_i} = g^{w_i} = v_i$. But then the prover will fail the first check. To see this, suppose for the sake of contradiction that the prover will pass the first check. We have that, $(u^{-1}w_i)^3 = (u^{-1})^3 CC_i = (u^{-1}t)^3 C_i$. Clearly, $(u^{-1}t)^3 C_i = C_i$ iff $u = t$. But, $u = t$ contradicts our assumption that the plaintext of C is not the discrete log of y. So, the prover will fail the first check in this case. Thus the prover will fail a given round with probability $1/2$. From this it follows that the proof is sound. QED.

The following is a sketch of the proof that this system constitutes a zero-knowledge proof system. This proof applies to the interactive version of our proof system. The Fiat-Shamir methodology and a random oracle assumption are used for the non-interactive proof of zero-knowledge. The poly-time probabilistic simulator S works as follows. S first puts C, the problem instance, in the output transcript P. S chooses $r_i \in_R Z_{2tn}^*$. S then flips a coin. If the result is heads, S computes $C_i = r_i{}^3 \bmod 2tn$, and $v_i = y^{r_i} \bmod p$. If the result is tails, S chooses $C_i = r_i{}^3/C \bmod 2tn$, and $v_i = g^{z_i} \bmod p$. The restartable verifier subroutine V^* is then invoked. V^*, given it's stored history, responds with heads or tails. If S guessed correctly, then (C_i, v_i) is added to P. Otherwise, this iteration is started over again. By induction on i, it can formally be shown that the probability distribution over the transcripts generated by S is the same as the distribution of those generated by the prover and the verifier.

We will now give a sketch of the proof that this proof constitutes a proof of knowledge. Suppose that the knowledge extractor is given both possible responses z_i, call them u_0 and u_1, where the subscript equals b_i, in a given round. It follows that the knowlege extractor can extract a value z by computing $u_1/u_0 = z$. Since $C_i = u_0{}^3 \bmod 2tn$ and since $CC_i = u_1{}^3 \bmod 2tn$ it follows that $u_1{}^3/u_0{}^3 = C = z^3 \bmod 2tn$. Thus, z is the plaintext of C. Also, since $v_i = y^{u_0} \bmod p$ and since $v_i = g^{u_1} \bmod p$ it follows that $xu_0 = u_1$. Therefore, $x = u_1/u_0 = z$, the value extracted. The knowledge extractor therefore extracts the plaintext of C which is also the log of y modulo p. Thus we have shown that criterion 2 of definition 1 is met.

Claim 2 *Assuming that RSA mod 2tn is secure, our auto-recoverable auto-certifiable cryptosystem is complete, sound and zero-knowledge proof of knowledge.*

Finally, the motivation for not allowing the CA to publish P will now be explained. If P is published for each user, then our system can be used to support a shadow public key infrastructure. To see this, note that a set of conspiring users can agree on the following way to abuse the system. It is agreed that the first iteration of the proof in which $b_i = 0$ will be used to display the shadow public key in the value for z_i. So, a conspirator can display a shadow public key in P as follows. He generates N public keys, and uses these N values as his N values for the r_i in the proof. Then, assuming that b_i will be zero at least once, he is able to display a shadow public key in P.

6 Depth-3 Escrow Hierarchy

Let us introduce the notion of escrow hierarchy by an example. Consider a scenario in which each U.S. state needs to be able to escrow the private keys of its residents, and the federal government needs to be able to escrow the private keys of all U.S. citizens. However, the state police of New York should not be able to successfully wiretap the communications of residents of California, and vice-versa. This application calls for an escrow hierarchy, which can be thought of as a depth-3 tree. The federal government is the root, the states are the middle nodes, and the citizens are the leaves of the tree. This defines by example what an escrow hierarchy is.

The following is how to realize such a system using our proposed system in conjunction with the algorithm from [YY98a]. The escrow authorities generate a shared composite n such that $q' = 2tn + 1$ is prime, and such that $p = 2q' + 1$ is prime. Here t is a small prime of the form $2t' + 1$ where t' is prime. Thus, from the root of the tree to the children of the root, the escrow system that is used is the one that is described in this paper. It is somewhat more difficult to generate an appropriate prime $2tn + 1$ in this case, since $4tn + 3$ must also be prime (so we have the same inefficiency as in [YY98a]).

Each child of the root (intermediate node) then generates a (potentially shared) public key $Y \bmod 2q'$. Thus Y is an ElGamal public key in ElGamal mod $2q'$.

The leaves corresponding to (i.e. under) each of these intermediate children then generate escrowed keys based on the values for Y using the algorithm from [YY98a]. Thus, the [YY98a] algorithm is used between the intermediate nodes and the users at the leaves. Note that in this case the generator that is used in Y may only generate a large subgroup of $Z^*_{2q'}$.

Using the arguments in this paper and in [YY98a], we can show how the hierarchical system is strictly preserved by the construction.

7 Conclusion

We presented a new implementation of an Auto-Recoverable and Auto-Certifiable cryptosystem based on generalized ElGamal and assuming the difficulty of generalized ElGamal, and modified RSA. By making a reasonable new cryptographic assumption, and by using the above assumptions we showed our scheme to be secure. We also introduced the notion of escrow hierarchy.

The new scheme can either be used for faster initialization, or as part of an escrow hierarchy, a notion we have presented herein. It also demonstrates an alternative implementation of auto-recoverable systems.

References

[BF97] D. Boneh, M. Franklin. Efficient Generation of Shared RSA Keys. In *Advances in Cryptology—CRYPTO '97*, 1997. Springer-Verlag.

[DDFY] A. De Santis, Y. Desmedt, Y. Frankel, M. Yung. How to Share a Function Securely. In *ACM Symposium on the Theory of Computing*, pages 522–533, 1994.

[ElG85] T. ElGamal.
A Public-Key Cryptosystem and a Signature Scheme Based on Discrete Logarithms. In *Advances in Cryptology—CRYPTO '84*, pages 10–18, 1985. Springer-Verlag.

[FMY98] Y. Frankel, M. MacKenzie, M. Yung. Robust Efficient Distrubuted Generation of RSA Keys. In *Symposium on Theory of Computing* (STOC) '98. ACM Press.

[FS86] A. Fiat, A. Shamir. How to Prove Yourself: Practical Solutions to Identification and Signature Problems. In *Advances in Cryptology—CRYPTO '86*, pages 186–194, 1987. Springer-Verlag.

[KL95] J. Kilian and F.T. Leighton. Fair Cryptosystems Revisited. In *Advances in Cryptology—CRYPTO '95*, pages 208–221, 1995. Springer-Verlag.

[Mi92] S. Micali. Fair Public-Key Cryptosystems. In *Advances in Cryptology—CRYPTO '92*, pages 113–138, 1992. Springer-Verlag.

[RSA78] R. Rivest, A. Shamir, L. Adleman. A method for obtaining Digital Signatures and Public-Key Cryptosystems. In *Communications of the ACM*, volume 21, n. 2, pages 120–126, 1978.

[VT97] E. Verheul, H. van Tilborg. Binding ElGamal: A Fraud-Detectable Alternative to Key-Escrow Proposals. In *Advances in Cryptology—Eurocrypt '97*, pages 119–133, 1997. Springer-Verlag.

[YY96] A. Young, M. Yung. The Dark Side of Black-Box Cryptography. In *Advances in Cryptology—CRYPTO '96*, pages 89–103, Springer-Verlag.

[YY97a] A. Young, M. Yung. Kleptography: Using Cryptography against Cryptography. In *Advances in Cryptology—Eurocrypt '97*, pages 62–74. Springer-Verlag.

[YY97b] A. Young, M. Yung. The Prevalence of Kleptographic Attacks on Discrete-Log Based Cryptosystems. In *Advances in Cryptology—CRYPTO '97*, Springer-Verlag.

[YY98a] A. Young, M. Yung. Auto-Recoverable and Auto-Certifiable Cryptosystems. In *Advances in Cryptology—Eurocrypt '98*. Springer-Verlag.

[YY98b] A. Young, M. Young. Finding Length-3 Positive Cunningham Chains and their Cryptographic Significance. In *Algorithmic Number Theory Symposium III*, 1998. Springer-Verlag.

A Secure Pay-per View Scheme
for Web-Based Video Service[*]

Jianying Zhou[1] and Kwok-Yan Lam[2]

[1] Kent Ridge Digital Labs
21 Heng Mui Keng Terrace
Singapore 119613
email: jyzhou@krdl.org.sg

[2] School of Computing
National University of Singapore
10 Kent Ridge Crescent
Singapore 119260
email: lamky@comp.nus.edu.sg

Abstract. With the development of high speed computer networks, video service on the Web has huge market potential in that the video service can be provided to subscribers with greater time and schedule flexibility compared to the current cable TV system. Under the *pay-per-view* (PPV) scheme, subscribers only need to pay for the programs that they have watched. A critical issue on PPV service is the capability of settling disputes over PPV service charges. This is especially important in the case that the Internet communication could be interrupted (by accident or deliberately) in the middle of a viewing session. This paper proposes a fair PPV billing protocol for web-based video service. With this protocol, a video service will be divided into small units, and a subscriber needs to submit cryptographic evidence which enables fair billing based on the number of units being provided in a viewing session. In addition, by the establishment of a one-way sequential link, the validity of evidence is maintained efficiently without any involvement of trusted third parties. Our scheme is light-weighted in terms of the storage requirement and computation overheads on subscribers, thus subscribers can request PPV service securely with their own smart cards regardless of their physical location.

Keywords: pay-per-view, video service, fair billing, validity of evidence

1 Introduction

Cable TV is a popular entertainment medium in our daily life. The charging mechanism for cable TV is very simple, where cable television companies pro-

---

[*] The research towards this paper was funded by the National Science and Technology Board of Singapore, and was conducted in the School of Computing, National University of Singapore.

vide *premium channels* on a monthly basis to subscribers who pay a flat fee irrespective of their viewing habit. A special device known as the *set-top box* (STB) should be installed by subscribers, which receives the encrypted signal from a premium channel, decrypts and decodes the compressed digital video and passes the signal to the television. The system does not permit subscribing or unsubscribing to these channels prior to the showing of some particular program.

Pay-per-view (PPV) service has the advantages over cable television service in that it can offer greater time and schedule flexibility to customers. With the development of high speed computer networks, it is possible to provide video services on the Web to customers with more flexibility. Under the PPV scheme, customers may choose to watch programs they are interested in at any time, and only need to pay for the programs that they have watched [6].

A critical issue on PPV service is to make provision for settling possible disputes over PPV service charges, especially in the case that the communication is interrupted (by accident or deliberately) in the middle of a viewing session. In order for the Web-based PPV service to be widely accepted, it is important that customers are not wrongly charged because of the more complex charging mechanism over a less reliable delivery medium.

In this paper, we propose a fair PPV billing protocol for web-based video service. With this protocol, a video service will be divided into small units, and a customer needs to submit cryptographic evidence which enables fair billing based on the number of units being provided in a viewing session. In addition, by the establishment of a one-way sequential link, the validity of evidence is maintained efficiently without any involvement of trusted third parties. Our scheme is light-weighted in terms of the storage requirement and computation overheads on customers, thus can be implemented in a resource scarce device such as a smart card.

The rest of the paper is organised as follows. We establish the model of PPV service on the Web and identify the security requirements in the next section. In Section 3, we present a simple PPV billing protocol and analyse its weakness. In Section 4, we propose a fair PPV billing protocol and demonstrate how to settle the billing problem with evidence collected in our protocol. In Section 5, we put forward an efficient approach to maintaining the validity of evidence. In Section 6, we assess the feasibility of protocol implementation in a smart card to support mobility of subscribers. Section 7 concludes the paper.

The following basic notation is used throughout the paper.

- X, Y: concatenation of two messages X and Y.
- $H(X)$: a one-way hash function of message X.
- $eK(X)$: encryption of message X with key K.

- $sS_A(X)$: party A's digital signature on message X with the private signature key S_A.
- S_A and V_A: party A's private signature key and public verification key.
- P_A and P_A^-: party A's public encryption key and private decryption key.
- $A \to B : X$: party A sends message X to party B.

2 PPV Service Model

Suppose a video service provider S offers PPV service on the Web. If a customer C intends to obtain PPV service from S, C needs to make a subscription to S. Thereafter, C will receive a bill periodically from S for video services C requested from S during the charging period. In general, we can divide PPV service into four stages:

1. Subscription
2. Browse
3. Request and View
4. Payment and Dispute Resolution

At Stage 1, C needs to provide his public key certificate issued by some *certification authority* (CA) [5] trusted by S, and his (email) address for receiving bills. After checking C's subscription information, S will open an account for C. Such an account may be maintained until C cancels his subscription or C's public key certificate expires.

At Stage 2, C can browse the catalogue of video programs provided by S, which may include the titles, abstracts, and duration of each program, as well as the price for a view of each of the listed programs. Once a choice is made, C enters Stage 3 when he sends a view request to S. The request contains enough information to enable S to charge the service request to C's account before video is delivered. C will be billed at Stage 4 for services he requested from S.

To provide a secure PPV service, we should first identify the risks that each party is subject to. The PPV service provider S is subject to the following risks:

S1. video stream may be tapped by a non-subscriber;
S2. C denies request for services;
S3. C denies receipt of the service he requested;
S4. C claims that the service was interrupted before completion.

On the other hand, the subscriber C is subject to the following risks:

C1. a hacker may masquerade as C to obtain free service;
C2. C is charged for a service he did not request;
C3. C is charged but did not obtain the (complete) service;
C4. C is overcharged for a service he requested.

To protect against risks **S1** and **C1**, entity authentication should be conducted between S and C, and video streams should be transmitted in cipher text. The remaining risks can be summarised as repudiation of billing which is addressed in this paper.

Repudiation is defined as "denial by one of the entities involved in a communication of having participated in all or part of the communication" [8]. Non-repudiation services protect the transacting parties against any false denial that a particular event or action has taken place. The basic non-repudiation services are [15]

- *Non-repudiation of Origin* (*NRO*) which provides the recipient of a message with evidence of origin of the message to protect against any attempt by the originator to falsely deny having sent the message.
- *Non-repudiation of Receipt* (*NRR*) which provides the originator of a message with evidence of receipt of the message to protect against any attempt by the recipient to falsely deny having received the message.

In the case of PPV service on the Web, it is desirable that subscribers cannot deny receipt of services they requested. On the other hand, subscribers should not be wrongly charged due to any billing error or security breach on the serving network. *Non-repudiation of Billing* (*NRB*) is a security service established between a service provider and its subscribers to enable the settlement of disputes over the correctness of service charges.

NRB could be built on *NRR* by demanding evidence of receipt from a subscriber being served. Some non-repudiation protocols exist for fair exchange of a message and evidence of receipt of the message [2, 3, 7, 15], thus achieving non-repudiation of billing. However, it is infeasible to achieve *NRB* in such a way if the content of a message to be transmitted is not completely fixed before the end of a transaction (e.g. a live program which is transmitted while actually happening), or if the service charge is irrelevant to the content of a message to be transmitted (e.g. the charge of a phone call). Instead, non-repudiation of billing for these services is mainly based on the duration of a communication session being connected. PPV service is provided with real-time connection between the service provider and the subscriber being served. This paper aims to propose a fair PPV billing protocol which makes the correctness of PPV service charges undeniable.

When a subscriber C requests a video program from S, he needs to provide S with evidence which can be used to prove that C is charged correctly for the service offered. S is responsible for maintaining the evidence until C has settled the bill. If C is in doubt of the bill, C can lodge a complaint to S and S can use the evidence to check whether C is wrongly charged. If both parties cannot reach an agreement by themselves, an arbitrator may be invoked to settle the dispute over the correctness of the bill. The arbitrator may ask S to present evidence to prove the service supplied to C. If S cannot present the evidence, C can reject the payment. Otherwise, C has to pay the bill.

3   A Simple PPV Billing Protocol – SPPV

The security of Stage 3 is the key to a successful PPV service. This is because PPV service has a complex charging mechanism and a subscriber is billed according to the video programs requested over the charging period. As disputes may arise concerning the correctness of a bill, it is important to establish certain evidence at this stage in order to enable the settlement of disputes at Stage 4. Such evidence is usually represented by digital signatures [9, 16]. Here we present a simple PPV billing protocol SPPV.

Suppose C is a subscriber at S, then S holds C's public key certificate. We assume that S's public key certificate is publicly available to its subscribers. Once C has chosen a video program to watch, C can make a view request as follows.

$$1. \; C \rightarrow S : Id, Pr, T_g, \; sS_C(S, Id, Pr, T_g)$$
$$2. \; S \rightarrow C : eP_C(K_s), \; sS_S(C, Id, T_g, K_s)$$
$$3. \; C \rightarrow S : H(C, S, Id, T_g, K_s)$$

In the above protocol, Id is the identifier of a video program, Pr is the price for viewing this program, T_g is the date and time that C's service request is made, K_s is a session key issued by S to C for deciphering the video stream to be transmitted.

Protocol SPPV is efficient for implementation. When making a view request, the subscriber C first generates a digital signature on his request as evidence and sends the signed request to the service provider S at Step 1. After verifying C's request, S issues a session key K_s to C at Step 2. Here the privacy of K_s is protected with C's public encryption key P_C while the authenticity of K_s is ensured with S's digital signature. The advantage is that C and S need not share a secret in advance. (The more secrets to be shared, the more difficult to manage these secrets.) By verifying S's digital signature, C can be sure that his view request is successful and K_s is the session key to be used for protecting the subsequent video stream. The reply from C to S at Step 3 makes S believe that C has received K_s and is ready for receiving the service.

Protocol SPPV provides a limited protection for the correctness of PPV service charges. Once S holds C's signed view request, C cannot deny the service charge. In other words, C has to be committed to the payment before viewing the program, which is unfair to C in the transaction. After submitting the view request, C has to wait for the service from S. However, C may not receive a *complete* service if the communication is suddenly interrupted, and it will be out of C's control to cancel his view request in such a case. Without S's agreement, C will be liable to the charge on any service he requested, even if the service is incomplete. Such a policy is necessary in protocol SPPV. Otherwise, C may terminate a service before completion thus deny the charge if he finds that the program is not interesting or if he cannot go on watching the program for other reasons.

4 A Fair PPV Billing Protocol – FPPV

As we pointed out in Section 3, protocol SPPV does not protect against the billing problem due to sudden interruption of communication in the middle of a viewing session. Such a scenario leaves subscribers in an unfair billing situation, and is especially undesirable in a network where bandwidth is not guaranteed such as the Internet. This section presents a fair billing protocol based on a combination of digital signature and one-way hash chain techniques originating from [13].

A *one-way hash chain* is constructed by recursively applying an input string to a one-way hash function [10], denoted as $H^i(x) = H(H^{i-1}(x))$ $(i = 1, 2, \cdots)$ where $H^0(x) = x$. According to the feature of one-way hash function, if x is chosen randomly and the hash chain is kept secret, given $H^i(x)$ it is computationally infeasible to find the input $H^{i-1}(x)$ except the originator of the hash chain. This forms the basis of our fair PPV billing protocol FPPV. The subscriber C can include a chained one-way hash value in his signed view request. Then C releases other chained hash values at a pre-defined interval during the service. S only needs to store the last hash value released by C as evidence to prove the duration of the service provided to C.

4.1 The Protocol

In the catalogue of video programs provided by S, the size of a charging unit L (e.g. 1 minute, 5 minutes, or 10 minutes etc.) and the number of units m for each program should be specified. Suppose C has browsed the catalogue and chosen a video program to watch. When C requests to view the program, C first chooses a random number n, and generates m chained one-way hash values as follows:

$$H^i(n) = H(H^{i-1}(n)) \quad (i = 1, 2, \cdots, m)$$

where $H^0(n) = n$. C keeps $H^0(n), H^1(n), \cdots, H^{m-1}(n)$ secret. Then C initiates the following *view request protocol*.

1. $C \rightarrow S : Id, Pr, L, m, H^m(n), T_g, \; sS_C(S, Id, Pr, L, m, H^m(n), T_g)$
2. $S \rightarrow C : eP_C(K_s), \; sS_S(C, Id, T_g, K_s)$
3. $C \rightarrow S : H(C, S, Id, T_g, K_s)$

After C makes a successful view request, C will release $H^i(n)$ $(i = m-1, m-2, \cdots)$ to S at a pre-defined interval L during the service [1]. S will check whether

---

[1] C can make use of the number of video frames he received from S as a counting mechanism.

$H(H^i(n)) = H^{i+1}(n)$. If true, S will overwrite the previous $H^{i+1}(n)$ and save the current $H^i(n)$ as a piece of evidence, and provide next unit of service to C. If S does not receive $H^i(n)$, or receives incorrect $H^i(n)$, S will cut off the service (with a warning in advance).

If the communication is interrupted accidentally in the middle of a service, the service can be continued from where it has stopped after the communication is recovered. Suppose the service was interrupted after C had released the jth chained hash value $H^{m-j}(n)$. C only needs to initiate the following *reconnection protocol*.

1. $C \to S : Id, T_g, j, H^{m-j}(n)$
2. $S \to C : eP_C(K_s), sS_S(C, Id, T_g, K_s)$
3. $C \to S : H(C, S, Id, T_g, K_s)$

A deadline may be defined for a valid reconnection request in the service policy. After receiving C's reconnection request, S will check whether the request is made before the deadline and $H^{m-j}(n)$ matches the last chained hash value held by S. If successful, the session key K_s will be re-established [2], and S will continue the service from the jth unit.

The above mechanism can support a more flexible charging policy in PPV service. Subscribers could be allowed to terminate a service before completion if they find that the program is not interesting or if they cannot go on watching the program for other reasons, and they may only be charged for the part of the program they have watched. This billing scheme does not provide *complete fairness* since the last unit of service may remain in dispute if the communication is terminated before completion of the service. Nevertheless, as long as the service provider S chooses an appropriate size of charging unit L, the possible loss of one-unit service charge can be limited to a negligible level.

4.2 Dispute Resolution

The PPV service provider S sends a bill to the subscriber C periodically. If C is in doubt of the charges, C can lodge a complaint to S and S will use the evidence collected at Stage 3 to check whether C is wrongly charged. If both parties cannot reach an agreement by themselves, a third party arbitrator may be invoked to settle the dispute over the correctness of the bill. The arbitrator may ask S to present evidence to prove the service supplied to C. If S cannot provide such evidence, the arbitrator will conclude that C is wrongly charged. Hence, S is responsible for maintaining the evidence until C has paid the bill.

Besides C's signed view request, the last chained hash value released by C in PPV service is vital for a fair settlement of the billing problem. For example,

---

[2] To avoid re-encrypting the video stream, S may choose the same session key as the one used before interruption.

the evidence of a *complete* service with the duration of $L * m$ supplied to C is

$$S, Id, Pr, L, m, H^m(n), T_g, \; sS_C(S, Id, Pr, L, m, H^m(n), T_g), \; H^0(n)$$

After receiving the above evidence from S, the arbitrator will check

- whether C's digital signature $sS_C(S, Id, Pr, L, m, H^m(n), T_g)$ is valid;
- whether $H^m(H^0(n)) = H^m(n)$ where $H^0(n)$ is the last chained hash value collected by S.

If the first check is positive, the arbitrator will believe that C made the view request. If the second check is also positive, the arbitrator will conclude that C was provided the service with a duration of $L * m$ and C is responsible for the corresponding charge Pr.

Since a service may be interrupted (by accident or deliberately) before completion, a billing policy should be defined for *incomplete* services. Suppose the above service was interrupted after S had received the jth chained hash value $H^{m-j}(n)$ from C. The arbitrator can make a similar check as above to see whether $H^j(H^{m-j}(n)) = H^m(n)$. If so, the arbitrator will conclude that C was provided an incomplete service with a duration of $L * j$. Depending on the billing policy for incomplete services, C will be liable for a charge accordingly.

5 Maintaining Validity of Evidence

In order to support undeniable billing in PPV service, digital signatures are generated and collected as non-repudiation evidence in our mechanisms SPPV and FPPV. As signature keys may be compromised and the validity of signatures may become questionable, additional security mechanisms need to be imposed on digital signatures [17].

A straightforward approach to secure digital signatures for non-repudiation requires that users interact with an on-line trusted *time-stamping authority* (TS) to get each newly generated digital signature time-stamped [1, 4, 11, 14] so that there is extra evidence to prove whether the signature was generated before the corresponding public key certificate was revoked and thus is deemed valid. Such an approach may be employed in high value business transactions where security is the most important requirement. However, it is probably not cost-effective in ordinary on-line transactions.

An efficient approach to secure digital signatures as non-repudiation evidence was proposed in [17], in which two different types of signature keys are defined.

- *Revocable signature keys* – the corresponding verification key certificates are issued by a *certification authority* (CA), and can be revoked as usual.
- *Irrevocable signature keys* – the corresponding verification key certificates are issued by users themselves and time-stamped by a *time-stamping authority* (TS). Such certificates cannot be revoked before their expiry.

The revocable signature key is used as a long-term master key to issue irrevocable verification key certificates while the irrevocable signature key is used as a temporary key to sign electronic documents. The digital signatures generated in such a way will remain valid until the corresponding irrevocable verification key certificates expire, thus can be exempted from being time-stamped by a time-stamping authority during on-line transactions.

The second approach can significantly improve the efficiency of mass on-line transactions. However, as the generation of irrevocable signature/verification key pairs needs much more computation and storage capacity, it seems infeasible to be implemented in a smart card. Here we put forward a new approach to maintain the validity of evidence for subscribers equipped with a smart card in PPV service.

The idea behind our approach is the establishment of a *one-way sequential link* of the subscriber C's signed view requests. The one-way sequential link has the property that any change to the order of C's signatures or insertion of a new signature to the link will be detected. If C wants to revoke his verification key used in PPV service, C only needs to ask the service provider S to countersign C's latest signed view request. With S's countersignature, C can deny other view requests which are signed with his revoked key but not in the countersigned link. Hence, S should not accept C's view request signed with his revoked key once S has confirmed C's revocation request.

Suppose C is going to make the view requests $Req_1, Req_2, \cdots, Req_i$. C can establish a one-way sequential link of his signed view requests $\sigma_1, \sigma_2, \cdots, \sigma_i$ as follows.

$$\sigma_1 = sS_C(Req_1)$$
$$\sigma_2 = sS_C(Req_2, H(\sigma_1))$$
$$\cdots$$
$$\sigma_i = sS_C(Req_i, H(\sigma_{i-1}))$$

For $1 < j \leq i$, S will check whether σ_j is linked properly to σ_{j-1} before accepting C's jth view request. Then we have the following claims.

Claim 1. $\sigma_1, \sigma_2, \cdots, \sigma_i$ *are sequential. That means, for $1 < j \leq i$, σ_j is generated later than σ_{j-1}.*

Proof: Since $H(\sigma_{i-1})$ is a part of the signed message in $\sigma_i = sS_C(Req_i, H(\sigma_{i-1}))$, $H(\sigma_{i-1})$ is a fixed value. According to the definition of a one-way hash function, it is computationally infeasible to find its input σ_{i-1}. Therefore, σ_{i-1} should have been generated before generating σ_i. For the same reason, σ_{j-1} $(j = i-1, \cdots, 2)$ should have been generated before generating σ_j. Hence, $\sigma_1, \sigma_2, \cdots, \sigma_i$ are sequential.

Claim 2. $\sigma_1, \sigma_2, \cdots, \sigma_i$ *are one-way linked. That means, for $1 < j \leq i$, it is computationally infeasible to generate a valid signature σ' which is linked between σ_j and σ_{j-1}.*

Proof: For $1 < j \leq i$, suppose $\sigma' = sS_C(Req', H(\sigma_{j-1}))$ is a signature to be inserted between $\sigma_{j-1} = sS_C(Req_{j-1}, H(\sigma_{j-2}))$ and $\sigma_j = sS_C(Req_j, H(\sigma_{j-1}))$. σ' should meet the requirement that $H(\sigma') = H(\sigma_{j-1})$ while $\sigma' \neq \sigma_{j-1}$. According to the definition of a one-way hash function, it is computationally infeasible to find such a value. Hence, $\sigma_1, \sigma_2, \cdots, \sigma_i$ are one-way linked.

If C thinks that his signature key S_C may have been compromised, or he does not want to request services from S any more after C made his ith view request, C can revoke his public key certificate submitted to S at subscription by initiating the following *revocation protocol*.

$$1.\ C \rightarrow S : \sigma_i$$
$$2.\ S \rightarrow C : sS_S(\sigma_i)$$

Once S receives C's revocation request, S checks whether σ_i is C's latest view request. If so, S confirms C's revocation request. Here we assume that C holds S's public verification key and thus can check S's countersignature $sS_S(\sigma_i)$. With evidence $sS_S(\sigma_i)$, C can deny all other view requests signed with S_C except $\sigma_1, \sigma_2, \cdots, \sigma_i$.

When C receives a bill from S and claims that σ_j is a signature forged by somebody else with S_C after the public key certificate had been revoked at S but S disagrees, C may provide evidence $sS_S(\sigma_i)$ to an arbitrator to prove that S had confirmed C's revocation request. Then the arbitrator will ask S to present C's one-way sequential link $\sigma_k, \sigma_{k+1}, \cdots, \sigma_i$ generated with S_C from the beginning of that billing period to check whether σ_j is a signature in the link. If not, C can deny it. Otherwise, C is liable for the corresponding charge.

The major advantage of this approach is that there is no involvement of a trusted third party in the process of key revocation. Hence, this approach will be very efficient in applications where a one-way sequential link of signatures can be established.

6 Supporting Mobility of Subscribers

To attract subscribers to make more frequent use of the video service, it is desirable that subscribers can securely request PPV service regardless of their physical location. Here we assess the storage requirement and computation overheads for executing protocol FPPV in a smart card.

A subscriber C needs to store

– cryptographic keys: S_C, P_C^- and V_S (128 bytes each), K_s (20 bytes);
– view request parameters: S (20 bytes), Id (10 bytes), Pr (5 bytes), T_g (14 bytes), L and m (2 bytes each).

The estimated memory for the above items are 457 bytes. The major demand for storage is the hash chain generated when making a view request. Suppose the minimum charging unit $L = 1$ minute, the upper-bound of a video program are 3 hours, then the maximum length of the hash chain $m = 180$. Each hash value is 20-byte long, thus $180 * 20 = 3600$ bytes are required to store the whole hash chain, and the total memory required in protocol FPPV are about $457 + 3600 = 4057$ bytes. Such a storage requirement is feasible for current smart cards with the average EEPROM size of $4 - 8K$ bytes.

Actually, we can reduce the storage of a hash chain at the cost of reasonable computation overheads if the hash chain is very long. For example, we may only store 9 hash values like $H^0(n)$, $H^{20}(n)$, $H^{40}(n)$, $\cdots$, $H^{160}(n)$ of the above hash chain. Then other chained hash values can be computed easily. Hence, the memory for the hash chain can be reduced to $9 * 20 = 180$ bytes.

When a subscriber C makes a view request, his major computation overheads are generating a hash chain and a digital signature, and performing a public key decryption and a signature verification. With the current smart card technology [12], these operations for a typical video length (i.e. a moderate value of m) can be finished within a few seconds. After making a successful request, C needs to release a chained hash value for each charging unit L during the service. Based on the above storage arrangement on the hash chain, C needs to execute at most 19 times hash operations to get the required hash value. For example, if C needs to release $H^{179}(n)$, it can be calculated from $H^{160}(n)$, which takes only a few milli-seconds. As we assume the minimum charging unit $L = 1$ minute, the required hash value can always be ready for release during the service.

The above analysis shows that protocol FPPV is light-weighted and can be implemented in a smart card to support mobility of PPV subscribers.

7 Conclusion

Pay-per-view video service on the Web has the following merits compared with the current cable TV.

– Subscribers can choose to watch the programs that they are interested in;
– Subscribers can watch these programs at any time;
– Subscribers only need to pay what they have watched.

This paper proposed a secure PPV scheme for web-based video service. The highlights of our scheme are

– *Non-repudiation of billing* – the correctness of a bill is incontestable;

- *Subscriber mobility* – subscribers can request PPV service securely by the use of their own smart cards;
- *Practical and efficient* – the validity of evidence can be maintained without invoking trusted third parties.

References

1. S. G. Akl. *Digital signatures: a tutorial survey.* Computer, 16(2):15–24, February 1983.
2. N. Asokan, V. Shoup and M. Waidner. *Asynchronous protocols for optimistic fair exchange.* Proceedings of 1998 IEEE Symposium on Security and Privacy, pages 86–99, Oakland, California, May 1998.
3. F. Bao, R. H. Deng and W. Mao. *Efficient and practical fair exchange protocols with off-line TTP.* Proceedings of 1998 IEEE Symposium on Security and Privacy, pages 77–85, Oakland, California, May 1998.
4. K. S. Booth. *Authentication of signatures using public key encryption.* Communications of the ACM, 24(11):772–774, November 1981.
5. CCITT. *Recommendation X.509: The directory – Authentication framework.* November 1988.
6. D. Cunningham and D. O'Mahony. *Secure pay-per-view testbed.* Proceedings of 1995 IEEE International Conference on Multimedia Computing and Systems, May 1995.
7. M. Franklin and M. Reiter. *Fair exchange with a semi-trusted third party.* Proceedings of 4th ACM Conference on Computer and Communications Security, pages 1–6, Zurich, Switzerland, April 1997.
8. ISO 7498-2. *Information processing systems - Open systems interconnection - Basic reference model - Part 2: Security architecture.* International Organization for Standardisation, 1989.
9. ISO/IEC 13888-3. *Information technology - Security techniques - Non-repudiation - Part 3: Mechanisms using asymmetric techniques.* ISO/IEC, 1997.
10. L. Lamport. *Password authentication with insecure communication.* Communications of the ACM, 24(11):770–772, November 1981.
11. A. J. Menezes, P. C. van Oorschot and S. A. Vanstone. *Handbook of applied cryptography.* CRC Press, 1996.
12. D. Naccache and D. M'Raihi. *Cryptographic smart cards.* IEEE Micro, 16(3):14–24, June 1996.
13. T. P. Pedersen. *Electronic payments of small amounts.* Lecture Notes in Computer Science 1189, Proceedings of Cambridge Workshop on Security Protocols, pages 59–68, Cambridge, April 1996.
14. B. Schneier. *Applied cryptography – Protocols, algorithms, and source code in C.* New York: John Wiley & Sons, 1996 (second edition).
15. J. Zhou and D. Gollmann. *A fair non-repudiation protocol.* Proceedings of 1996 IEEE Symposium on Security and Privacy, pages 55–61, Oakland, California, May 1996.
16. J. Zhou and D. Gollmann. *Evidence and non-repudiation.* Journal of Network and Computer Applications, 20(3):267–281, London: Academic Press, July 1997.
17. J. Zhou and K. Y. Lam. *Securing digital signatures for non-repudiation.* (manuscript)

Author Index

Lecture Notes in Computer Science

For information about Vols. 1–1474
please contact your bookseller or Springer-Verlag

Vol. 1511: D. O'Hallaron (Ed.), Languages, Compilers, and Run-Time Systems for Scalable Computers. Proceedings, 1998. IX, 412 pages. 1998.

Vol. 1512: E. Giménez, C. Paulin-Mohring (Eds.), Types for Proofs and Programs. Proceedings, 1996. VIII, 373 pages. 1998.

Vol. 1513: C. Nikolaou, C. Stephanidis (Eds.), Research and Advanced Technology for Digital Libraries. Proceedings, 1998. XV, 912 pages. 1998.

Vol. 1514: K. Ohta, D. Pei (Eds.), Advances in Cryptology – ASIACRYPT'98. Proceedings, 1998. XII, 436 pages. 1998.

Vol. 1515: F. Moreira de Oliveira (Ed.), Advances in Artificial Intelligence. Proceedings, 1998. X, 259 pages. 1998. (Subseries LNAI).

Vol. 1516: W. Ehrenberger (Ed.), Computer Safety, Reliability and Security. Proceedings, 1998. XVI, 392 pages. 1998.

Vol. 1517: J. Hromkovič, O. Sýkora (Eds.), Graph-Theoretic Concepts in Computer Science. Proceedings, 1998. X, 385 pages. 1998.

Vol. 1518: M. Luby, J. Rolim, M. Serna (Eds.), Randomization and Approximation Techniques in Computer Science. Proceedings, 1998. IX, 385 pages. 1998.

1519: T. Ishida (Ed.), Community Computing and Support Systems. VIII, 393 pages. 1998.

Vol. 1520: M. Maher, J.-F. Puget (Eds.), Principles and Practice of Constraint Programming - CP98. Proceedings, 1998. XI, 482 pages. 1998.

Vol. 1521: B. Rovan (Ed.), SOFSEM'98: Theory and Practice of Informatics. Proceedings, 1998. XI, 453 pages. 1998.

Vol. 1522: G. Gopalakrishnan, P. Windley (Eds.), Formal Methods in Computer-Aided Design. Proceedings, 1998. IX, 529 pages. 1998.

Vol. 1524: G.B. Orr, K.-R. Müller (Eds.), Neural Networks: Tricks of the Trade. VI, 432 pages. 1998.

Vol. 1525: D. Aucsmith (Ed.), Information Hiding. Proceedings, 1998. IX, 369 pages. 1998.

Vol. 1526: M. Broy, B. Rumpe (Eds.), Requirements Targeting Software and Systems Engineering. Proceedings, 1997. VIII, 357 pages. 1998.

Vol. 1527: P. Baumgartner, Theory Reasoning in Connection Calculi. IX, 283. 1999. (Subseries LNAI).

Vol. 1528: B. Preneel, V. Rijmen (Eds.), State of the Art in Applied Cryptography. Revised Lectures, 1997. VIII, 395 pages. 1998.

Vol. 1529: D. Farwell, L. Gerber, E. Hovy (Eds.), Machine Translation and the Information Soup. Proceedings, 1998. XIX, 532 pages. 1998. (Subseries LNAI).

Vol. 1530: V. Arvind, R. Ramanujam (Eds.), Foundations of Software Technology and Theoretical Computer Science. XII, 369 pages. 1998.

Vol. 1531: H.-Y. Lee, H. Motoda (Eds.), PRICAI'98: Topics in Artificial Intelligence. XIX, 646 pages. 1998. (Subseries LNAI).

Vol. 1096: T. Schael, Workflow Management Systems for Process Organisations. Second Edition. XII, 229 pages. 1998.

Vol. 1532: S. Arikawa, H. Motoda (Eds.), Discovery Science. Proceedings, 1998. XI, 456 pages. 1998. (Subseries LNAI).

Vol. 1533: K.-Y. Chwa, O.H. Ibarra (Eds.), Algorithms and Computation. Proceedings, 1998. XIII, 478 pages. 1998.

Vol. 1534: J.S. Sichman, R. Conte, N. Gilbert (Eds.), Multi-Agent Systems and Agent-Based Simulation. Proceedings, 1998. VIII, 237 pages. 1998. (Subseries LNAI).

Vol. 1535: S. Ossowski, Co-ordination in Artificial Agent Societies. XV; 221 pages. 1999. (Subseries LNAI).

Vol. 1536: W.-P. de Roever, H. Langmaack, A. Pnueli (Eds.), Compositionality: The Significant Difference. Proceedings, 1997. VIII, 647 pages. 1998.

Vol. 1538: J. Hsiang, A. Ohori (Eds.), Advances in Computing Science – ASIAN'98. Proceedings, 1998. X, 305 pages. 1998.

Vol. 1539: O. Rüthing, Interacting Code Motion Transformations: Their Impact and Their Complexity. XXI,225 pages. 1998.

Vol. 1540: C. Beeri, P. Buneman (Eds.), Database Theory – ICDT'99. Proceedings, 1999. XI, 489 pages. 1999.

Vol. 1541: B. Kågström, J. Dongarra, E. Elmroth, J. Waśniewski (Eds.), Applied Parallel Computing. Proceedings, 1998. XIV, 586 pages. 1998.

Vol. 1542: H.I. Christensen (Ed.), Computer Vision Systems. Proceedings, 1999. XI, 554 pages. 1999.

Vol. 1543: S. Demeyer, J. Bosch (Eds.), Object-Oriented Technology ECOOP'98 Workshop Reader. 1998. XXII, 573 pages. 1998.

Vol. 1544: C. Zhang, D. Lukose (Eds.), Multi-Agent Systems. Proceedings, 1998. VII, 195 pages. 1998. (Subseries LNAI).

Vol. 1545: A. Birk, J. Demiris (Eds.), Learning Robots. Proceedings, 1996. IX, 188 pages. 1998. (Subseries LNAI).

Vol. 1546: B. Möller, J.V. Tucker (Eds.), Prospects for Hardware Foundations. Survey Chapters, 1998. X, 468 pages. 1998.

Vol. 1547: S.H. Whitesides (Ed.), Graph Drawing. Proceedings 1998. XII, 468 pages. 1998.

Vol. 1548: A.M. Haeberer (Ed.), Algebraic Methodology and Software Technology. Proceedings, 1999. XI, 531 pages. 1999.

Vol. 1551: G. Gupta (Ed.), Practical Aspects of Declarative Languages. Proceedings, 1999. VIII, 367 pgages. 1999.

Vol. 1553: S.T. Andler, J. Hansson (Eds.), Active, Real-Time, and Temporal Database Systems. Proceedings, 1997. VIII, 245 pages. 1998.

Vol. 1557: P. Zinterhof, M. Vajteršic, A. Uhl (Eds.), Parallel Computation. Proceedings, 1999. XV, 604 pages. 1999.

Vol. 1560: K. Imai, Y. Zheng (Eds.), Public Key Cryptography. Proceedings, 1999. IX, 327 pages. 1999.

Vol. 1567: P. Antsaklis, M. Lemmon, A. Nerode, S. Sastry (Eds.), Hybrid Systems V. X, 445 pages. 1999.

Vol. 1570: F. Puppe (Ed.), XPS-99: Knowledge-Based Systems. VIII, 227 pages. 1999. (Subseries LNAI).